The BBC Today: Future Uncertain

EDITED BY
JOHN MAIR, RICHARD TAIT
and
RICHARD LANCE KEEBLE

Published 2015 by Abramis academic publishing

www.abramis.co.uk

ISBN 978 1 84549 656 2

Printed and bound in the United Kingdom

Typeset in Garamond 11pt

Abramis is an imprint of arima publishing.

arima publishing
ASK House, Northgate Avenue
Bury St Edmunds, Suffolk IP32 6BB
t: (+44) 01284 700321

www.arimapublishing.com

Contents

Acknowledgements

Thanks to all the authors who (like the editors) receive no fee nor royalties. Special thanks to Richard and Pete Franklin, of Abramis, our excellent and as ever efficient publishers. And thanks to the BBC for existing – long may it continue. That's enough thanks (eds).

John Mair, Oxford
Richard Tait, London
Richard Lance Keeble, Withcall, Lincolnshire

The Contributors

Steven Barnett is professor of communications at the University of Westminster and an established writer, author and commentator who specialises in media policy, broadcasting, regulation, and journalism ethics. He has acted several times as specialist adviser to the House of Lords select committee on communications, and over the last 30 years has directed numerous research projects on the structure, funding, and regulation of communications. He is on the management and editorial boards of the *British Journalism Review*, has authored a number of books, and writes frequently for the national and specialist press. His most recent book, an edited collection on *Media Power and Plurality*, was published by Palgrave Macmillan in 2015.

Patrick Barwise is emeritus professor of management and marketing at London Business School and a visiting senior fellow in media and communications at the LSE. He joined LBS in 1976 after an early career with IBM. He has published widely on management, marketing and media. His 1988 book, *Television and its Audience* (with Andrew Ehrenberg), has never been out of print and his 2004 *Simply Better: Winning and Keeping Customers by Delivering What Matters Most* (with Seán Meehan) won the American Marketing Association's annual book prize. He is also chairman of Which?, but writes here in a personal capacity as an independent academic.

Colin Browne is chairman of the Voice of the Listener and Viewer. He was director, corporate affairs at the BBC from 1994 to 2000, having previously been director, corporate relations at BT. From 2000 to 2009 he was a partner and senior consultant at Maitland, one of the UK's leading financial and corporate communications consultancies and is a past member of the Communications Consumer Panel. He currently has his own company providing strategic communications advice, and is a non-executive director of the Centre for Effective Dispute Resolution (CEDR).

Anna Carragher was controller, BBC Northern Ireland, between 2000 and 2006 and head of programmes, BBC Northern Ireland, from 1995 to 2000. She was editor of European and correspondent programmes, BBC Radio, from 1992 to 1995 and had previously been the producer of *Any Questions* on Radio 4 and *Question Time* on BBC 1. She worked as a producer on a number of BBC radio and television programmes including *Newsnight*, *Breakfast Time* and the *Today* programme. She is the electoral commissioner with particular responsibility for Northern Ireland, a member of the board of the Arts Council of Northern Ireland and a board member of the Equality Commission for Northern Ireland.

Ian Carter is editorial director of KM Media Group, an independent family-owned publisher with interests in newspapers, websites, radio and television across Kent. He is a former senior broadcast journalist for the BBC and serves on the working party set up to build relations between the corporation and the regional press.

Catherine Chapman is a freelance journalist and former MA student at Brunel University London.

Fiona Chesterton is a former controller of adult learning at the BBC and had a long career in television production, commissioning and journalism, at both the BBC and Channel 4. In 2008, she was made a fellow of the Royal Television Society for services to broadcasting. She writes book reviews for the London School of Economics *Review of Books* online.

Alex Connock is managing director of Shine North and chairman of the Royal Television Society North West. He has held visiting academic positions at MMU, Manchester Business School, Oxford's Reuters Institute for the Study of Journalism. Sunderland University, Salford University and INSEAD. He writes here in a personal capacity.

Diane Coyle is a professor of economics at the University of Manchester, and was vice-chairman of the BBC Trust until April 2015. She is also a former member of the Competition Commission and the Migration Advisory Committee.

Howard Davies is chairman of the Royal Bank of Scotland and professor at Sciences Po in Paris. He was a member of the Burns committee which advised the Blair government on the 2006 BBC charter review.

Farrukh Dhondy was born in India, came to Britain on a scholarship to Cambridge University and lives in Britain. He is a writer of fiction, biography, TV screenplays and journalism and was for fourteen years the multicultural commissioning editor of Channel 4.

David Elstein is chairman of the Broadcasting Policy Group.

Alice Enders is director of research at Enders Analysis, a leading UK-based supplier of independent research and consultancy on media, technology and telecommunications.

Rona Fairhead is chairman of the BBC Trust, the BBC's governing body. She is currently on the board of HSBC Holdings plc and PepsiCo Inc and is non-executive chairman of HSBC Northern America Holdings Inc. She is also a UK trade and investment business ambassador. She was chairman and CEO of the Financial Times Group from 2006-2013, having previously been group finance director of its parent company, Pearson plc. Before joining Pearson, Rona held a variety of senior positions in financial and global businesses.

Suzanne Franks is professor of journalism at City University London. She joined BBC TV as a trainee and later worked on programmes such as *Newsnight*, *The Money Programme*, *Watchdog* and *Panorama*. She left to found an independent production company and through that was involved in the televising of parliament. Since gaining a PhD she has published widely on the reporting of humanitarian crises and the history of the BBC. Her recent books include *Famine, Aid, Politics and the Media* (Hurst 2013) and *Women and Journalism* (I. B. Tauris 2013).

Ivor Gaber is professor of journalism at the University of Sussex and a former political journalist for BBC TV and Radio, ITN, Channel 4 and Sky News.

Michael Grade (Lord Grade of Yarmouth) is chairman of Pinewood and Shepperton Film Studios which provides the BBC with studio facilities. He is a contributor to BBC programmes and a Conservative peer. He began his career as a newspaper journalist, became director of programmes at LWT from 1977 to 1981; director of programmes, BBC television from 1986 to 1987; chief executive of Channel 4 from 1988-1997; chairman of the BBC from 2004 to 2006 and executive chairman and chief executive of ITV from 2007 to 2009.

James Heath is director of policy at the BBC. He oversees public policy development, government relations and regulatory affairs at UK and EU levels. Previously, James was controller of strategy for the BBC's journalism division, advising on portfolio strategy for its news, sport and local services. He has also worked as a policy/public affairs advisor at ITV/Granada plc, the British Chambers of Commerce and the Labour Party.

Sylvia Harvey is visiting professor in the School of Media and Communication at the University of Leeds. She has published on film history and policy, on the political economy of media and on broadcasting policy and regulation. She is a founder member of the Sheffield International Documentary Festival, a trustee of the Showroom Cinema and of the Voice of the Listener & Viewer.

Dan Hind is an author and publisher. His books include *The Return of the Public: Democracy, Power and the Case for Media Reform* and *The Magic Kingdom: Property, Monarchy and the Maximum Republic*.

Lis Howell is professor of journalism and director of broadcasting at City University London. She was formerly a BBC local radio producer; managing editor at Sky News; director of programmes for the Living Channel and senior vice-president of Flextech Television. She was also the first female head of news in ITV, she won an RTS award for coverage of the Lockerbie plane disaster, she managed Sky News coverage of the first Gulf War from Saudi Arabia, and she produced a knitting strand for *This Morning*! She also writes for OurBeeb and appears regularly on BBC Radio 4's *The Media Show*.

Jacquie Hughes is an experienced journalist and academic whose career spans print, radio, television and includes more than a decade at the BBC (latterly as a commissioning editor). She has held senior management roles in the independent sector, and has worked as a reporter, producer/director, executive producer and editor across all broadcast formats including live, documentaries, investigative current affairs and drama-documentaries. She has worked on strategy and standards at the BBC Trust, and authored various reports on the state of British media practice. A keynote speaker at many industry events and a visiting lecturer in Strasbourg, Bournemouth and Durham, she currently runs the Master's journalism programme at Brunel University and is specialist adviser to the Lords communications committee. Her on-going interests include standards and ethics of practice, the role of regulation and the dynamics of the public/private sector landscape.

Richard Lance Keeble has been professor of journalism at the University of Lincoln since 2003. Before that he was the executive editor of the *Teacher*, the weekly newspaper of the National Union of Teachers and he lectured at City University London for 19 years. He has written and edited 30 publications on a wide range of subjects. He is joint editor of *Ethical Space: The International Journal of Communication Ethics* and the winner of a National Teacher Fellowship in 2011 – the highest prize for teachers in higher education. In 2014, he was given a Lifetime Achievement Award by the Association for Journalism Education.

Roger Laughton joined the BBC in 1965 and worked as a director in Bristol and, from 1969, with *Nationwide*. He was deputy editor, *Pebble Mill at One*, between 1973 and 1977 and editor, features, Manchester from 1977 to 1980. He moved to London to lead the network features department in 1980 which staged *Live Aid* in 1985. Amongst his other production credits were *Brass Tacks*, *Great Railway Journeys of the World* and *River Journeys* (a BAFTA winner). In 1986, he launched the BBC's daytime service including two daily helpings of *Neighbours*. His final role with the BBC was as director, co-productions, BBC Enterprises, between 1987 and 1990. He left the BBC to lead MAI's bid to win the ITV franchise for the South in 1990. The bid was successful and he was appointed CEO of Meridian TV in 1991. As ITV consolidated, Meridian merged with Anglia and HTV to become United Broadcasting – where he acted as CEO from 1994 to 1999. In 1999, he left ITV to head the Bournemouth Media School. Since 2005, he has served on a number of boards and is currently chairman, Arts University Bournemouth.

Professor Justin Lewis is dean of research at Cardiff University. He has written widely about media, culture and politics.

David Liddiment has had a distinguished career in television as a programme maker and broadcaster. He was director of programmes for the ITV Network from 1997 to 2002, delivered the MacTaggart lecture in 2001 and was awarded the Royal Television Society Gold Medal in 2003. He is co-founder and non-executive director of independent producer All3media and a BBC trustee.

David Lloyd is visiting professor of journalism, City University London, and former head of news and current affairs, Channel 4 TV.

John Mair has taught journalism at the Universities of Coventry, Kent, Northampton, Brunel, Edinburgh Napier, Guyana and the Communication University of China. He has now edited fourteen 'hackademic' volumes over the last five years on subjects ranging from trust in TV, the health of investigative journalism, reporting the 'Arab Spring' to three volumes on the Leveson Inquiry. He and Richard Lance Keeble invented the sub-genre. John also invented the Coventry Conversations which attracted 350 media movers and shakers to Coventry University while the podcasts of those have been downloaded five million times worldwide. Since then, he has launched the Northampton Chronicles, MediaMondays at Napier and most recently the Harrow Conversations at Westminster. In a previous life, he was an award-winning producer/director for the BBC, ITV and Channel 4 and a secondary school teacher.

Tom O'Malley is emeritus professor of media, Aberystwyth University. His publications include *Closedown? The BBC and Government Broadcasting Policy 1979-92*, London: Pluto, 1994; with Clive Soley, *Regulating the Press*, London, Pluto, 2000; with David Barlow and Philip Mitchell, *The Media in Wales*, Cardiff: Cardiff University Press, 2005; with Janet Jones (eds) *The Peacock Committee and UK Broadcasting Policy*, London: Palgrave Macmillan, 2009. He is co-founder and co-editor of the journal *Media History* (Routledge) and a member of the national council of the Campaign for Press and Broadcasting Freedom.

Peter Preston edited the *Guardian* from 1975 to 1995. He is currently a director of the Guardian Foundation, a media commentator for the *Observer* – and a founding partner of the new European Press Prize.

Neil Midgley is a freelance journalist. He has been covering media and television for the last ten years, mainly for the *Daily Telegraph*. During seven years on staff at the *Telegraph*, he edited the television pages and then moved to the newsroom, where he was a full-time reporter on the industry as assistant editor (media). Since going freelance in 2011, he has written for publications including the *Telegraph*, *MediaGuardian* and *Radio Times*, as well as being a regular media pundit on television and radio. He has served for six years on the advisory committee for the Edinburgh TV Festival, and on awards juries for the Royal Television Society, Bafta and Freesat. Journalism is his second career: in the 1990s, he was a litigation lawyer for firms including Linklaters and Debevoise & Plimpton.

Elis Owen is a freelance programme consultant currently mentoring *It's My Shout*, a project which introduces young people into television and film making. From 2009 to 2011, he was head of English language commissioning BBC Wales; from 2007 to 2009, managing director ITV Wales, from 1997 to 2007 programme controller ITV Wales, and from 1993 to 1997, head of news and current affairs ITV Wales.

Gillian Reynolds has been radio critic of the *Daily Telegraph* since 1975. Previously she was radio critic of the *Guardian* (1967-1974). In between, she was founding programme controller of Radio City, Liverpool's first commercial radio station. She chaired the Radio Academy Festival (for 12 years), the Sony Awards (4 years), the Charles Parker Archive Trust (30 years). She received the Media Society Gold award (2004), the Radio Independents Group Gold Award (2014) and the Voice of the Listener & Viewer award for public service (2015).

Marcus Ryder is the editor of current affairs BBC Scotland. He executive produces all of the television current affairs output produced by Scotland Current Affairs for BBC Scotland, the News Channel and BBC Network. He has executive produced more than twenty *Panorama* programmes including *The Money Farmers*, *The Return of the Secret Policeman*, *All Work and Low Pay*, *Disabled or Faking It?*, *Surgery's Dirty Secrets* and *Smoking and the Bandit*. He sits on the BBC Scotland Diversity Champions Group and is the chair of the RTS Diversity Group.

Jean Seaton is professor of media history at the University of Westminster and director of the Orwell Prize for political writing and journalism. She has written widely on broadcasting history, conflicts, security, politics and the media. Her books include (with James Curran) *Power Without Responsibilty: The Press, Broadcasting and Internet in Britain*, and *Carnage and the Media: The Making and Breaking of News about Violence* (Penguin). Her official history of the BBC, *'Traitors and Pinkoes': The BBC and the Nation 1974-87*, was published by Profile Books in 2015.

Maurice Smith is a journalist, consultant and documentary producer based in Glasgow. He was business editor of BBC Scotland from 1989 to 1999 before setting up his own business, TVI Vision. Before that he was a journalist with the *Herald* newspaper. He is the author of *Paper Lions* (Polygon Books, 1994) on the Scottish press and national identity, and continues to contribute to various publications.

After studying at Queen's University, in Belfast, **Raymond Snoddy** worked on local and regional newspapers, before joining *The Times* in 1971. Five years later he moved to the *Financial Times* and reported on media issues before returning to *The Times* as media editor in 1995. At present, Snoddy is a freelance journalist writing for a range of publications. He presented *NewsWatch* since its inception in 2004 until 2012. The programme was launched in response to the Hutton Inquiry, as part of an initiative to make BBC News more accountable. His other television work has included presenting Channel 4's award-winning series *Hard News*. In addition, Snoddy is the author of a biography of the media tycoon Michael Green, *The Good, the Bad and the Ugly*, about ethics in the newspaper industry, and other books. Snoddy was awarded an OBE for his services to journalism in 2000.

Jon Snow is a *Channel 4 News* presenter.

Richard Tait is professor of journalism at the School of Journalism, Media and Cultural Studies, Cardiff. From 2003 to 2012, he was director of the school's Centre for Journalism. He was editor of *Newsnight* from 1985 to 1987, editor of *Channel 4 News* from 1987 to 1995 and editor-in-chief of ITN from 1995 to 2002. He was a BBC governor and chair of the governors' programme complaints committee from 2004 to 2006, and a BBC trustee and chair of the trust's editorial standards committee from 2006 to 2010. He is a fellow of the Society of Editors and the Royal Television Society, treasurer of the International News Safety Institute and an independent trustee of the Disasters Emergency Committee.

Aidan White is the director of the Ethical Journalism Network, a global coalition of media professional groups promoting ethics, good governance and self-regulation in journalism. He was previously a journalist with the *Guardian* and for 24 years the general secretary of the International Federation of Journalists based in Brussels.

Andrew Whitehead was the editor of BBC World Service News for six years to March 2015, and was also a BBC Delhi correspondent and a Westminster-based lobby correspondent, a radio news presenter and an award-winning documentary maker in a career in BBC News stretching over thirty-five years. He has a PhD in history and is an honorary professor at the Institute of Asia and Pacific Studies, Nottingham, and visiting senior research fellow at the King's India in London. He is the author of *A Mission in Kashmir*, an account of the origins of the Kashmir conflict in 1947, based largely on personal testimony.

Brian Winston holds the Lincoln chair at the University of Lincoln. He is concerned with new media technologies, documentary film and free expression – on which his latest books are *A Right to Offend* (2012) and *The Rushdie Fatwa and After: A Lesson to the Circumspect* (2014).

Preface:
My BBC – by Jon Snow

The *Channel 4 News* presenter reveals the beginning of his 'true love affair' with the corporation. Now the World Service remains in his soul, he is addicted to Radio 4 while Radio 3 'brings solace' whenever he needs it. How dare the government seek to diminish it!

I was eighteen when I discovered the BBC World Service. Of course, *Listen with Mother*, Children's Hour, and *Uncle Mac*, had already long previously introduced me to the BBC Home Service. But the World Service was to prove a positive lifeline.

My discovery was rooted in Uganda. Never having been on a plane, never having even been out of England, I found myself in 1967 on the banks of the Nile in a little, two-room shack on the edge of Kamuli College in a small village called Namasagali. Bereft of phones and radio communications, I was some fifteen miles on a mud road from the nearest post office.

The traumatic shock of being propelled from the shelter of my Yorkshire home to this green and distant place, 150 miles from Kampala, was more than I could bear. But on my second home-sick, tearful night, the headmaster, Father Grimes, gave me an old valve radio with ten bands of short-wave. So began my true love affair with the BBC. The news, the variety, the voices, the constant interference, combined to weave this link to all that I had known before and remained so for the year that I was there.

These days I depend as strongly as ever on a much bigger BBC than ever existed then. But the World Service remains in my soul – visited on late nights and early mornings when home. When abroad I refer to it constantly and nowadays, far from valves, I consume it online. In these days, too, I worry about the starvation of the World Service, the failure of government to recognise it as the stunning, envied manifestation of the UK's 'soft power'. The decisions to squeeze the corporation, and to fail to invest in it, flow from the decision of government no longer to fund it directly. It leaves me increasingly convinced that such a decision can only have been taken by politicians who have never been anywhere – particularly in the developing world.

For the rest, I am a Radio 4 addict. Whisper it softly, but from my own non-BBC roots at LBC (the first legal, commercial radio station ever to broadcast in the UK), I have been convinced that radio is the ultimate medium – not least because the pictures are so much better. The stimulation of all the senses by radio is unique. The BBC's deployment of the medium is without parallel anywhere in the world. In the car, at home, at my desk, on my phone, Radio 4 is in and out of my life every day that I am in the UK. Abroad it is increasingly with me online.

Mentioning online, the BBC has few if any challengers.

As a choral scholar at Winchester Cathedral who sang Bach and Tallis at eight-years-old, Radio 3 rattles and succours my bones. From Handel to Howells, from Fauré to Finzi, it cushions my news and current affairs and brings solace whenever I need it.

The quality of the BBC's television output remains world beating. In short, the creation and maintenance of the BBC as the greatest broadcaster in the world goes to the very core of what the word 'British' means.

So why have I never worked for this great national and global asset that I depend upon and admire so much? Well, it's a hard question to answer. In part, it's because I am somewhat non-conformist. In part, beyond a tentative approach quarter of a century ago, I have never been asked. I like the freedoms offered by the other public broadcaster, Channel 4. It was established to be different. I guess I feel myself, though in part deeply conventional, also to be different. But make no mistake, if anyone ever tries to diminish or destroy the BBC, they will have to contend with a myriad of people who, like me, will be manning the ramparts to defend it.

I'm delighted that my former boss Richard Tait and good friend John Mair have decided to compile this book. Though whether they will approve of my introduction as true BBC hands themselves, I can't say.

Section 1:
What Sort of BBC Do We Want?

Conservatives tactic from start [handwritten annotation]

Richard Tait

In February 2014, this book's predecessor asked: *Is the BBC in Crisis?* Although memories of the horrors of 2012 and 2013 have faded a little, it is hard to avoid the feeling that the BBC has not fully recovered from the largely self-inflicted wounds of that period. It now faces the shortest and potentially the most difficult charter review process in living memory. *a written constr constitution* [handwritten annotation] Shortest, because the then-coalition government decided to postpone any consideration of the BBC until after the general election in May 2015 and there is now not much more than a year to determine the new charter. And most difficult, because, instead of a widely predicted coalition or minority government which would probably have been content to leave fundamental debates about the future of the BBC to another day, the BBC now has to deal with a majority Conservative government, many of whose supporters are looking for radical change, *political reform* [handwritten annotation] and a secretary of state who knows his brief (from the BBC's point of view) uncomfortably well after a decade as chairman of the Commons culture and media committee.

The writers in this opening section approach the BBC from very different perspectives, but on one thing they are agreed – the *status quo* is not an option. As chairman of the BBC from 2004 to 2006, Michael Grade helped pull the BBC round after its last great crisis – the Hutton report of 2004. In a unique career, he has been the BBC's director of television, Channel 4's chief executive and the executive chairman of ITV. Nowadays he is chairman of Pinewood Shepperton and a Conservative peer.

He is in no doubt that the only option for the BBC is radical change – the BBC needs to become smaller and more agile and take a hard look at its existing portfolio of services. He thinks it is telling that the government has had to appoint an external panel to ask the difficult questions which the management should be asking itself. The challenge, he suggests, is whether the BBC – an organisation he cares about and supports – has the will and the culture to embrace change. 'I just wish,' he writes, 'those responsible for charter review would get out more.'

Another voice with commercial media experience but a deep commitment to the BBC is that of Rona Fairhead, the chair of the BBC Trust, who took over in the autumn of 2014 after ill health forced chair Lord Patten to step down. As a former chief executive of the Financial Times Group, one of the world's most successful and respected media brands (and then still in UK ownership), she understands the challenges the BBC faces from market changes and new technologies. But her focus, rightly, is on the key role of the trust to represent the interests of the licence fee payers.

The trust's research into what licence fee payers actually want from the BBC is crystal clear – 'audiences have higher expectations of the BBC than of other broadcasters, and they want the BBC to be held to higher standards'. There is no evidence that the public want it to become a niche broadcaster – 'there isn't a lot in broadcasting that audiences *don't* want from the BBC'. The BBC's future is too important to be left to the politicians and the lobbyists – 'the public have the right to play a central role in deciding the future of their BBC'.

That public involvement was conspicuous by its absence in the July 2015 deal over the licence fee. Raymond Snoddy has been the most authoritative of UK media commentators since his twenty years as the media specialist on the *Financial Times* showed how it should be done. Here he unravels the fascinating inside story of the brutal, short and very political negotiations over the licence fee with threats of service closures being announced on budget day and last-minute changes of position. In the end, the government and the BBC both gave ground – but the deal leaves the scale and scope of a future BBC still to be resolved.

Neil Midgley, one of the new generation of media journalists, casts a critical eye over the BBC's options in those negotiations to come – showing how many services could be affected by even the modest budget cut backs implied by the licence fee deal. He writes: 'It's looking likely that the government will force the BBC to make cuts in some areas – possibly genre by genre, programme by programme, making the BBC up its game in terms of innovation.' The arguments over budgets will, at heart, be about the purpose of the BBC. 'Hall will want to preserve a populist BBC that justifies universal funding – whereas Whittingdale has already come out in favour of distinctly public service offerings, which will not be replicated by commercial rivals.'

For James Heath, the BBC's director of policy and a key figure in preparing the BBC management's vision of its future, to be published in September 2015,

4

this is the central debate. He does not believe that the BBC's role is simply to fill the gaps left by 'market failure'. He writes: 'The case for the BBC starts from a different set of considerations about the sort of society we want to live in. The BBC exists to deliver a public mission.' Far from 'crowding out' the private sector, he argues that public funding has a vital role in supporting the UK's vibrant media market. He accepts that the BBC is not 'a perfect institution that does not need to change', but he stresses: 'The BBC works in practice because it works in theory.'

Any decision on the future size of the BBC in the UK will also have international implications. Alice Enders, economist and media industry analyst, shows that the BBC is now one of the UK's only significant global media players. In France, Germany and Japan, for example, the public broadcasters are no longer in the international game – in this, as in other areas, the current BBC is on its own. And the fate of ABC in Australia and CBC in Canada, modelled on the BBC, is a cautionary tale – both have suffered budget cutbacks after the election of centre-right governments and suffered 'a disproportionately reduced international presence'.

According to Brian Winston, one of the UK's leading media academics, 'no broadcaster is an island'. He worries about the continuing Murdoch influence on British media policy since the secret 1981 lunch with Margaret Thatcher that handed Rupert Murdoch dominance of the UK newspaper industry. The first critic to talk about reducing the BBC's 'scale and scope' – now the focus of so much debate, in precisely those terms – was James Murdoch in his 2009 Edinburgh MacTaggart lecture. Winston does not have much time for the 'constitutional conventions' which are meant to protect the BBC from the politicians – quoting Dicey's view that such conventions are 'fictions ... the most fanciful dreams of *Alice in Wonderland*'. The bell tolls, he warns – and not just for the BBC. As fundamental issues are debated – and decided – in the few short months that remain of the old charter, the stakes have never been higher.

Sky set up as rival to BBC

A Smaller BBC?

The corporation needs a radical approach to survive and the *status quo* is simply not an option, argues Michael Grade

It is so easy to criticise the BBC, and too often the corporation makes it all too easy. Executive pay-offs, Savile, McAlpine, mismanagement of public money (£100 million written-off on a failed digital project) – they provide a regular supply of ammunition to their enemies. Little wonder the BBC is accused of being too big, too complex and too difficult to manage.

When criticised, the responses are mostly too defensive, too threatening or full of post-rationalisation. Apologies usually have to be dragged out of the management, too little and too late. This all points to an institutional mind-set which is out of touch and out-of-date – in short, inward-looking. Until the arrival of John (Lord) Birt, the BBC was oblivious to the seismic political shift heralded by Thatcherism. In today's economic times, when the government of the day is struggling to get the nation's balance sheet back into manageable shape, the BBC gives the impression that it is immune to such outside forces.

Leading *Sunday Telegraph* columnist Janet Daley recently wrote of its current condition: 'The truth is that the BBC is now such a huge, self-referring, inbred institution that it can no longer trust its own judgement.' I am sure this must happen to all ageing institutions, whether public or private. In the BBC's case, which has publicly and politically to justify its existence every ten years, it could become a fatal flaw. That must not happen. The BBC, at its core, is too important in so many ways, both culturally and commercially, to be allowed to continue to self-harm. I would personally 'die in the ditch' for the BBC and its monopoly funding. But it has to change.

Public institutions that do not have to live or die by a profit-and-loss account have to invent other key performance indicators to judge their own progress. These KPIs usually boil down to acquiring more 'turf', plus, of course, increased public funding. No institution, I will wager, has ever scored better on these latter measures than the British Broadcasting Corporation. It has survived regular charter reviews, a full-frontal ideological attack (the Thatcher years) and endless inquiries (Annan and Peacock, to name just two). But, like Pac-Man of yesteryear, it just keeps coming.

'Auntie the mistress of token sacrifices'

As a result of its Darwin-esque survival instincts, it now has a guaranteed annual income of around £3.7 billion. Moreover, it has gone forth and multiplied, occupying sizeable chunks of the new, valuable radio and television digital spectrum and is a major player in the online space. Despite customary pleas of poverty, it has managed recently to absorb the costs of the World Service, the Welsh Fourth Channel and other miscellaneous items. Now it has absorbed licence fee concessions for pensioners. No matter how the private sectors of programme-making and facilities-supply have developed, the BBC carries on doing what it has always done, paying lip-service only to the changes around it. 'Auntie' is the mistress of token sacrifices!

And the media landscape inhabited by the BBC is flourishing like never before. Sky, ITV, Channels 4 and 5, plus BT and hundreds of digital channels, have transformed modern viewers' choice, not to mention online services. At the onset of yet another charter review, this is the right time for even its most committed supporters to ask the BBC to think how it can *voluntarily* adapt and continue to justify such unfashionable and, some would argue, unnecessary public intervention in such a dynamic and expanding market.

Is it too much to hope that the BBC, just for once in its history, could *volunteer* a plan for a radical rationalisation of its size, scope and complexity? To do so would not be a 'denial of the faith'. It would disarm its enemies, transform political perceptions and enhance its independence for the foreseeable future. I can dream, can't I? I have always been, and remain, a 'believer' in the very idea of the BBC. I have twice worked inside the corporation, so I feel qualified to understand its great strengths, and its weaknesses.

Keeping the rest of broadcasting 'honest'

The basic case *for* is that, with secure and adequate public funding through the compulsory licence fee, the BBC is able to keep the rest of the domestic sector 'honest'. By this I mean that at its best, its guaranteed monopoly funding enables it to take risks, avoid patronising audiences in search of ratings, and provide a rich diet of British-made programmes for British viewers with only one overall purpose: to educate, inform and entertain. It is a key engine for growth and exports in our valuable creative industries. It is a bulwark against foreign ownership of our media, which is proceeding apace: Channel 5 is US-owned as are many of our most successful independent producers.

There are worrying signs that the BBC is playing its usual hand in the charter review process. Reams and reams of strategy papers, 'evidence' and, somewhat disingenuously, cost comparisons with Sky etc, are pouring out of Broadcasting House. These will conveniently ignore that the public has a choice in the private sector but *no* choice in paying for the BBC – and warn of Armageddon if the BBC loses so much as one of its activities.

The questions that cannot be avoided

Secretary of state John Whittingdale has convened a special panel to try to answer the many questions the BBC puts huge effort into avoiding. What is now the core mission of a public sector media broadcaster in an age of almost intimidating choice? What can it give up in order to remain relevant and to have enough scale to matter? What is its core mission? How should it be funded?

The future of the BBC can only be secured long term (with its compulsory licence fee) if the corporation takes a long hard look at its activities and services and embarks on a zero-based, bottom-up justification for every one of its myriad activities. It is telling that these questions now have to be researched by a committee of politically-appointed outsiders. As an old BBC hand myself, the detailed questions to which I am looking for answers are:

- how many digital television channels does the BBC really need, is six too many?

- can the News Channel demonstrate it represents value for money? If so, should it move to online only?

- is there a case to privatise Radios 1 and 2 and, maybe 5?

- should they give up all in-house television drama, light entertainment and documentary production?

- is the publisher/broadcaster model appropriate now that the independent sector is a proven creative powerhouse?

- should *all* physical production (except for news) be out-sourced, including post-production and studios?

- how can the extensive property portfolio be further rationalised?

- should online viewing and listening be encrypted and should the licence fee include an *optional* online supplement to unlock online services?

- is it fair to commercial competitors that the BBC is free to cross-promote radio across television channels and *vice versa*, thus providing it with a massive advantage?

Impartial news, domestic, nations and international should be at the core of the BBC's future. *But* the BBC must be able to answer effectively how ITN, privately-funded, manages to service three national networks on a fraction of the BBC's news resources. The BBC's enemies would like to see the corporation reduced simply to an elitist ghetto, redressing a narrow market failure, which they define as niche, uncommercial, unpopular programming.

There is market failure in today's burgeoning media space. That failure I prefer to define as risk-taking and innovation. It includes drama, entertainment, factual, documentaries, arts, the whole gamut of genres and genres yet to be invented.

Yes to *Strictly*, No to *The Voice*

The BBC is paid for by everyone and everyone should get value at some time from some service. So it is *yes* to *Strictly*, highly original, high class, popular family entertainment but *no* to *The Voice*, as unoriginal a format as ever I saw.

In the cut-throat competition that is the private sector, risk-taking is hard to find these days. It is understandable. Their advertisers and shareholders correctly expect immediate results. The BBC has none of these inhibitors. It has a monopoly source of revenue, so reaching out and failing is not financially punishing. Its mission *must* be to strive at all times in all genres to take risks. Its commissioning processes are in dire need of being streamlined to allow for this. It is *not* a badge of shame to lose share of audience, provided from time to time it can produce wonderfully compelling, popular programmes such as *Strictly Come Dancing*, *Bake Off* and *Masterchef*. (One caveat here: it is impossible to predict how the BBC is impacted by the devolution agenda across the UK until parliament has reached a post-election consensus. The economic implications for the corporation of a new constitutional settlement are too uncertain and must be left for another day.)

The BBC has been unable to resist government impositions to fund digital switch-over, the World Service and S4C out of its existing licence fee revenues – proof to its enemies that it always has more money than it really needs, but also undermining its independence. With a drastically reduced scale and scope (devolution adjustments excluded), it would be demonstrable that there are no more funding projects that government departments, desperate to make savings, can continue to dump on a bloated BBC.

A *much smaller* BBC would be simpler and more efficient to manage and govern. It would have to make the structural changes, which have been postponed by years of 'salami-slicing' budgets. It would have the money to do what is asked of it well with demonstrable efficiency. It would present less of a threat to the exciting, innovative new media markets. In short, it would be a much smaller target for those growing numbers who do not believe in the idea of the BBC – either for ideological or commercial reasons. Once all of these questions are answered, that will be the time to look at the governance structure, but not before.

No doubt I will be 'spun' as a heretic for departing from BBC orthodoxy. But, I want the BBC to survive. It is a most valuable national asset, recognised the world over. I just wish those responsible for charter review would get out more.

Tomorrow's BBC

Rona Fairhead considers how we can build the BBC most effectively for the next generation. She argues that, while there is need for reform, the BBC should remain a universal service, independent from politicians, bringing a wide range of benefits to everyone in the UK

The UK has built something special in the BBC. That's what our audience surveys tell us. It is a very British institution with an enduring mission which countries around the world respect and would love to call their own. It's certainly not perfect. But it is something of real and lasting value. It informs us. It educates us. It entertains us. It creates economic wealth through support for key industries like music and television production and plays a critical role in the UK's position as a creative powerhouse. It brings editorially independent news into people's homes throughout the four nations of the UK on television, radio and online. It brings people together to witness and enjoy significant events in our national life. And through the quality of its content, it encourages other broadcasters to up their game, improving standards across the board to the benefit of all viewers.

But it is also clear that the BBC needs to reform in a number of areas including its costs, the complexity of its structures, its governance, how it works with other parts of the industry and the way it serves an increasingly disparate nation.

The formal charter review debate has now begun. The over-arching question for that debate is: what is the right BBC for the next generation? And from that come other questions. What should its role and mission be? Should it still seek to serve everybody in return for a licence fee that we all pay? How can it best serve generations to come, both in terms of its programmes but also the wider benefits it brings to society and the economy? How can it best maintain its independence from politicians and commercial interests? How can it partner more and stimulate, but not crowd out, the competition? When does it need boundaries and what form should they take, including around its online services?

And how can it most effectively and efficiently serve audiences when it faces increasing financial constraints that will entail ever tougher choices? While we are still in the foothills of charter review, I will set out the thoughts of the trust on these questions, largely rooted in what the public have told us over the past eight-and-a-half years. Despite the incessant noise around it, the future of the BBC needs to be driven by evidence and fact, not by prejudice and not by vested interest.

First, and most profoundly, there is good evidence that audiences very much want the BBC to continue to be part of their lives and that they believe that a significant public benefit arises from the existence of a strong, independent BBC that provides a universal service. That is to say a BBC that provides programmes people love at a lower cost than would be possible for a niche broadcaster, and that brings a multitude of other benefits, like jobs, economic growth, social cohesion and enhanced international standing. That's why 97 per cent of the population still use the BBC every week and 46 million of us use it every day. The trust's research shows an extraordinarily high level of public support for the Reithian mission to inform, educate and entertain (although not necessarily in the order Reith originally expressed it). Four out of five believe the BBC achieves its mission objectives.[1] And it is worth stressing that the public strongly back the 'entertainment' part of the package. They expect their BBC to give them high quality entertainment as well as high quality drama, and high quality coverage of the great events – from state occasions, to moments of high political tension, to iconic sporting moments – that bring the nations together. The trust has seen no evidence that the public want less entertainment from the BBC. What they want is a broad range of programmes with a common theme – and that's quality. Audiences take it as axiomatic that the BBC should set higher editorial standards than they demand of other broadcasters – not just in terms of accuracy and impartiality and fairness and respect, but in the way the BBC goes about the business of making its programmes. That's why, on those occasions when the BBC fails the test, audiences feel genuinely let down.

Significant majorities also support the idea of a BBC that provides something for every household; that reflects lives as they are lived in the different nations and regions and communities that make up the UK; that contributes to UK prosperity; provides programmes that bring people together; gets the UK public talking and debating. They also still want a BBC free of advertisements, commercially independent. Paradoxically, while audiences largely want the BBC to remain true to its past, they also want it to embrace the future: to experiment, and to lead them into new technologies with content they can trust. The truth is – and it's sometimes a difficult one for governments to accept and for the BBC to live up to – there isn't a lot in broadcasting that audiences *don't* want from the BBC, and most of them are prepared to pay for it.

It is important to acknowledge from the outset that, in addition to what it actually broadcasts, the BBC also brings very significant wider benefits. These are many and diverse. For example, the BBC is a hot-house for nurturing and training talent in the broadcasting industry. While it is important that the BBC does everything it can to hold on to its best people, it is also right that it provides a training ground from which the rest of the industry benefits. Indeed, it is inevitable – and healthy too – that some of the top talent the BBC develops both on and off air will leave to work in other parts of the industry. A recent independent study for the trust found that 49 per cent of ITV's factual, lifestyle, entertainment and comedy talent began their careers at the corporation.[2]

Bringing benefits to the UK economically and internationally
The BBC brings important benefits to the UK internationally, most notably through the World Service, which in 2015 reached 210 million people, going above 200 million for the first time. People around the world have respect and affection for the BBC – Kofi Annan, the former UN secretary general, called the World Service 'Britain's greatest gift to the world'. This has tangible knock-on benefits for the UK, encouraging people to do business, visit and study here. This respect for the World Service also helps the BBC to make programmes in other parts of the world and attract global talent. Perhaps most importantly, the World Service plays a key role in bolstering the UK's 'soft power'. A recent analysis, launched by the strategic communications consultancy Portland,[3] ranked the UK top for soft power in a league table of global leaders and found that it performed particularly strongly in relation to culture, digital, and global engagement.

The BBC incentivises its domestic competitors to improve the quality of their programmes to stay in the game. When Michael Grade was chief executive of Channel 4 he liked to say: 'It's the BBC that keeps us honest'[4] – the existence of the BBC gives its competitors an incentive to compete on quality rather than on purely commercial criteria. This produces higher quality across the whole UK ecology. Anyone looking at the generality of, say, US television, where public service broadcasting plays a much smaller role than in the UK, would be unlikely to disagree with this analysis. This is the case even though there are clearly examples (*House of Cards, Breaking Bad, Game of Thrones* spring to mind) across a narrow range of genres where the US system produces some extraordinarily high quality output – but at a price already way beyond the BBC's capacity to pay.

The evidence shows that the UK would be a far less formidable force in world markets if the BBC did not exist. According to the DCMS,[5] the UK creative industries employ 1.7 million people. They account for 5 per cent of the UK economy. They are responsible for more than £17 billion of exports. It is generally accepted that the existence of the BBC underpins a significant part of this success, particularly in the film, television and music sectors. The corporation's commercial arm, BBC Worldwide, acts as a global showcase, not just for BBC productions, but for programmes from a wide range of UK independents. In 2013/14, Worldwide paid more than £116 million to UK independent rights holders in upfront rights investment, profit share and royalties.[6]

At its foundation, the economic value of the BBC relies on a strong intellectual property framework to both protect and exploit its creative content in the UK and globally. Without the protection that this affords, the BBC and other content creators would find our strength as an economic powerhouse diminished and our power in global markets significantly weakened. It is, therefore, imperative that the BBC maintains a strong intellectual property regime.

The UK pop music industry – a world leader – freely acknowledges the BBC's key role in finding and developing new talent and creating an audience for it.[7] When the trust reviewed the BBC's music radio services recently, the BPI, the trade body representing the UK's recorded music industry, told us: 'The BBC is a fundamentally important part of the ecosystem for British music, and for the UK creative industries as a whole. BBC Radio is a critical part of the success of British music and the recorded music sector.'[8] Overall, this adds up to a real economic benefit. A study by Deloitte[9] found that each pound of the BBC licence fee produced two pounds of economic value for the UK, adding some £8 billion to GDP.

Nonetheless, the trust is clear that the BBC must do much more by way of partnerships and collaboration. The trust wants to see a more open BBC, actively seeking to broker alliances right across the cultural and creative spectrum, sharing its content and its technologies, acting as a catalyst, a platform, and a connector for new kinds of creative endeavours that deliver real benefits to all the partners involved, as well as to the wider creative economy – and thereby to the public. In particular, we want to see whether the BBC can partner more with local media who in some cases may no longer have the resources to adequately cover areas like local government and court reporting. The trust would encourage the BBC to help plug the democratic deficit here. To achieve all this, the BBC needs to become easier and more welcoming to work with, less bureaucratic, more agile, with fewer managerial layers – all issues where there has been progress but where more needs to be done. But, even while pressing the BBC hard to do more, and to make the structural and attitudinal changes needed to enable it to do more, we should not underestimate the contribution it already makes to the UK's creative industries and the economic benefit this generates for the wider public.

A BBC for everyone

So the evidence suggests that the BBC maintains public support (and our consultation process will further test the level of that support), has an enduring mission and brings real benefits across a broad spectrum of areas, but there remains the question of whether it should be a universal service. Some argue that the BBC should address only areas of market failure, with a schedule consisting of news and current affairs, children's, science, the arts, religion and so on. We recognise that the BBC can't be all things to all people, but we fundamentally support a BBC that everyone pays for and from which everyone benefits. This is not just in terms of its programmes, but the wider benefits that I have just set out and the economies of scale that enable the BBC to produce great programmes at a cost-effective rate that makes them available to all.

By definition, a BBC limited to areas of market failure would benefit principally the commercial interests of its competitors, so it is hardly surprising that some of them find this prospect attractive. It is essential that we don't get seduced by a short-term market failure argument with long-term irreversible consequences. It is, of course, right that the BBC constantly needs to evolve; the deliberations we have been going through about the future of BBC Three show the BBC taking this process seriously, however painful it may be. But we are concerned that some changes to the BBC could be irreversible. If we end up cutting the BBC back to an irreducible minimum, we should be under no illusions about the cultural, societal, educational and economic benefits that will be lost, in addition to the great programmes that would go.

Ever more acute pressure on BBC budgets

The problem for the BBC, of course, is not lack of aspiration to meet audience expectations, but ever more acute pressure on budgets. This stems in large part from five years of the licence fee being frozen, and increasing additional burdens placed on it – most recently the budget decision to give the BBC full responsibility for the over-75s television licence concession from 2020. As the trust has already set out,[10] we accept that this was a decision the government was entitled to take. But it should make the BBC wary of, ever again, accepting money under the direct control of government. The BBC's role is to hold politicians to account – and any ability to influence this through the control of funding has a potentially chilling effect on the BBC's independence. Nor can we endorse the process of agreeing a financial framework when the public, who – let us not forget – pick up the bill, were by-passed. As for the decision on the over-75s itself, we argued, along with the director general, for additional measures that, we believe, make the BBC financially sustainable in something like its current form: measures that include what the government have assured us about the licence fee rising in line with CPI over the charter period. It is on that basis that we agree with the chancellor's statement that he has given the BBC a sustainable income for the long term.

The immediate question, though, is where the budget decision leaves the charter review process. It is essential that we now have an open and honest discussion with licence fee payers about what sort of BBC they want for their money, given that the financial framework has been set. We have already started that conversation but it might ultimately mean presenting the public with pick-and-mix options to establish their priorities.

The trust is determined this charter review should establish that future changes to BBC funding should require public consultation and some form of parliamentary scrutiny. This will help protect both the BBC's financial and its editorial independence, for the two are entwined. Research carried out for the trust shows clearly that the public see a need for independent scrutiny and regulation, but they want this done by a separate body representing licence fee payers, not by politicians. That independence has needed defending over decades, not just from governments but also from parliament, with a growing tendency in recent years for select committees to question BBC executives about detailed editorial decisions. We believe that this charter review gives us a chance to codify the relationship between the BBC and the state, and the BBC and its public, so that the terms of engagement are clear, the processes transparent, and the BBC can be seen to be *both* accountable *and* independent. → *so the public realise the great loss if it were to go.*

Era of rapid technological and market changes

One undeniable fact is that the context within which the BBC will operate during the next charter period will be one of rapid technological change. The public have made it very clear they have a voracious appetite for the opportunities that new technologies offer. The BBC cannot sit still here, and audiences do not want it to. It has a strong history of initiating highly-valued technological change – the iPlayer being only the most recent example. But the iPlayer is now more than seven years old – which makes it venerable in digital time-scales. Everyone wonders where the next great innovation in delivery will come from, so the BBC must have the technical and research capacity, if not to invent new technologies, at least to adapt and exploit them.

Technology is not the only area of rapid change. The competitive environment in which the BBC operates is also changing fast. 2014 saw an extraordinary process of consolidation in the UK independent sector – home of some the BBC's most important creative partners. Super-indies became mega-indies as three of the top four production companies were taken over by international groups that dwarf the BBC. Meanwhile, global giants such as Google, Apple, Amazon and Netflix are all investing heavily in content. We need to see clarity from the BBC about how it intends to respond to these dramatic changes in its competitive environment.

Across many fronts it is clear that demands on the BBC budget will only increase. Significant new costs will arise from the need to construct new online delivery while maintaining existing broadcast networks. There is strong public demand for more tailored services for the nations and regions. Rights costs for some key genres are spiralling upwards, with high-end drama and sports-rights being particularly demanding. Where sport is concerned, there may be a case for new regulation to protect certain crown jewel events that bring the nations together if we are to be able to keep them on free-to-air networks. But even if that were achieved, the problem of the rapidly escalating cost is not going away.

Giving the public value for money

You might not believe it if you rely on what some of the BBC's harshest competitors in the press report, but actually the corporation has a good record of becoming steadily more efficient in recent years, and we know it can do more. The trust is determined that the BBC becomes a leaner organisation, with less complexity and clearer responsibilities. We are confident that the management recognises this need and can rise to the challenge. The BBC also needs to build further on the work that BBC Worldwide is doing to increase other sources of funding, and that in turn will reduce the pressure on the licence fee. We want to explore options for commercial partnerships or investment that could strengthen Worldwide's position and deliver long-term growth. However, we oppose outright privatisation because of the dramatic impact that would have on long-term revenue and on up-front investment in producing public service content. The global exploitation of its intellectual property rights is a critical part of the future funding of the BBC.

But nobody should be under doubt that budget pressures on the scale that the BBC is facing, together with the responsibility for paying the licence fee for the over-75s, will lead to some impact on programmes and services. The charter review public consultation will be critical to determining the nature of the changes that entails.

As to how the BBC is paid for, our research currently shows that the licence fee remains, by some margin, the system that commands the most support among the public. It has the advantage of being widely understood and accepted. We welcome the government's commitment to modernise the licence fee by closing the iPlayer loophole that lets people watch television programmes on demand without a licence as long as they are not viewed 'live'. The trust has an open mind about the longer term, and as traditional broadcast services perhaps make way for online delivery in the future, technology could offer new funding opportunities too. However, the trust's clear view is that any model needs to be universal – it must offer something for everyone. A subscription model for the BBC's public services would be incompatible with this, although it is worth exploring for the BBC's commercial services. In the meantime, we are consulting licence fee payers about the funding options put forward in the green paper, including a universal household levy and a combination of public funding and 'top-up' subscription services.

The question of governance

Finally, there is the question of governance. This is not the place to explore this question in any depth. Any system of governance has both strengths and weakness. The trust's strength has been in bringing transparency and accountability to the BBC's range of services, each one with its own licence setting out what the trust requires it to deliver within its headline budget. The trust's service reviews have given both audiences and the whole industry a voice in assessing the BBC's performance. The trust has shown its willingness to curb the BBC's ambitions when they would not have served audience interests well or would have caused undue impact on the BBC's competitors. We have set – and effectively policed – the highest editorial standards in broadcasting, putting complainants and the BBC on an entirely equal footing in the hearing of appeals.

And the trust has been instrumental in driving efficiencies from the BBC over years of frozen funding.

But there have been failures too, often exacerbated by the blurred lines of accountability in oversight and governance. So we think reform of BBC governance – intelligent reform – is necessary, and we have set out our proposals to bring greater clarity over responsibilities and accountabilities.[11] In brief, our view is that the BBC needs to be run by a stronger unitary executive board with an independent chairman and a majority of non-executive directors. It would have sole responsibility for running the BBC and its strategy and corporate governance. The BBC's services would be scrutinised by an external regulator, taking over the trust's responsibilities for quality control and accountability. It would regulate the BBC's market impact and ensure that it abided by fair trading principles. We think it needs to be a bespoke regulator for a whole range of reasons. Audiences have higher expectations of the BBC than of other broadcasters, and they want the BBC to be held to higher standards. And we believe the BBC's regulator should have a public role in providing guidance on what would be a sufficient level of funding to enable the corporation to fulfil its public purposes and meet the expectations of the public.

If the regulation of the BBC is to be kept beyond the immediate direction of ministers, any future regulator should be established, like the BBC itself, under royal charter. The new regulator would continue to provide a buffer between BBC management and government to ensure the BBC's independence is maintained – a matter of central importance to the public.

Whatever the ultimate BBC governance solution set out in the new charter, and however the responsibilities are shared between regulator and board, we are clear that the system must fulfil three roles:

- regulation to apply the appropriate checks and balances to what is a major market intervention;

- oversight of the BBC's strategy, operations and management, and

- representation of licence fee payers to ensure the public voice is heard, that value for money is achieved and that quality and editorial standards are met.

And so to return to the beginning: what is the right BBC for the next generation? Answering this will be the fundamental challenge of charter review. And it now needs to be answered within a defined funding package. What we do know is that people value the BBC. As its owners, they rightly have huge expectations of it; expectations that need to be met as far as possible within these ever tighter funding constraints and in the face of arguably the greatest external challenges the BBC has confronted in its lifetime.

It is clear to me and my fellow trustees that the *status quo* is not an option. We need to be clear about the BBC's future priorities, and exactly what changes need to be made. But this should all happen through a proper debate where the public's voice is heard loud and clear. The BBC's future is simply too important to be settled behind closed doors.

Importance of public engagement

And it needs to be a debate based on evidence, not anecdote. To help achieve this, as representatives of the licence fee payer, the trust has launched its most comprehensive programme of public and industry engagement, including a public consultation, seminars throughout the UK, greater use of social media to canvass views and engage in debate, and more surveys and polling.

The public have the right to play a central role in deciding the future of their BBC. We will do everything we can to encourage them to seize the opportunity. They have all grown up with the BBC. Now they must say what BBC they want to hand on to the next generation.

Notes

[1] http://downloads.bbc.co.uk/bbctrust/assets/files/pdf/news/2015/audience_research.pdf, accessed on 24 July 2015

[2] http://downloads.bbc.co.uk/bbctrust/assets/files/pdf/review_report_research/managing_talent/managing_talent.pdf, accessed on 24 July 2015

[3] http://www.portland-communications.com/wp-content/uploads/2015/07/The-Soft-Power-30_press-release.pdf, accessed on 24 July 2015

[4] http://www.bbc.co.uk/pressoffice/speeches/stories/bpv_grade.shtml, accessed on 24 July 2015

[5] https://www.gov.uk/government/publications/creative-industries-economic-estimates-january-2015/creative-industries-economic-estimates-january-2015-key-findings, accessed on 25 May 2015

[6] http://www.bbcworldwide.com/annual-review/annual-review-2014.aspx, accessed on 25 May 2015

[7] ibid

[8] http://downloads.bbc.co.uk/bbctrust/assets/files/pdf/our_work/music_radio/bpi.pdf, accessed on 24 July 2015

[9] http://downloads.bbc.co.uk/aboutthebbc/insidethebbc/howwework/reports/pdf/bbc_economic_impact_2013.pdf, accessed on 25 May 2015

[10] http://downloads.bbc.co.uk/bbctrust/assets/files/pdf/news/2015/letter_chancellor_sos.pdf, accessed on 24 July 2015

[11] http://www.bbc.co.uk/bbctrust/news/speeches/2015/oxford_media_convention, accessed on 25 May 2015

How BBC Warnings of Financial Meltdown brought Government to Negotiating Table

Imminent announcements of major eye-catching service closures by the corporation won major concessions from the government, Raymond Snoddy reports exclusively

The BBC feared all along that the department of work and pensions (DWP) had never given up on its desire to pass on to the corporation the financial responsibility for free licence fees for the over-75s, introduced without ceremony or warning by the then-Labour chancellor Gordon Brown in 2001. Yet until almost the last minute the BBC hoped the deeply controversial action would not be taken.

Iain Duncan Smith had tried once in 2010 and failed. He planned to try again as a relatively easy way of helping to fund the DWP's contribution towards the £12 billion cut in public spending promised during the 2015 general election campaign by George Osborne, the chancellor of the exchequer. Such a policy would cost more than £650 million a year initially, and would then rise steadily as a result of an ageing population to more than £750 million.

At stake, apart from the cost, was the important principle that the BBC licence fee should not be used as an arm of social service policy. It was that principle which led the majority of the members of the BBC Trust under the chairmanship of Sir Michael Lyons in 2010 to decide they would resign *en masse* unless the government backed down. It did and the BBC lived to fight another day. For months the BBC was reassured that the government would not try again to impose the cost of free licences on the BBC. Several times after the May 2015 general election when the BBC asked, the corporation was told not to worry, the Treasury was opposed to such a charge on the licence fee. Gradually, however, the tone changed and the answers became more equivocal, the caveats more noticeable.

James Purnell, the BBC's head of strategy and former Labour culture secretary, is experienced at reading the political runes, listening to what is not said, as much as to what civil servants and politicians are actually saying. At an internal meeting in the BBC on Friday, 26 June 2015, the strategy head warned that a new attempt to impose free licence fees for the over-75s was now a distinct possibility, although he had no idea how or when it might happen.

'No room for the BBC to negotiate on principle'

Purnell was prescient. The calls from John Whittingdale, the recently appointed secretary for culture, media and sport (DCMS) to Lord Hall, the director general of the BBC, and Rona Fairhead, who chairs the BBC Trust, came at 9.45 am on Monday, 29 June. There had been tough inter-government negotiations involving the Treasury but ultimately the imperative to cut public spending, with DCMS under pressure from the DWP, carried the day. A final decision had been taken and government ministers, perhaps learning from the dramatic brinkmanship of five years earlier, made it clear there was no room for the BBC to negotiate on the principle.

Whittingdale and his officials explained that although the over-75s decision had been made, it did not mean that the BBC could not get the money back in another form as part of the much longer royal charter review process. BBC executives recognised the political cleverness of the manoeuvre. It would have been very hard, and might even have appeared irresponsible, for Tony Hall to threaten to resign, when at least in theory, the game was still on and there was apparently a lot to play for.

It was likely that the BBC Trust, much changed in political complexion from the days of Sir Michael, would not even seriously consider resigning, which anyway might turn out to be an empty gesture this time as the trust itself could well be abolished as part of the charter review.

The talks between the two sides got under way in the search for balancing compensation for the free licence fee decision, or mitigation as it came to be called. Hall met officials the day after and on Wednesday 1 July there was a much more heavyweight meeting between Hall, Osborne and Whittingdale with the cabinet secretary Sir Jeremy Hayward in attendance. There was little sign of any movement on the basic government position that mitigation would be a matter for the charter review, although conciliatory noises were noticeable.

The following day, Thursday 2 July, in a small concession, Whittingdale called Hall and said that the BBC would be spared £50 million of the £150 million annual payment the corporation has been required to pay towards improving broadband rollout in the UK since the 2010 settlement. Anything else would have to be negotiated during the charter process. The call could have done little to lift Hall's mood. That very day he had been forced to announce that a £150 million hole was opening up in the BBC's finances for 2016/17 because an unexpectedly large number of people were giving up on their television sets and, therefore, not having to pay the BBC licence fee. Instead, they were exploiting a loophole and using their laptops, Xboxes and smart phones to watch recorded online material, including recorded BBC programmes via the iPlayer, that they were making no contribution to funding. More than 1,000 jobs would be lost as a result of a new round of cost-cutting, most of them in middle management, following a simplification of the BBC's structure. The process would include the merger of a number of divisions.

The BBC director general tried to soften the public relations blow of yet more financial problems at the corporation by announcing that a new independent study by consultants PwC (PricewaterhouseCoopers) published that day had ranked the BBC amongst the most efficient public sector organisations. The BBC's overhead costs were around 8 per cent and were due to fall to 7 per cent, compared with the public sector average of 11.2 per cent and the regulated industry average of 8.8 per cent.

On the financial discussions with the government the issue was now completely clear. As far as the government was concerned there was no opportunity for further compromise before charter review. If the government had been prepared to be more flexible the BBC would have been in a more difficult, equivocal position. As it was this outcome was completely unacceptable and had to be opposed vigorously.

'Devastating consequences' of government proposals

During the previous several days Treasury officials had been reluctant to accept the BBC's account of the potentially devastating consequences of what the government was suggesting. After all, last time the BBC had managed to absorb a licence fee that had been frozen for six years and taken on the additional cost of paying for the World Service, the Welsh Fourth Channel and Caversham monitoring services on top. More than 2,000 jobs had been lost but the BBC had still been able to protect and pay for all its existing services plus the new responsibilities. One of the BBC executives involved, explaining the Treasury attitude, said:

> The Treasury officials didn't believe we couldn't make those cuts without service closures. One of the things in retrospect … was that Mark Thompson [the previous DG] made the previous round of cuts without closing any services while back-loading all the difficult [financial] stuff. Let's try again and if it doesn't work we'll know we have gone far enough.

So that evening Lord Hall and his executives made it clear the BBC would have to reject the proposals and campaign against them in public. The BBC was facing an overall financial hit of close to £1 billion a year including that day's £150 million savings. George Osborne was told in words of one syllable, and with numbers to back up the BBC case, exactly what the consequences of the government's plans would be:

- BBC Two would close.

- BBC Four would close.

- All BBC local radio stations would go off the air.

- The national radio news services for Scotland, Wales and Northern Ireland would also be shut down.

The BBC director general did his very best to convince the chancellor that this was no idle threat or negotiating tactic but a matter of grim and prudent financial reality.

The BBC has only the most limited borrowing ability and was in danger of running out of money, a process that could begin accelerating if more viewers began exploiting 'the loophole'. Because of the financial background the BBC could not go on spending money it did not have on such services, in the hope that some undefined mitigation could be achieved much later in the royal charter negotiations. There was actually a danger that one of the most famous broadcasters in the world could go broke unless urgent action was taken.

The BBC announcement on the service closures would come on the day of the summer budget, or more probably the day after. If not exactly overnight, the actual closures could not be long delayed because of the financial imperatives involved. The sceptical Treasury officials were given the numbers to back up the BBC case that the world's most highly regarded public service broadcaster was facing financial meltdown because of the proposed policies of the Conservative government. The proposed service closures had been carefully selected. With the imposition of the over-75s free licence fee, the BBC had to do everything it could to keep in touch with young audiences so services like Radio 1 or even BBC One could not be jeopardised.

Echoes of 2010 stand-off between government and BBC

In the talks there were eerie echoes of the all-night negotiations five years earlier during a stand-off between the coalition government and the BBC when George Osborne faced the then-director general, Mark Thompson, across the Treasury table. The issues were remarkably similar, the sense of drama and crisis equally palpable even though the outcome was rather different.

Then, on Monday 18 October 2010, Thompson and Sir Michael were invited to the department of culture, media and sport to be told by the then-culture secretary, Jeremy Hunt, rather plaintively and with a shrug of the shoulders, that the government had decided after all to make the BBC take responsibility for the free licences for the over-75s. The two men were shocked and thought they had been successful over a week of negotiations in persuading the government to change its mind and reject the over-75s policy. But the imperative of the imminent Comprehensive Spending Review had apparently prevailed, just as the promised £12 billion in public spending cuts had this time.

A rather disconsolate Thompson was on the train home to Oxford and members of the BBC strategy team were in the pub drowning their sorrows when the BBC director-general received a message to return to London immediately. There had been a change of mind. The Lib Dems' media spokesman Don Foster, who was opposed to the over-75s plan as a 'disgraceful' dipping into the licence fee, had been active in alerting the office of deputy PM Nick Clegg about the attitudes and likely behaviour of the BBC Trust.

That afternoon BBC executives called everyone they could think of who might influence Osborne including Lib Dem business secretary Vince Cable. The threat of mass resignations at the BBC Trust following a meeting planned for the following morning was expertly deployed. Only two trust members, former banker Anthony Fry and Dame Patricia Hodgson, the former BBC executive who currently chairs Ofcom, had made it clear they had no intention of resigning.

Thompson got off the Oxford train when it stopped at Slough, crossed platforms and returned to his office to take part in what would become all-night negotiations. Once again the choice was clear. The BBC could escape paying for the over-75s and a planned 'scale and scope' inquiry if it was prepared to accept, within 12 hours, a frozen licence fee and the BBC World Service, Welsh Fourth channel and Caversham costs, plus some of the start-up costs for Hunt's pet project – local television services – and the contribution to broadband rollout.

The deal was done and Thompson declared that the all-night horse-trading represented 'the best of the available outcomes for the BBC, and actually a pretty good outcome'. It was a conclusion that was not universally shared, not least in the BBC. Of the method by which the deal was done, without consultation with either parliament or people, the then-chairman of the House of Commons media select committee, John Whittingdale, declared that it had been wholly wrong. 'No future licence fee negotiation must be conducted in the way of the 2010 settlement,' Whittingdale pronounced last year before going on to do exactly the same as Hunt, but with less apparent reticence.

Dramatic government change of heart overnight

This time, too, there appeared to have been a dramatic change of heart overnight. Tony Hall and Rona Fairhead went to see George Osborne, who had largely taken over the negotiations from Whittingdale, in his office at the Treasury at 11am on Friday 3 July and found him suddenly to be in 'a very constructive mood'. Significant 'mitigations' of the cost of the over-75s licence fees would be possible after all. Where once it had been the threat of BBC Trust resignations that had made the difference, this time it was imminent BBC announcements of major eye-catching service closures, which could have overshadowed the impact of the budget measures, that had brought the government to the negotiating table.

Other influences were almost certainly deployed behind the scenes on some of the key players in the drama. When she heard about the government's ultimatum on the over-75s, Diane Coyle, the economist and former senior member of the BBC Trust, called Lord Patten, the former chairman of the BBC Trust and Conservative politician, to inform him about what was happening. It is not known whether Lord Patten was subsequently in contact informally with his old political colleague George Osborne but he was certainly outspoken about the government's 'awful' plans to make the BBC pay for pensioners' free licence fee on BBC Radio 4's *The World at One*. In remarkably cutting language for a former Conservative cabinet minister, the former BBC Trust chairman called John Whittingdale an 'adolescent ideologue'.

Coyle believes that the government action on the over-75s is 'profoundly unconstitutional', quite apart from what she calls the dodgy process by which it was imposed. 'I am amazed that parliament hasn't made more of a fuss about a welfare policy being outsourced,' says Coyle, who tracks the tendency for increased top-slicing of the licence fee back to an obscure change of licence fee definition in 2006 that was barely noticed at the time. The Office of National Statistics decided that the licence fee was a tax rather than a service charge. The change, which Coyle believes was a misjudgement by the ONS, opened the door to the raft of top-slicing measures that have happened subsequently, culminating in the recent imposition.

Government change of heart on 'mitigations'

Following the government's change of heart on mitigations, the BBC would, indeed, take on the full cost of the over-75s television licence concession, but at least it would be phased in from 2018, with the full liability being met by the BBC from 2018/19. The DWP contribution towards the cost would fall from £468 million in 2018/19 to zero by 2020/21. Crucially from the government's point of view the deal on free licence fees would be honoured throughout the current parliament as promised.

Equally crucially from the BBC's stance, after that, the corporation would take over control of the policy. The BBC interprets this as meaning that from the next parliament it can do whatever it decides on free licences. This could include abolishing the concession or introducing means testing to reduce the cost, though considerably unpopularity among the over-75s could result.

There was a list of other mitigations, some more bankable than others. The broadband ring-fence would fall to £80 million in 2017/18, £20 million in 2018/19, £10 million in 2019/20 and down to zero by 2020/21. The government would also legislate next year 'to modernise the licence to cover public service broadcast catch-up TV' but did not explain in detail how that was to be done. The BBC's contribution to funding the Welsh Fourth Channel would be cut in proportion to any other cuts in overall licence fee funding.

There were two other important matters in the package. The government pledged that it would carefully consider the case for decriminalisation of the non-payment of the licence fee in the light of the recent report by an independent review team led by David Perry QC – which found against decriminalisation – and the need for 'the BBC to be funded appropriately'. No decision would be taken in advance of charter review although MPs have in the past expressed strong support for decriminalisation. The BBC has warned such a step would inevitably mean fewer people paying the licence fee and the corporation could lose up to £200 million a year as a result.

The most important, and most problematical, mitigation involved the licence fee and inflation. The government said it 'anticipated' that the licence fee would rise in line with the Consumer Price Index (CPI) over the next charter review period. Two enormous conditions were, however, imposed on the unfreezing of the licence fee. The first is that the BBC has to demonstrate efficiency savings equivalent to those being made in other parts of the public sector. If PwC is right, this condition can probably be met by the BBC.

The other is potentially far more serious. CPI will be subject to the conclusions of the charter review in relation to 'the purposes and scope of the BBC'. This is a phrase subtly different from the more traditional 'scale and scope' and one that could have serious consequences for the range of BBC services currently on offer.

Appetite for smaller BBC

Whatever the difference in nuance turns out to mean in practice, there seems to be an initial government appetite for a smaller BBC and one that no longer seeks to 'chase ratings' or try to be 'all things to all people'. The approach appears to be reflected in the composition of a panel of eight expert advisers set up by Whittingdale whose technical adviser is Ray Gallagher, for many years a Sky executive who was also an adviser to Whittingdale's Commons media select committee.

The majority of the new panel, led by Dawn Airey, a former chief executive of Channel 5 who now works for Yahoo, have either worked for the BBC's commercial rivals, or in the past have declared themselves in favour of a narrower range of BBC services. Lord Patten, in a debate in the House of Lords, described the advisory panel as 'a team of assistant grave-diggers' who would help the culture secretary 'bury the BBC that we love'.

Broadcasting consultant Clare Enders, who is not on the panel of experts, has warned that linking CPI with 'purposes and scope' can only be seen as an area of major uncertainty and doubt for the corporation. Enders Analysis also pointed out that, contrary to Osborne claims about the BBC's 'imperialist' ambitions – although he was mainly referring to online – the corporation's share of total British television revenues is in long-term decline as a percentage. In 2010, the BBC had a 22 per cent share of television revenues in the UK. By 2016 that is forecast to fall to 17 per cent and on downwards to 12 per cent by 2026.

In her letter to chancellor Osborne following the negotiations, Fairhead referred to 'the assurance that the licence fee (£145.50) will rise in line with inflation over the next charter period'. The conditions attached to the 'anticipation' that the licence fee will rise in line with CPI and what scale of BBC service it would apply to appear to fall a long way short of an 'assurance'.

Privately, BBC executives accept there is a hole that politicians can push their way through if they want to undo the deal. They believe, however, that the undertakings, such as they are, were given in good faith and represent 'an insurance policy' against future risk. Better to have such an insurance policy as a base to argue from rather than starting totally afresh in the charter negotiations. 'If we play the politics right there is a bit of growth in this parliament and then in the next parliament it's all to argue for,' explained one executive.

Director-general Hall, as BBC director generals tend to do following tense negotiation with government, declared that overall the deal was a fair one for the corporation. He wrote in the *Observer* that 'although the BBC used this pre-budget window of opportunity to reach a fair deal, it is not a process we should have chosen and it is not a process that should be repeated'. Lord Hall went on to reject criticisms that the BBC's independence had been undermined: 'There has been no fundamental change in the relationship between government and corporation. Nor will there ever be on my watch. Our independence is precious and will never be negotiated away.' The cost of the over-75s had been 'more than matched by the deal coming back'.

On the financial balance sheet of the negotiations, James Heath, the BBC's policy director, argued that the effect of the agreement would be 'flat cash funding' for BBC content and services over the first five years of period, after implementing a programme of £1.6 billion of cumulative savings over the current charter period by 2016/17. Others have been more negative about the deal and have suggested that, in fact, rather than being cash neutral, the BBC could be down as much as 10 per cent even before any 'purpose and scope' determinations come into play.

Sir Michael Lyons is perfectly placed to set July's latest bout between the government and the BBC into context. For Sir Michael in 2010, two basic principles were at play: the licence fee should not be confused with general taxation and if the government wanted to get rid of the free licence fee it should have had the courage to take action itself rather than trying to shift the charge on to the BBC. The second was that in the general economic gloom that prevailed at the time, the corporation had to play its part in the deficit reduction challenge through taking on a number of broadcasting costs being funded by the government at the time. Sir Michael believes it is outrageous and 'a complete breach of faith' for the government to accept the savings imposed on the BBC and then come back for a second huge bite of the cherry five years later. He says:

> I do not want to say it was a great negotiation in 2010 and a poor set of negotiations in 2015 but in 2010 we negotiated off the table the scale and scope review which is still on the table this time so they [the BBC] have gained nothing at all. We saw the fundamental threat of both the scale and scope review and the move of welfare payments and acted accordingly. I do not wish this to sound like we were heroes.

But at least the threat of resignation by a majority of trustees put the government off – it turns out only until the next time. The problem is the cumulative effect on the BBC. It took on board the raft of new costs to avoid the over-75s licence fees and the scale and scope review. The extra costs from 2010 remain, and the savings needed to absorb them, while the BBC has had to take on the additional cost of the free licence fees plus the uncertainty of what will come out of the 'purpose and scope' review.

What would Sir Michael Lyons have done if he had been chairman of the BBC Trust in 2015? Would he have resigned? 'I think I would have had to resign because they were simply coming back for something that they had already done a deal on. I am sure I would have resigned. On the other hand you have to be desperately cautious how you say and present these things. If I had been the chairman that might have been exactly what they had wanted,' he says with a laugh.

Crumbs of hope in challenging times ahead

BBC executives looking for crumbs of hope in the challenging times ahead, point to the heavy involvement of George Osborne in the final negotiations. The chancellor, they think, has changed his stance from believing that the days of the licence fee are numbered. Now there are signs that he sees the BBC, albeit a more efficient BBC that he is happy to squeeze, as a potentially important component of one-nation Toryism.

It is a slim hope to hang your hat on but one that is more preferable to the apparent ideological hostility to the BBC of John Whittingdale.

The Next Round of BBC Cuts: Where Will the Axe Fall?

The licence fee settlement really isn't that bad for the BBC, argues Neil Midgley – it's the green paper and charter renewal where DG Tony Hall will run into real problems

How deep will the BBC have to cut when the next royal charter and licence fee settlement take effect in 2017? After the licence fee deal was announced in July 2015 – with the BBC taking on responsibility for free licences for the over-75s – a cacophony of hand-wringers spoke out to bewail its horrors. It was a 'bullying backroom deal' and a 'scandal', wrote former BBC trustee Diane Coyle in the *Guardian*, which would involve 'a profound cut to the BBC's ability to deliver its services'. Former director general John Birt told the House of Lords communications committee that there had been 'another raid' on the BBC's finances. Steven Moffat, Stewart Lee, Jonathan Dimbleby, a raft of letter-writing Hollywood stars: the list of doom-sayers goes on.

I wonder, though, if any of this tin-hat brigade has looked at the figures in detail. I have, and my calculations show that the licence fee deal protects the BBC's annual income – in real terms – until April 2019 (see graph 1, below). And looking at the BBC's cumulative income over the next licence-fee period gives an even more surprising result: there is no real-terms cut until April 2020 (see graph 2, below). This licence fee deal is hardly the raid on BBC finances that has been so widely lamented.

How can that be so, given the huge liability for free TV licences for the over-75s? Well, for a start, the BBC's obligation to pay for the over-75s only kicks in gradually, rising over three years from 2018 (from £200 million in the first year to £745 million in the last). And 2018 is the second year of the next charter and licence fee. In 2017, the BBC will start to feel the benefit of the three sweeteners that it negotiated in that 'bullying backroom deal'. Its current obligation to help fund broadband rollout will gradually be phased out, netting the BBC £70 million in 2017 and rising to £150 million in 2020. The licence fee will be index-linked, meaning no more inflationary erosion to existing budgets. And the so-called 'iPlayer loophole' will be closed, forcing people to have a television licence to watch catch-up shows online, which the BBC estimates will bring in £100 million a year.

Income boost for BBC in 2017 and 2018

All of which means that in 2017 and 2018, the BBC will actually receive a real-terms boost to its income (of 4.4 per cent in 2017 and 0.8 per cent in 2018 – see graph 1).

And, because of those additional receipts early in the licence fee settlement, the cumulative income received by the BBC will not be cut, in real terms, until 2020. (In the financial year 2019/20, the BBC's cumulative income under the settlement will reach £11.857 billion – whereas simply index-linking its income from the last year of the previous settlement would have raised an almost identical figure of £11.862 billion. It is only in 2020/21 that the cumulative figures really turn against Hall, with £15.475 billion under the settlement vs an index-linked figure of £15.975 billion.)

True enough, my calculations do show a real-terms drop in *annual* income of 5.1 per cent in 2019, and 12 per cent from 2020 onwards. Cutting 12 per cent – or £450 million – from the BBC's annual budgets will be a real challenge. But it is not the full £700 million of over-75s liability that has been so widely reported. And to repeat: the cut is fully cushioned for the next four and a half years, giving director general Tony Hall plenty of time and room for manoeuvre.

I should say that, like any predictive numbers, my calculations come with a health warning. They are based only on publicly available sources, including the summer budget document – not on complex computer models. And there are variables which mean that they could change either way. The BBC might benefit from household growth, meaning that more people (under the age of 75) pay the licence fee. And there is another valuation of the BBC pension fund in 2016 which – if interest rates rise as predicted – could see the pension deficit shrink, and with it the BBC's contributions, which are currently running at £185 million a year.

On the other hand, the licence fee deal requires the BBC to demonstrate that it is undertaking efficiency savings 'at least equivalent to those in other parts of the public sector' – whatever that means. And then, of course, comes the biggest imponderable of all. Culture secretary John Whittingdale's green paper on the future of the BBC – which, of course, cunningly came after the licence fee deal – wonders aloud whether the BBC is of the right scale and scope. In other words: at the beginning of 2017, when the new royal charter begins, should there be a pre-emptive swing of the axe – so that when all these licence fee mechanisms kick in, they do so with a much-diminished baseline for the BBC?

Graph 1.
BBC annual income – index-linked baseline vs July 2015 settlement

	16/17	17/18	18/19	19/20	20/21	21/22
Graph line 1: July 2015 settlement	3,800	4,046	3,984	3,827	3,618	3,701
Graph line 2: index-linked baseline	3,800	3,876	3,954	4,032	4,113	4,196

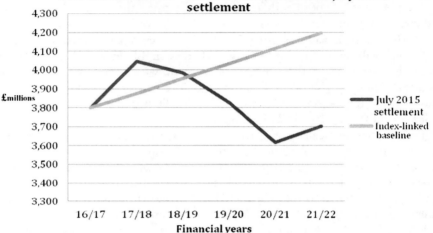

Graph 2.
BBC cumulative income – index-linked baseline vs July 2015 settlement

	16/17	17/18	18/19	19/20	20/21	21/22
Graph line 1: July 2015 settlement	3,800	4,046	8,030	11,857	15,475	19,176
Graph line 2: index-linked baseline	3,800	3,876	7,830	11,862	15,975	20,171

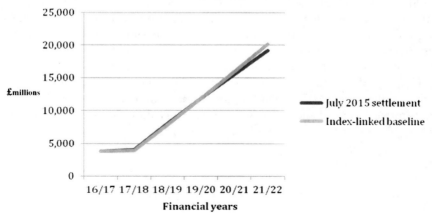

Notes

1 Baseline figure for BBC income of £3,800,000 in 2016/17 is taken from the Treasury's summer budget 2015, p. 109. Available online at https://www.gov.uk/government/uploads/system/uploads/attachment_data/file/4432 32/50325_Summer_Budget_15_Web_Accessible.pdf

2 These graphs assume CPI inflation at the Bank of England's target figure of 2 per cent

3 The differences between the index-linked baseline figures and the July 2015 settlement figures come from four agreements made between the BBC and the government as part of the settlement

3.1 That the BBC will take on liability for free TV licences for the over-75s, in stages, rising from £200 million in 2018/19 to the full liability of £745million in 2020/21 (Treasury summer budget 2015, p. 74)

3.2 That the licence fee will be modernised to cover catch-up TV online, bringing extra income estimated by the BBC itself at £100 million a year from 2017/18 (see blog by BBC head of policy James Heath, 9 July 2015. Available online at http://www.bbc.co.uk/blogs/aboutthebbc/entries/efa49056-e32f-4e8a-b2b4-cb215e6a0bc1)

3.3 That the current 'broadband ring-fence' from licence fee income will be phased out – the benefit to the BBC rising from £70 million in 2017/18 to £150 million in 2020/21 (and onwards); see John Whittingdale statement to the House of Commons, 6 July 2015. Available online at http://www.publications.parliament.uk/pa/cm201516/cmhansrd/cm150706/debtext/1 50706-0001.htm#1507066000598)

3.4 That the licence fee will rise in line with CPI inflation – also John Whittingdale's statement to the House of Commons, 6 July 2015

As that negotiation really gets going in the autumn, it will not just be Tory ideology that Hall, Rona Fairhead, BBC Trust chair, and their lieutenants have to fight. Their sharpest problem is that Whittingdale knows where the bodies are buried. He spent ten years as chairman of the Commons culture, media and sport select committee, writing hundreds of pages of reports on the corporation. So, for example, the green paper distinguishes between Saturday night entertainment hit *Strictly Come Dancing* (a BBC invention, which makes millions of pounds around the world for licence fee payers) and Saturday night entertainment hit *The Voice* (an off-the-shelf foreign format, which required no innovation on the BBC's part and will only ever cost it money). No other culture secretary of recent memory would have been able to put the BBC's output under such an uncomfortable microscope.

Are Radio 1 and 2 'too commercial'?
The green paper also took aim at Radio 1 and Radio 2 for being too mainstream and commercial, which prompted BBC head of radio Helen Boaden instantly to write a blog protesting how distinctively public service they are. She would say that, wouldn't she? But other voices share the government's concern. Independent radio consultant Francis Currie suggests 'a radical restructure of the BBC radio proposition, in which it does fewer things – but makes them distinctive and puts them in the shop window, and stops playing ratings games'. Currie points to the documentaries on Radios 1 and 2 that get shunted to the edges of the schedule, and seldom repeated, while those stations' peak time programmes arguably resemble Capital or Heart.

Currie also singles out local radio as the BBC's 'problem child', saying that it has lost '5 per cent of its audience, and 10 per cent of its listening hours, during the last 12 months'. Put together, the 40 local stations are also the biggest item in the radio budget, at £149.6 million in 2013/2014 (compared to Radio 4 at £120.6 million). Falling between the news division and the radio division, local radio tends to be unloved within BBC management – but escaped big cuts last time around after a passionate campaign by listeners.

Again, commercial radio competitors have ideas about where the BBC could wield its axe. 'Just as they are using BBC Three to spearhead online TV viewing, why not use Radio 1 to drive DAB listening, by taking it off FM?' suggested one source. 'That would also have the advantage of saving them significant transmission costs.'

So it's looking likely that the government will force the BBC to make cuts in some areas – possibly genre by genre, programme by programme, making the corporation up its game in terms of innovation. Those cuts could come as early as 2017. But if the rest is left to Hall – with a £450 million gap to bridge by 2021 – where will he wield his axe?

One possible target is sport, where the BBC competes with Sky, BT and commercial radio. 'Look at what we do in sport,' said Tony Hall in a speech early in 2015, 'where we show 3 per cent of all the hours but attract 45 per cent of all the viewing.' With a Tory government in place, that statistic may not serve the BBC well.

Sport is both populist and costly. Viewers take *Match of the Day*, Wimbledon, Formula 1 and the World Cup for granted as BBC events – but that does not make the BBC immune from rampant inflation in the sports rights market, described as 'eye-watering' by one commercial television source. In 2011, then-director general Mark Thompson saved £150 million with a single deal to share Formula 1 with Sky – which, as he put it, made 'savings that otherwise might have meant deeper cuts in other services'. At the same time, the BBC considered dropping Wimbledon, which would have saved 'tens of millions a year' in rights payments. And in recent months, Discovery has swooped for the rights to the Olympics – which came as a real shock to the BBC, and which punches a big hole in its sport strategy.

The BBC does not publish its sports budget – estimated by the *Daily Mail* at £240 million a year in 2013 – but Ofcom calculated that BBC One's budget went up by £55 million in 2012, when it offered wall-to-wall coverage of the Olympics. With tens if not hundreds of millions of pounds at stake, rivals are quick to highlight areas where they say the BBC's muscle distorts the market. A commercial radio source said: 'Why does Radio 5 Live have to do so much Premier League football? One estimate calculated that it spends more on those rights alone than talkSPORT's entire annual budget.'

Hall is also likely to look at the BBC's non-core TV channels for savings: those other than BBC One and BBC Two – namely BBC News channel, BBC Four, CBBC and CBeebies. Children's programming could be used to shore up the schedules of BBC One and BBC Two – or it could go the way of BBC Three. 'I fear losing kids' programming to online access only,' said Simon Spencer, executive producer at Sony Music Entertainment and member of the Bafta children's committee. 'Kids' shows should be available on a platform they can easily find, without the necessity of navigation through the myriad of internet choices. Watching online also leads to a solitary experience, which is arguably not ideal for pre-schoolers.'

What is to become of highbrow BBC Four?
Then there's the highbrow BBC Four – beloved of broadsheet newspaper critics, but unpopular among BBC management. According to one senior BBC insider, BBC Four 'was lucky not to be closed last time around – it's the obvious one to be cut next'. The highbrow arts channel has already shrunk, with budget cuts and the downgrading of its channel controller role to channel editor (reporting to BBC Two controller Kim Shillinglaw).

However, supporters of BBC Four both inside and outside the BBC point to its unique remit, and worry that drastically cutting it – or folding it entirely into BBC Two – would mean that some types of programming would be lost forever. 'Before the budget cut, BBC Four used to do dramas,' said Nicolas Kent, creative director of indie Oxford Film & Television, remembering a unique strand of biopics that stretched from Enid Blyton to Alan Clark. 'That's left a gap that hasn't been filled anywhere else. The fear is that narrowing BBC Four's remit will make our culture poorer as a result.'

One channel that seems to be safe – for now – is BBC News. Senior BBC managers recognise just what a PR disaster it would be to threaten such an obviously public-service offering, at the same time as championing (say) their Saturday night entertainment. Yet some inside the BBC's news division believe that its chief, James Harding, 'hates' the News channel and would close it if he could.

Which highlights the tension that could end up at the heart of this charter renewal process: what is appealing to Tony Hall could face significant obstacles from Whittingdale. Hall will want to preserve a populist BBC that justifies universal funding – whereas Whittingdale has already come out in favour of distinctly public-service offerings, which will not be replicated by commercial rivals. Much will hang on the outcome of that clash of ideas during charter renewal – rather than on the licence fee deal that has already been done.

- This chapter is based on features that appeared in the 5 June and 12 June 2015 editions of *Broadcast* magazine

Why Do We Have the BBC?

The BBC undeniably works in practice – but it also works in theory while the rationale for the BBC and for public service broadcasting is as strong now as ever, according to James Heath

'It's weird but it works' is sometimes used to describe the BBC. The implication being that if the BBC did not exist there would be no need to invent it in today's media market. This chapter explores the case for the BBC. On any measure, the BBC is a world-class organisation, hugely valued by the British public and admired globally. The BBC undeniably works in practice – but it also works in theory. Moreover, the rationale for the BBC and for public service broadcasting (PSB) is as strong now as ever.   *(Green Paper)*

First, the advantages of the BBC are concrete and demonstrable. The BBC's services reach 97 per cent of UK adults every week.[1] The public chooses to spend over one billion hours of their time watching or listening to BBC television and radio every week – that is eight-and-a-half hours of TV per person per week and more than ten hours of radio per adult per week.[2] The BBC is the most used public service in the country.

Second, far from becoming an anachronism in the digital world, the corporation has kept pace. BBC Online is the only British representative in the world's top 100. Reach of BBC services has been stable over the last ten years, despite an explosion of competition and choice. Looking back at last year's output, the BBC remains in rude creative health. It provides great programmes and services at an affordable price (40p per day) to everyone – from *Wolf Hall*, *The Honourable Woman* and our coverage of World War One anniversaries to *Strictly*, *Bake-off* and *EastEnders'* live 30th birthday week. British audiences rate the quality of their television higher than any other nation, and within that they rate the BBC's services highest of all.[3]

So the BBC works in practice but what about the theory. What is the policy rationale for institutions like the BBC, in today's world? Now that broadcasting is subject to greater competition, why not leave it entirely to the market, especially as the market already has a big role?

This debate should start with the goals we want to achieve – what does a good outcome look like in the different spheres of our lives? The next step is to determine the means to deliver these goals. What is the best mix of market-based and public solutions? What is the best way to allocate and fund services with different purposes? The choices made will vary by area and will depend on the weight attached to social and moral criteria as well as to economic efficiency. Defining the boundaries of markets is not a scientific exercise; it ultimately comes down to judgements.

We know that, under many conditions, markets are a great way to organise the production and distribution of goods and services in an economy. They do so in broadcasting too. Yet we also know that markets on their own can fail to deliver optimal outcomes for a variety of reasons – the power of monopolists, the existence of negative and positive externalities, the costs to consumers of a lack of information, or the under-provision of 'public goods', particularly where some can free-ride. These failures can require governments to intervene.

The justification for the BBC, however, does not rest on the doctrine of 'market failure'. While modern media markets do exhibit some of the above characteristics and the BBC's presence can help correct them, this is not *why* we have the BBC. The case for the BBC starts from a different set of considerations about the sort of society we want to live in. The BBC exists to deliver a public mission.

The public interest

In the UK, we believe it is important to have a broadcasting system that meets the needs of the public as consumers but also meets their needs as citizens. We want a range of high quality original British content to be widely available and widely consumed. This is because we legitimately regard access to culture, media and information as fulfilling a basic human need, regardless of an individual's ability to pay for them. It is how many of us find out what matters and how we expand our horizons. When everyone takes part it confers benefits on our well-being and cohesion, our democracy, and our education. Broadcasting – in particular from the BBC – brings families and the country together in a particularly British way. BBC's *Year of Science* reached more than 45 million people and Professor Brian Cox credits it with an increase in those studying science. *Democracy Day* on the BBC marked the 750th anniversary of England's first parliament and helped awareness of the anniversary almost double overnight.[4]

The best means to achieve these goals overall is a mix of public and private institutions with different remits and funding models. The 'competition for quality' between the BBC, the commercial public service broadcasters (ITV, Channel 4 and Five) and subscription broadcasters such as BSkyB, has led to higher levels of investment and better, more varied output. Ofcom's latest PSB review shows there continues to be strong public support for the purposes of PSB, which go beyond correcting market failures.[5] The PSBs remain the engine of UK original content investment, providing 80 to 85 per cent of total investment each year.[6]

The BBC is a unique, vital *part* of this successful ecology. Along with other public services with similar motivations – such as universities, public libraries, museums, and art galleries – the BBC ensures everyone has access to content that informs, educates and entertains. The fact that just about the whole UK population uses the BBC – 46 million people each day – makes it central to our democracy and our shared culture. It is part of what makes Britain, Britain. And as I have argued elsewhere, it is the public purpose of the BBC that explains why it is funded by the licence fee model.[7]

BBC and market success

As well as enhancing the quality of life in the UK, the BBC makes the creative economy work better. Few other countries are in better creative shape than the UK. Over a sustained period the creative industries have grown much faster than the economy as a whole, in terms of gross value added (GVA), exports and employment. This competitive strength has not come about by accident. We have created a media system in this country that is driven by:

- an astonishing strength and depth of creative talent – the writers, directors, producers, musicians, actors and those involved back-stage;

- a creative network with strong connections and talent flows between its different constituent parts – between TV and film, radio and music, and broadcasting and the performing arts; and

- public-private competition: in broadcasting, as in culture and the arts, we have a mixed ecology of publicly funded and commercial organisations that compete to the benefit of all. Public funding – now at only around a fifth of total TV revenues – has supported rather than crowded-out a vibrant UK media market.

The BBC's public service remit requires it to invest in new, home-grown creative ideas and talent, and the licence fee enables it to do so at scale. Analysis by Frontier Economics has identified the principal channels through which the BBC supports private sector growth.[8]

First, the BBC is the single, biggest investor in TV and radio. At its simplest, it uses the licence fee to discover and fund the best British ideas and talent – whether in-house or from independent companies – and connect them with an audience at home and abroad. The BBC invested around £2.2 billion of licence fee income directly in the creative sector in 2013/14.[9] £1.2 billion of this total was invested outside of the BBC, with around £450 million in small and micro-sized creative businesses. Some 86 per cent of its creative suppliers are small or micro-sized. While the licence fee accounts for around 20 per cent of UK TV broadcast revenues, it is converted into around 40 per cent of the investment in original UK TV content.

Second, the BBC is the best 'shop window' to the world for British talent and programme-makers. Many of the TV programmes invested in by the BBC go on to generate big economic returns through secondary sales and exports (from *Wolf Hall* to *Silent Witness*). BBC Worldwide distributes both BBC programmes and those of independent producers, and is the largest in the world outside the major US studios.

Third, as Ofcom's PSB review highlighted, the BBC is the cornerstone of the PSB system.[10] When the BBC performs well, commercial broadcasters raise their game to compete for audiences, which challenges the BBC to aim higher – in a positive feedback loop not a zero-sum game. The same is true of news, where the BBC was one of the first to create the market for online news, and Britain now has two of the top three newspaper websites in the world.

Fourth, the 'ripple effects' from the BBC's investments go well beyond broadcasting. The BBC iPlayer was the catalyst for the development of UK's video-on-demand market – now by far the largest in Europe. As Reed Hastings, chief executive of Netflix, put it: 'The iPlayer really blazed the trail. That was long before Netflix and really got people used to this idea of on-demand viewing.'[11]

The BBC is recognised as being indispensable to the UK's position as a global music leader.[12] Radios 1 and 2, in particular, discover and promote new home-grown music talent and exposure on their airwaves drives music sales. More than half of the music recordings played on British radio or television last year were only played by the BBC.[13] As I heard one music executive put it, the BBC makes the hits that others play.

Finally, the BBC strengthens the productive capability of the creative sector and, critically, spreads the benefits of growth across the UK. It does this by discovering and championing the next generation of British on-screen and back-stage talent. In the past 12 months, *BBC Introducing* has discovered 27 artists who have subsequently signed to major and significant indie record labels. Oscar-winning directors such as Danny Boyle and Tom Hooper, or global acting stars such Martin Freeman and Daniel Craig, all had early breaks on the BBC.

The BBC also strengthens the creative sector by acting as an 'anchor tenant' for media/digital clusters across the UK – in Manchester/Salford with MediaCityUK, in Bristol with the Natural History Unit, in Cardiff with the drama village and in Glasgow with Pacific Quay. Alex Connock, managing director of Shine North, describes, in his chapter, how the BBC's scale investment in MediaCityUK kickstarted a thriving production campus spanning 3,000 workers and major television companies and digital start-ups.

Even if you accept that the BBC has some economic benefits, there remains the question of whether the right mix to deliver the outcomes we want from broadcasting is one with a diminished public broadcaster. Or put another way, would the UK creative economy be just as successful without the BBC? For the answer to be 'yes', you would need to believe that: a) the BBC crowds-out private investment to a significant degree, so that its economic effects are not truly additional, and b) that the broadcast market, funded by subscriptions and advertising alone, would fill the investment gap left by the BBC. Such assumptions are based on theories that misread how the mixed broadcasting ecology works.[14] More importantly, they are not supported by the evidence. As the BBC's spend on UK public services has fallen in real terms over the last five years due to the last licence fee settlement, so investment in original British content has gone down.[15] This is a real-life experiment in what happens with a smaller BBC.

In the global media race, the risk is less of the BBC crowding-out the market than the BBC being crowded-out. In revenue terms, the BBC is small compared to the global media companies now in the UK. In five years' time, it has been forecast that the licence fee will account for around 15 per cent of UK TV revenues. BSkyB's operating profits in the UK are now broadly the same as the BBC's investment in original UK TV content.[16]

The future BBC

None of my argument should be taken to mean that the BBC is a perfect institution that does not need to change or address legitimate criticisms. But it is wrong to see the BBC as a deviation from an idealised market norm. Rather, it is the result of a collective choice about the nature of the society we want to live in. It is also a key source of the UK's competitive advantage in global media.

The challenge, as with many other public institutions, is how to modernise the BBC so it stays relevant to audiences while preserving what is unique and special about it. The right question to ask is: 'How can we make the BBC better in the public interest?'

The internet has opened the UK to global competition on a completely new level. New entrants such as Netflix and Amazon are re-defining scale as they target a single, global English-language audience. The need for the BBC will be as great as ever in this world. It will have a major role to play in investing in and creating high quality British content, in supporting a thriving and distinctive British culture, and in bringing together the whole nation as well representing the voices and communities of its different parts. In news and information, the BBC will be a trusted place where audiences go to find out what is really happening and why.

Understanding why and how the BBC benefits the UK and its creative economy allows us to chart a future path for the organisation. The BBC's purpose will remain as important as ever but the means to deliver it will need to change. The corporation must become more open, more personal, more mobile, and a pioneer in internet content. It must act as an enabler for others as well as a creator, helping to grow the British creative economy. We have started the journey in this charter by, for example, our plans to increase creative competition, reinvent BBC Three online, and maximise the money spent on programmes and services. We must go much further and faster in the next charter, in order to reinvent our mission and our services for the internet age. We will publish our proposals for the future of the BBC in September 2015 and test them with the public.

The charter review process is now underway with the launch of the government's green paper. This charter review matters much more than most. It is about something bigger than the BBC – it is about the future of British creativity and story-telling, the sustainability of PSB, and the idea that universal access to cultural experiences of merit and ambition is a good in itself. The choices we make will shape our future.

Notes

[1] GfK for the BBC, *Cross-Media Insight Survey*, c6,000 UK adults per quarter, overall BBC average weekly reach 15 mins or more claimed, 2014/15

[2] Radio Joint Audience Research (RAJAR) 2014/15; Broadcasters' Audience Research Board (BARB) 2014/15

[3] In an international survey of 14 countries, people in different parts of the world were asked to rate the quality of their biggest channels. Viewers in the UK were most satisfied with their television and BBC One rated highest on quality and BBC Two came third, out of 66 major television channels. Populus, 500 respondents per country, October 2013

[4] Populus for the BBC, 1,054 UK adults 18+, 19 Jan 2015; 1,075 UK adults 18+, 21 January 2015. From 19 per cent awareness the day before Democracy Day to 34 per cent awareness the day after

[5] http://stakeholders.ofcom.org.uk/binaries/consultations/psb-review-3/statement/PSB_Review_3_Statement.pdf, accessed on 2 August 2015

[6] Source: Public Service Content in a Connected Society, Ofcom December 2014. The precise figure depends on the methodology used. Sports rights spend is excluded

[7] http://www.bbc.co.uk/blogs/aboutthebbc/entries/9637e45d-c96c-36c6-9e3f-af141e81cab4, accessed on 2 August 2015

[8] The Frontier Economics analysis considers: 'first round impacts', relating to the BBC's direct investments in content and technology; 'second round impacts', covering the commercial exploitation of intellectual property and the output in creative industries that are generated by the BBC's direct investments; and 'spillover impacts', capturing the wider benefits that result from the BBC's investments. See http://downloads.bbc.co.uk/aboutthebbc/insidethebbc/reports/pdf/bbc_report_contribution_to_the_UK_creative_industries.pdf, accessed on 2 August 2015

[9] The BBC invested a further £1.5 billion of the licence fee in other (largely digital and high-tech) UK industries on activities that support content creation and distribution, according to Frontier Economics.

[10] Ofcom PSB review report, p. 72

[11] See *Telegraph* article, 5 October 2014

[12] *Music Week* cover, 27 July 2015

¹³ http://www.bbc.co.uk/blogs/aboutthebbc/entries/2494f2c0-1eb0-4608-9a30-b836387e36d4, accessed on 2 August 2015

¹⁴ http://downloads.bbc.co.uk/aboutthebbc/insidethebbc/howwework/reports/pdf/bbc _report_public_and_private_broadcasting_across_the_world.pdf, accessed on 2 August 2015

¹⁵ According to Ofcom, total investment in original television (excluding sport) in the UK fell in real terms from £2.6 billion to £2.4 billion between 2008 and 2013 (in 2013 prices). Since 2008, there has been a c.15 per cent real-terms fall in investment in new, original UK programmes by the public service channels from £2.4 billion in 2008 to £2 billion in 2013 (again excluding sport). The non-PSB channels have increased their investment but this does not make up the shortfall.

¹⁶ In the 12 months to June 2015, BSkyB recorded operating profits of £1.35 billion.

Assessing the BBC's International Presence

Within its peer group including the Australian ABC and Canadian CBC/Radio, there are no publicly-funded broadcasters comparable to the BBC in terms of the scale of its international audiences and the activity of its commercial subsidiary, according to Alice Enders

Looking at the BBC from international perspective has suddenly become relevant in the light of the 'existential crisis' faced by the BBC in July 2015, triggered by the surprise licence fee settlement and the green paper on the future of the BBC. Despite high levels of support among audiences, public service broadcasters in Australia (ABC) and especially in Canada (CBC), have similarly undergone budget shock in the context of wider austerity programmes implemented by elected politicians of the centre-right. However, public service broadcasters in Britain and Canada have borne disproportionately sharp cuts to their budgets, suggesting that these corporations are being asked to make a contribution to budget repair – and then some more.

The cuts at ABC and CBC have disproportionately reduced international presence, and this is a major risk for Britain as well, even though the green paper speaks approvingly of the manner in which the BBC successfully brings 'the UK to the world and the world to the UK' (section 4e of the BBC's royal charter, 2006). In addition to the World Service and BBC.com, a critical channel is BBC Worldwide (BBCWW), the pipeline to external sales for both BBC in-house and commissioned productions. The green paper laconically encapsulates the policy issue being put to stakeholders as the partial or complete 'privatisation' of this operation. In fact, the BBC is unique among PSB corporations in terms of the scale of its global audiences and the revenues realised from secondary sales of BBC made and commissioned productions. This unique success could be among the casualties of what appears to be a highly politicised process of change at the BBC.

A trio of broadcasting corporations: ABC, BBC, CBC/Radio Canada

Looking at Australia and Canada, ABC and CBC/Radio Canada are each to some degree modelled on the BBC, their core mission being stated identically, which is to 'inform, enlighten and entertain'. Each of these corporations is ostensibly independent of political institutions in terms of the administration of their budgets, fulfilment of public purposes and programming choices. However, ABC and CBC/Radio Canada are each reliant on annual budget allocations from the central government, meaning they endure annual 'political' budgeting exercises, scrutiny and pressure. They are nominally independent, but operationally dependent on political institutions, thus making for a precarious existence from year-to-year, impacting on the continuity of programming commitments. By contrast, the BBC's arrangement of a multi-year settlement for an identifiable household licence fee is clearly superior, despite the departure from practice in 2010. The BBC may be said to endure periodic rather than annual pressures from political institutions.

A striking recent experience in common has been budget shock after elections won by centre-right parliamentary majorities:

- In Australia, ABC has had its aggregate government funding cut by $254 million from $5.5 billion to $5.2 billion for 2015-20, to be financed by back-room efficiency gains rather than programming cuts, and a termination of the contract to supply Australia Network, a service aimed at expatriates.

- In Britain, the BBC's licence fee settlement announced in parliament on 6 July 2015 may loosely fulfil the pledge contained in the Conservative Party's electoral mandate to continue the freeze on the corporation's resources imposed in 2010. The Office of Budgetary Responsibility has calculated that real government expenditure on the corporation for the period of the next charter 'would fall by 19.9 per cent between 2015-2016 and 2020-2021, compared to a 0.8 per cent real fall in assumed total public services spending over the same period'.[1]

- In Canada, following the outright majority won by the Conservative Party in the May 2011 federal election, Prime Minister Stephen Harper handed down a 2012 budget that provided for $115 million to be cut over three years from the government funding of $1.1 billion (10 per cent) made available to CBC/Radio Canada,[2] followed by the elimination of the Canadian Radio-television and Telecommunications Commission's local programming improvement fund, worth another $40 million to the CBC, and reduced funding from the Canada media fund.

These budget shocks to the trio of broadcasting corporations also have in common the fact that they were decided by federal politicians without reference to the views of television audiences or, indeed, other layers of government (notably regional) that could be affected. This trio enjoys strong and persistent levels of support in their populations, as surveys indicate:

- In Australia, a large majority (84 per cent) of people believe the ABC, also known as 'Auntie', performs a valuable role; in terms of the quality of programming, an especially striking finding is that 78 per cent of adults described ABC TV programming as 'very' or 'quite good' in early 2014, compared to just 43 per cent for commercial television.[3] Looking back, the quality gap of the commercial television sector had narrowed on the launch of new Australian programmes between 2007 and 2011, when 51 per cent of adults said the quality was good, then reversing again subsequently.

- In Canada, where the CBC offers French and English language programming, each of these segments received high scores of 7 or higher on a 10-point scale (where 1 means disagree/strongly disagree and 10 means strongly agree) for each of the aspects of its mandate that was measured (informative, enlightening, entertaining, available on new platforms), noting that the softening in Anglophone ratings since the federal budget 2012 cuts took effect.[4]

- In the UK, the BBC similarly enjoys high scores in surveys, obtaining an average score of 7.4 when television audiences were asked to rate their 'overall impression' of the BBC on a scale of 1 to 10 (where 1 means extremely unfavourable, and 10 means extremely favourable), noting the regional variation in scores in Wales (7.7), in England (7.5), Northern Ireland (7.2), and then Scotland (6.6).[5]

Among all three, the scale of the decline in government expenditure was greatest in Canada. The CBC's precarious revenue situation was then compounded by the reduction of advertising revenues (26 per cent of $1.87 billion of revenues in 2013-2014) due to soft audiences for primetime programming and the catastrophic loss of media rights for the National Hockey League (NHL) to Rogers Communications for the next 12 seasons, as of the 2014/15 season,[6] the most important sporting event.[7] With its own costs rising, the CBC reports cutting staff by 650 over three years, and to the funding of news and other programming, to balance the 2013-2014 budget. Since every $1 of CBC expenditure contributed $3.63 in tangible value to the Canadian economy (not to speak of the intangible benefits), the net impact of reducing government expenditure on the CBC by $115 million is estimated to be $386 million, demonstrating the knock-on effects of such cuts on the wider creative economy.[8]

In terms of programming, ABC, BBC and CBC each have in common a focus on the provision of an ample supply of impartial news and current affairs programming; in the case of CBC, this provision is in two official languages, a further burden on costs. This aspect is among the core differences between public sector and commercial broadcasting, the latter being known to invest less in 'hard' news.[9] ABC, in Australia, for example, prides itself on its independent news coverage and recently highlighted the extensive coverage it provided of the 2013 federal election campaign, a core contribution to voters and societal discourse and exchange.

It is also possible that editors and/or proprietors of commercial television suppliers will opt to support one political party over another where they are not enjoined, as is the case of the UK, to adopt the position of 'due impartiality and due accuracy and undue prominence of views and opinions', notably with respect to the conduct of elections or referenda, under Ofcom's Broadcast Code.[10]

ABC, BBC and CBC/Radio Canada also have a focus in common on funding originating works (audio and audio-visual), rather than buying in foreign productions, more prominent at commercial broadcasters. The aim is to supply programming that reflects stories of relevance back to their respective populations, thus also sustaining the professionalisation of the audio-visual sector, including the creation of businesses, the acquisition of skills and training by young people:

- In Australia, ABC is self-regulated and interprets its role as making a unique range of programmes and perspectives that reflect Australian people, culture and history, that 'only it would tell', reporting that 66 per cent of content broadcast on ABC1 between 6am and midnight was Australian-made, a higher share than commercial television.[11]

- In Canada, Canadian content must make up at least 75 per cent of the CBC's broadcast day (80 per cent for prime time) for each of the French and English language programming, which the corporation comfortably exceeds.

- In the UK, the BBC is required (as are commercial PSBs) to broadcast a majority of 'European works', which it meets mainly through the broadcasting of UK works.

This naturally leads on to another of the core missions of public sector broadcasting, namely connecting expatriates with news and current affairs of their home country and/or projecting an image of the country to the world that sustains reputation and drives exports of goods and services, including tourism. This function has been noticeably impaired in the case of Australia and Canada, respectively, in the latter case due to the depth of the expenditure cuts required to balance the 2013-2014 budget, which led international activities to be disproportionately reduced.

The threat to BBC Worldwide
The green paper on the future of the BBC approves of the way the BBC is bringing the UK to the world and asks how this could be made more effective

(Question 7). At the same time, the government has put on the agenda the option of partially or fully privatising BBC Worldwide (Question 14), even though the success of BBCWW is functionally related to the success of the BBC in bringing the UK to the world. This is an example of the absence of 'joined-up thinking' and evidence-based policymaking in the green paper. The BBC brings the UK to the world through two main channels:

- Radio, TV and online services, including BBC World Service, BBC Global News (BBC World News Television Channel and bbc.com/news), BBC Media Action (the charity), and BBC Worldwide's BBC-branded direct to consumer services – a combined weekly reach of 308 million unique users (outside the UK), according to the 2015 edition of the Global Audience Measure (GAM).[12]

- BBC programmes made or commissioned are sold by BBC Worldwide to third-party broadcasters and other platforms.

The BBC is uniquely successful amongst its direct 'peer group' of public service broadcasters in terms of:

- achieving scale international audiences for its news services, providing them with quality news on a par with its UK news services, and

- monetising BBC content in 'secondary' sales to other broadcasters and platforms via BBC Worldwide.

The BBC plans to build its international audience to reach 500 million by 2022. This large and growing international presence of the BBC does more than bring the UK to the world since, as a result of this activity, people are encouraged to buy UK goods and services, including through tourism. The UK is also the second top exporter of audio-visual products and services, behind the United States.

Why do BBC international services appeal?

Quality
The BBC Trust has laid out guidelines for the corporation's public service remit to bring the UK to the world, which emphasises the accuracy, impartiality and independence of its news service as the primary value.[13] The BBC stakes a claim to being the most trusted news organisation globally.

Supplied in English and 27 other languages
To optimise its reach globally, the BBC provides versions of its international news services in English and other languages. The BBC World News TV Channel is delivered in 12 languages. BBC World Service English has the single largest audience, with 52 million weekly unique users (up 25 per cent on 2014), of a total World Service audience of 210 million. BBC.com is supplied in

English and 27 other languages, including Spanish, French, Portuguese, Arabic, Hindi, Russian and Mandarin.

Multi-platform and multi-device

BBC World Service has been transformed from a primarily radio-based service with two TV channels to a multimedia broadcasting operation with an increasing digital presence. According to GAM 2015, television overtook radio to be the leading platform for international BBC services, with a weekly audience of 148 million, compared to 138 million for radio, and 55 million for BBC.com. The BBC has created dedicated apps to allow its services to be consumed across connected devices, including smartphones, tablets, computers and connected TVs.

The BBC World Service Group received annual funding of £245 million in 2014/15 (about £10/year per licence fee paying household), the first year in which the BBC has funded these services from the licence fee. BBCWW sells BBC-commissioned content globally and is the most successful commercial subsidiary of a state broadcaster judging by the scale of its annual revenues of just over £1 billion in 2013-2014, £38.50 per licence fee paying household. These were generated from secondary sales in the UK (one-third), the US (one-third) and the rest of the world (one-third). After deducting the expenses of BBCWW from revenues, BBCWW returned £174 million to the BBC and £116 million to independent rights-holders.

Britain ranks first among PSB nations

Within the UK's peer group of France, Germany and Japan (which have similarly-sized or somewhat larger populations than the UK), there are no publicly-funded broadcasters that are comparable to the BBC in terms of the scale of its international audiences and the activity of its commercial subsidiary. In our view, this is down to several critical success factors for the BBC:

- English, the *lingua franca* of global audiences, the leading second language in Europe and spoken in the US, the single largest market by far for audio-visual content.

- Limited fragmentation of BBC activities and funding to regions, enabling resources to be devoted to funding programming of national and international resonance. By contrast, in Germany, the regional public broadcasting layer consisting of ARD attracts 75 per cent of funding, while the national level consisting of ZDF is relatively impoverished with revenues of $3 billion in 2014 (compared to £3.7 billion for the BBC).

- A strong, well-funded commercial subsidiary in BBCWW. France's TV France International, the organisation of original content producers, has a staff of just 10 and attends trade fairs to place its programming

Another factor that the BBC has nothing to do with helps explain its international success: the absence of a publicly funded media organisation in the United States, where the Public Broadcasting Service (PBS) is, in fact, a charity. As a result, the programmes sold by BBCWW into the US fill a niche in the market for 'high-quality' programming that US audio-visual producers do not wish to contest. PBS *Masterpiece Theatre* on Sunday evenings is the regular home of British-produced television programmes such as *Sherlock*, *Wolf Hall*, *Poldark* and *Downton Abbey*.

Thanks to its UK and international activities, the BBC brand was said to be worth $6 billion by BrandFinance in 2015, was ranked 15th overall among British brands, and 226th globally.[14] In relation to other media companies, the BBC was ranked 11th overall and was the second leading British brand in the media segment, behind Sky. Uniquely, the BBC is the only publicly funded media company in the top 500 brands in 2015.

Conclusions

The prevailing fiscal trend being to austerity, it is unavoidable that public service broadcasting, even if financed by a household licence fee as is the case of the BBC, should come under pressure. ABC, as communications minister Malcolm Turnbull said when announcing the cut to funding, had to contribute to the 'overall budget repair strategy'.[15] However, as the data presented above indicates, public service broadcasters in Britain and Canada have suffered disproportionately large declines in funding, despite enjoying high levels of support in the public at large. In no instance have the authorities concerned consulted the public or weighed carefully the costs of not being able to fulfil remits to the creative economy in terms of investment in the delivery of independent news and the funding of domestic audio-visual productions.

Notes

[1] Office for Budget Responsibility (OBR) *Economic and Fiscal Outlook*, July 2015, page 136. Available online at http://cdn.budgetresponsibility.independent.gov.uk/July-2015-EFO-234224.pdf, accessed on 27 July 2015

[2] CBC is funded by the federal government, while the provincial and local governments undertake the majority (64 per cent) of government expenditure (IMF, Canada 2012 Article IV Consultation, February 2013, see http://www.imf.org/external/pubs/ft/scr/2013/cr1340.pdf). According to the 2012 federal budget plan, the cuts to the heritage portfolio, of which the CBC is the most prominent part, were identified subsequent to a review of federal expenditure. Total savings under the review, which spanned a number of federal programme areas, were estimated at $5.2 billion, representing 6.9 per cent of an aggregate review base of $75.3 billion. This represents less than 2 per cent of expected federal programme spending in 2016-2017. See http://www.budget.gc.ca/2012/plan/anx1-eng.html#a2

[3] *ABC Appreciation Survey: Summary Report*, July 2014. Commercial television consists mainly of FoxTel, the satellite and cable TV pay-TV provider, and some free-to-air channels and local television

[4] *CBC/Radio-Canada Annual Report* 2013-2014, pages 33 and 37. Available online at http://www.cbc.radio-canada.ca/site/annual-reports/2013-2014/pdf/cbc-radio-canada-annual-report-2013-2014.pdf, accessed on 25 July 2015

[5] NatCen, *Purpose Remit Survey UK*, report autumn 2014. Available online at http://www.natcen.ac.uk/media/863672/ara-2013-14.pdf.=, accessed on 25 July 2015

[6] In November 2013, the NHL concluded an exclusive agreement with Rogers for 12 years, ending 61 years of CBC engagement in the sport. Through a sub-licensing agreement, CBC audiences will still be able to view *Hockey Night in Canada* and the final of the Stanley Cup. However, Rogers assumes control over content, on-air talent and the creative direction of *Hockey Night in Canada*. CBC will not be able to realise revenues from the sale of advertising

[7] *CBC/Radio Canada Annual Report* 2013-2014, page 19. Available online at http://www.cbc.radio-canada.ca/site/annual-reports/2013-2014/pdf/cbc-radio-canada-annual-report-2013-2014.pdf, accessed on 25 July 2015

[8] Deloitte and Touche. Available online at http://cbc.radio-canada.ca/_files/cbcrc/documents/latest-studies/deloitte-summary-findings-en.pdf, accessed on 25 July 2015

[9] In Australia, 62.6 per cent of hard news stories were aired on public service outlets, 61.5 per cent in Britain and 53.4 per cent in Canada. See Cushion, Stephen (2012) *The Democratic Value of News*, London: Palgrave Macmillan, Table 3 p. 74

[10] Ofcom, Guidance Notes, Issue Five, 21 March 2013. Available online at http://stakeholders.ofcom.org.uk/binaries/broadcast/guidance/831193/section5.pdf, accessed on 25 July 2015

[11] The Australian Communications and Media Authority (ACMA) regulated Australian content on commercial television by mandatory standards: Australian Content Standard (ACS) and Television Program Standard 23 – Australian Content in Advertising. The ACS requires all commercial free-to-air television licensees to broadcast an annual minimum transmission quota of 55 per cent Australian programming between 6am and midnight. In addition, there are specific minimum annual sub-quotas for Australian (adult) drama, documentary and children's programmes

[12] The Global Audience Measure (GAM) measures the combined reach of the BBC's international news services and direct-to-consumer BBC branded channels. The measure nets out overlapping audiences and also consumption on multiple devices

[13] BBC Trust, Purpose remits, March 2013, states: '(a) Provide international news broadcasting of the highest quality. The BBC's journalism for international audiences should share the same values as its journalism for UK audiences: accuracy, impartiality and independence. International audiences should value BBC news and current affairs for providing reliable and unbiased information of relevance, range and depth. (b) Enable audiences and individuals to participate in the global debate on significant international issues The BBC should inform conversation and debate with impartial and accurate coverage and through discussion'

[14] See http://brandirectory.com/league_tables/table/global-500-2015

[15] See http://www.news.com.au/entertainment/tv/government-to-reduce-abc-funding-by-254m-over-five-years/story-e6frfmyi-1227128448197

No Broadcaster is an Island

**The fragility of the BBC's independence from the state cannot continue
to be ignored, argues Brian Winston.
Nor can its overall future be discussed in a silo**

That fateful lunch at Chequers…

4 January 1981: a day as fateful for the BBC as 30 July 1954 when the Television
Act, breaking its broadcasting monopoly, received the royal assent; or 1 January
1927, when that monopoly was established by a royal charter transforming the
British Broadcasting Company into a corporation.

On that day in 1981, the Prime Minister, Margaret Thatcher, entertained
Rupert Murdoch to a secret *tête-à-tête* lunch at which a change-making deal was
struck. At least, in the opinion of Harold Evans, it led to 'a coup that
transformed the relationship between British politics and journalism. … She was
trailing in the polls, caught in a recession she had inherited, eager for an assured
cheerleader at a difficult time. Her guest had an agenda too…' He wanted to add
The Times and *The Sunday Times* to the *News of the World* and the *Sun* which he
already owned and was concerned about competition regulations. She assured
him that he need not be. *The Times* could be his (Evans 2015).

Mudoch's control of 40 per cent of UK national newspaper circulation
followed this useful lunch. Well, why not? If all competition law does is count,
then 40 per cent is not a monopoly. Sky Television was added in 1983 and again,
why not? Television isn't newspapers. Revealed as a shibboleth was any
assumption that a market place of ideas with a plurality of voices was a necessity
for a democracy. It was not, after all, the eighteenth century anymore and such
outmoded notions had no place in that brave neo-liberal dawn. And, so, for the
BBC, what was a broadcasting monopoly in 1927 and a competition in 1954
became today's death threat.

During the 2015 general election that returned him to office, David Cameron
had dismissed a BBC news story about him as 'rubbish'. 'I'm going to close
them down after the election,' he promised. The BBC's political editor, Nick

Robinson, wondered about the threat: 'Joke? Expression of frustration? All three? No one could be sure' (Martinson 2015: 32). But on 11 May 2015, it became clearer. Cameron gave the culture, media and sport portfolio to John Whittingdale, a man dubbed 'a sound right-winger and a devoted Thatcherite' (Anderson 2015), once 'Thatcher's toy boy' (cited in Higgins 2015: 28) and now 'the Tory minister for Murdoch' (Holmes 2015: 40).

Fifty days after that, the BBC's director general, Lord Hall, following talks with George Osborne, the chancellor of the exchequer, was informed that the cost of free licences for the over-75s (a Blairite pre-election bribe of 2001 now running at some £630 million a year) would, in the future, be shouldered by the corporation itself. Even for an organisation with a £3.7 billion annual income, this could not be thought small change. Then, on 17 July, Whittingdale unveiled a green paper – a consultation document: *BBC Charter Review: A Public Consultation* (DMCS 2015).

'Being funded by a universal hypothecated tax, the BBC feels empowered and obliged to try and offer something for everyone, even in areas well-served by the market. ... The scale and scope of its current activities and future ambitions is chilling' is not what this document says. Those words were James Murdoch's in his notorious Edinburgh MacTaggart lecture in 2009 (Murdoch 2009). Whittingdale, in introducing his green paper, is more emollient, but the echoes are clear: 'What should the BBC be trying to achieve in an age where consumer choice is now far more extensive than it has been before? What should its scale and scope be in the light of those aims and how far it affects others in television, radio and online?' (Whittingdale 2015: 2). And who but the Murdochs and their fellow media oligarchs can he have in mind when he writes of the BBC 'affecting others *in*' (not merely consuming) broadcasting?

No broadcaster is an island, each is a piece of the media continent, as is every media platform – the newly electronic as well as the time-honoured press. It is now clear that the mutually beneficial relationship sealed that January day 34 years ago meant no good to the BBC – how much is only now finally becoming clear. It was damaging not only in the obvious sense that another significant percentage of its audience was about to be lost. More worryingly, Murdoch's political hold over the politicians in turn implied that their hold over the BBC could be unduly influenced in his favour. But we choose not see that. Harold Evans told the *Toronto Star* he was 'astonished by the lack of curiosity about a shocking story [e.g. the 1981 secret Thatcher/Murdoch concordat] that has been lying around on the pavement like a gold coin waiting for somebody to pick it up' (Knelman 2015: E3). He should not be.

Independence
Until Whittingdale, cognitive dissonance had more or less allowed us to ignore the implications of the BBC's charter and agreement (Secretary of state for culture, media and sport 2006a, 2006b, 2011). We pay little attention to the fact that the minister is mentioned 78 times in the 61 pages of the current agreement.

Among other powers, he chooses and pays the BBC's trustees. We, though, believe that a force-field known as 'conventions' protects the BBC and its 'independence'; and perhaps even after the summer of 2015 some still do. However, 'constitutional conventions' are, according to A. V. Dicey, who invented the concept in the nineteenth century, 'fictions … the most fanciful dreams of *Alice in Wonderland*' (cited in Ward 2004: 33). The black-letter law enables threats like Cameron's, but trusting the 'conventions' is all the BBC actually has to protect it. And, long before the very public assault of 2015, our faith in the reality of the 'conventions' could only be sustained by ignoring all evidence to the contrary. The secrecies of power-broking (such as private luncheons at Chequers) made this easy. Things come to light but usually decades later and with the non-effect Evans notes.

It is, for example, rumoured that Thatcher consulted Murdoch on the appointment of Marmaduke (Duke) Hussey as chair of the BBC board of governors in 1986 (Seaton 2015: 319-320). His first major act was to sack the director general, Alasdair Milne (ibid: 322-325). Milne was defenestrated after years of Thatcherite hostility which began, just after his appointment in 1982, with her backbenches frothing with indignation that the BBC news, in reporting the Falklands War, spoke of 'British troops' not 'our forces' (Milne S. 2015). Official historian Jean Seaton describes Murdoch's intervention as 'extraordinary' as, indeed, it was (Seaton 2015: 307); but what is truly extraordinary it that all these incidents are greeted with such insouciance.

The drip of stories does not stop with Murdoch's lunch and Milne's fall. For example, there is DG Greg Dyke's defenestration in January 2004 over Andrew Gilligan's *Today* report on Saddam Hussein's supposed weapons of mass destruction (Kuhn 2005: 101). We knew about it quickly enough but, so far, it is hard to know exactly if, on this occasion, the BBC was pushed or jumped of its own accord. It could well have jumped. It has form in this regard. Astonishingly for an organisation that vaunts its 'independence', undercutting it can start with the BBC leadership itself 'seeking guidance' from Westminster.

Consider DG Sir Ian Trethowan's servile shopping of a ground-breaking *Panorama* on MI5 in 1981 to the spooks and then, at their behest, in banning it (Campbell nd). Or Lord Normanbrook, the chair of the governors, running to the Home Office in 1965 to check if the vivid anti-nuclear drama, *The War Game*, was OK to broadcast (Chapman 2006: 85). (It wasn't.) Or DG Sir Ian Jacob putting the frighteners on any current affairs producer tackling the nuclear issue in 1955 (Milne, C. 2015: 24). Or the prevention of Lord Beveridge coming to the microphone in 1942 to explain his (best-selling) report on welfare, that crucial template of the post-war social settlement (Briggs 1995c: 547-559.) Or, the *de facto* neutering of the somewhat radical talks department in 1934 on the eve of that decade's charter renewal for fear that its record might cause difficulties (Briggs 1995b: 206). Or (starting as one means to go on) the founding DG, John Reith, not allowing the unions on air for the nine days of the 1926 general strike

– 'the strike having been declared illegal' (Briggs 1995a 330, 347, 351; Cardiff and Scannell 1991: 42).

To be fair, there are even rarer known contrary occasions where the BBC is recorded as having spoken truth to power. Most notable is chairman Charles Hill's initial defiance of the home secretary, Reginald Maudling's attempt to stifle the reporting of the troubles in Ulster in 1972 (Briggs 1995d: 907). And, no doubt, day-to-day, unreported improper interferences are resisted in, shall we say, a Paxmanesque style. But, even though it prides itself on being a 'trusted' news source, it is hard when reviewing such of the record as can be known not to see a thread of pusillanimity running through it. The BBC does not seem to have within its DNA much of a 'publish and be damned' instinct. To say that 'it has become pathologically risk-averse' (Church 2015) is, in the light of history, to give it rather more credit than it is due. It has always tended to timorous caution but, certainly since the Hitler war created the circumstances in which it was eventually allowed to shine, it has been Teflon-coated. The current DG Lord Hall need not expect to be contradicted, except by the flicker of evidence, when he talks in public of the BBC news 'ethos, and the hard discipline of BBC training and neutrality'.

It is a mark of extreme radicalism, it would seem, to challenge this rhetoric. Yet these glimmers of impropriety smack of the relationship of politicians and the media in eighteenth century Hanoverian Britain – but, when it comes to the BBC, 'smack' is all we allow them to do. We no longer smell the stench that necessarily accompanies any financial bond between government and media.

Come dancing?

Robert Walpole, thus far Britain's longest-serving premier (1721-1742) was a byword for corruption, not least because of his financial relationship to the press. A free press was held in high esteem: 'the Palladium of all the civil, political and religious rights of an Englishman' ('Junius' 1772: iv). But it was utterly subverted by Walpole and his cronies through the stamp duty, manipulation of the mails and 'subsidies'. In the 1730s, he used £50,000 – £4.25 million in today's money – to bribe toady editors and hacks (Barker 1998: 85). That we may be in the slightest echoing such goings with, dare one say, the licence fee is beyond the pale. Hanoverian corruption? Do me a turn (as my father-in-law used to say)! Doesn't happen here anymore: despite the MPs' expenses racket, Britain is still perceived as the fourteenth least corrupted nation on earth (Transparency International 2015). And, of course, at stake here is not the corruption of personal enrichment but that of power and influence. The licence fee system might involve the passing of large sums of money from the state to an organ of opinion, but any resemblance to Walpole's recycling of taxation into subsidies is deemed merely coincidental. Nevertheless, tax money, however, hypothecated or not, is as much the Achilles' heel of the BBC's independence as it was of any eighteenth century denizen of Grub Street.

And, suddenly, thanks to Whittingdale, in 2015 that truth becomes unavoidable. To the toxicity of Cameron-style attacks over news coverage is now added the *faux-naïf* complaint about popularity. Well, not a complaint we understand, merely a reasonable query: why use tax money to produce programming which private entities can provide? It is a question that the BBC is hard pressed to answer and before the Second World War, it did so, essentially, by not making much of a fist of low-brow programming. 'A jam session?' the controller of programmes, queried his staff in 1938. 'We must introduce some sort of supervision to prevent this sort of thing' (cited in Scannell and Cardiff 1991: 189, 191). Hitler helped the BBC's 'Light Entertainment' to have brilliant war, only to fall back towards elitism with the peace. The head of drama in the late 1940s dismissed an innocuous radio soap as being 'socially corrupting by its monstrous flattery of the ego of the "common man"' (cited in Briggs 1995c: 37). 'Auntie' BBC was only laid to rest in the 1960s under the pressure of competition.

Ever since John Reith escaped the clutches of the postmaster general in 1928 by promising never to cause any trouble, any parliamentary non-news related complaints about programming – sex and violence, say – have been swatted away by the government of the day as not being its business. Moreover, has any MP ever risen in the House of Commons to complain that the corporation is planning yet another dramatisation of Jane Austen when Thomas Love Peacock remains untouched? Whittingdale echoes this apparent non-interventionism, upon which rests the corporation's political independence, when he says: 'Even if I wanted to close down *Strictly Come Dancing*, which I don't, it would be completely wrong of the government to try and decide which programmes the BBC should make and which it shouldn't' (Martinson and Plunkett 2015: 6).

But it is disingenuous to pretend that without popularity the licence fee is not endangered. He who pays the piper calls the tune, after all. Indeed, if the BBC cedes its hard-won capacity for light entertainment and is forced to retreat into a Reithian elitist ghetto, as sure as night follows day, it would be 'completely' right for the politicians to abolish a tax on operating a receiver, which is what the licence fee is, when the proceeds go only to one broadcaster who isn't used by the majority of those paying the tax. And, whoops, there goes the BBC!

Hard questions

John Whittingdale says: 'We also need to ask some hard questions in charter review if we are to ensure the future success of the BBC, and indeed UK broadcasting' (Whittingdale 2015:2) but the agenda of charter renewal does not come close to addressing them, not least because 'UK broadcasting' is involved and UK broadcasters include media conglomerates. The last time we asked hard questions of them, at the feet of my Lord Leveson, answer came there none. The best we do in looking beyond the BBC silo are Ofcom's public service reviews but even they restrict the definition of broadcasting competition to the BBC, ITV, C4, C5 and SC4. This has the Orwellian result of making the BBC the monopolist (Ofcom 2014). News International, remember, is no such thing – it is not, curiously, even a public service broadcaster.

The BBC's mission, as the *BBC Charter Review* reminds us, is to 'inform, educate and entertain'. When we are assured in the consultation document that 'The government is, therefore, committed both to the future of the BBC and to its underlying Reithian mission' an eyebrow can surely be raised. The information function, at its heart the news service, is compromised by the public funding source being controlled by politicians – and they are themselves not truly independent of the BBC's rivals. And it is those last who demand that the BBC cease and desist from entertaining. That leaves, in the broadest sense, education but that function drips elitism and elitism is fatal to the universality of the licence fee.

That need not be, of course. If we were dealing with the marketplace of ideas rather than just the marketplace, the principle of an hypothecated tax – or some other public subvention – could by defended. As it is, Tony Hall is right to protest: 'I don't think we are just there to be a market failure BBC', although that role could be an honourable one (Martinson and Jackson 2015: 2). In 1927, one of John Reith's most brilliant early moves was to save the Henry Wood Promenade concerts from collapse because of the withdrawal of commercial sponsorship. In the same spirit, in March 2014, Tony Hall announced close 'partnerships' with the National Theatre, the Tate Gallery, the Hay Festival of Literature and Arts, the Royal Academy and Glyndebourne (BBC 2014). To be such a hub could well justify the use of public funds. But not in today's cold neo-liberal light. As it is, the implicit invitation to play the market failure role is a poison chalice.

Despite five pages in the consultation document on 'the BBC's values' and 'the BBC's public purposes', there is, in truth, little here beyond lip-service about the quality and value of culture. No proposed examination of the BBC's need to compete to protect its claim on the public purse. No (how could there be?) inquiry into the market's failures. The only thing that truly matters here are questions that 'persist around the distinctiveness of the programmes the BBC delivers, and whether it uses its broad purposes to act in too commercial a way, chasing ratings rather than delivering distinctive, quality programming that other providers would not' (Whittingdale 2015: 2). James Murdoch would not disagree.

Silo

To talk only of the BBC's governance, finance and management failings in a converged digitised multi-platform, internationalised, conglomerate-dominated world is to be rearranging the deckchairs. No broadcaster is an island, so how can any policy remotely pertinent to long-term realities emerge from such limited exercises as this? Above all, how can we square the market, with so limited a number of 'speakers', with the market place of ideas where creating a cacophony of voices is the objective?

Unless we can answer that, the bell tolls, and not just for the BBC.

References

Anderson, Bruce (2015) Competition will force the BBC to save itself – or die, *Daily Telegraph*, 20 June. Available online at http://www.telegraph.co.uk/news/bbc/11688991/Competition-will-force-the-BBC-to-save-itself-or-die.html, accessed on 21 June 2015

BBC (2014) Tony Hall announces greatest commitment to arts for a generation, 25 March. Available online at http://www.bbc.co.uk/mediacentre/latestnews/2014/bbc-arts-release, accessed on 24 June 2015

Barker, Hannah (1998) *Newspapers and English Society 1695-1855*, Abingdon, UK: Routledge

Briggs, Asa (1995a) *A History of Broadcasting in the UK, Vol. 1*, Oxford: Oxford University Press

Briggs, Asa (1995b) *A History of Broadcasting in the UK, Vol.2*, Oxford: Oxford University Press

Briggs, Asa (1995c) *A History of Broadcasting in the UK, Vol 3*, Oxford: Oxford University Press

Briggs, Asa (1995d) *A History of Broadcasting in the UK, Vol.5* Oxford: Oxford University Press

Campbell, Duncan (nd) Banning *Panorama*, Duncan Campbell.org. Available online at http://www.duncancampbell.org/content/banning-panorama, accessed on 21 June 2015

Cardiff, David and Scannell, Paddy (1991) *A Social History of British Broadcasting 1922-39*, London: John Wiley and Sons

Chapman, James (2006) The BBC and the censorship of the *War Game* (1965), *Journal of Contemporary History*, Vol. 41, No. 1, January pp 75-94

Evans, Harold (2015) How Thatcher and Murdoch made their secret deal, *Guardian*, 28 April. Available online at http://www.theguardian.com/uk-news/2015/apr/28/how-margaret-thatcher-and-rupert-murdoch-made-secret-deal, accessed on 13 June 2015

Hall, Tony (2014) Speech at the 'Future of the licence fee' seminar, City University, London, BBC Media Centre, 10 July. Available online at tp://www.bbc.co.uk/mediacentre/speeches/2014/dg-city-university, accessed on 21 June 2015

Holmes, Jon (2015) Left field: Before celebrating the fall of Fifa's Sepp Blatter, English football should get its own house in order, *New Statesman*, 12 June

'Junius' (1772) *Junius: Stat Nomis Umbra*, London: Henry Sampson Woodfall

Knelman, Martin (2015) Harold Evans on a dirty deal and a tarnished press, *Toronto Star*, 6 May. Available online at http://www.thestar.com/entertainment/2015/05/05/harold-evans-on-a-dirty-deal-and-a-tarnished-press.html, accessed on 26 June 2015

Kuhn, Raymond (2005) Media management, Seldon, Anthony and Kavanagh, Dennis (eds) *The Blair Effect 2001–2005*, Cambridge: Cambridge University Press pp 94-111

Martinson, Jane (2015) What was ignored was that Salmond picked the fight, not me, *Guardian*, 22 June. Available online at http://www.theguardian.com/media/2015/jun/21/nick-robinson-bbc-lung-cancer-cybernats, accessed on 26 June 2015

Martinson, Jane and Jackson, Jasper (2015) Nick Robinson: PM threatened to 'close down' BBC, *Guardian*, 22 June. Available online at http://www.theguardian.com/media/2015/jun/21/nick-robinson-cameron-threatened-close-down-bbc-election-bus, accessed on 26 June 2015

Milne, Claudia (2015) *The BBC's Imperial Culture, Political Independence & Panorama 1953-1959* (unpublished MA, Sheffield Hallam University)

Milne, Seumas (2015) Review of Jean Seaton's *'Pinkoes and Traitors'*: My father, the BBC and a very British coup, *Guardian*, April 27. Available online at http://www.theguardian.com/books/2015/feb/27/seumas-milne-on-pinkoes-and-traitors-by-jean-seaton-review-my-father-the-bbc-and-a-very-british-coup, accessed on 13 June 2015

Murdoch, James (2009) Edinburgh International Television Festival MacTaggart Lecture, 28 August. Available on line at http://image.guardian.co.uk/sys-files/Media/documents/2009/08/28/JamesMurdochMacTaggartLecture.pdf, accessed 20 July 2015

Ofcom (2014) *Public Service Broadcasting Annual Report 2014*, 15 December. Available online at http://stakeholders.ofcom.org.uk/broadcasting/reviews-investigations/public-service-broadcasting/annrep/psb14/, accessed on 24 June 2015

Secretary of state for culture, media and sport (2006a) *Broadcasting: Copy of Royal Charter for the Continuance of the British Broadcasting Corporation: Presented to Parliament by the Secretary of State for Culture, Media and Sport by Command of Her Majesty*, October, CMD 6925, London: Stationery Office

Secretary of state for culture, media and sport (2006b) *Broadcasting: An Agreement Between Her Majesty's Secretary of State for Culture, Media and Sport and the British Broadcasting Corporation Presented to Parliament by the Secretary of State for Culture, Media and Sport by Command of Her Majesty*, July, CMD 6872, London: Stationery Office

Secretary of state for culture, media and sport (2011) *Broadcasting: An Agreement Between Her Majesty's Secretary of State for Culture, Olympics, Media and Sport and the British Broadcasting Corporation Presented to Parliament by the Secretary of State for Culture, Olympics, Media and Sport by Command of Her Majesty*, February, CMD 8002, London: Stationery Office

Transparency International (2015) *Corruption Perceptions Index 2014: Results*. Available online at https://www.transparency.org/cpi2014/results, accessed on 18 June 2015

Ward, Ian (2004) *The English Constitution: Myths and Realities*, Oxford and Portland, Oregon: Hart

Whittingdale, John (2015) 'Foreword', *BBC Charter Renewal Public Consultation*, Department of media, culture and sport. Available online at https://www.gov.uk/government/uploads/system/uploads/attachment_data/file/44570, accessed 20 July 2015

Section 2:
Who Rules the BBC?

Richard Lance Keeble

As Shakespeare's Henry IV complained: 'Uneasy lies the head that wears a crown.' Indeed, when appointed on 31 August 2014, in the wake of a series of serious BBC controversies, Rona Fairhead may well have expected to face an 'uneasy' period as chairman of the BBC Trust. The *Guardian* even welcomed her to the job with an editorial suggesting her time as chair would be a 'certainly disagreeable experience'.[1]

Since its formation in the early 1920s, the BBC's governance and regulation have been the focus for endless debate of 'infinite variety' (to maintain the Shakespearean theme). Not surprisingly, Rona Fairhead's first months as chairman were eventful. In March 2015, her suggestion that the corporation be overseen by a tough external regulator instead of being allowed to govern its own affairs, had the *Daily Mail* predictably thundering: 'Head of BBC Trust calls for it to be axed.'[2] In July 2015, after the BBC agreed secretly with the government to shoulder the £700 million cost of providing free television licences for the over-75s from 2020, she was accused of being a 'lame duck' by shadow culture secretary Chris Bryant.[3]

So as the debate over the BBC's governance hots up in the approach to charter renewal, this section of *The BBC Today* aims to provide historical context, detailed analysis of the issues – and some insightful suggestions for the way ahead.

First Howard Davies brings his enormous experience and knowledge of broadcasting governance issues to the table: chairman of the Royal Bank of

Scotland and professor at Sciences Po in Paris, he was a member of the Burns committee which advised the Blair government on the 2006 BBC charter review. For Davies, a BBC board, independently chaired with a majority of non-executives, would provide efficient decision-making and operational effectiveness. Ofcom would take on the role of regulatory oversight, including competition issues – and while complaints should initially be handled by the corporation, dissatisfied complainants should have access to Ofcom. Alongside this, a public service broadcasting commission would recommend the allocation of licence fee funding between the BBC and others. He concludes:

> The BBC Trust is a dead regulator walking. A new governance model is slouching towards Westminster to be born. The green paper, on this issue, certainly asks the right questions, But there will – and should – be many arguments about the precise details. The overriding aim must be to create a structure which wins public confidence and which will attract strong people. The BBC deserves a board with the backbone to defend its independence, and stand up to meddlesome politicians, and also a regulator which does not bow to political winds.

David Liddiment has had a distinguished career in television and recently spent two terms as a BBC trustee. Throughout that period, he says, the trust owed nothing to the management of the BBC and everything to the licence fee payer. 'Therefore, we had a mandate to be as forceful as necessary to ensure that the organisation was efficiently run, did not waste public money, and delivered a distinctive suite of services to the public.' At the same time, he admits there was insufficient clarity as to where key responsibilities lay between the executive board and the trust.

So what's the way ahead? Liddiment argues for a second tier of governance independent both of the corporation and of the commercial regulator, but solely accountable to the public for the proper conduct of the BBC – and with the reserve power to dismiss the chair with the expectation that his or her non-executives would follow.

Next Steven Barnett, professor of communications at the University of Westminster and a regular media commentator on broadcasting, places the issues in a useful historical context, arguing that Mrs Thatcher's victory in May 1979, intriguingly, 'may well have saved the BBC'. For the man she appointed as home secretary, Willie Whitelaw, was a supporter of both the BBC and the licence fee, and ensured not only an adequate funding settlement, but more importantly, a 15-year charter, the longest in BBC history.

Barnett also has some positive words for the embattled trust. He suggests that, in its response to the July 2015 green paper on the future of the BBC, the trust demonstrated that it could stand up for a strong corporation 'not emasculated by the commercial self-interest of its competitors'. 'With a clearer demarcation of responsibilities between the trust and executive, given time and support, it could develop into a perfectly adequate mechanism of governance which would preserve both regulatory plurality (keeping Ofcom at a distance from the BBC) and avoid the perils of yet more structural inventions and organisational instability.'

Finally, Richard Tait, a distinguished journalist, former BBC trustee and chair of the trust's editorial standards committee from 2006 to 2010, seriously questions whether giving Ofcom powers over BBC journalism is really the best option. He continues:

> For those who thought those days of censorship were long gone, the recent revelation of a Home Office proposal to give Ofcom, up to now a post-transmission regulator, powers to take pre-emptive action against extremist content was a shock to the system. ... Whoever does end up regulating the BBC's coverage of politics, Islamist extremism and security issues (to take just three of the more contentious areas) it is absolutely essential that such regulation, as at present, is on a strictly post-transmission basis.

Recently, the BBC Trust suggested that all BBC content regulation should be in the hands of a bespoke, independent BBC regulator paid for out of the licence fee. Tait agrees. This view, he says, accepts the opinion poll evidence that the public want an independent body to adjudicate on BBC editorial complaints. 'But it argues, correctly in my view, that this is better achieved by a bespoke regulator whose focus is entirely on the BBC.'

Notes

[1] http://www.theguardian.com/commentisfree/2014/aug/31/guardian-view-bbc-trust-rona-fairhead,accessed on 1 August 2015

[2] http://www.dailymail.co.uk/news/article-2980284/Head-BBC-Trust-calls-axed.html, accessed on 1 August 2015

[3] http://www.theguardian.com/media/2015/jul/10/lame-duck-bbc-trust-chair-should-quit-labour-chris-bryant, accessed on 1 August 2015

Slouching towards Westminster: A New Governance Model for the BBC

The BBC Trust is a dead regulator walking, according to Howard Davies. 'The BBC deserves a board with the backbone to defend its independence, and stand up to meddlesome politicians'

When John Whittingdale's appointment as secretary of state for culture, media and sport was announced immediately after the 2015 general election, every Guardianista in the country went into a collective swoon. The man who declared that the licence fee was 'worse than the poll tax' (Furness 2014) in charge of the BBC? This must presage the end of civilisation as we know it and, as the bard said, life will from now on be weary, stale, flat and unprofitable.

For once, the Guardianistas might be right, though the licence fee seems likely to survive in some form. Whittingdale himself has said he expects it to survive until 2026, at least, and that reports of its imminent demise have been much exaggerated. But it could be appreciably smaller if *The Voice* and *Strictly Come Dancing* are scrapped, and radio is reduced to *The Archers* and the shipping forecast. The green paper (DCMS 2015) which introduced the public consultation on the charter review raised these and many other issues, discussed elsewhere in this volume. It also raised, yet again, the issue of how the corporation should be governed and regulated – a hardy perennial which has flowered every ten years since the BBC was conceived.

The end of the BBC Trust

The questions raised in the green paper are apparently open. One of the 'strategic options' for future governance remains 'a model based on the trust'. But I suspect the civil service draftspeople were simply being polite. Whittingdale himself has been quite categorical about the trust's manifold sins. In a speech in 2013, he said: 'I was always unhappy with the trust to begin with,' and went on: 'I was always of the view that actually the BBC should be run in a traditional corporate structure with a board of directors with non-executives on it and it should be regulated by an external regulator, probably called Ofcom'

(Plunkett 2013). He sees such an arrangement as far preferable to the half-in, half-out arrangement put in place by Tessa Jowell a decade ago, whereby the trust was an unclassifiable creature, neither man nor beast: half-regulator, half cheerleader. As Whittingdale acutely observed: 'The BBC Trust remains far too close to the BBC and blurs accountability.' He drew particular attention to the bizarre arrangement whereby the chair of the trust might use the courtesy title of the 'chairman of the BBC', a deal struck between Tony Blair and Michael Grade, specifically to keep the latter on board – though quite quickly he left. The curious ancestry of this strange arrangement was described in the predecessor volume in this series (Davies 2014).

Even before Whittingdale's appointment it was clear that opinion in the Conservative Party on how the BBC should be governed was on the move. After five years defending Blair's structure, especially during Chris Patten's reign as chair of the trust (2011-2014), senior party figures began to show awareness of the curiosity of the arrangements they inherited. During the election campaign, George Osborne told *Radio Times* that 'the trust arrangement has never really worked. I've never understood why the BBC is frightened of regulation by Ofcom. It is not as if ITV is poorly regulated. Ofcom has proved itself to be a robust regulator' (see Lynch 2015). (That, as Osborne surely knows, may be exactly why the corporation has always been nervous about this idea.)

So now that the government seems to have given up on it, who is now left defending the trust and all its works? The chairman, surely? Well, not quite, as Rona Fairhead herself has realised, a little belatedly, that there is a 'fault line in the blurred accountabilities' (Fairhead 2015) between the trust and the BBC's management it is supposed to oversee. She argues that the corporate governance responsibility should be in the hands of a new unitary board, with an independent chair (in other words, not chaired by the director general as the executive board still is today) and with the non-executives in a majority, as the UK corporate governance code now requires. Regulation should be handled by a body external to the corporation, without the odd two-hattedness of the current structure. 'The cleanest form of separation,' she suggests, 'would be to transfer the trust's responsibilities for regulation and accountability to an external regulator. That way there should be no possibility of vagueness or uncertainty about who will be held responsible for what, when the chips are down' (ibid).

Morale among trust staff must now be hitting new lows. Their own chairman, who might have been expected to defend and justify their role, has abandoned them in their hour of need. With friends like that, who needs enemies? All their hard work on public value, and some of what they have done has been interesting and illuminating, has been set aside.

But in Fairhead's defence she was only accepting what had become inevitable. John Whittingdale's parliamentary committee, which has performed its role of holding the executive to account in an exemplary way in recent years, concluded in its 2015 report, *The Future of the BBC*, that the trust should be abolished and be replaced by a unitary board to run the corporation from day-to-day, on the one hand, and a public service broadcasting commission (PSBC), on the other (culture, media and sport select committee 2015). The committee, in effect, went right back to the formula proposed by the Burns committee of which I was a member in 2004, as part of the last charter review. With this degree of consensus on display, and an almost universal view that the Blair/Jowell scheme has been a decade-long disaster, what is left to discuss? Can we not simply get on with a change along the lines proposed by the parliamentary committee, and be done with it?

That may well be how things turn out, but there are two important issues to resolve, one of process and one of substance.

Process and substance

Previous charter reviews have been accompanied by an inquiry, carried out by a wise person or persons, designed to tease out the major issues, and to allow a process of public consultation on them. Last time, the Burns committee hosted a series of public evidence and consultation sessions. I remember them well. Some of them were sleep-inducing. But while a cynic might argue that nothing new emerges from this kind of exercise it, nonetheless, plays a role in building consensus around a set of propositions. People like to have their say, and it is right to give them the opportunity. This time the new secretary of state has appointed a group of advisers, some of whom have firm and somewhat hostile views about the BBC's mission. But it seems that their advice will be given in private. There is no mention of a chair of the group, or of the publication of an independent collective report. That strikes me as unfortunate. Whatever emerges from this charter review needs to attract a degree of consensus support. Last time, the trust model was holed beneath the water line from the start, as it emerged from ministers' fertile minds and was implemented without due process. There is a serious risk that whatever the government now decides will not be seen to have been submitted to appropriate scrutiny.

Scrutiny and debate are important, because while the death of the trust is almost universally supported today – though Sir Michael Lyons, its first chair, has tried to mount a rearguard action – there is less agreement on how its responsibilities should be reallocated. The green paper suggests two other options: 'a new standalone regulatory organisation, such as the public service broadcasting commission ... and moving more regulation to Ofcom while abolishing the trust.' Both would, if I understand the paper correctly, sit above a unitary board.

How should we evaluate the strengths and weaknesses of these two options? David Elstein has suggested a helpful taxonomy, which illuminates the arguments (Elstein 2015). He argues that the BBC's governance system, broadly defined, needs to carry out three principal functions:

- to promote operational effectiveness;

- to provide consistent regulatory oversight, and

- to judge the quality of the output.

Taking these functions in turn, the role of providing efficient decision-making and operational effectiveness would be the responsibility of the BBC board, and it is hard to see why such a board should not be structured along lines which have now emerged as best practice in the private sector. In other words, it should be independently chaired, and be endowed with a majority of non-executives who can take responsibility for 'corporate hygiene', a category which includes transparent accounting and a disciplined approach to financial control and remuneration, something which has been conspicuously lacking at the BBC in the past. They need half a dozen people with solid experience in well-run companies, universities or charities, to apply themselves to the slightly unusual circumstances of the corporation. The roles are clear: it will not be hard to find them.

Some care and attention is needed to the arrangements for making appointments to that board. There should be an independent element in the selection process, perhaps provided by the civil service commission. In the recent past the appointments made to the BBC governors or to the executive board have at times seemed to be excessively political: in future that should be avoided as far as possible. These are important questions on which a proper charter review committee could have offered an informed view.

Future regulation

The other two elements are more problematic. A decade ago there was a good deal of nervousness in Broadcasting House about the prospect of making the BBC subject to the kind attentions of Ofcom. Some of those concerns have dissipated as Ofcom, under Ed Richards until recently, and now under former Treasury official Sharon White, has matured into a better-respected body, which has demonstrated an ability to maintain its independence and to reach well-balanced views. But there remains uncertainty about precisely what Ofcom would do, and whether a separate public sector broadcasting commission (PSBC) would be a preferable model or, indeed, whether both are required.

The select committee's preferred arrangement was that Ofcom should be the final arbiter of complaints against the BBC. Elstein agrees, though he would perhaps give the BBC's internal processes greater weight. So far, so uncontroversial.

But what would a public sector broadcasting commission do, and how would it interface with Ofcom? The Burns committee, which I believe invented the name, saw the commission as having an important role in funding. It would receive licence fee funding and distribute it to the different broadcasters with a public service obligation (Burns committee 2005) Obviously, the great majority of the money would go to the BBC itself in present circumstances, but some would be routed to S4C, Channel 4 and ITV, and perhaps elsewhere. That would give the PSBC an obvious locus in relation to quality, but without a view of competing offerings it would be difficult for it to decide on an appropriate funding distribution.

The select committee model is a little different. The PSBC would not be the principal funding channel, though 'it could recommend withholding some funding from the BBC in cases where there was a persistent disregard for the views of licence fee payers'. That would still be a powerful sanction and, indeed, would be seen more as a punishment mechanism than a funding formula. There is a danger, though, that it could be used in retribution for a programme the government did not like.

Returning to Elstein's views, my own preference would be for the role of regulatory oversight, which includes competition issues – such as whether the BBC is operating in such a way that it is damaging completion in national local markets – to be undertaken by Ofcom. I find it difficult to see how a regulator focused solely on the BBC can properly address those market dominance questions. Similarly, it is impossible for the BBC to rule on complaints against itself: certainly the trust never achieved the requisite degree of separation to be credible in that role. So while complaints should initially be handled by the corporation, dissatisfied complainants should have access to Ofcom. That is the way things work in financial services, and the regulators monitor companies' complaint handling procedures closely.

As for quality control, this seems to me to be largely a matter for the BBC board itself, though I can see an argument for some external oversight. That oversight would be far sharper if the body carrying it out had a credible sanction to deploy. I doubt whether the sanction proposed by the select committee of withholding funding in egregious cases would work easily in practice, which takes me back to the Burns model. I prefer an arrangement whereby the PSBC would recommend the allocation of licence fee funding between the BBC and others. I believe a solution along these lines, with some contestability of funding – initially at the margin perhaps – would be the best guarantor of a strong and independent BBC (Davies 2005). But reasonable people may reach different views on that issue, and the BBC will certainly resist it, which is another argument for hearings at which the cases for and against can be challenged and assessed.

It is clear that the governance debate has moved on a long way in the first six months of 2015. The BBC Trust is a dead regulator walking. A new governance model is slouching towards Westminster to be born. The green paper, on this issue, certainly asks the right questions, But there will – and should – be many arguments about the precise details. The overriding aim must be to create a structure which wins public confidence and which will attract strong people. The BBC deserves a board with the backbone to defend its independence, and stand up to meddlesome politicians, and also a regulator which does not bow to political winds.

References

Department for culture, media and sport (2015) *BBC Charter Review: Public Consultation.* Available online at https://www.gov.uk/government/consultations/bbc-charter-review-public-consultation, accessed on 23 July 2015

Burns committee (2005) *Independent (Burns) Panel's Final Advice to the Secretary of State,* 27 January. Available online at www.culture.gov.uk, accessed on 28 May 2015

Culture media and sport select committee (2015) *The Future of the BBC,* 26 February. Available online at www.parliament.uk/business/committees, accessed on 28 May 2015

Davies, Howard (2005) *Life after Hutton: Reviewing the BBC Charter.* Available online at www.lse.ac.uk/publicevents, accessed on 28 May 2015

Davies, Howard (2014) Need for clarity at the corporation on who is responsible for what, Mair, John, Tait, Richard and Keeble, Richard Lance (eds) *Is the BBC in Crisis?* Bury St Edmunds: Abramis pp 260-267

Elstein, David (2015) Does the governance and regulation of the BBC need to be changed? 3 April. Available online at https://www.opendemocracy.net/ourbeeb/david-elstein/does-governance-and-regulation-of-bbc-need-to-be-changed, accessed on 28 May 2015

Fairhead, Rona (2015) *BBC Governance: The Case for Intelligent Reform,* Oxford Media Convention. 4 March. Available online at http://www.bbc.co.uk/bbctrust/news/speeches/2015/oxford_media_convention, accessed on 28 May 2015

Furness, Hannah (2014) BBC licence fee 'worse than poll tax', says John Whittingdale, *Daily Telegraph,* 28 October. Available online at http://www.telegraph.co.uk/culture/tvandradio/bbc/11192145/BBC-licence-fee-worse-than-poll-tax-says-John-Whittingdale.html, accessed on 28 May 2015

Lynch, Gerald (2015) Chancellor George Osborne wants BBC to be regulated by Ofcom, gizmodo, 14 April. Available online at http://www.gizmodo.co.uk/2015/04/chancellor-george-osborne-wants-bbc-to-be-regulated-by-ofcom/, accessed on 28 May 2015

Plunkett, John (2013) Jimmy Savile scandal damaged Lord Patten, says culture committee chair, 1 May. Available online at http://www.theguardian.com/media/2013/may/01/jimmy-savile-damaged-lord-patten, accessed on 28 May 2015

Protecting the Public Interest

Former BBC Trustee David Liddiment sees the charter review period as a vital opportunity both to improve the corporation's governance and safeguard its independence and unique public purposes

First an admission: when I first put my mind to writing this chapter I felt less than enthusiastic about returning to the 'post-crisis' debate about BBC governance. Was there really anything new to say? Hadn't the political die been comprehensively cast? Wouldn't cutting old arguments new ways be read as a defence of a structure perceived to have failed? The charter review is about so much more than governance, but getting this right after the agony and recriminations of the latter trust years is a prerequisite to the survival of an independent BBC as a robust public service in an increasingly commercial world. So here goes.

I entirely accept that there is a political imperative for reform. I acknowledge the structural and constitutional imperfections inherent in the original trust that – alongside the human ones – led to the apparent failures of governance so publicly and painfully aired in the final years of my time there. But let's just remind ourselves that, when it was set up, the new structure was a wholesale improvement on what went before. It felt very different in culture and represented real and positive change from the patrician hand of the old-style governors. The trust now included people from a wide range of backgrounds with specific experience relevant to the supervision of a major public broadcaster, all of whom shared a commitment to making the new structure work in the interests of the licence fee payer. That it didn't, quite, had in my view as much to do with misjudgements, bad timing, and uneven leadership as with its structural flaws. The trust was manifestly not, as its detractors now like to claim, a system doomed to failure from the outset. It did hold BBC management to account – on occasion insufficiently robustly, it is true – and it scored some notable goals in the public interest that I will not rehearse again here. But there was one constitutional flaw that, in retrospect, could be considered fatal.

Personally, I never felt any discomfort or conflict of interest in being part of a body that was in essence 'the BBC'. My view, from my first year in 2008 and throughout my two terms there – shared, I know, by many of my fellow trustees – was that we owed nothing to the management of the BBC and everything to the licence fee payer and, therefore, we had a mandate to be as forceful as necessary to ensure that the organisation was efficiently run, did not waste public money, and delivered a distinctive suite of services to the public.

However, because of our constitutional position as the embodiment of the corporation – but with insufficient clarity as to where key responsibilities lay between the executive board and the trust – there was always the unspoken constraint that our actions might undermine the authority of the director general. Where we did (more often than not) take a hard line, this set up unhelpful tensions with the executive board and led to inevitable power plays between personalities about who was really in charge.

The imperative to rein back executive pay, for example, was evident to the trust long before the executive board and its remuneration committee took action (at the trust's insistence) to get the issue under control – with a serious loss to the BBC's credibility with the public. More recently, proposals from the director general outlining far-reaching changes to in-house production and the closure of BBC Three as a broadcast service were made public without any meaningful prior consultation with the trust – supposedly the body charged with setting the BBC's strategy. Neither scenario demonstrates best practice in governance and regulation.

So how can things be improved?
So much is water under the bridge. How can it be made better? A governing body that sits fully outside the BBC seems now not only inevitable but sensible. This distancing started in the trust with its separate building and support staff but breaking the traditional constitutional link seemed at the time a revolution too far. In retrospect this was a mistake. So will a newly-constituted unitary board backed by lighter-touch Ofcom regulation now fit the bill? I don't think so.

The communications regulator has extensive powers and responsibilities focused on the technological and economic needs of commercial markets. As a former secretary of state pointed out at the last charter review.[1]

> Given its range of responsibilities across the commercial section, it may be difficult for Ofcom to devote itself fully to upholding the public interest in BBC services and programmes, in defending the independence of the BBC itself, or in satisfying the need for direct accountability to licence fee payers. It might not be obvious to the licence fee payer how Ofcom was going to resolve any conflict between what was good for the BBC and what was good for the commercial sector. Significant organisational change would be

needed were it to be entrusted with the guardianship of the BBC. Ofcom is not at present responsible for the direct oversight of public spending on the scale represented by the licence fee. Such a change would be likely to lead to greater confusion of responsibilities rather than clarity.

I, too, would be worried that a regulator whose principal focus must be the proper conduct of the commercial broadcast market would have an inherent conflict of interest if it also had to represent the public interest in the biggest intervention in that market. And, as I have said before, light touch regulation of the BBC is the last thing the corporation needs and the public deserves.

Faith in the efficacy and probity of the unitary board as the front line in this new governance model may also be misplaced. It is ironic that the trust's perceived diligence failings over the Digital Media Initiative and severance payments have resulted in a clamour for a unitary board when there have been so many recent similar (and worse) failures by such boards in the private sector. There is plenty of evidence to indicate that non-executives can too easily be captured by the businesses they are supposed to be supervising. It is bad enough when this happens in a major bank or supermarket chain; if it happens in a corporation paid for by £3.7 billion of the public's money, it is unforgiveable.

Need for second tier of governance
All of this argues for a second tier of governance that is independent both of the corporation and of the commercial regulator, but is solely accountable to the public for the proper conduct of the BBC. To get it right this time a number of conditions need to be met. The new body must have clearly articulated functions that flow from its principal purpose – to hold BBC management to account in the public interest. These should include:

- appointing the non-executive chair of the BBC board (who becomes effectively the BBC chair);

- approving all non-executive board appointments;

- approving the appointment of a new director general;

- overseeing and ratifying the board's broad strategy to ensure it is aligned with the BBC's charter responsibilities and public purposes;

- monitoring delivery on those public purposes;

- approving any changes to them;

- setting or amending service licences;

- reviewing performance against their requirements in periodic reviews, each service to be reviewed at least once during a charter period.

Setting regulatory sanctions at an appropriate level for a public corporation will always be problematic: hefty financial penalties or 'special measures' flying squads are not the answer here. Nevertheless, the new body should have the reserve power to dismiss the chair with the expectation that his or her non-executives would follow.

This is not the cheapest or simplest option, though it could be done for about the same, or perhaps a bit less, than the present trust costs now – about 0.21 per cent of licence fee income.[2] But it does meet the requirement for a clear separation of powers and avoids the conflict of interest inherent in going the Ofcom route. But, most importantly, its very existence would be an explicit acknowledgement of the unique role the BBC plays in our democracy: an independent public broadcaster with no political or commercial allegiances, directly paid for by the public and – through this body – properly accountable to them.

There is an additional opportunity during this charter review period to improve clarity and so make for a smoother working relationship between management and governing body in future. The BBC's public purposes and their associated purpose remits, first established by the trust, should be revisited. Without losing proper nuances or scope for subtlety, anything mealy-mouthed should be excised. Both parties need to be clear about their respective roles but above all there should be absolutely no doubt about what the BBC is for. That is what will ultimately bind in a common purpose those running the BBC with those who govern it.

Safeguarding reputation as beacon of Britain's creative and inclusive culture

For the body eventually given the job, representing the public interest goes far beyond the relatively straightforward functions of ensuring that public money is wisely spent or that the BBC's activities don't unfairly impact the commercial market. It has the formidable task of safeguarding the corporation's independence, its role in our democracy, its cultural value and its reputation at home and abroad as a beacon of Britain's creative and inclusive culture.

I wish it, whatever 'it' is, every success. In particular, I wish it strength of purpose and wise and consistent leadership. Because, however watertight you make a governance model on paper, you can never legislate for human behaviour. My eight years on the BBC Trust were some of the most frustrating but also the most fascinating and worthwhile of my life in broadcasting. However history judges its successes and failures, I count it a privilege to have been involved. I hope those entrusted with governing the BBC in future will feel the same.

Notes
[1] *Review of the BBC's Royal Charter: A Strong BBC, Independent of Government*, DCMS, March 2005

[2] *BBC Report and Accounts*, 2014/15, July 2015

Beware the Governance Trojan Horse

With a clearer demarcation of responsibilities, the BBC Trust could develop into a perfectly adequate mechanism of governance which would preserve both regulatory plurality and an independent voice for licence payers, argues Steven Barnett

Historical context: How Thatcher saved the BBC

The last time the BBC was so vulnerable to a general election result, its unlikely saviour was Margaret Thatcher – or, perhaps more accurately, her party's election victory in 1979. It is not often appreciated that the Labour government of 1974-1979, first under Harold Wilson and then under Jim Callaghan, was largely unsympathetic to the BBC. With the royal charter of 1964 due to expire at the end of July 1976, and with the country mired in severe economic difficulties, a distracted government with a tiny working majority agreed to a short-term, three-year charter extension. A further two-year extension was then granted in April 1979, just weeks before the general election. In the meantime, the Labour government had made its intentions clear.

In its broadcasting white paper published in 1978, the government had proposed that each of the BBC's television, radio and external services be supervised by a service management board in order to improve economic efficiency. Under these proposals, 'about half' of the members of each board were to be appointed by the home secretary from outside the BBC, a clear threat to the BBC's political independence (Home Office 1978: 19). Des Freedman quotes an editorial reaction from the Murdoch-owned *News of the World* which today reeks of irony: '....the proposal in the Government's off-White Paper to intimidate the proud BBC into craven impotence is no laughing matter. It is malicious. It is sinister. It is appalling' (Freedman 2003: 107). While the Labour Party's 1979 manifesto made no specific reference to these proposals, its arts and media section was clear that 'On broadcasting, the Labour government will implement the proposals in its white paper'. Furthermore, it promised to 'phase out the television licence fee for old age pensioners during the lifetime of the next parliament' without any commitment to replacing the lost revenue (Labour Party 1979).

At the same time, as Jean Seaton has recounted in her fascinating analysis of that period in her official history, the Labour government kept the corporation on a short funding leash through incremental annual increases in the licence fee. This was partly dictated by soaring inflation which left the BBC in a submissive position, but partly also by a willingness to 'tether' the BBC to government during a period of industrial turmoil and cuts imposed by the International Monetary Fund. In Seaton's words, with three hand-to-mouth licence fee settlements in succession, 'Labour came close to tying the BBC into general expenditure without a fig leaf to protect political independence' (Seaton 2015: 44).

So Thatcher's victory in May 1979 may well have saved the BBC. Its survival was not, of course, down to her own support for an institution she deeply distrusted – as later events were to prove – but through the man she appointed as home secretary: Willie Whitelaw. A supporter of both the BBC and the licence fee, he ensured not only an adequate funding settlement but more importantly a 15-year charter, the longest in BBC history – quite possibly, as Seaton suggests, 'to put it beyond the prime ministerial career of Mrs Thatcher' (ibid: 26). If so, it was a canny and successful strategy. While Mrs Thatcher failed to impose her favourite BBC 'solution' of obliging it to take advertising (even once Whitelaw's influence had waned) through the Peacock committee, she had no natural opportunity through an expiring charter to launch a root-and-branch inquiry into the BBC's right to exist.

Within months of her leaving office in November 1990, her successor, John Major, made it clear that he had no problem with the BBC. His re-election in 1992 meant that, despite the usual mutterings of opposition on the right of his party, the next charter in 1996 was concluded without a great deal of anxiety. And the Labour government of Tony Blair – which was significantly more comfortable with the BBC than previous Labour or Conservative governments – was never a serious threat. While abolishing the BBC governors, Labour's 2006 charter and accompanying agreement emerged with a much more transparent and codified structure, a new governance mechanism in the BBC Trust, and more detailed public service obligations laid down in the charter and agreement, all within a spirit of safeguarding and strengthening a much-prized British institution. And while David Cameron's coalition government may have sliced 16 per cent off the BBC's income under cover of 'austerity measures', its dates fell outside the span of charter renewal.

40 years on: A new Conservative government and a perfect political storm
So we come to the new charter, and four factors which make this, potentially, a perfect political storm for the BBC. First, there is an uncomfortably short time span between May 2015's general election and charter expiry at the end of 2016.

Last time around, then-culture secretary Tessa Jowell kicked off the process in December 2003, allowing almost three years for a lengthy consultation process which involved the public as well as industry and civil society stakeholders, and which included a comprehensive programme of qualitative, quantitative and deliberative research. The results fed into a green paper published in March 2005 (in advance of the general election in May) followed by a white paper in March 2006. That two-and-a-half-year process will, this time, be crammed into a few months, allowing little time for serious debate and consultation.

Second, the renewal process will be conducted by a Conservative government which, after unexpected electoral success, will be at its most energised and least vulnerable for the twelve months in which the future of the BBC will be decided. If Prime Minister David Cameron is willing to take on the right of his party over renegotiations with Europe, he may be rather more eager to compromise over their demands for a major overhaul of an institution which many have long despised on both ideological and partisan grounds. Their mood will not have been helped by the traditional complaints of left-wing bias by their own campaign team, despite clear evidence that the BBC – like other broadcasters – was directly influenced by the rabidly partisan campaigning of the right-wing press (Lewis 2015).

Third, that visceral hostility from the right of the governing party will be echoed and magnified by large sections of the national and regional press which are more antagonistic to the BBC now than at any time in its history. Not only do several editors – and the commentators they employ – share the Conservative right's impatience with public funding, but their proprietors are increasingly infuriated by a universally available and trusted 'free' source of news which (in their view) hinders their already fragile publishing business models. The tone of commercial self-interest was set by the *Sun*, in the wake of John Whittingdale's appointment as culture secretary, whose leader column on 12 May 2015 ('Licence to kill') combined both bias and competition arguments: it was, raged the editorial, 'payback time' after 'decades of BBC bias against the Tories, subtle and blatant'; moreover, the BBC 'intrudes into markets where private firms should thrive instead' and should be 'radically shrunk so it focuses on first-class original TV and radio'.

On the same day, the *Daily Mail* condemned the BBC's 'bloated bureaucracy and entrenched Left-wing bias', while the *Daily Telegraph* managed both to blame the BBC for pre-election polls underestimating the Tory share of vote ('This set of Left-of centre assumptions … contributes to a reluctance among voters to say they support the Conservatives') and to make a blatantly self-interested link between the BBC's news operation and the press: 'Why does the BBC need to have such an all-encompassing digital news operation in competition with newspapers that do not have the luxury of a tax to support them? The BBC's broadcasting model is as outdated as the vast state-funded monolith that runs it.'[1]

How different is today's dominant anti-BBC newspaper rhetoric from those desperate days of Labour government manipulation in 1977-1978. As well as the *News of the World*, there were supportive articles in the *Economist* and *The Times* in a period when '[t]he BBC continued to receive a broadly positive press' (Seaton op cit: 45). Moreover, Jean Seaton's predecessor as BBC official historian, Asa Briggs, was equally clear about the potentially destructive impact had there been similarly hostile press coverage when the BBC started. He told her in an interview: 'Had Northcliffe and Beaverbrook seen the BBC as a rival in the same way, then the corporation would have been strangled at birth.'

Finally, the new culture secretary, generally seen as on the right of the party, is a long-term BBC critic. As chairman of the culture, media and sport select committee for the last ten years, he is well versed in the issues and – as has been widely reported – has described the licence fee as 'worse than the poll tax' and unsustainable in the long term. That in itself need not be problematic. As I wrote just after his appointment, not only was Whittingdale widely regarded as a fair and effective select committee chairman who listens to arguments, but 'he was clear in his comments about the future of the licence fee that he was thinking beyond the next ten years – in other words, any move towards subscription or other funding solutions would have to wait until the 2026 charter' (Barnett 2015). That longer-term thinking appears to be confirmed in the government's green paper on charter renewal which states explicitly that it is 'minded to consider [subscription] as an option for the longer term' rather than the short or medium term (Department for culture, media and sport 2015: 102). The shotgun funding deal between chancellor George Osborne and DG Tony Hall – which saw the BBC agree to take on the cost of licence fees for the over-75s in return for very little – will impose another real-terms revenue reduction that will certainly have a detrimental impact on BBC services. It should not yet, however, represent an existential threat to the institution itself.

Where the real threats lie: Culture select committee report and green paper proposals

Where, then, does the real charter renewal threat to the BBC lie if not in a wholesale restructuring of its funding? The answer lies in two key ideas buried in one of the last select committee reports of John Whittingdale's chairmanship on the future of the BBC, published in February 2015 (Culture, media and sport select committee 2015) which are not surprisingly echoed in his green paper.

First is top-slicing of the licence fee. The select committee report recommended that, while the BBC should be the *principal* recipient of the licence fee, 'a small proportion should be made available for other public service content priorities such as supporting local and regional journalism, and children's broadcasting'. This would be part of a broader strategy to reduce the BBC's size because it 'needs to be able to make bigger, braver decisions on its strategy and inevitably must do less in some areas'. There was no mention of which particular areas should be in the firing line, not least because every service and every aspect of the BBC's output attracts loyal and appreciative audiences who protest loudly at the prospect of losing their favourite programmes (e.g. when 6 Music was threatened with closure by DG Mark Thompson in 2010). Precisely the same top-slicing idea appears in a whole page of the green paper devoted to 'contestable funding', on the basis that 'a small amount of contestable funding could introduce greater diversity of providers and greater plurality in public services provision' (op cit: 114). The notion of a smaller BBC runs through the green paper like letters through a stick of Blackpool rock. It is hard to see this emphasis on reduction as anything other than a sop to the BBC's increasingly vocal competitors who fear both subscription (which would potentially compromise the revenues of Sky, Virgin and BT) and advertising (equally opposed by ITV, Channel 5 and other advertising-funded channels).

Second is another bone for commercial competitors: a call for more stringent controls on the BBC's freedom to manoeuvre. Under the terms of the current charter, any new BBC service or 'significant change' to an existing service must be subjected to a public value test. This includes a 'market impact' study, carried out by Ofcom, to identify any detrimental effect on commercial competitors. While this was an entirely proportionate response to competitor concerns about the BBC overreaching itself, the select committee recommended a much lower threshold which would 'trigger public value and market impact tests where there is *prima facie* evidence of the BBC crowding out others' endeavours and having an adverse market impact'.

While not explicitly transferred to the green paper, this proposal is implicit in the questions which ask:

- whether the PVT suffers from 'either taking too long to deliver or missing a change that did not meet the threshold of significance'; and

- whether service licences 'may not hold the BBC to a high enough standard or contain enough specific details about output' (ibid: 145).

Further restrictions on the BBC's freedom to programme would strike at the heart of its ability to provide a comprehensive service of size and scale reaching out to the whole nation. By definition, the BBC is an intervention in the market. Commercial rivals who love to blame every conceivable problem on the BBC – from ITV's complaints about *Strictly Come Dancing* to commercial radio's lack of profitability to regional newspaper groups' closure of newspapers – will certainly enjoy the frequent references to criticisms from competitors. By indulging them as comprehensively as this green paper does, there is a very real risk of constraining the BBC to the point where it would barely be able to function.

A new governance structure and a Trojan horse

In the select committee report, both these proposals would be achieved through a new governance structure which would essentially become a Trojan horse for a desiccated BBC. It proposed that the BBC Trust be abolished and replaced by a public service broadcasting commission (PSBC) which would have 'discretion to carry out public value tests on BBC services' as well as 'a role in allocating a proportion of the licence fee … on a competitive basis to the BBC and others for production of PSB content'.

Ironically, the PSBC construct is 25 years old and was first mooted by the Conservative MP Damian Green. In a report for the right-wing Centre for Policy Studies in 1991, he proposed a public service broadcasting authority (PSBA) which would distribute to the BBC a steadily diminishing proportion of licence fee revenue (Green 1991). Not only is the proposal ancient history, so is the rebuttal: two years later, in response to the Major government's green paper on charter renewal which floated a similar idea, I wrote: 'As in Australia and America [the BBC] would become increasingly irrelevant and marginalised, losing public sympathy and affection: a cultural backwater for the intellectual and artistic elite with a rapidly diminishing presence in the global communications battle' (Barnett 1993: 81). *Plus ça change.* Once again, this same concept is mirrored in one of the three governance options advanced by the green paper: a 'standalone' regulator which could, amongst other new powers, have responsibility for 'allocation of any contestable funding' (ibid: 139).

It has become a conventional wisdom that the BBC Trust does not work, a conclusion which is surely premature for an organisation which is less than ten years old. Ironically, one of the best defences of the trust model comes from a passage in the green paper which rehearses the advantages of strengthening the existing system rather than replacing it: that all organisational change 'takes time, costs money and introduces disruption, risk and uncertainty'. It does not, however, advance perhaps the most persuasive argument of all, which relates to the provenance and rationale of the trust model: that it should be, in the words of the culture secretary, Tessa Jowell, who established it, 'the eyes and ears of the licence payer', representing their interests in guaranteeing the BBC's independence, efficiency, quality and integrity. In its response to the green paper – which firmly establishes the case for universality as well as a legitimate entertainment role for the BBC – the trust itself demonstrated that it can fulfil the role of standing up for a strong BBC which is not emasculated by the commercial self-interest of its competitors (BBC Trust 2015). Perhaps that is why it is consistently pilloried by a press which has much to gain from a smaller BBC.

Those who seek a perfect solution for BBC governance will be forever disappointed because there is no counsel of perfection for an institution which is by definition intimately intertwined with the market and the state, but separate from both. With a clearer demarcation of responsibilities between the trust and executive, given time and support, it could develop into a perfectly adequate mechanism of governance which would preserve both regulatory plurality (keeping Ofcom at a distance from the BBC) and avoid the perils of yet more structural inventions and organisational instability. My fear is that the mantra of 'abolish the trust' is becoming a convenient pretext for a new governance structure which will become the Trojan horse that we avoided nearly 25 years ago.

Notes

[1] *Daily Mail*, 12 May 2015. Available online at
http://www.dailymail.co.uk/debate/article-3077589/DAILY-MAIL-COMMENT-
Cameron-s-sure-touch-nation-s-tiller.html, accessed on 14 June 2015. *Daily Telegraph*, 12
May 2015. Available online at http://www.telegraph.co.uk/news/bbc/11597679/The-
BBCs-views-and-structure-are-outdated.html, accessed on 14 June 2015

References

Barnett, Steven (2015) Is the BBC safe in the hands of our new culture secretary, John
Whittingdale? *New Statesman*, 12 May. Available online at
http://www.newstatesman.com/politics/2015/05/bbc-safe-hands-our-new-culture-
secretary-john-whittingdale, accessed on 9 June 2015

Barnett, Steven (1993) Gift horse or Trojan horse? Some thoughts on an Arts Council of
the Airwaves, Barnett, Steven (ed.) *Funding the BBC's Future*, London: British Film
Institute pp 75-83

BBC Trust (2015) *Initial response to the Government's Green Paper on BBC Charter Review*, July.
Available online at
http://downloads.bbc.co.uk/bbctrust/assets/files/pdf/about/how_we_govern/charter
_review/green_paper_response.pdf, accessed 24 July 2015

Culture, media and sport select committee (2015) *Future of the BBC*, HC 315, The
Stationery Office

Department for culture, media and sport (DCMS) (2015) *BBC Charter Review: Public
Consultation*, Cm116, The Stationery Office

Freedman, Des (2003) *Television Policies of the Labour Party 1951-2001*, London: Frank Cass
Publishers

Green, Damian (1991) *A Better BBC: Public Service Broadcasting in the '90s*, Policy Study No.
122, London: Centre for Policy Studies

Home Office (1978) *Broadcasting*, Cmnd.7294, HMSO

Labour Party (1979) *The Labour Way is the Better Way*, 1979 election manifesto. Available
online at http://www.politicsresources.net/area/uk/man/lab79.htm, accessed on 31
May 2015

Lewis, Justin (2015) Newspapers, not BBC, led the way in biased election coverage, *The
Conversation*, 15 May. Available online at https://theconversation.com/newspapers-not-
bbc-led-the-way-in-biased-election-coverage-41807, accessed on 9 June 2015

Seaton, Jean (2015) *'Pinkoes and Traitors': The BBC and the Nation 1974-1987*, London:
Profile Publishing

The Politicians and the BBC: What Price Independence?

The aftermath of a bruising election campaign is the worst possible time for the BBC to be negotiating its long term future – and trying to preserve its financial and editorial independence, argues Richard Tait

The 2011 Parliament Act has been bad news for the BBC. It means the two periods of maximum potential political intervention and/or interference in the BBC – charter renewal every ten years and licence fee negotiations every five – now coincide almost exactly with the dates of UK general elections and will do so for the foreseeable future.

General elections are always fraught times for relations between MPs and broadcasters. James Harding, the BBC's new director of news, was taken aback by the ferocity of attacks on the BBC from all the parties. He described the election campaign as both 'fun' and 'hell on wheels':

> Labour was angry about the focus on the SNP, the Tories regularly questioned our running orders and editorial decisions, the Lib Dems felt they weren't getting sufficient airtime, the Greens complained about being treated like a protest movement not a party, UKIP railed against what they saw as an establishment shut-out, the DUP felt Northern Ireland parties were being treated as second class citizens, the SNP questioned what they saw as metropolitan London bias at the BBC (Harding 2015).

Some of the parties linked their complaints to threats about what they would do to the BBC after the election. Nigel Farage, the leader of UKIP, called for the licence fee to be cut and *Newsnight* replaced (Farage 2015); the Democratic Unionist Party (DUP) leader, Nigel Dodds, said the BBC charter should be in the hands of a royal commission to ensure that the DUP was guaranteed fair treatment by the BBC (Watt and McDonald 2015). Tom Baldwin, Labour's spin doctor, accused the BBC of caving in to Conservative bullying: 'BBC executives and journalists have told me that there were regular, repeated threats from senior Tories during this election campaign about "what would happen afterwards" if they did not do as they were told and fall into line' (Baldwin 2015). The then-culture secretary, Sajid Javid, criticised what he said was anti-Tory bias in a Radio 4 discussion and said the review of the charter would have to consider balance in news coverage (Chapman 2015).

The danger for the BBC in this sort of environment is that the politicians begin to chip away at that independence from political interference which is what has up to now distinguished the corporation from most public broadcasters in the world. The licence fee is meant to insulate the corporation from direct government influence or control over how it spends its budget; the BBC's journalism must be accurate and impartial, but it, rather than the government or some third party, has always been the judge of how well it meets that obligation. Both those key elements of independence are now at risk.

Financial independence

Over the last twenty years, different governments have encroached more and more on the principle that the licence fee was to pay for the BBC and that the BBC, regulated by its governors and more recently the trust, did not take political instruction on how to spend it. There has been much criticism of the most recent deal on the licence fee, and it was certainly a particularly brutal example of the harsh reality that a determined government can more or less do what it wants to the BBC, but unlike Captain Louis Renault in *Casablanca* who declared himself 'shocked, shocked' that gambling had been going on in Rick's Café, while pocketing his winnings, we should also recognise the increasingly questionable deals that preceded it.

Take, for example, the ill-fated Jam project on digital learning, launched in 2006 after three years of planning, which wasted as much money as the Digital Media Initiative (DMI). Potentially a good idea, it was also in tune with the Blair government's education priorities. The project was not well managed (to put it politely) and the government, which had initially encouraged the BBC as part of the digital curriculum, changed its mind and abandoned its support for the project in 2007 when it was challenged on competition grounds (Chesterton 2014: 219-220). The BBC's huge investment in Salford was part of a very necessary shift away from London – but it was also expected to bring big economic benefits to one of Labour's heartlands – the politicians hoped for 15,000 jobs and £1.5 billion in investment. So insistent on Salford was the Blair government that the trust was required to confirm (on the very day of the licence fee announcement) that BBC North would go ahead. It was made, effectively, a condition of the 2007 settlement (House of Commons *Hansard* 2007).

At the same time, worries about the sustainability of commercially-funded public service broadcasting led to the argument that some of the licence fee should be top-sliced and go to support it. Before the 2006 charter review, both Ofcom and Lord Burns, the government's adviser, argued for quite similar forms of taking money from the licence fee and giving it to an external body to spend on non-BBC public service broadcasting (Culture, media and sport committee 2015: 88-89). The BBC fought the principle of top-slicing the licence fee and giving it to a separate organisation on the grounds that it would undermine support for the licence fee (Holmwood 2009).

However, Labour began to raid the BBC budget in a different way – by putting pressure on the corporation to take on new responsibilities which would otherwise have been general public expenditure. It got the BBC to agree it to help pay for digital switchover. It then proposed to top slice the licence fee (Digital Britain 2009: 141-157) for, as a first project, the ill-fated Independently Financed News Consortia. Paying for them would have been part of the licence fee settlement in 2010 had Labour won the election (Tait 2012).

The last two licence fee deals – of 2010 and 2015 – have clearly moved us into different territory in terms of the scale of the erosion of the BBC's financial independence. On both occasions, the BBC ran, immediately after the general election, straight into a chancellor of the exchequer determined to cut public spending and equally determined that the BBC should make a significant contribution to his emergency budget by taking on costs which had been central governnment's.

After the 2010 agreement, licence fee payers found themselves funding S4C, the World Service, the roll out of rural broadband and subsidising commercially run local TV stations at a total bill of around £500 million as these costs were transferred from the government's account to the BBC's. These commitments could just about be reconciled with the BBC's public purposes and were (more or less) under BBC control. However, the BBC management and the trust dug in their heels and threatened resignation over George Osborne's demand in 2010 that the BBC paid for free licences for the over-75s. With the support of the Liberal Democrats a more acceptable deal was done in a few breathless days (Snoddy 2014: 85-86).

History repeats itself

The culture, media and sport committee was unimpressed. It warned sternly that 'No future licence fee negotiations must be conducted in the way of the 2010 settlement'. However, history repeated itself with an almost eerie precision in July 2015 when George Osborne, in the course of a similar week of closed doors negotiations, took the cost of free licences for the over-75s out of the social security budget and put it on the BBC's tab at an estimated cost of £700 million by 2020, and potentially rising further as the population aged.

The BBC bowed to the inevitable in return for an agreement which offered it some significant benefits – the return of indexation of the licence fee after seven years of freeze, the chance to claw back the money being lost to people who only viewed online, the end of the top slice to fund rural broadband. The pensioner perk would be phased in over three years and the BBC would (perhaps) be under no obligation to maintain it in full after 2020. The odds on decriminalisation of non-payment of the licence fee lengthened – not least licence fee was looking increasingly like general taxation (Snoddy

_____ial terms it was as good a deal as the BBC could have hoped for – and the government got a big chunk of the social security budget off its books in perpetuity. But where does it all leave the BBC's independence? Lord Birt, the former director general, said it was seriously damaged; Lord Hall, the current director general, disagreed (Gayle 2015). Which of them is seen to be right in the long term will depend mainly on how much freedom the BBC will have to manage its own budget. The prospect of top slicing has not gone away – the green paper both asks if some funding should be made available for other providers to deliver public service content and raises the possibility of the licence fee supporting digital radio switchover or regional news (DCMS 2015: 55-57).

The settlement is far from generous – it will mean re-prioritisation of budgets and services, perhaps some service closures, and certainly some tough decisions about where the BBC does – and does not – spend its money. Tony Hall has some ambitious plans for the BBC's digital future and they will need to be funded as well, if necessary by cuts elsewhere. Will the new BBC management and governance structure be free to make those decisions without political interference?

The green paper asks the key question here – whether the level of funding for certain services and programmes should be protected (DCMS 2015: 55). Will the commitments to World Service, S4C and local TV, for example, be 'ring-fenced' or can the BBC reduce those budgets as well as those of its core services? Can it decide at some stage in the future that, say, keeping football rights for a mass audience is a higher priority than free TV licences for wealthier pensioners who can easily afford £3 a week? Will it have a board with the determination as well as the power to make those very tough (and quite political) decisions?

Only when the answers to those questions begin to emerge will we know how much damage has been done to the BBC's financial independence. If the 2010 and 2015 commitments were to be ring-fenced the BBC could find itself in a very few years' time spending only two thirds of its licence fee income on the services the public values and which, in the main, it thinks the licence fee is meant to fund.

Editorial independence

And just as worrying, the structures which are meant to protect the BBC's journalistic independence are not going to survive charter renewal in their present form. What replaces them and how effective they will be in the future should concern anyone who cares about the maintenance of freedom of expression.

The most likely change to the regulation of the BBC's journalism could mark a major break with the past. Since its formation in 1926, the BBC has been the final arbiter of its own journalism. The BBC set its own editorial standards and adjudicated on its own editorial complaints in the key areas of accuracy and impartiality (BBC Trust 2006: 25-28). Any effective system of editorial regulation has to work in two very different ways. It has to be independent of management to give confidence to the outside world that the organisation is being properly held to account but it also has to protect the integrity of the organisation from external pressures.

After a long debate during the 2006 charter review process, the new BBC Trust kept responsibility for accuracy and impartiality. Ofcom regulates the commercial sector for accuracy and impartiality, but not the BBC. The BBC argued that impartiality and accuracy were so central to its political independence that it should retain the final word in these areas and that the BBC Trust was sufficiently independent of the BBC management to do the job effectively.

This time round, it is already clear that this part of the 2006 settlement is under serious threat. The culture, media and sport committee report in March 2015 recommended that the trust should be abolished and replaced with a unitary board and an external regulator. It suggested that two of the trust's key responsibilities in protecting the BBC's independence should be split and given to different bodies. The new board and chairman should take over the role of defending and protecting the BBC's independence. But the final arbiter of whether the BBC's journalism was accurate and impartial should pass to Ofcom (Culture, media and sport committee 2015: 108-110)

The Ofcom option

Two Ofcom old hands, Richard Hooper and Ed Richards, told the committee that transferring that responsibility to Ofcom was the right move. Hooper, a former deputy chair, argued that Ofcom's judgements on accuracy and impartiality would be more respected because they were from an independent body, not a BBC in-house regulator; Richards, a former chief executive, stressed Ofcom's independence of government and assured the committee that in his time he had never been pressurised by senior politicians (ibid: 110-111).

The green paper does not go quite so far in recommending this solution – it raises the interesting question whether impartiality, as one of the BBC's values, should be set out and codified to allow the BBC's performance to be judged and measured (DCMS 2015: 19). And it is very complimentary about Ofcom's overall performance (ibid: 68). It is pretty clear where the debate is going, but I wonder whether giving Ofcom powers over BBC journalism is really the best option.

Some of the BBC's critics support the Ofcom option because they believe it will 'sort out' the BBC and shift the corporation's editorial stance more towards their view of the world. They are likely to be quickly disillusioned. From my own experience of BBC and Ofcom complaints handling from 2004 to 2010, the BBC's procedures are now similar to Ofcom's; far from being a soft 'in-house' regulator, the trust's adjudications in favour of complainants often upset senior

BBC people both behind and in front of the camera. Comparing Ofcom and BBC Trust judgements on similar complaints suggests no difference in approach in the overwhelming majority of their decisions.

Both bodies have experienced and independent-minded people running their editorial boards. The current chair of the Ofcom content board is Tim Gardam, a former director of television at Channel 4 and before that a senior BBC executive; the current chair of the BBC Trust's editorial standards committee is Richard Ayre, a former deputy chief executive of BBC News (and a recent member of Ofcom's content board).

The culture committee was right to say that the BBC system has its critics. I am sure some of them have a point – these are, in the end, often quite fine judgements and the BBC Trust (like Ofcom) sometimes gets it wrong. But equally, some unhappy complainants will never be satisfied. They have strong, sincerely held and unshakeable views on the rightness of their cause – whether it be the Israeli-Palestinian conflict, or the European Union, climate change or UK politics. They will never be convinced by any regulator that a broadcaster has been impartial because, ultimately, they want to see their own news values, their own use of language and their own choice of evidence take priority over others. Shifting responsibility for dealing with their complaints to Ofcom will not change that.

And moving responsibility for impartiality and accuracy to Ofcom is a very big decision, with major implications for both organisations. Ofcom's new chief executive, Sharon White, while promising the culture media and sports committee that Ofcom 'will do the best possible job' if asked to regulate the BBC for accuracy and impartiality, pointed out the BBC received 250,000 complaints a year to Ofcom's 25,000 (Plunkett 2015). The BBC also has different editorial standards in a number of key areas and the public's expectations of it are different. The BBC's dominant share of the broadcast news and current affairs market means it attracts far more editorial complaints than ITN or Sky; the BBC's role as an international broadcaster means apparently arcane arguments over, say, who should or should not be called a terrorist or what is the correct term to describe the organisation that calls itself Islamic State have a global resonance.

For the broadcast regulators are not just complaints handlers. They issue the codes and guidelines by which the broadcasters are judged; their decisions over a period of time can produce a 'case law' of precedents which can also affect the way broadcasters approach issues and the language they use. A regulator's handling of complaints about past programmes can change what viewers see in the future. In the 1990s, when I was at ITN, we found the Broadcasting Standards Council (whose writ extended to the BBC as well as us) was increasingly critical of our use of war footage from Bosnia – we felt, rightly or wrongly, that we were being pressurised to sanitise terrible violence at a time when successive British governments were determined not to intervene (Simms 2001). We pushed back and managed to persuade the regulator to allow us a little more latitude, but I still feel we did not always report the story as we should have done – on occasions what the viewers saw did not adequately represent the terrible violence, particularly against civilians..

The regulator as censor

It is not so very long ago that the broadcast regulators (part of whose job was meant to resist political pressure) were being bullied by the politicians into direct censorship of programmes. Until it was replaced by the ITC in 1992, the Independent Broadcasting Authority (IBA), the commercial television regulator, had the power to pull programmes from the schedule. Under pressure from the then-Labour government, the IBA stopped Thames Television broadcasting a number of programmes on Northern Ireland in the 1970s (Potter 1990: 207-213). In 1985, the BBC governors caved in to a request from the Conservative home secretary, Leon Brittan, and stopped the transmission of a *Real Lives* documentary on Northern Ireland, breaking the convention that they did not preview programmes and left decisions on transmission to the director general as editor-in-chief (Seaton 2015: 313-317).

On at least one occasion, regulatory plurality trumped censorship – in June 1978, Roy Mason, the Labour government's Northern Ireland secretary, got the IBA to pull a Thames Television *This Week* programme about the alleged maltreatment of suspects at the Castlereagh interrogation centre in Northern Ireland. The next day BBC *Nationwide* decided to cover the story, using some of the Thames film which had been banned on ITV (Taylor 1978).

For those who thought those days of censorship were long gone, the recent revelation of a Home Office proposal to give Ofcom, up to now a post-transmission regulator, powers to take pre-emptive action against extremist content was a shock to the system. In April 2015, the then-culture secretary, Sajid Javid, wrote to the Prime Minister opposing Teresa May's idea, which, apparently in response to television interviews after the murder of British army fusilier Lee Rigby in May 2013, would turn Ofcom into a censor. Javid rightly said it would involve 'a fundamental shift in the way UK broadcasting is regulated', moving away from the current framework of post-transmission regulation which takes account of freedom of expression (Travis 2015).

The proposal (and at time of writing, July 2015, it remains only a proposal) was a warning sign that broadcasters' reporting of Islamist extremism and, in particular, their coverage of those who appear to sympathise with terrorist violence could bring them on to a collision course with the government, rather as television interviews with Sinn Fein caused such tensions during the thirty years of the IRA campaign. The current row over what the BBC should call Islamic State could be an indication of more serious trouble ahead (Smith 2015).

History teaches us that the really toxic arguments between broadcasters and politicians are always over security issues – terrorism in Northern Ireland, weapons of mass destruction, Al-Qaeda and now Islamic State. The current situation is all the more difficult because of worries over radicalisation – how do broadcasters balance the need to report all sides of a complex conflict with the risk of being accused of encouraging radicalisation, even inadvertently? How much airtime should be given to apologists for terrorism? How do you report these stories impartially if some views and people are off-limits? In any case, do broadcasters really matter as much as they once did in the new world of social media and online grooming?

Although in recent years the BBC governors and the trust found themselves under external pressure on a number of occasions from complainants to preview contentious programmes on the grounds that it was already clear that they would breach the BBC's editorial guidelines, the answer was always that the decision to broadcast lay with the director general as editor-in-chief who was then accountable post-transmission. Whoever does end up regulating the BBC's coverage of politics, Islamist extremism and security issues (to take just three of the more contentious areas) it is absolutely essential that such regulation, as at present, is on a strictly post-transmission basis.

The dawn of the 'super-regulator'?
In the UK, media regulation is split among a range of bodies and it is sometimes inconsistent. But it also reflects the fact that there are real differences in the roles and responsibilities of different media organisations (Fielden 2011). As convergence means print, broadcast and online media, currently all regulated in very different ways, are all heading for the same space, spreading responsibility around different regulators may still have some advantages over the creation of a single 'super-regulator' which could, in a worst case, do the government of the day's bidding in ways which may inhibit freedom of expression.

Even though the newspapers are putting more and more emphasis on their online presence, they have clearly won the argument, with this government at least, that – despite Leveson – their comparatively light touch system of self regulation should not change much and they certainly want nothing to do with Ofcom. Indeed, when Leveson suggested some Ofcom involvement in press regulation, David Cameron rejected the idea out of hand, reminding MPs that the chair of Ofcom was appointed by the secretary of state and adding '… we also have to consider that Ofcom is already a very powerful regulatory body. We should be trying to reduce concentrations of power rather than increase them' (House of Commons *Hansard* 2012).

Although Ofcom is currently well and independently run and has done a good job regulating commercial broadcast journalism, that is not, in itself, an overwhelming reason for giving it responsibility for the BBC's editorial independence. The BBC Trust has suggested that all BBC content regulation should be in the hands of a bespoke, independent BBC regulator paid for out of the licence fee (BBC Trust 2015: 21-23). It recognises and accepts the opinion poll evidence that the public want an independent body to adjudicate on BBC editorial complaints. But it argues, correctly in my view, that this is better achieved by a bespoke regulator whose focus is entirely on the BBC.

The scene is set for a re-run of the arguments last time round. Earlier in the summer the decision in favour of Ofcom looked as though it had been taken before the consultation had begun, perhaps on the assumption that Ofcom would take over all BBC governance. But Sharon White, the new chief executive, has made clear she does not think Ofcom is the right organisation to be responsible for the rest of BBC governance. The more likely overall solution is, as the trust has effectively now recommended, a unitary board and a bespoke BBC regulator. So the trust's proposal has a chance – it combines independence of regulation with the recognition that the BBC's journalistic role in the UK is unique and its regulation, therefore, needs a specific solution.

Changing the regulation of BBC journalism, however it is done, is a big decision. The mess which the politicians made of the BBC's governance ten years ago should not give anyone great confidence that radical change always make things better. Moving responsibility for impartiality and accuracy to Ofcom may not be as unproblematical as the culture committee hoped; a bespoke regulator could well be a better solution. But whichever way the argument is settled later in 2015, at the very least I recommend anyone concerned about freedom of expression in the UK to keep a close eye on how any new system works in practice, who is appointed to the key regulatory and supervisory roles and what guidelines and rules the BBC is asked to observe. 'Scale and scope' matter, of course, but if the BBC is not independent it is no use to anyone.

References

Baldwin, Tom (2015) The BBC was not in the pocket of Labour this election. Quite the opposite, *Guardian*, 13 May 2015. Available online at http://www.theguardian.com/commentisfree/2015/may/13/bbc-labour-election#img-1, accessed on 15 June 2015

BBC Trust (2006) *From Seesaw to Waggon Wheel: Safeguarding Impartiality in the 21st Century*, London: BBC Trust

BBC Trust (2015) *Initial Response to the Government's Green Paper on BBC Charter Review*, London: BBC Trust

Chapman, James (2015) BBC accused of 'anti-Tory bias' by culture secretary Sajid Javid who threatens review of how the corporation is governed, *Daily Mail*, 29 April. Available online at http://www.dailymail.co.uk/news/article-3059974/Media-minister-warns-BBC-anti-Tory-bias-Senior-Conservatives-express-anger-left-leaning-slant-broadcasters.html#ixzz3d3Sjezqn, accessed on 15 June 2015

Chesterton, Fiona (2014) Who cares about BBC education? Mair, John, Tait, Richard and Keeble, Richard Lance (eds) *Is The BBC in Crisis?* Bury St Edmunds: Abramis pp 215-222

Culture, media and sport committee (2015) *Future of the BBC*, 26 February, London: Stationery Office

Department of culture, media and Sport (DCMS) (2015) *BBC Charter Review Public Consultation*, London: DCMS

Digital Britain (2009) *Final Report*, June, London: Stationery Office

Farage, Nigel (2015) Nigel Farage calls for BBC to focus on core programming, tackle political bias and scrap *Newsnight*, 3 May. Available online at http://www.ukip.org/nigel_farage_calls_for_bbc_to_focus_on_core_programming_tac kle_political_bias_and_scrap_newsnight, accessed on 17 June 2015

Fielden, Lara (2011) *Regulating for Trust in Journalism*, Oxford: Reuters Institute for the Study of Journalism

Gayle, Damian (2015) Tony Hall rejects claims licence fee deal turns BBC into a branch of the DWP, *Guardian*, 7 July. Available online at http://www.theguardian.com/media/2015/jul/07/tony-hall-licence-fee-deal-bbc-dwp-george-osborne, accessed on 7 July 2015

Harding, James (2015) *Speech at Voice of Listener and Viewer*, 2 June. Available online at http://www.bbc.co.uk/mediacentre/speeches/2015/james-harding-speech-vlv-2-june-2015, accessed on 17 June 2015

Holmwood, Leigh (2009) BBC's Mark Thompson attacks plans to 'top-slice' licence fee, *Guardian*, 24 June. Available online at http://www.theguardian.com/media/2009/jun/24/bbc-mark-thompson-top-slice, accessed on 10 July 2015

House of Commons *Hansard* (2007) *BBC Licence Fee*, 18 January, Col. 933. Available online at http://www.publications.parliament.uk/pa/cm200607/cmhansrd/cm070118/debtext/7 0118-0006.htm

House of Commons *Hansard* (2012) *Leveson Inquiry*, 29 November, Col. 452. Available online at http://www.publications.parliament.uk/pa/cm201213/cmhansrd/cm121129/debtext/1 21129-0003.htm#12112958000004, accessed on 17 July 2015

Plunkett, John (2015) Ofcom could take on BBC regulation but not governance, says Sharon White, *Guardian*, 21 July 2015. Available online at http://www.theguardian.com/media/2015/jul/21/ofcom-bbc-regulation-governance-sharon-white, accessed on 22 July 2015

Potter, Jeremy (1980) *Independent Television in Britain: Volume 4 Companies and Programmes*, London: Macmillan

Seaton, Jean (2015) *'Pinkoes and Traitors': The BBC and the Nation 1974-1987*, London: Profile

Simms, Brendan (2001) *Unfinest Hour: Britain and the Destruction of Bosnia*, London: Allen Lane

Smith, Dominic (2015) BBC rejects MPs' calls to refer to Islamic State as Daesh, *Guardian*, 2 July 2015. Available online at http://www.theguardian.com/media/2015/jul/02/bbc-rejects-mps-calls-to-refer-to-islamic-state-as-daesh, accessed on 20 July 2015

Snoddy, Raymond (2014) BBC licence fee negotiations – past and future, Mair, John, Tait, Richard and Keeble, Richard Lance (eds) *Is The BBC in Crisis?* Bury St Edmunds: Abramis pp 84-89

Tait, Richard (2012) Self-inflicted wounds? The decline of local news in the UK, Mair, John, Fowler, Neil and Reeves, Ian (eds) *What Do We Mean by Local?*, Bury St Edmunds: Abramis pp 5-17

Taylor, Peter (1978) Reporting Northern Ireland, *Index on Censorship*, Vol. 7, No.6. Available online at http://cain.ulst.ac.uk/othelem/media/docs/freespeech1.htm, accessed on 10 July 2015

Travis, Alan (2015) Theresa May's plan to censor TV shows condemned by Tory cabinet colleague, *Guardian*, 21 April 2015. Available online at http://www.theguardian.com/world/2015/may/21/mays-plan-to-censor-tv-programmes-condemned-by-tory-cabinet-colleague, accessed on 10 July 2015

Watt, Nicholas and McDonald, Henry (2015) Democratic Unionists: We'd seek review of BBC in hung parliament talks, *Guardian*, 28 April. Available online at (http://www.theguardian.com/politics/2015/apr/28/democratic-unionists-wed-seek-review-of-bbc-in-hung-parliament-talks, accessed on 7 July 2015

Section 3:
The Money Programme: Who will pay and What does it Pay for?

Richard Tait

The July 2015 deal on the licence fee does not mean the end of the debate about how best to fund the BBC in the long term. As this section demonstrates, no issue is more important to the long-term future of the BBC – and on no issue are there more polarised views. The licence fee has been, since 1923, one of the foundations of the BBC's relationship with the public; it has helped preserve it from capture by political or commercial interests, and it has allowed it, unlike its competitors, to plan with some certainty of income. Now it looks as though this charter could mark its last decade as the BBC's core funding mechanism.

David Elstein, after a career at the top of commercial television with Thames, Sky and Channel 5, is unashamedly in the radical camp that thinks this is happening not before time. He challenges the argument that the licence fee is a guarantor of quality and independence. He sees the licence fee rather as creating perverse incentives to produce unoriginal programmes in the search of ratings to justify a universal levy – and the recent deal has seen the BBC obliged to accept 'a dubious bargain' with the politicians.

He believes the licence fee is doomed and that the BBC would be a more independent and a more distinctive broadcaster if it moved to subscription. He also worries about the decline of commercial public service broadcasting and believes that a system of contestable funding should support it. Both ideas have growing political support. Both are anathema to the BBC – but, as he writes, not even Sherlock Holmes could make sense at this stage of the current convoluted

91

and deceptive politics of charter renewal where the only certainty is that 'the game was afoot and there was all to play for'.

A trenchant critic of the recent licence fee settlement is Diane Coyle, economist and until the summer of 2015 deputy chair of the BBC Trust (and acting chairman for four months while the government found a replacement for Lord Patten). She says that 'the government's recent £745 million raid on the licence fee is unacceptable'. Her focus is on the economic contribution of the BBC to the competitiveness of a vital sector of the UK economy, in programme making, training and technology. The BBC should be 'investing in skills and enabling the rest of the sector to succeed and innovate, too, in global markets increasingly dominated by large-scale entities'. She argues that the BBC's role in the creative economy makes a case for increasing, not reducing, the scale of the BBC: 'The government should not presume to know the answer in advance of a public debate and better evidence.'

Charter debate 'like Hamlet without the prince'
For Patrick Barwise, management and marketing emeritus professor at the London Business School and a long-time supporter of the licence fee, the chance of a rational decision about the level of the fee has gone: 'Much of the charter renewal debate will also be like Hamlet without the prince, with the funding – on which almost everything else hinges – already decided.' The impact of the deal is worse for everyone. 'Apart from a few commercial and political vested interests and the minority of households that include at least one member aged 75-plus and for whom the above disadvantages are worth less than 40p per day, it is hard to think of anyone in the UK who would be better off.'

The level of the licence fee is a key determinant of the amount of first-run content on British screens and that the public may well pay more for a better service. Barwise argues that it would actually be in the public interest for the licence fee to be increased by more than inflation. 'The outcome would clearly be better for the UK public as viewers, listeners and citizens, as well as for producers and the creative industries.'

But whatever the level, can the licence fee survive for another ten years? Jacquie Hughes, of Brunel University, is not sure. She argues that its survival is not a matter of corporate life or death and that at present the licence fee is the best option. But the BBC will have to work harder to earn it: she points to the worrying fact that while 79 per cent of the public believe it is important that the BBC has lots of fresh and new ideas, only 56 per cent believe the corporation delivers – 'a staggering 23 point performance gap'.

In the long term, however, she thinks the licence will probably have to be replaced by a household fee, on the German model. If we do go down that road, however, there need to be some clear protections of the BBC's independence – the level of tax should either be set by an independent panel (the German model) or by parliament on advice from Ofcom. She believes that whatever model is adopted the corporation 'needs to be given a clear flight path to change, with an indicative timescale, coupled with long-term policy commitment to the future size and independence of the BBC'.

Licence fee: Why the broadcasters are missing the point

Peter Preston, former editor the *Guardian* and now media commentator, takes a very different approach. He thinks the broadcasters are missing the point. 'The music industry has had to change radically. The written press is in the throes of change. Television itself is in flux. Why should the BBC stay a stagnant pond of calm amid so much turbulence?' He does not think it is necessary to work out exactly what role subscription should play to realise that 'for the BBC, abandoning some or all of the licence fee is a no-brain solution'.

The BBC's conservatism on the licence fee, he argues, is likely to be swept away by the digital transformation of the media industries – even Lord Reith, he thinks, might find the BBC's current position past its sell-by date. He suggests, for example, a core news and current affairs service funded by government grant with optional paid-for channels on demand that would still offer a bargain compared, say, with Sky. Subscription – or household tax? Or is there a way of adapting the licence fee to the digital world? The current settlement, built round the licence fee, should give us all a little time to resolve these questions – but no one should be in any doubt what a big decision it will be.

Saving both the BBC *and* public service broadcasting: It's elementary, dear Watson

What is the connection between BBC funding and funding public service broadcasting? David Elstein enlists the help of a famous sleuth to delve through the politics of charter review

The BBC's favourite detective flared his nostrils as the evidence tumbled out. First – he told the intrepid Watson – came a report in February 2015 on the future of the BBC from the House of Commons culture, media and sport committee, with many intriguing elements:

- calling for replacement of the BBC Trust;

- forecasting a limited life for the television licence fee but advocating closure of the 'catch-up loophole';

- supporting decriminalisation of licence fee evasion;

- suggesting the BBC 'reduce provision in areas that are over-served, as the BBC must inevitably do less in some areas';

- warning against the dangers of the BBC trying to provide 'something for everyone', and

- supporting the idea of a public service broadcasting commission to oversee provision of public service content from the BBC or third parties.

The BBC welcomed the report.

'Does that not strike you as odd, Watson? Do you recall The Adventure of Silver Blaze? *The dog that did not bark?' 'Ah, Holmes, there have been so many reports, from MPs who were once ministers and others who never will be. That is why we have the long grass. The BBC does not concern itself with such documents.'*

Then there was general election result on 7 May 2015. To the BBC's consternation, not only was David Cameron confirmed as Prime Minister – after resisting steady BBC pressure (including veiled threats of 'empty chairs') to participate in a series of broadcast leader debates during the campaign – but he was returned to Downing Street with a clear Tory majority.

11 May was worse. Cameron's first choice as the new culture secretary, Boris Johnson, declined the offer, not wanting to render his last year as full-time Mayor of London an object of mockery. Instead, the long-standing chairman of the Commons culture committee, John Whittingdale, was appointed. Some Conservative newspapers crowed triumphantly that this unreconstructed Thatcherite would cut the BBC down to size. Mandarins at New Broadcasting House glanced nervously over their shoulders.

For Whitto (as we shall call him), it was a bolt from the blue, ministerial ambitions having long since evaporated. Now, as probably his only cabinet posting, he would oversee renewal of the BBC charter and the setting of the BBC licence fee. His old committee's report had called for the swift setting-up of an expert panel, alongside publication of a green paper and a public consultation, so as to provide time for a white paper early in 2016 ahead of the expiry of the BBC charter at the end of that year. True to form, Whitto named his panel and issued his green paper within two months of taking office.

'Is not this entirely commendable, Watson? Do what you said you would do? And surely speed is of the essence?' 'I cannot disagree, Holmes.'

But first came a nasty surprise for the BBC. Just ahead of publishing his green paper, Whitto telephoned the BBC's urbane DG Lord (Tony) Hall, and told him that the chancellor, George Osborne, wanted to re-open the question of free television licences for the over-75s (a dotty benefit brought in by Gordon Brown to mollify elderly voters after Tony Blair lost his nerve in 1999, abandoning – under pressure from Sky and ITV – the idea of a digital licence fee to fund the BBC's digital ambitions, and instead hiking up the basic licence fee, just before an election).

In 2010, the coalition government had tried to persuade the BBC Trust to take on this expensive bribe. They refused, but grudgingly accepted a raft of other departmental spending obligations, such as World Service radio, costing almost as much, along with a frozen licence fee (amusingly, Whitto's Commons committee accused the trust of breach of fiduciary duty in not resigning *en masse* at this outrage). The combined impact of this double whammy was to reduce BBC spending power by some 26 per cent.

Now the BBC did not even have the Lib Dems to help them repel a determined chancellor: in five days of frantic negotiation (even faster than the six-day ambush of 2010), Tony Hall chose discretion over valour and – with the BBC Trust's consent – 'volunteered' to take on the over-75s concession, in exchange for some of the 2010 financial obligations being removed, and inflation-proofing of the licence fee, assuming its basic level (and the BBC's scope and scale) survived the charter review process. A further 10 per cent reduction in BBC spending power by 2021 was the minimum likely impact of this dubious bargain (former BBC Trust chairman, Sir Michael Lyons, dismissed as 'preposterous' Hall's claim to have 'settled' the BBC's financial future).

When the expert panel – the 'Whitto Eight' – was announced, another former BBC Trust chairman, Lord Patten, gloomily pronounced them the assistant grave-diggers at the BBC's funeral. Other one-time BBC dignitaries deplored the financial settlement as unconstitutional and a disaster. The BBC's leadership was as much criticised for caving in to pressure as were ministers for applying it.

> *'Did our man Hall not anticipate this line of attack?' 'It is certainly true, Holmes, that the chancellor had made quite clear his intention to reduce expenditure on benefits by £12 billion a year.' 'And this over-75s concession amounts to 5 per cent of that?' 'Indeed, but the prime minister had promised not to abolish it.' 'So pinning it on the BBC, as previously attempted, would honour the promise, but remove the obligation from the Treasury.' 'Correct.' 'I conclude this turn of events was not that surprising, my dear Watson.'*

A change of tack

It was time for a change of tack. Ahead of the promised green paper, 29 celebrities decided to publish a spirited defence of the BBC. The corporation's press office denied all knowledge of this open letter. Attack dogs in the Tory press quickly worked out that a top BBC executive had composed the letter and asked some pals to sign (many of them earned substantial sums working for the BBC): a miscue, if not an actual own goal. The next day, the BBC's annual report and accounts were published: more fodder for the ravening hacks.

Staff numbers have risen by 300. Salary costs are nearing a billion pounds a year. Annual technology costs are £166 million; property £162 million; finance and operations £85 million; divisional costs £85 million; development £83 million; marketing £70 million – total support and development costs £766 million. The pension deficit is £948 million. Finance lease obligations amount to £1.932 billion. BBC Online costs £201 million. BBC News Channel costs £63 million.

> *'But the BBC tells us it has made hundreds of millions of pounds of savings; and delivered some very good programmes. Did not the Tory press report this, Watson?' 'I fear not.'*

Time for the BBC to adopt some rugby tactics: get your retaliation in early. Come the publication of the green paper on 16 July 2015, the corporation had its response out within seconds: 'We believe that this green paper would appear to herald a much-diminished, less popular BBC.' BBC supporters and spokespeople spoke of an ideological attack, based on a neo-liberal belief in a smaller state (and so a smaller state broadcaster): all in all, a 'Tory agenda'. Labour's shadow culture secretary enthusiastically joined the chorus.

'But is this wise, Watson? What does the green paper actually say about a smaller BBC?'

'Well, Holmes, there is one sentence on page 25 of the 76-page document that notes the argument that, given the amount of choice now available, there might be a case for a more focused BBC, and that "a smaller BBC" could see a reduced cost for the licence fee and reduced market impact. But the 19 questions the public are invited to answer during the consultation on the green paper do not overtly include that option.'

'So: 19 questions! Are these loaded against the BBC, as the critics say?' 'No, Holmes, they seem balanced and reasonable, and – frankly – blindingly obvious.' 'Which would explain why the Daily Mail *called it terribly mild – how disappointing for the slavering Tory press.'*

It was worse than disappointing. The green paper calls the corporation 'one of this nation's most treasured institutions'. It says the government wants 'the BBC to continue to adapt and thrive'. It calls the BBC 'much-loved', and 'an international benchmark for television, radio, online and journalism ... trusted and relied upon at home and abroad'. It confirms the 'need for the state to intervene in the market', that 'the rationale for a publicly-funded BBC ... remains strong even in the current media age', and that 'the BBC remains highly-valued and well-used by the majority of people within the UK'. Not surprisingly, little of this actually found its way into coverage of the green paper by the Tory newspapers.

Holmes frowned. He was sure that BBC News, on the day of the green paper's publication, had led with a report that Radio 1 or Radio 2 might be forced to take advertisements: yet, reading the document, he saw that advertising was explicitly rejected as a way of funding the BBC. The same report had claimed the document said the BBC should not be producing the entertainment show *Strictly Come Dancing*; yet the green paper actually praised that programme as UK-originated successful risk-taking, comparing well with the expensive imported format for *The Voice*. Had BBC editorial swallowed BBC corporate propaganda uncritically? Had the reporter even read the green paper?

Clearly, that excellent script writer Steven Moffat hadn't. ('What was that show he worked on, Watson? *Sherlock* something?') He condemned it as an attack on the BBC, without saying what exactly in it constituted an attack. Perhaps the whole idea of charter review offends some supporters of the BBC (the director of *Wolf Hall*, Peter Kosminsky, publicly stated just that view). Anything other than a pat on the back and a brisk 'good effort, chaps', followed by lengthy renewal of the charter, was seemingly frightful.

Was the suggestion that the BBC might aim at more distinctiveness so unreasonable? Did not the BBC Trust say the same? Was not demographic 'targeting' already the norm, not just for BBC channels, but individual BBC programmes? Why would 'better' targeting be damaging? Was more focus on the 'underserved' equivalent to a 'much diminished BBC'? Holmes noted that the green paper revealed how BBC TV devoted just 0.01 per cent of its transmissions to education, and BBC Radio 0.001 per cent , without ever saying that the BBC was failing in delivery of one-third of its 'information, education and entertainment' mission.

Indeed, the green paper emphasised how the iPlayer 'loophole' would be closed by legislation – something the BBC had spent a year requesting. Of course, observed Holmes, this was a fairly worthless concession, as the BBC had no means of differentiating between those watching on-demand services such as Netflix or YouTube and the catch-up services of BBC One, BBC Two, ITV, Channel 4 and 5. Payment of the licence fee to watch catch-up, just for those five channels, would effectively be voluntary – if as many students coughed up as the BBC hoped over-75s would (10 per cent), the rate of drop-out from the licence fee would fall from the present 700,000 a year (which is what is driving the call for a change in the law) to 630,000.

The subscription option

The green paper was also gentle in pushing the BBC's pet hate – subscription. It noted that it might take many years to upgrade millions of televisions that lacked a conditional access module (CAM). It failed to note that the only reason for this was the BBC's deliberate abuse of its control of the Freeview project to prevent the inclusion of CAMs in Freeview set-top boxes (STBs): even requiring removal of pre-existing CAMs from STBs equipped with them so as to meet the Freeview standard. The purpose was quite explicit: create a barrier to any possible move towards subscription. It is odd that a supposedly neo-liberal government is willing to indulge such Luddite behaviour. As it happens, the average cost of a television set or STB upgrade is £15, so the cost per household, given a two- to three-year notice period before encryption of BBC transmissions, may be £10 per annum: scarcely an insurmountable obstacle.

Even more curious is the failure to observe that more than 60 per cent of homes are already equipped with cable, satellite or YouView boxes, immediately capable of providing access to encrypted BBC channels. The green paper emphasises how 95 per cent of homes will have access to superfast broadband by the end of 2017: so there will be three clear routes to a full subscription system well ahead of 2020.

Equally curious is the green paper's suggestion that one of the options for a combination of a 'basic' licence fee and a subscription service would be for the iPlayer to be encrypted. What degree of reduction in the licence fee that would allow is not explained, yet the idea of encrypting the iPlayer anyway (still allowing licence fee payers free access), rather than vainly attempting to 'close the iPlayer loophole', is not explored at all. It would, after all, be entirely logical: at the moment, viewers must pay to watch BBC programmes live, will have to pay to buy them online after the 30-day iPlayer window once BBC Store is launched in October 2015, already have to pay to buy boxed sets of those programmes, and must subscribe to a pay-TV system to see them again on the

UKTV service, which is half-owned by the BBC. For the only 'free' use to be the iPlayer window is very strange: changing the law to include catch-up in the licence fee regime seems Canute-like in its wishful thinking.

Indeed, it is hard not to see something of the Freeview CAM tactic in the BBC's decision to launch the iPlayer seven years ago knowing full well no licence fee was required for its use, and then – having hooked millions of users – to campaign for any future use to cost £145.50 a year. In the days of John Bloom and Rolls Razor washing machines, this was called 'bait and switch'.

The rapid growth of subscription packages in the last two years strongly suggests the BBC is missing an opportunity. 16.7 million of the UK's 26 million homes subscribe to Sky, Virgin Media, BT or TalkTalk (the number grows by a million homes a year). Netflix now has 4 million subscribers and Amazon 1.7 million, with annual growth rates of 57 per cent and 42 per cent respectively. The annual growth of Sky's flexible pay-lite offering, Now TV, has been even faster – 236 per cent. The BBC's seeming lack of confidence in its ability to persuade viewers to pay directly for its content (despite constantly touting it as being an irresistible bargain at 40p a day) should not deter ministers. And if a subscription service is launched, the possibility of rolling it out across Europe and beyond must surely make appeal.

The notion of separating BBC services as between 'basic licence fee' and 'subscription top-up' is acknowledged in the green paper as being tricky: the BBC claims to have researched putting BBC One and BBC Two in 'basic' and then finding that demand for a 'digital top-up' was minimal. So how about all public service content in the basic and all entertainment in the top-up? If so, the proposition seems remarkably close to the idea contained in the Broadcasting Policy Group's *Beyond the Charter* (2004): 'Brilliant,' says Whitto, according to the *Guardian*; its 19 recommendations nicely echoed by the green paper's 19 questions.

The BPG recommended that BBC entertainment be funded solely by subscription, with public service content financed by central government or a small licence fee; and that such content funding be fully contestable – a notion explored in the Commons committee report and the green paper. Of course, the BPG's concern was not just how to fund the BBC (though it certainly regarded subscription as in every way superior to the licence fee) but how to fund public service broadcasting (PSB), which it saw as facing a seemingly inevitable decline: growing audience fragmentation would undermine commercial PSB revenues whilst the need to preserve broad public support for the licence fee would push the BBC towards preserving audience share and reach, even at the expense of quality.

Ofcom has confirmed in its latest report on PSB (July 2015) that the fall in supply of first-run originated programming by the PSB system (the BBC channels, plus ITV1, Channel 4 and 5), which started in 2004, has continued in almost a straight line ever since. The £3.3 billion spent in 2004 has declined to £2.5 billion in 2014 (£2 billion if sport is excluded) – a level last seen almost 20 years ago. The predicted decline in commercial PSB supply was eased by the 2003 Communications Act which set up Ofcom as the monitor of PSB, but also explicitly allowed the commercial PSB channels to abandon certain unprofitable genres of output, such as arts, religion and children's. That BBC supply would fall in parallel (a fall that began well before the freezing of the licence fee) may have been less predictable, other than for those, such as the BPG, who noted the perverse incentives of licence fee funding.

The Ofcom Public Service Broadcasting report

The latest report from Ofcom makes dismal reading, and should at the very least be factored into the green paper process: resolving the many issues facing the BBC must take into account the crisis in PSB, and the need to find a way of funding the kind of public service content that has been marginalised or abandoned in the last ten years. Ofcom tells us that the supply of religion and ethics programming has 'all but ceased'. Education has almost vanished (just 52 first-run hours across the whole system – a drop of 84 per cent since 2008). What is left of arts and classical music is mostly confined to concert performances on BBC Two and BBC Four. Children's is almost exclusively a BBC preserve, but confined to its specialist digital channels: nothing appears on BBC One, BBC Two, BBC Three or BBC Four.

Even supposedly key entertainment genres – comedy and non-soap drama – have been substantially displaced by low-cost features and factual programmes. Drama spend has dropped by 44 per cent in six years, and comedy by 30 per cent. In one important respect the two systems – BBC and commercial PSBs – have diverged: the BBC has spread its money thinly, reducing hours far less than spend, while the commercial PSBs have concentrated their resources on fewer, higher-value hours. Either way, the audience has lost out. ITV now offers its viewers barely two hours a week of proper drama: 20 years ago, anything less than six hours would have been unthinkable. The BBC offers the public large volumes of daytime dross.

Unfortunately, Ofcom itself has proved to be a poor guardian of PSB, unable to influence the BBC and partly complicit in the performance of its own commercial licensees. It persists with attitude research, even after a previous embarrassment of finding wide satisfaction with 5's original drama (of which there was none). This time, it finds a rising positive response – by 12 percentage points since 2008 – to the assertion that the PSB system shows new programmes made in the UK (despite the sharp decline in supply), and an 11 point rise in support for the belief that 'it provides a wide range of high quality and UK-made programmes for children' (again, despite the reported decline in supply).

Having embraced the concept of a public service publisher in 2007 (abandoned the next year) and having attempted to push through the idea of licence fee-funded independently financed news consortia in 2010 (torpedoed by the election that year), Ofcom has reverted to its initial mistaken belief that contestable funding of PSB involves 'undue bureaucracy', as compared with institutional funding. Obviously, Ofcom has not yet caught up with Tony Hall's joke about reducing BBC management layers from ten to seven (it was a joke, wasn't it, Tony?).

The role of the public service broadcasting commission (PSBC)

At least the BBC Trust has addressed quality control issues, even if not always broadly enough. If – as the green paper and the Commons committee strongly suggested – the trust is likely to be replaced, that function must not be lost in the maw of Ofcom. Inescapably, the conclusions of the Burns committee – set up by Tessa Jowell as culture secretary but whose recommendations were ignored by her – seem ever more prescient. The correct way to restore the public service element in publicly-funded broadcasting is to create a public service broadcasting commission (PSBC), tasked with managing and allocating PSB funds, whether derived from a licence fee, a household levy or mainstream tax receipts.

A PSBC would not need to oversee the whole of the BBC – just the output for which it sought and received public funding. The BBC has hinted heavily that if ever it were forced into subscription funding, it would be the 'market failure' content that it sloughed off, not the entertainment. Yet the latest licence fee settlement, with its minimum reduction in BBC spending power of 10 per cent, will surely result in the same outcome (unless the green paper process forces it into a more explicitly public service role, risking marginalisation of the BBC, and a reduced public willingness to fund it through a compulsory mechanism backed by criminal sanctions – the dreaded downward spiral).

In the ponderous language of the Ofcom report, 'further reduction in real-terms funding may lead to a bigger fall in investment than we have seen in this review period (2008-2014), with possible implications for the volume, range and quality of output that the PSB system can deliver as a result'. The Commons committee, in re-visiting the Burns committee report, adopted so much of it that its own report included an annex noting the minor variations it suggested. The green paper includes the PSBC (as advocated both by Burns and the Commons committee) as an option in reform of BBC governance. It also devotes a section to contestable funding of public service content. But it fails to draw the threads together, by recognising the symbiotic relationship between BBC funding, PSB funding, contestability and governance: it will be up to the public, in their responses, to do that job for it.

The green paper not only rejected advertising as a means of funding the BBC, but also general taxation. Unexpectedly (at least as far as the *Daily Telegraph* was concerned, in its second-guessing of what might be in the green paper), it discarded one of the options in the Commons committee report: a Finnish-style ring-fenced sliver of income tax. Like the BBC, it seemed most attracted by a household levy (perhaps German-style, with exemptions for the poorest). Yet negotiating such a levy through our current devolved government structure might be extremely tricky. The SNP has made no secret of its wish to take control of BBC assets north of the border, and turning the licence fee into a household levy will certainly open the door to Holyrood essentially achieving that aim.

A deeper plot?

There are those who see a Machiavellian plot in that scenario: a cynical Osborne/Sturgeon plot to slice and dice the BBC. They say we need to look beyond the 'reasonableness' of the green paper, and of Whitto himself, and recognise the forces at work. The BBC management's response to the green paper, and the campaign it is trying to foster, has more than a tinge of such thinking. Indeed, one might almost detect a note of *après nous, le deluge*.

Oddly, the BBC Trust's own response to the green paper (a good deal less gloom-laden than that from the executive) expressed some interest in the option of a basic licence fee combined with a subscription for premium content. But it rejects the full subscription option, asserting that 'this would seem at odds with the principle of a universal public service BBC, which should continue to provide its content free at the point of use to all households on an equal basis'.

Holmes smiled at the realisation that membership of the BBC Trust appears not to require any basic knowledge of logic. After all, subscription-funded BBC content would be available to all households on an equal basis, just like licence fee-funded BBC content, and after payment of the required sum (monthly subscription or annual licence fee), it would be free at the point of use. The only difference was that non-payers would be able to continue watching non-BBC content without penalty. Oh, well.

Watson had become animated. 'I have been looking deeper, Holmes. The idea of a PSBC in the 2005 Burns document seems very similar to the idea of a public broadcasting authority in the BPG report the previous year. And the original PSBC idea can be found in the Peacock report from 1986. In fact, the home secretary who appointed Peacock summarised his report in the House of Commons thus: "A BBC funded by subscription, but supplemented by an Arts Council-like body funding those programmes whose ratings alone would not keep them going, combines the highest possible degree of choice for the consumer with the central features of public service broadcasting as we have known it."

'Given that Tony Hall and the chairman of the BBC Trust have called for politicians to cease to have any influence over the level of BBC funding, it would seem to me that for the BBC to establish a direct relationship with consumers would be the best outcome for that institution, and creating a PSBC the best way to place public service content, funded contestably, within a protected and guaranteed structure.'

'My dear Watson! Elementary!'

Holmes puffed contentedly on a cheroot. In just six months, the green paper would be supplanted by a white paper. The main battle would commence. Meanwhile, the game was afoot, and there was all to play for.

The Scale of the BBC

The BBC's charter should include explicit reference to its strategic role in the creative sector, including technological innovation, investing in skills and enabling the rest of the sector to succeed and innovate. To deliver these benefits in global markets, the BBC needs to be bigger, not smaller, according to Diane Coyle

The scope of the BBC's activities and its size (and hence also the level of the licence fee) are – or should be – linked; just one of the reasons why the Conservative government's July 2015 £745 million raid on the licence fee was unacceptable. This chapter looks at the scope and scale of the BBC through a particular lens: as a strategic public intervention in an extremely successful sector of the UK economy. What should its *economic* role be in the next charter period?

The economic aims of public service broadcasting can be divided into two broad categories, with different emphasis placed on each at various times in the history of the British broadcasting industry and the BBC:

- driving technological innovation, and so supporting the supply chain, market entry and economic growth, and

- addressing market failures.

For all the part played by negotiations and lobbying in shaping the structure of the broadcasting industry, and the size and role of the BBC, over the years, the outcome has been a real British success story. According to the latest department of culture, media and sport (DCMS) figures, the output of the UK's creative industries amounted to 5 per cent the economy, and had grown 9.9 per cent in 2013, making it the fastest-expanding sector with a growth rate three times that of the economy as a whole (DCMS 2015).

However, technology, market structure and user demands are all changing significantly. With the arrival from the 1990s of multi-channel digital services, there were predictions of big changes in television viewing habits. But with hindsight, that technological switch does not seem to have had much effect, whereas fast broadband and online innovation are proving highly disruptive of established patterns. The changing content-consumption behaviour of young people is the clearest evidence for this, with significant change in the habits of successive cohorts. For example, Ofcom found that children aged 12-15 now spend more time online than watching television; children's listening to radio is in decline (Ofcom 2014a).

The market and technological context is, therefore, changing rapidly now. What scale and character of BBC would enable it to continue to play a positive role in the economic success of the wider creative sector?

Making markets

Technological change has been the impetus for the development of a broadcast sector from the beginning. The economist, Ronald Coase, described the origins of the BBC and the early debate about its function in a series of papers published in 1947, 1948 and 1954, and a 1950 book (Coase 1947, 1948, 1950 and 1954). In his account of the policy debates, the Post Office played a leading role. It was a technological innovator in the early 20th century, up to the research carried out on programmable computers at its Dollis Hill research unit after the Second World War. An experimental broadcast by Dame Nellie Melba from Marconi's Chelmsford station in 1920, sponsored by the *Daily Mail*, had encouraged a proliferation of amateur, low-power radio stations. The Post Office wanted orderly use of spectrum to prevent interference, licensing of transmitting and receiving equipment, and a clear run for British manufacturers of radio equipment when it became apparent from US interest in the opportunities that there was a good market for the taking. Under Post Office co-ordination, the British manufacturers grouped into two consortia and then one, as the British Broadcasting Company.

Marconi collection https://www.mhs.ox.ac.uk/marconi/exhibition/broadcasting.htm
[Dame Nelli Melba's microphone for the 1920 broadcast: http://www.bbc.co.uk/ahistoryoftheworld/objects/p0lN-tRe1l2P_QyzRwKFEA; publication permission sought]

Coase quoted P. P. Eckersley, who had been in charge of the experimental Marconi broadcasts: 'Broadcasting came about because those interested came over from the States and pointed out what vast sums of money were being made there, what interest broadcasting was creating, and how England was getting left behind. This I think was the great stimulant.'

The industrial policy calculations, therefore, dominated the debate at this early stage. Coase, one of the all-time most influential economists on questions of industrial organisation, argued in his papers that the interventions helped explain why Britain had a 'regular television service' many years before the US. Without access to the BBC's engineers and transmitters, John Logie Baird's broadcasts would not have resulted in a sustained service reaching a large audience. But Coase also described the continuing debate from the start about the advantages and disadvantages of the BBC's early monopoly. He argued that BBC opposition thwarted the innovation of radio broadcasting via the electricity mains (not that this technology succeeded anywhere), and warmly welcomed the arrival of commercial competition in broadcasting in the 1950s.

Technology and programme content have always gone hand-in-hand in the industry, and the importance of national technology or industrial strategy is too often ignored in the debate about the BBC. Public policy has a central role in doing the basic technological research, which is both a pure public good and usually too risky for investment by commercial players, and also in creating the conditions for its commercial implementation. For example, it is now widely recognised that US government funding and granting of monopoly status to some entities enabled innovations that have translated into the subsequent success of America's computer and software industries, from the development of the transistor at Bell Labs to the foundation of the internet.[1]

The BBC's researchers and engineers have made important contributions over the decades, including standards setting. As required by the royal charter, the results are widely shared to benefit the UK economy.[2] The contributions range from television, FM radio and colour television to compression technologies such as NICAM and DVBT2.[3] One particularly well-known project was the BBC Micro, which played an essential role in developing the interest and skills of the founders of the highly successful British video games industry (Radcliffe and Salkeld 1983). Commercial companies also undertake R&D spending and innovate, both in terms of broadcast and online technologies and in their programming but, of course, prefer *not* to share the results widely.

How the BBC supports the industry supply chain

This is one way the presence of the BBC has supported the industry supply chain, and is worth emphasising because of its low profile in public debate. Other important examples include the training and experience gained by the many people who work at the BBC and then move on to the commercial sector; the commissioning of programmes from the independent sector, enabling many individuals to set up and sustain to a viable size their own companies; and the bringing to market of large numbers of new musicians, again giving them the initial platform and exposure needed to achieve commercial success. Thus, the UK is one of the only countries to be a net exporter of music; the only other examples are the US, whose musicians benefit from the scale of their domestic market, and Sweden (UK Music 2014).

Competition for the BBC from the commercial sector in production and in services has, without question, been good for audiences. The policy aim has to be a balance of intervention to provide both public benefits and also vigorous competition in the market, a balance that needs constant vigilance as technology and market structures change over time.

What is the state of competition in the relevant markets now? Along the supply chain, market structure has changed significantly in the past 25 years. In terms of the content viewed, heard or read by audiences, the share of all the PSBs including the BBC has declined, although less quickly in the multi-channel era than was once expected. The share of cable and satellite broadcasters and of online services has increased, and the latter is now rising rapidly. In terms of revenues, there has been a major transformation, with the BBC's revenues dwarfed by cable and satellite and digital providers' revenues. Even in news, where the BBC's scale of operation and audience share remain relatively large, there are many well-funded competitors.

So the BBC monopoly about which Ronald Coase wrote is long gone. Looking at the television channels, according to BARB (Broadcasters' Audience Research Board), BBC TV's audience share is 33 per cent, compared with 22 per cent for the ITV portfolio, 11 per cent for the Channel 4 portfolio, 8 per cent for Sky, and 6 per cent for Channel 5. In terms of revenues, the BBC's £5 billion a year (including BBC Worldwide) compares with £3 billion for ITV, £7.6 billion for Sky, £4.2 billion for Virgin Media, and £4.3 billion for BT's consumer division, not to mention the epic scale of revenues at the large American digital companies.[4] Large American companies have recently purchased Channel 5 and Virgin Media. Even in news, where the BBC's share in people's consumption is relatively high, only one in five people rely only on (all) television and radio for their news, and just over two in five now use the internet or an app. A minority, just over a quarter, rely on only one news provider (Ofcom 2014b).

When it comes to production, the UK has a vigorous independent production sector. This is again a highly competitive market, although one that has been consolidating in the mid-ranks and above into a smaller number of super-indies mostly with US owners.[5] In 2014, three of the four UK super-indies were taken over by international groups with UK broadcast interests, creating groups with large turnover (for example, £1 billion annually in the case of Shine/Endemol).[6] This consolidation means the charter renewal discussions about the successor arrangement to the WOCC (Window of Creative Competition) will be timely. Along with the BBC's anticipated proposals for its in-house production, this will be an opportunity to ensure its activities are geared towards maintaining a competitive market with scope for new entry, and growing the overseas market for UK producers.

At the distribution end of the supply chain, the risk to the UK economy, and to the UK PSBs, is increasing market concentration and the emergence of extremely powerful gatekeepers. In the ISP market, just four competitors (BT, Virgin Media, TalkTalk and Sky) have an 86 per cent market share in fixed broadband (Ofcom 2013). The most-accessed websites in the UK are Google (.com and .co.uk), Facebook, YouTube and Amazon, followed then by bbc.co.uk.[7]

So the BBC has to compete vigorously for audiences and attention; the idea that it is protected from competition because it has licence fee income is incorrect, although the pressures are certainly different compared with commercial rivals. (In just the same way, state-funded schools can compete for pupils with each other and with the private sector.) There is no evidence that the BBC's services have crowded out commercial activity, and this is even less likely to be a risk with the transition to online. What's more, the nature of the competition in Britain, because there is a mixed economy of the BBC alongside a commercial sector, is not just for the biggest audiences but also for range and quality of programmes.

Trends towards market consolidation
However, there are emerging risks to this healthy situation for the UK's creative sector. The most significant is that the economies of scale in broadcasting (traditional and online distribution) are huge and increasing – reflected in the trends toward market consolidation mentioned above. The fixed costs of making and distributing programmes are higher because of higher production values including HD quality, higher costs of premium content and star talent of all kinds, and increased distribution costs including running both traditional and online distribution together. With the marginal costs of adding audience numbers low, the winner-take-all dynamic in online markets is powerful. American content and distribution companies are at an enormous advantage because of the large scale of their domestic market, which has given them a platform from which to address global markets at a low incremental cost.

The success of the online players in attracting eyeballs and hence advertising revenue has already damaged newspapers around the world, not just in the UK. In a 2010 study, the OECD found that the newspaper market had declined in 28 member countries in 2006-2009, with the largest decline by some margin in the US, followed by the UK, Greece, Italy and Canada (OECD 2010). In her Cudlipp memorial lecture, Emily Bell, of Columbia University, said of journalism:

> All news outlets need numbers in the web economy that are vastly greater than they had in an analogue world, firstly to make the economics work and secondly to have an impact. The demands of web scale economics

have torpedoed the local news model; they have also driven great invention and a new set of entrepreneurial skills into journalism (Bell 2015).

She also noted the pressure in news to produce content that will 'go viral', which is very different from the priorities arising from traditional news values.

Traditional broadcasters of all kinds will be facing a similarly difficult competitive challenge from online providers in the years to come. All the UK-based PSBs suffer disadvantages of scale compared to the American digital titans. It is sometimes argued that the digital technologies have made niche content viable, with providers able to offer 'bundles' of channels proving a range of content; but the more frequently-observed strategy is bidding for premium content.[8] Given its restricted supply, this is an increasingly costly strategy, again reinforcing the advantages of scale. The need to seek ever-greater scale to stay viable is driving commercial media behaviour, consolidation being one manifestation.

There is no strong evidence that a wholly commercial television market would produce public service programming for large audiences. There are, of course, some high quality programmes made in the almost-wholly commercial US market, but these form a small proportion of total origination in a large market and represent a high-cost premium offer by subscription services rather than a universal service offer; for example, the acclaimed series *House of Cards* cost $3.8 million per episode and surveys suggest it reaches about 7 per cent of Netflix subscribers (Wallenstein 2015).

In global markets where the commercial imperative is to achieve scale, prospects for any kind of local content look economically fragile, whether that is local newspapers, drama made for regions or the devolved nations, programming in minority languages, children's programming, or anything reflecting the specifics of a country's culture and politics.

The now-rapid move to online distribution and the overwhelming importance of economies of scale are changing the market context and posing serious challenges to the UK's creative sector as a whole, and to its ability to provide the range of output desired by people in the UK. The BBC's charter should include explicit reference to its strategic role in the creative sector, including technological innovation, investing in skills and enabling the rest of the sector to succeed and innovate, too, in global markets increasingly dominated by large-scale entities. There is growing understanding in economic research of the importance, in increasingly global markets, of pinning supply chains to specific locations by developing a thicket of skills and companies that make it harder for activity to relocate. Technical infrastructure, research, skills and standards setting are specifically identified as key elements in achieving this, requiring a public-private strategy to deliver them (see Tassey 2014).

Market failures

Alongside the strategic arguments about the status of British industry (what we would now call the creative sector, originally the radio and television manufacturers), there have also always been powerful arguments about the BBC's function in addressing market failures in broadcasting.

In the debate in the 1980s – reflected in the Peacock commission report of 1986 – it was often said that digital, multi-channel television undermined the argument for public service broadcasting outside narrow 'market failure' niches, because the technology made it possible to exclude people who had not paid a subscription. Proponents of a smaller BBC said it should, therefore, just provide niche services and let audiences choose and pay for the rest in the market. This line of argument is mistaken, as it was never the technical infeasibility of exclusion that was the market failure; indeed, the licence fee has always been an effective exclusion mechanism, just legal rather than technical.

Broadcasting involves a range of other market failures. What's more, new technologies are clearly *expanding* the market failures, not shrinking them. It remains a public good (in the economic sense) because consumption of programmes is largely non-rival (your watching a broadcast programme does not stop me doing so). There are also, as discussed above, very large economies of scale. In online services there is often zero or near-zero marginal cost of serving one more user. Digital content, therefore, increasingly has the characteristics of a natural monopoly.

There are many externalities in broadcasting as well, the most important economic one being the scarcity of a common resource, spectrum, and the risk of interference. Contrary to earlier expectations, spectrum scarcity is getting worse, not better, because of the rapid expansion of demand for mobile broadband. Other externalities include the merit or good character of some kinds of broadcasts (they are good for you or you would enjoy them, even if you would choose something else), and the civic and cultural importance of shared experiences, cultural references and political debate. This is, of course, the main reason the BBC's universality is so important and hence its need to provide a wide range of programming appealing to as many people as possible, rather than just narrow 'market failure' niches. The increasing global nature and large scale of the content industry anyway seems to be increasing rapidly the scope of market failure to provide a number of types of national and local content, as noted already.

The licence fee happens to be an economically efficient form of pricing a near-zero marginal cost good: it is an all-you-can-eat subscription with a price of zero for incremental consumption. Its civic function is even more important: it is a permit giving people access to the open space of the public internet, unmanipulated by large gatekeepers beyond the reach of the UK's democratic process (Ageh 2015).

Conclusions

This chapter has argued that both rationales for the role of the BBC, whether creative sector strategy or market failure, are stronger than in the past, and support increasing the scale of the BBC. The charter debate should recognise

5

Diane Coyle

these rationales explicitly in updating the BBC's purposes. There are various ways a responsibility to the whole of the sector could be expressed, including as now training, R&D, and standards, but also going beyond this to encompass explicit supply chain co-operation and co-operation in global markets. The public purpose, that in the current charter requires the BBC to support new digital technologies, needs re-writing to set out explicitly these wider responsibilities.

What scale of BBC is needed to deliver for the sector? A shrunken BBC is unlikely to be able to either thrive itself or assist other UK firms from the commercial PSBs to the UK-based independent producers in global and increasingly online markets with huge economies of scale. We do not have good enough information on the BBC's contribution to the economy, or analysis of the scale below which its contribution would become impossible.[9] The government should not presume to know the answer in advance of a public debate and better evidence.

The BBC Trust's research showed that 55 per cent of people want the level of the licence fee to be set by a body independent of government;[10] an independent commission could gather the economic evidence and consider what size the BBC serving the whole economy needs to be, and what shape its strategic partnership with the creative sector ought to take. However, in a world of consolidation into ever-larger (and mainly US-based) digital and media corporations, it would be better for the British creative sector to have a bigger BBC explicitly charged with operating for their benefit.

Notes

[1] There is a large literature on the *de facto* industrial policy of the US, especially with regard to high tech industries. See, for example, *The Idea Factory: Bell Labs and the Great Age of American Innovation*, Jon Gernter (Penguin, New York, 2012); *Accidental Empires*, Robert X. Cringely (Addison Wesley, New York, 1992); AnnaLee Saxenian, *Regional Advantage: Culture and Competition in Silicon Valley and Route 128* (Harvard University Press, 1996); *How The Internet Became Commercial*, Shane Greenstein (Princeton University Press, forthcoming)

[2] See http://www.bbc.co.uk/rd/about/our-purpose, accessed on 11 June 2015

[3] See downloads.bbc.co.uk/rd/pubs/reports/1990-06.pdf and http://www.bbc.co.uk/rd/projects/dvb-t2, accessed on 3 June 2015

[4] Figures from latest annual reports

[5] The sector has a large number of small companies. Mediatique found that the market share of the top ten indies had risen from 53 per cent in 2005 to 67 per cent in 2009. A recent report by O&O for PACT (the trade association representing the commercial interests of UK independent television, film, digital, children's and animation media companies) noted that importance of global scale for the creation of 'super indies'. See http://www.pact.co.uk/support/document-library/documents/oando-report-on-tv-producer-consolidation-march-2015/, accessed on 3 June 2015; O&O, in their 2014 report for Ofcom, *The Evolution of the TV Content Production Sector* (see http://stakeholders.ofcom.org.uk/binaries/broadcast/reviews-investigations/psb-

111

review/psb3/The_evolution_of_the_TV_content_production_sector.pdf) note that consolidation has occurred in the mid-tier companies and a few mergers among the largest ones

[6] Shed was acquired by Warner Brothers international TV, All3Media was acquired by Discovery Networks and Liberty Global. In autumn 2014, it was announced that Shine Group – acquired by News Corp in 2011 – would merge with Endemol under the 21st Century Fox group (subject to regulatory clearances). In late 2014, the largest remaining UK-owned independent producer, Tinopolis, was put up for sale

[7] See http://www.alexa.com/topsites/countries/GB, accessed on 11 June 2015

[8] See fuller discussion in Diane Coyle and Paolo Siciliani, *Is There Still A Place for Public Service Television: Effects of the Changing Economics of Broadcasting*, Robert Picard and Paolo Siciliani (eds) Reuters Institute for the Study of Journalism, September 2013

[9] This is because the ONS does not include its output in GVA or its spending on R&D in the national figures. These omissions need to be remedied, and the BBC returned to its status as a public, non-financial corporation in the national accounts. The 2006 decision to reclassify it to central government was an error of judgement with several adverse consequences, not least for the BBC's independence

[10] ICM survey *Future Priorities for the BBC: An Audience View*, February 2015. Available online at http://downloads.bbc.co.uk/bbctrust/assets/files/pdf/news/2015/audience_research. pdf, accessed on 11 June 2015

References

Ageh, Tony (2015) *The BBC, The Licence Fee and the Digital Public Space.* Speech at Royal Holloway University of London, 10 March. Available online at https://www.royalholloway.ac.uk/harc/documents/pdf/tonyageh.pdf, accessed on 31 May 2015

Bell, Emily (2015) Hugh Cudlipp memorial lecture. Available online at http://www.theguardian.com/media/2015/jan/28/emily-bells-2015-hugh-cudlipp-lecture-full-text, accessed on 31 May 2015

Coase, R. H. (1947) The origin of the monopoly of broadcasting in Great Britain, *Economica*, New Series, Vol. 14, No. 55, August pp 189-210

Coase, R. H. (1948) Wire broadcasting in Great Britain, *Economica*, New Series, Vol. 15, No. 59, August pp 194-220

Coase, R. H. (1950) *British Broadcasting: A Study in Monopoly*, London and Cambridge, MA: Longmans Green and Harvard University Press

Coase, R. H. (1954) The development of the British Television Service, *Land Economics*, Vol. 30, No. 3, August pp 207-222

Department of culture, media and sport (DMCS) (2015) *Creative Industries Economic Estimates*, 13 January. Available online at https://www.gov.uk/government/uploads/system/uploads/attachment_data/file/3946 68/Creative_Industries_Economic_Estimates_-_January_2015.pdf, accessed on 11 June 2015

OECD (2010) *The Future of News and the Internet*, Paris. Available online at http://www.oecd.org/sti/ieconomy/oecdexaminesthefutureofnewsandtheinternet.htm, accessed on 29 May 2015

Ofcom (2013) *Facts and Figures*. Available online at http://media.ofcom.org.uk/facts/, accessed on 2 June 2015

Ofcom (2014a) *Children and Parents: Media Use and Attitudes Report*. Available online at http://stakeholders.ofcom.org.uk/market-data-research/market-data/communications-market-reports/cmr14/uk/uk-1.040, accessed on 2 June 2015

Ofcom (2014b) *News Consumption in the UK*. Available online at http://stakeholders.ofcom.org.uk/market-data-research/other/tv-research/news-2014/, accessed on 2 June 2015

Radcliffe, John and Salkeld, Robert (eds) (1983) *Towards Computer Literacy: The BBC Computer Literacy Project 1979-83*, BBC. Available online at http://www.dcs.bbk.ac.uk/~rgj/Towards%20Computer%20Literacy.pdf, accessed on 29 May 2015

Tassey, Gregory (2014) Competing in advanced manufacturing: The need for improved growth models and policies, *Journal of Economic Perspectives*, Vol. 28, No. 1, Winter pp 27-48

UK Music (2014) *Measuring Music*, September. Available online at, http://www.ukmusic.org/assets/general/UK_MUSIC_Measuring_Music_September_2014.pdf, accessed on 11 June 2015

Wallenstein, Andrew (2015) Netflix ratings revealed: New data sheds light on original series' audience levels, *Variety*, 28 April. Available online at http://variety.com/2015/digital/news/netflix-originals-viewer-data-1201480234/, accessed on 2 June 2015

Evaluating the July 2015 Licence Fee Settlement

Patrick Barwise analyses the July 2015 settlement, concluding that, compared with reinstating the inflation-indexed licence fee with no additional top-slicing, it will be worse for consumers, producers, citizens and the economy

This chapter aims to evaluate the BBC's controversial July 2015 licence fee (LF) settlement. The analysis suggests that, compared with reinstating an inflation-indexed LF with no net increase in top-slicing, the consequences of the settlement will be worse for viewers, listeners and producers, worse from a welfare and citizenship perspective, and worse for the UK economy. The chapter also shows that, despite all the complexity and uncertainty surrounding broadcasting policy, a reliable analysis with clear practical implications is perfectly feasible, provided it uses the available evidence – of which there is plenty. In essence, the settlement involved:

(a) the BBC, by 2020/21, paying for free TV licences for all households with at least one member aged 75-plus;

(b) in return for the government phasing out the BBC's broadband subsidy and reducing its grant to the Welsh language channel, S4C, and

(c) reinstating an inflation-indexed LF, updated to cover PSB catch-up viewing (HM Treasury and DCMS 2015).

I start with the likely shape of the UK television market in 2016 (revenue and content investment for the BBC, the commercial PSBs and the non-PSBs). With this starting-point, I project the shape of the market in 2021, assuming the July 2015 settlement is enacted and with a number of other stated assumptions (Scenario 1). For comparison, I then project a second scenario (Scenario 2): what the market would be like in 2021 if, instead of enacting the settlement, the government dropped points (a) (free TV licences) and (b) (no broadband subsidy and reduced S4C grant) but with everything else the same. Scenario 2 incorporates point (c) (inflation-linked LF, updated to cover PSB catch-up viewing) and all the other assumptions in Scenario 1. In terms of revenue and content investment, the only difference between the two scenarios is that Scenario 1 assumes a large net increase in top-slicing, because the cost of free licences will be much more than the saving on broadband subsidy and S4C, while Scenario 2 assumes no change in the level of top-slicing.

To evaluate the July 2015 settlement, I analyse the differences between the two scenarios from the perspectives of consumers and content producers and from a wider social and economic perspective, including the welfare implications (because, as well as reducing the BBC's LF revenue, the settlement also shifts the cost of free licences from taxpayers to the majority of households with no member aged 75-plus). The analysis draws heavily on my previous work at the Reuters Institute (Barwise and Picard 2012, 2014) but uses more recent data. Readers wanting more detail can download these reports for free. The chapter concludes with a summary of the evaluation and some comments on the need to reframe the debate. To keep it to a reasonable length, the analysis is simplified in three ways, each of which could be addressed by further research:

1. it covers only BBC Television, the core service accounting for the bulk of LF expenditure;

2. it mainly takes a consumer perspective, focusing on the choice and value for money of UK television – not just the BBC – and only briefly discussing social, cultural, economic and welfare issues;

3. it directly explores just two possible options for the future level of the LF. However, the approach can be easily adapted to show the likely consequences of other options.[1]

The UK television market in 2016

Barwise and Picard (2014: 54-55) used commercial television revenue forecasts to 2016 kindly provided by Toby Syfret, of Enders Analysis (EA), in late 2013. For this chapter, I asked EA to update its forecasts with the same definitions as before (ibid: 18-19) but using the latest available data (personal communication).[2] Since 2013, pay TV subscriptions, television advertising and online television have all grown faster than expected. Table 1 shows the revised projections for television revenue, total content investment and first-run UK content investment in 2016, the last year of the current BBC charter, using the same assumptions about content investment as a percentage of revenue as in Barwise and Picard (ibid).

Table 1: UK Television Revenue and Content Investment in 2016

2016 £s	Revenue (£bn)	Total Content Investment (£bn)	First-Run UK Content Investment (£bn)
BBC TV[3]	2.61 (17%)	1.55 (22%)	1.46 (40%)
Commercial PSBs[4]	3.48 (23%)	2.14 (31%)	1.55 (42%)
Non-PSBs[5]	8.89 (59%)	3.28 (47%)	0.68 (18%)
Total	14.98 (100%)	6.97 (100%)	3.69 (100%)

By 2016:

- The real (inflation-adjusted) revenue of BBC TV will have fallen by almost 15 per cent since the 2010 settlement, while all the commercial TV revenue streams will have grown in real terms. The combined effect will be to reduce the BBC's TV revenue share to its lowest ever figure of 17 per cent.

- The commercial PSBs' revenue share, still largely based on advertising, will be 23 per cent – marginally lower than in 2012.[6]

- The non-PSBs' revenue share will have increased even further, from 54 per cent in 2012 to 59 per cent in 2016, because of the cuts in BBC revenue and the continuing growth of pay and, especially, online TV subscriptions (ibid: 13, 19, 23).

- This will reinforce the non-PSBs' dominance of total content investment (projected 47 per cent share in 2016). The annual cost of the new Premiership contract (£1.7 billion from 2016/17) will alone be about 10 per cent higher than BBC TV's total content budget (£1.5 billion).

- However, despite recent increases, the non-PSBs will still account for only about 18 per cent of first-run UK content investment, which will still be dominated by the BBC (40 per cent) and the commercial PSBs (42 per cent) with their much higher investment in UK content as a percentage of revenue.

By the time of charter renewal, updated estimates will be available, but are unlikely to change this picture materially.

Scenario 1: The market in 2021 if the 2015 settlement is enacted

Scenario 1 assumes all the terms of the settlement, plus the following:

1. LF evasion is not decriminalised (at least until all television viewing devices have conditional access technology so that evaders can be excluded[7]); evasion rates remain constant; the BBC continues to be gifted spectrum for DTT but receives no retransmission fees; and Scotland stays in the UK.

2. The percentage of BBC revenue going to BBC TV remains constant.

3. The number of households with television licences grows at 0.5 per cent per annum, reflecting continuing population growth.[8]

4. The net contribution from the BBC's commercial activities remains constant in real terms.

Point 3 means that, without the increase in top-slicing, the real LF revenue of BBC TV would grow by 0.5 per cent per annum to £2.68 billion by 2021. The Office for Budget Responsibility (OBR) estimates that the annual cost of free licences at the end of the five years will be £745 million in real terms (Jackson 2015). However, this will be partly offset by phasing out the broadband subsidy, estimated at £80 million per annum (ibid), and reducing the S4C grant (by, say, £15 million per annum). The net increase in top-slicing will therefore be about £650 million per annum at that point.[9] Attributing 70 per cent of this to television, the net result will be a reduction of £453 million[10] in the real revenue of BBC TV in 2021 estimated above, from £2.68 billion to £2.225 billion. Again, revised estimates are unlikely to change the position very materially.

Relative to the £2.61 billion in 2016 (Table 1), the projected BBC TV revenue of £2.225 billion in 2021 corresponds to a reduction of almost 15 per cent in real terms over the five years. This is less than the 20 per cent cut estimated by the OBR (ibid) because it also includes the savings on broadband and S4C and an increase in TV households. Based on discussion with industry experts, I assume the following real annual growth rates for the commercial broadcasters over the same time period 2016-2021:

- commercial PSBs: +1.6 per cent per annum (+8.3 per cent over the five years);

- non-PSBs: +2.4 per cent per annum (+12.6 per cent over the five years).

The reasons for the difference are that the commercial PSBs will still be largely reliant on traditional advertising, a relatively mature market, although with some subscription, targeted advertising[11] and online TV revenue; and vice versa for the non-PSBs (which include the fast-growing pure-play online television operators as well as the established pay TV companies and non-PSB commercial channels). The expert consensus is that these numbers fall well within the likely range and that the non-PSBs (including the online-only players) will grow faster than the commercial PSBs. For simplicity, I also assume that all three types of broadcaster invest a constant percentage of revenue in content and, within that, in first-run UK content. This seems broadly realistic:

- The BBC's overheads are already less than 8 per cent of revenue (PwC 2015). Its commitment to personalisation will increase technology and distribution costs, making it hard to increase content investment as a percentage of revenue. 94 per cent of its content investment is already in first-run UK programmes.

- The commercial PSBs invest a slightly higher percentage of revenue in content than BBC TV.[12] More than 70 per cent of this is first-run UK content. They are unlikely to increase these investments faster than their revenue growth.

- The pay TV operators are more likely to increase their content investment over time as a percentage of revenue, but their ability to do so will be limited by their high marketing, account management, technology and distribution costs; the non-PSB commercial channels will continue to see the UK largely as a way of generating revenue from existing US content; and a growing proportion of non-PSB revenue will be accounted for by online television players with even higher non-content costs. The overall effect is unlikely to be a significant increase in content investment as a percentage of revenue, except perhaps for sports rights.

These assumptions lead to the figures in Table 2. Comparing this with Table 1, we see that, over the five years, total UK television revenue is projected to grow by 6.8 per cent and total content investment by 5.2 per cent, while first-run UK content investment will be unchanged (all in real terms).

Table 2. Scenario 1: July 2015 Settlement
UK Television Revenue and Content Investment in 2021

Constant 2016 £s	Revenue (£bn)	Total Content Investment (£bn)	First-Run UK Content Investment (£bn)
BBC TV	2.225 (14%)	1.32 (18%)	1.24 (34%)
Commercial PSBs	3.77 (24%)	2.32 (32%)	1.68 (46%)
Non-PSBs	10.01 (63%)	3.69 (50%)	0.77 (21%)
Total	16.005 (100%)	7.33 (100%)	3.69 (100%)

Scenario 2: No increase in top-slicing
Scenario 2 is identical to Scenario 1 except that the level of top-slicing remains unchanged rather than increasing to fund free TV licences. Specifically, points 1 (no decriminalisation, etc) and 2 (constant proportion of BBC revenue allocated to TV) are unchanged. For simplicity, I also conservatively assume no change in point 3 (0.5 per cent per annum growth rate of TV homes paying the LF) although, because of the ageing population, the growth rate for all households (Scenario 2) will in practice be slightly higher than for those with no one aged 75-plus (Scenario 1). On point 4, I assume that, without the cut in the BBC's first-run commissions, the contribution from its commercial activities grows annually by the equivalent of 0.5 per cent of LF revenue. Combining this with point 3 means that, without the increase in top-slicing, BBC TV revenue would grow at 1 per cent per annum in real terms, or 5.1 per cent over the five years. Relative to the almost 15 per cent reduction in Scenario 1, the BBC figures for 2021 in Scenario 2 are therefore 23 per cent higher.[13]

To model the overall UK television ecology with a 23 per cent bigger BBC TV (relative to Scenario 1) we also need to allow for some possible 'crowding out' of commercial broadcasters. As in Barwise and Picard (2014: 19-24), I therefore assume that the commercial broadcasters' revenue and content investment would be higher if the BBC were smaller. International comparisons actually cast doubt on this assumption. In fact, the evidence is that, far from crowding out commercial broadcasters' content investment, well-funded public broadcasters may even force them to invest *more* in order to 'compete on quality' (ibid: 46-47). Nevertheless, I here conservatively assume that, because BBC TV's 2021 revenue would be 23 per cent higher in Scenario 2 than in Scenario 1, the commercial broadcasters' revenue would be fractionally lower. Further, I assume that their total and first-run content investment would also be lower by the same proportion. For simplicity, I assume that the magnitude of this 'crowding out' effect is consistent with the 'base case' in Barwise and Picard (ibid: 19-24).[14] The result is a 1 per cent reduction in the commercial PSBs' revenue, total content investment and first-run UK content investment in Scenario 2, and a 3 per cent reduction in the equivalent figures for the non-PSBs, all relative to the Scenario 1 figures in Table 2.

Combining these estimates with those for BBC TV gives the figures in Table 3. There are, of course, many uncertainties around these but the policy issue is to do with the *differences* between the two scenarios. Most of the uncertainties (for instance, about the future growth of commercial broadcasters' revenue and content investment) largely cancel out, so the policy implications are unaffected. In other words, there is much less uncertainty about the difference between the two scenarios (which is what matters for evaluating the policy) than there is about the scenarios themselves.

The overall picture of UK television in Table 3 is extremely rosy. Comparing it with Table 1, viewers are paying no more for the LF in real terms than five years before (although they are, on average, paying about 7 per cent more for pay and online TV and, indirectly, about 4-5 per cent more for TV advertising)[15] but benefit from significantly higher real investment in both total content (+8 per cent) and first-run UK content (+7 per cent). By the same token, producers are benefiting from the 7 per cent real increase in the value of UK commissions.

Table 3. Scenario 2: No Increase in Top-Slicing
UK Television Revenue and Content Investment in 2021

Constant 2016 £s	Revenue (£bn)	Total Content Investment (£bn)	First-Run UK Content Investment (£bn)
BBC TV	2.74 (17%)	1.63 (22%)	1.53 (39%)
Commercial PSBs	3.73 (23%)	2.30 (31%)	1.66 (42%)
Non-PSBs	9.71 (60%)	3.58 (48%)	0.75 (19%)
Total	16.18 (100%)	7.51 (100%)	3.94 (100%)

Comparing the two scenarios

To evaluate the July 2015 settlement, the key comparison is between the two scenarios. Comparing Table 2 with Table 3, we see that, by 2021, the settlement will have had the following effects, relative to the outcome with no increase in top-slicing and everything else held constant:

1. Total UK television revenue will be just over 1 per cent lower (£16.005 billion vs £16.18 billion) and even more dominated by the non-PSBs (63 per cent vs 60 per cent). BBC TV's revenue will be almost 19 per cent lower (£2.225 billion vs £2.74 billion) and its revenue share will have fallen further to only 14 per cent rather than remaining almost steady at 17 per cent. The commercial PSBs' revenue share will be one point higher at 24 per cent, but even more dominated by the non-PSBs.

2. Total content investment will be about 2.4 per cent lower (£7.33 billion vs £7.51 billion) and, again, even more dominated by the non-PSBs (50 per cent vs 48 per cent). Most of the non-PSBs' content will, of course, be available only to those paying a subscription.

3. First-run UK content investment will be reduced by just over 6.3 per cent relative to Scenario 2 (£3.69 billion vs £3.94 billion, a reduction of £250 million per annum), entirely wiping out the real growth in UK commissions in Scenario 2.

The 19 per cent cut in BBC income in Scenario 1, relative to Scenario 2, will also lead to a similar percentage reduction in resources for:

- BBC Radio, which accounts for over half of radio listening and the great majority of original UK content investment.

- BBC Online, the UK's only global top ten online service and the only one, apart from Wikipedia, without adverts.

- The BBC World Service – the most trusted international news source in the world.

- S4C, BBC Monitoring, local TV, children's TV and the BBC's learning and development (e.g. digital skills) and training activities.

- Distribution technologies such as the iPlayer.

- The BBC's contribution to the creative industries (Frontier Economics 2015) and the wider economy.

- The BBC's numerous contributions to the UK's national culture, society and democracy. Many of these are contested but only the BBC's strongest critics argue that its overall impact on UK citizens is negative, especially with a growing proportion of UK broadcasting US-owned and controlled.[16]

Welfare implications

As chancellor, Gordon Brown introduced free television licences, with no consultation, in 2001. This is a badly targeted use of taxpayers' money (because it applies to all households with at least one member aged 75-plus, regardless of household size or income) and, as a subsidy, is marginally regressive (because better-off people live significantly longer than poorer people). The July 2015 settlement switches the funding to the majority of households with no member aged 75-plus. This makes the policy equally badly targeted (still subsidising all households with at least one member aged 75-plus) and even more regressive, because the cost is shifted from taxpayers (who tend to be better off) to young adults, working-age families and younger pensioners, regardless of income. If anything, the resulting reduction in programme choice disproportionately harms poorer people because they watch more free-to-air television and listen to more radio. In welfare terms, this was always a bad policy. The 2015 settlement makes it slightly worse.

Relative to Scenario 2, most households – all those with no member aged 75-plus – will suffer a clear reduction in choice and value for money as a result of the settlement. They will be paying the same for the LF but their overall programme choice will be reduced by 2.4 per cent and, more important to most viewers (especially those with only free-to-air TV), their choice of first-run UK television content will be cut by 6.3 per cent and radio significantly more. Even for the minority of households with at least one person aged 75-plus, many would probably prefer paying the 40p per day LF to losing 6 per cent of original UK television content and all the other service reductions listed above. Among both groups, the exact impact will vary between households, depending on whether they switch to pay TV, or upgrade their pay TV contracts, to compensate for the 19 per cent reduction in BBC programme budgets (ibid: 33-42). But the great majority will be clearly worse off as both consumers and citizens, as will UK producers.

Evaluation summary

Compared with maintaining the real level of the LF with no net increase in top-slicing, and holding everything else constant, the July 2015 settlement will be:

- worse for most viewers;
- significantly worse for radio listeners;
- marginally worse for online users (less free, trustworthy, advertising-free content);
- significantly worse for the UK's international image and 'soft power' (reduced BBC World Service and BBC Worldwide);
- worse for those benefiting from the other activities funded by the LF (S4C, children's television, etc);

- worse for UK producers, other creative industries (authors, actors, musicians, etc) and the wider economy (lower employment, growth and exports; higher imports);

- marginally worse in welfare terms;

- and also – most would agree – worse in multiple ways for the UK's national culture, society and democracy.

In fact, apart from a few commercial and political vested interests and the minority of households that include at least one member aged 75-plus *and* for whom the above disadvantages are worth less than 40p per day, it is hard to think of anyone in the UK who will be better off under Scenario 1 versus Scenario 2.[17]

This conclusion is extremely robust partly because it makes optimistic assumptions, especially about the settlement leading to reduced 'crowding out' of commercial content investment, but mainly because it is based on the difference between two scenarios in which the *only* differences in the inputs are the level of top-slicing and how the free licences are funded. Both scenarios contain many uncertainties but these are almost entirely irrelevant. For instance, it might be that online television revenue and content investment grow much faster than I have assumed. But, if that happens, the resulting non-PSB figures will be higher under both scenarios (Tables 2 and 3). Unless the level of the LF hugely impacts the growth of online television – which is unlikely – the difference between the two scenarios will not be materially affected and the policy implications will be unchanged.

The July 2015 settlement is not, in itself, a disaster. But it continues or even accelerates the pattern of aggressive salami-slicing of BBC funding started in 2010, the long-term effects of which we explored in Barwise and Picard (ibid: 56-60). The BBC's share of television revenue will have fallen from 22.2 per cent in 2012 and 17.4 per cent in 2016 to about 13.9 per cent in 2021, an 8.3 percentage point drop in just nine years. Almost half of this would have happened even if the LF had been inflation-indexed with no increase in top-slicing, because of the continuing growth of commercial broadcasters. But at least half is attributable to the 2010 and 2015 settlements.

Whether the salami-slicing continues after 2021 partly depends on whether the BBC can phase out free TV licences for the growing number of households with at least one member aged 75-plus. This will be difficult for an already weakened BBC in the face of almost certain hostility from most national newspapers, many politicians and, of course, those getting free licences. But it may be achievable if the BBC replaces the scheme with a cheaper one aimed at the much smaller number of households (including many with no one aged 75-plus) for whom the 40p per day LF is a genuine burden. The pressure to reduce BBC funding is not coming from the public, despite relentless anti-BBC propaganda. The evidence is that the public is highly satisfied with the BBC's services and most would be willing to pay a higher LF in order to get more good programmes. That is especially clear when their preferences are researched properly, using methods that spell out the genuine policy choices and trade-offs (see Barwise 2006) rather than through poorly designed or disingenuous surveys that misleadingly imply that the LF can be cut indefinitely with no reduction in programme quality or choice.[18]

Reframing the debate

> 'The BBC's output today – compared to 30 years ago – blazes with inventiveness, skill and brilliance. We will miss it bitterly when it is gone'
> (McKay 2015: R25).

We need to reframe the debate. There is a fatalism that assumes that it is written in the stars that the BBC must get ever smaller until it either disappears – as implied by the above quotation from a *Daily Telegraph* review of Jean Seaton's (2015) official history of the BBC 1974-1987, '*Pinkoes and Traitors*' – or is reduced to an irrelevant rump like PBS in America (Barwise and Picard 2014: 62-63).

One reason for the fatalism may be the idea that technology change makes the BBC irrelevant or non-viable. This is nonsense. Technology change presents both threats and opportunities but is almost entirely about distribution. It has minimal bearing on the need for continuing investment in high-quality original UK content (Barwise and Picard 2012: 43-44). While the BBC is still funded by a universal LF (or household levy), the best way to achieve that is by – at least – re-indexing the LF or levy to general inflation and avoiding further top-slicing.

Another reason for the fatalism may be an assumption – usually implicit – that without such a large public intervention the market would offer greater choice and value for money, in pure consumer terms, than the current mixed (but now more than 80 per cent commercial) economy. In Barwise and Picard (2014), we showed that that assumption is wrong, even with optimistic assumptions about how much more the commercial broadcasters would invest in content if there were no BBC. So far, none of those arguing for a smaller BBC has even attempted to challenge this analysis.

If the BBC eventually disappears, this will be the result of successive incremental policy choices, not because of technology or market forces. In Barwise and Picard (ibid: 63) we wrote: 'The danger ... is not from any of the more radical proposals to take an axe to the BBC or the licence fee, since, if seriously put forward, they would be likely to produce a strong backlash from the public. Instead, the more likely scenario is a continuation of the current salami-slicing policy, leading ineluctably to a smaller and smaller BBC within a bigger and bigger ... television market.' The July 2015 settlement precisely fits this description. This chapter shows that it is *demonstrably* against the public interest.

Notes

[1] For instance, an even deeper cut in the real value of the LF. e.g., UKIP's Nigel Farage has proposed a 67 per cent cut to £48.15 with even worse consequences for UK broadcasting and the public (Hope 2015). It could also be applied, with minimal modification, if the LF were replaced with a household levy. Directionally, the conclusions would be unaffected

[2] At the time of writing the forecasts prepared by EA are internal, but they will be published later in the summer

[3] Assumes total and first-run BBC TV content investment of 59.2 per cent and 55.8 per cent of revenue, respectively. These and the other figures in the table are based on estimates in Barwise and Picard (2014: 19, 23, 27-28, 55), updated using recent industry data

[4] ITV, C4/S4C, C5, including their portfolio channels. Assumes (a) 0 per cent of pay TV revenue, 74.5 per cent of advertising and sponsorship revenue, 10 per cent of online TV revenue and 38 per cent of other commercial revenue, (b) total and first-run content investment of 61.4 per cent and 44.4 per cent of revenue, respectively

[5] All other commercial channels and pay/online TV operators. Assumes total and first-run content investment of 36.9 per cent and 7.6 per cent of revenue, respectively

[6] TV revenue in 2012: total £12.29 billion, commercial PSBs £2.98 billion, a 24 per cent share (Barwise and Picard 2014: 19, 23)

[7] Given the large installed base of viewing devices and the high cost of retrofitting conditional access technology, there is no realistic prospect of universal CAT before 2026. At the time of writing (July 2015), we are still waiting for David Perry QC to report on decriminalisation

[8] The current rate of household growth is about 0.75 per cent per annum (source: ONS) but I here assume a continuing reduction in households with television licences as a percentage of total households, partly mitigated by updating the LF to include PSB catch-up viewing

[9] £745m minus £80 million minus £15 million

[10] 70 per cent of £650 million

[11] Eg Sky's AdSmart. For homes in the system, the broadcaster loads a library of commercials onto the STB. Each household has a profile of demographic and other data, including postcode, enabling advertisers to target particular segments. The commercials are placed seamlessly into the broadcast stream in the target homes, replacing the broadcast commercials in those spots. AdSmart is still available only for live viewing of commercial breaks in non-live broadcasts, but it and other similar systems, DTT and online systems will become increasingly important over the next few years

[12] This is the commercial PSBs' content investment as a percentage of their revenue, which is mainly their share (almost 75 per cent) of *net advertising revenue* (NAR), the money they receive for commercial airtime. From a societal and economic viewpoint, the more relevant figure is their share of *TV advertising expenditure*, the total amount companies spend on TV advertising, including agency commissions and commercial production costs – about 15-20 per cent higher than NAR (Barwise and Picard 2014: 33-34). Relative to this higher figure, the commercial PSBs invest roughly 53-54 per cent in

content and 40 per cent in first-run UK content, significantly less than BBC TV but still much more than the non-PSBs

[13] Using detailed figures, in Scenario 1 BBC TV's real revenue is 14.8 per cent lower in 2021 than in 2016. In Scenario 2, it is 5.1 per cent higher than in 2016. Comparing the two, the Scenario 2 projection is 1.051/(1 minus 0.148) equals 1.23 times the Scenario 1 figure.

[14] This projects that, if there had been *no* BBC TV in 2012, the commercial PSBs' revenue would have been 6.7 per cent higher and the non-PSBs' revenue 22.2 per cent higher. Expressing this relative to what the commercial broadcasters' 2012 revenue would have been if there had been no BBC TV, the BBC's crowding impact becomes a 6.3 per cent reduction for the commercial PSBs (1 minus (1/1.067)) and an 18.2 per cent reduction for the non-PSBs (1 minus (1/1.222)). BBC TV's actual revenue share in 2012 was 22 per cent. Rescaling its crowding out effect to its 14 per cent projected share in 2021 under Scenario 1 (i.e. multiplying the impacts by 14/22, implying a stable, linear relationship), these become a 4.0 per cent reduction for the commercial PSBs and an 11.6 per cent reduction for the non-PSBs, relative to the 'base case' projection if there were no BBC TV. Again rebasing the numbers and assuming a linear relationship between BBC TV's revenue and market impact, a 23 per cent increase implies a 1.0 per cent reduction in the commercial PSBs' revenue (i.e. 23 x 0.040/0.960 per cent) and a 3.0 per cent reduction for the non-PSBs (23 x 0.116/0.884 per cent), all relative to the figures in Table 2. These estimates are conservative; i.e. they probably overstate the impact of crowding out, but the uncertainty around them is insufficient to impact materially the results of the analysis in this chapter

[15] Real pay and online TV subscriptions up about 10 per cent (the main driver of the non-PSBs' 9.2 per cent increase in revenue) through a combination of higher ARPU and higher penetration. With a 2.5 per cent cumulative increase in the number of households, the net effect is an increase of about 7 per cent per household. Real advertising revenue per household (the main driver of the commercial PSBs' 7.2 per cent increase in revenue) would also be 4-5 per cent higher, indirectly funded by consumers (Barwise and Picard 2014: 33-34)

[16] The Americans themselves do not share our governments' relaxed attitude towards foreign ownership of broadcasting. No Brit would be allowed to own the smallest radio station in Tuscaloosa

[17] The situation may be even worse than this. The government is also making the reinstatement of an inflation-adjusted LF dependent on (a) charter renewal not leading to any reduction in the aims and scope of the BBC and (b) the BBC demonstrating efficiency cuts 'at least equivalent to those in other parts of the public sector' (HM Treasury and DCMS)

[18] A particularly misleading question relates to advertising funding. At least 25 per cent of the public respond positively to the suggestion that some or all of the LF could be replaced by advertising. Although this has never, to my knowledge, been directly researched, the indirect evidence is that these people assume that the only difference would be a lower LF and having to put up with advertising breaks on the BBC. In reality, all analysts agree that almost 100 per cent of the BBC's advertising revenue – some say more than 100 per cent – would be diverted from other advertising-funded channels, leading to a sharp reduction in content investment, especially for the BBC and the commercial PSBs (Barwise and Picard 2014: 20 and Appendix A). It is unlikely that more

than a handful of respondents would favour replacing LF funding with advertising once they understood the likely consequences

References

Barwise, Patrick (2006) *The BBC Licence Fee Bid: What Does the Public Think?* Report for the BBC governors, April. Available online at http://downloads.bbc.co.uk/bbctrust/assets/files/pdf/our_work/govs/barwise06.pdf, accessed on 16 June 2015

Barwise, Patrick and Picard, Robert G. (2012) *The Economics of Television in a Digital World*, Oxford University: Reuters Institute for the Study of Journalism. Available online at http://reutersinstitute.politics.ox.ac.uk/publication/economics-television-digital-world, accessed on 16 June 2015

Barwise, Patrick and Picard, Robert G. (2014) *What If There Were No BBC Television?: The Net Impact on UK Viewers*, Oxford University: Reuters Institute for the Study of Journalism. Available online at http://reutersinstitute.politics.ox.ac.uk/publication/what-if-there-were-no-bbc-television, accessed on 16 June 2015

Frontier Economics (2015) *The Contribution of the BBC to the UK Creative Industries*. Report prepared for the BBC, April. Available online at http://downloads.bbc.co.uk/aboutthebbc/insidethebbc/reports/pdf/bbc_report_contribution_to_the_UK_creative_industries.pdf, accessed on 16 June 2015

HM Treasury and DCMS (2015) *Arrangements for Over-75s TV Licence Concession from 2017/*. Letter from George Osborne and John Whittingdale to Lord Hall, 3 July 2015. Available online at https://www.gov.uk/government/uploads/system/uploads/attachment_data/file/443735/Letter_from_George_Osborne_and_John_Whittingdale_to_Tony_Hall_FINAL.PDF, accessed on 12 July 2015

Hope, Christopher (2015) Nigel Farage: I want to cut the BBC licence fee to less than £50 a year, *Daily Telegraph*, 21 April. Available online at http://www.telegraph.co.uk/news/politics/ukip/11551322/Nigel-Farage-I-want-to-cut-the-BBC-licence-fee-to-less-than-50-a-year.html, accessed on 12 July 2015

Jackson, Jasper (2015) BBC spending to be cut by 20% in real terms over five years, says OBR, *Media Guardian*, 8 July. Available online at http://www.theguardian.com/media/2015/jul/08/bbc-spending-cut-budget-20-real-terms-five-years?CMP=ema_546, accessed on 12 July 2015

McKay, Sinclair (2015) The trouble with Auntie, *Daily Telegraph* review section, 28 March

PwC (2015) *BBC Efficiency Review: An Update on the BBC's Overheads*, July. Available online at http://downloads.bbc.co.uk/aboutthebbc/insidethebbc/reports/pdf/bbc_report_pwc_update_overheads_efficiency_review.pdf, accessed on 11 July 2015

Seaton, Jean (2015) *'Pinkoes and Traitors': The BBC and Nation 1974-1987*, London: Profile Books

How Best to Fund the BBC?

Jacquie Hughes argues that, as the PSB market and the BBC's function within it change over the next decade, it seems both inevitable and rational that the government consider collection of monies based on a household fee, similar to the German model

The summer budget of 2015 saw an audacious raid on the coffers of the BBC, courtesy of an 'agreement' that the BBC would take on a government welfare benefit – free TV licences for the over-75s. Few had seen it coming, and the widespread expressions of shock that the deal had happened under the nose of the imminent charter review process were only amplified by knowledge that this was the second time in five years that proper process – and the BBC's independence – had come under direct government threat.

In October 2010 – as part of another bruising and hurried financial settlement between government and the corporation – the current fee was frozen and top-sliced. The BBC was forced to fund the World Service, make programmes for Welsh language broadcaster S4C and meet the cost of rolling out broadband internet access to rural areas. Plans to force it to take on the cost of free licence fees for the over-75s were only resisted when several members of the BBC Trust threatened to resign.

Following the 2015 'settlement', few missed the chance to point out that the man whose paw prints were all over it – new culture secretary John Whittingdale – had, only five months earlier, issued a report from his then DCMS select committee office damning in its criticism of the earlier deal:

> The 2010 settlement demonstrated that the BBC's independence can be compromised by negotiations with the government of the day that lack transparency and public consultation. ... No future licence fee negotiations must be conducted in the way of the 2010 settlement: the process must be open and transparent, licence fee payers must be consulted and parliament should have an opportunity to debate the level of funding being set and

any significant changes to funding responsibilities. We recommend that the independent panel and charter review process consider the appropriate length of licence fee settlements and the period in which they should be reviewed and changes made.

Any small satisfaction derived from quoting Whittingdale's own report's findings back at him soon faded with the realisation of how significant an act this was. Former BBC trustee Diane Coyle called it 'profoundly unconstitutional' and the National Union of Journalists (NUJ) was poised to mount a legal challenge on the grounds it breached the corporation's rules on governance, amongst other things.

All very regrettable, but not least because both incidents serve only to highlight the fragility of one of the supposedly strongest and most oft-quoted qualities of the licence fee: that, unlike other funding arrangements, its one-step remove from direct government funding nature affords the BBC a shield of independence. Unless this principle can be restored and strengthened the licence fee offers no more protection than any other funding form.

It's an old story...
How long have we been talking about how to fund the BBC, and more specifically, the licence fee? Only since 1923 ... In the beginning, broadcasting was very much viewed as a utility: the need to negotiate spectrum allocation internationally as well as mediate the competing demands of domestic wavelength users (the armed forces, merchant shipping, emergency services, telecommunications) suggested government intervention, as did the need to finance it.

Unlike other forms of cultural activity, radio and television were enjoyed in people's own homes and, as others have pointed out, appeared as natural resources, available at the turn of a switch. It was not immediately obvious how to pay for something which undoubtedly cost money (Scannell 2002: 46). So, broadcasting was originally financed partly by a tariff on the wireless itself, and partly through a licence fee. In the early days, the fee was referred to as a 'subscription': wireless owners paid their 10 shillings in return for broadcasting services. Only later did this change into a tax on households with television sets.

Since then, eleven government-instigated committees have wrestled with various aspects of broadcasting, not least the tension between the view of public service broadcasting as 'an expression of cultural values and the view that it is predominantly a commercial activity; a tension which is besieging the entire broadcasting ecology today' (Noonan 2008). The licence fee – both in principle and practice – has been shaken around, threatened with abolition, warned it was a funding mechanism whose time was up, yet managed to survive: even the hawkish Peacock report (1986) (see *Telegraph* 2014) concluded that a licence fee was still 'the least worst' way to fund the BBC. Almost thirty years on from Peacock, the latest major report into the future of the BBC echoed this view:

In the short-term there is currently no better alternative to the licence fee but as a minimum the licence fee must be amended to cover catch-up television as soon as possible. ... A broadcasting levy on all households is the preferred alternative but a degree of subscription for BBC services could be a possibility in the future (DCMS 2015).

However, five months later, the green paper on charter renewal raised all the same questions again, asking people to ponder how we should pay for the BBC and if funding should be top-sliced. If we accept that producing, broadcasting and distributing creative content costs money, then the only real question is how much money and who should pay? And the choices have always been these: we can each make individual consumer decisions and buy what we want (the pay TV, subscription model), we can accept advertisements or sponsorship as subsidy for production, or we can agree that intervening in the media market and collecting a universal levy is the right thing to do. If the latter, then payment can be collected from general taxation (as for other, non-discriminatory, universal services such as health and education), or via a ring-fenced tax such as the current licence fee.

That's the nub of it. If there were a simple, universally agreeable way of paying for public broadcast services, it would have been settled upon by now. We only have to look at how public service broadcasting (PSB) is funded in other countries with similar broadcasting systems to find evidence of the 'political messiness and contestedness' (Tambini 2014) of broadcasting policy worldwide; the terms of the debate around funding PSB are much the same as those found in the UK.

Criticism of the licence fee is easy: it is a regressive flat tax; it's unfair if viewers only want to watch commercial TV as they still have to pay; it's expensive to administer; it encourages evasion; its device-dependency looks increasingly redundant; it offers no mechanism by which to judge consumer satisfaction. And the fact that it is set by government implies a level of political control. But criticism of the fee on principle or moral grounds can often mask vested interests, political or commercial motives. By contrast, supporters of the mechanism claim it offers stability of funding, preserves the independence of the BBC, spreads the cost widely making it value for money and enables the BBC to focus on quality output.

The problem with the debate to date is that discussion of the licence fee has become conflated with discussion of the essential role and purpose of the BBC. The corporation has gone to great lengths to promote the idea that fulfilment of its objectives is intrinsically linked to a licence fee of scale. Any change to the level of funding or mechanism would, they say, undermine the key principles of PSB. This is obviously not the case: the objectives of PSB remain the same regardless of the funding mechanism. Debating whether the BBC has delivered them is important when assessing if the corporation is still worthy of its privileged status, but consideration of the merits or demerits of the licence fee as a funding mechanism (compared to all other possible methods) must be decoupled from this debate. As former *Guardian* editor Peter Preston ably put it:

> We're not talking the end of civilisation: merely ends, ways and means. It's probably a bad idea to try to send people to court for not paying up. Let's just settle down quietly – pushing meddling politicos out of action – and decide, as sentient stakeholders, what we want to do next (Preston 2014).

Do the current funding arrangements protect the BBC's independence?

That the licence fee establishes a direct bond between citizens and broadcaster and that the BBC's shareholders are its audience (not the government) are the simplest expressions of the mechanism as a guarantor of independence. To fund the BBC from more general taxation would, the argument goes, break that bond and undermine independence, leaving the BBC at the whim of political forces and fiscal pressure. Even the current hawkish green paper acknowledges this much. But in truth, the licence fee has proved barely any better a protector. As described earlier, events of the last five years suggest the licence fee's claim to offer a shield of independence from government are all but sunk. The 2010 and 2015 settlements aside, even a cursory look at the history of the BBC reveals governments repeatedly and unashamedly prepared to wield control of the licence fee as a threat to secure their own objectives. The BBC's courting of government in an attempt to evade restrictions on its reporting has been a feature since the beginning of its existence. This has made the BBC susceptible to bullying as at various times 'it was implied that the licence fee might not be allowed to rise or its licence to broadcast terminated altogether' (Curran and Seaton 1981: 118).

Most academics and observers agree that whenever the BBC asks parliament to increase the licence fee (or even not reduce it) it becomes vulnerable to political pressure. Add in any combination of rising costs, inflation, general spending cuts the political game is set. Since 1991, the whole of the licence fee has been granted to the BBC. As we have seen, this point of principle has been quietly but fundamentally broken in the past decade, which now puts association of the licence fee mechanism with the independence argument further into question. And as Coyle and others have pointed out, a seemingly obscure judgement by the Office for National Statistics in 2006 effectively redefined the fee as a tax, and BBC and BBC Worldwide borrowing scores against the public borrowing requirement – further eroding the corporation's financial independence.

The dominant status of the BBC in the media landscape, especially the news supply, also exposes it to far greater political scrutiny than any other broadcaster. In late 2013, Conservative Party chairman Grant Shapps made what was described as 'the most explicit threat by a cabinet minister against the broadcaster' when he suggested the BBC could lose its exclusive right to the licence fee, while making clear his real target was the tone of the BBC's news reporting. This, he claimed, was biased against the government (see Ross 2013).

The licence fee: Upholding universality?

Supporters of the licence fee cite its association with universality as one of its core strengths. Collecting the fee from every household commits the BBC to providing something for everyone – no section of the audience who pays for the BBC is left uncatered for. Yet critics point out a paradox. Striving for universality has forced the BBC to chase share (and reach) very closely because any weakening of performance here would undermine the same principle. So as not to fall prey to political enemies (keen to argue that it no longer merits public funding), the BBC is forced to pursue ratings battles with its commercial rivals and attract a respectable share of the audience – a strategy that, in turn, leads to conformity in programming and editorial policy, the antithesis of the innovation and distinctiveness supposedly afforded by the privilege of public funding. According to David Elstein (2014):

> The BBC is forced to offer high volumes of middle-of the-road or populist output, most of which is indistinguishable from that of the commercials sector ... a good 90 per cent of television output lacks real distinctiveness, let alone the independence of market share measures that the purity of the licence fee funding is meant to allow.

There is another challenge associated with the commitment to universality given the rapidly converging, connected world. Changing demographics – particularly the gap between younger and older audience's habits – are already beginning to challenge the notion of universal reach via traditional services and channels. Yet it is clear the BBC's claim that only the licence fee prompts a commitment to universal provision – which, in turn, is an unquestionably positive characteristic – is, indeed, questionable and in need of radical reconsideration given changing viewing habits and technology.

BBC licence fee: Value for money?

There is a strong consumerist argument for a licence fee-funded BBC, especially when set against the subscription costs of pay TV and broadband connections. With the fee levied on all households with televisions (regardless of levels of consumption), the BBC can rightly trumpet its claim over '40p a day for all that' (four television channels, ten national radio stations, a network of local radio stations, and an internationally acclaimed website).

While a majority of UK adults (57 per cent) judge the licence fee 'good value for money', a worrying 43 per cent do not, many citing affordability as a concern. Approval is higher in England (58 per cent) and Wales (60 per cent) than in Scotland (50 per cent) or Northern Ireland (47 per cent). BBC management was a factor cited by 20 per cent of those in the 'value for money' camp and 31 per cent opposing camp (BBC Trust 2013).

Since 2008, the BBC has analysed and reported on the economic impact of the licence fee on the broader economy and creative sector and found that the effect of its £4 billion spend on television, radio and online services is 'multiplied' as it ripples through the economy. In brief, £2 of economic value are created for every £1 of licence fee investment. The BBC has also helped the independent production sector grow from generating £1.3 billion in revenues in 2005 to £3.1 billion in 2013 (ibid). This makes a compelling case for the claims of the licence fee as seed-corn for the creative economy *per se*, and one supported by industry trade body PACT and many other media analysts.

One of the most important ways the BBC could reclaim the 'value for money' agenda is to open its spending plans and performance to third-party scrutiny. Currently, by reference to the charter, the BBC is exempt from the National Auditing Office's rights to examine public institutions for efficiency and effectiveness, in other words, value for money. The BBC and some supporters are resistant to formalising the NAO's scrutiny of the BBC, but this should be agreed by way of withdrawing or limiting that exemption during this charter review process, or giving the NAO full financial auditor status. Its terms of reference can be so designed to prevent involvement in the editorial or creative risk aspects of the BBC. Financial responsibility and transparency have nothing to do with independence of operation.

The licence fee: A guarantee of quality?
Guaranteed over a known period and affording the BBC freedom from shareholder pressure, advertiser influence and the need to chase ratings, the licence fee should allow the BBC to concentrate purely and simply on providing high quality, distinctive, innovative, challenging content that is highly regarded by all viewers. How then can we best judge quality in the context of the BBC?

One simple measure is audience share: are viewers attracted to BBC content in sufficiently high numbers compared to alternative offerings? Another measure is to ask if audiences find BBC output sufficiently distinctive, original and innovative, compared to that on offer from other providers. Almost all of the UK (96 per cent of UK adults) uses the BBC each week, and these audiences spend a considerable amount of time with BBC services (around 19 hours per week, on average). The public consumes the BBC for substantial periods of time across multiple platforms. Almost nine in ten people watch BBC TV overall each week. The BBC also emerges as a global leader on quality – in a recent international survey of 14 countries, BBC One was rated highest out of 66 major television channels.

The BBC Trust surveys adult opinion on various statements of significance and delivery every year. Of the view: 'The BBC makes high quality programmes or online content', some 83 per cent cite this as important and 76 per cent feel the BBC delivers on it. However, there is a considerable gap – and serious questions to be addressed – about the BBC's commitment to distinctive and innovative programming. Of the statement: 'The BBC has lots of fresh and new ideas', 79 per cent of respondents agreed this was important, but only 56 per cent felt the BBC delivered on it – a staggering 23 points performance gap. More significantly, this performance failure has been a repeat finding since 2009

(BBC Trust 2013). Former Ofcom chair Ed Richards said these were legitimate issues for the BBC to address:

> If I were running one of the commercial broadcasters I would feel very strongly about those sorts of matters. ... I think they are the absolute essence of what the BBC management must have at the front of its mind, along with the BBC Trust, because the question must always be that this is the use of public money, and the use of public money must be focused on the core public purposes and the distinctiveness and the distinctive contribution that the BBC makes in the context of a wider market.

Overtaking this performance gap is the failure to serve all nations and regions equitably: only 59 per cent of people agree that the BBC is good at representing their nation/region in its drama and other entertainment content and in its main UK news content.

The theory that the BBC's privileged funding position creates competition for quality across the sector is certainly plausible and *realisable* and is one of the stronger arguments for ongoing financial intervention on the current model.

Conclusion

At present, the licence fee is still the best way of associating payment with consumption of service. It should be rebranded to represent the right to consume PSB on any platform at any time, and extended to every UK household, regardless of equipment or consumption levels. This model would future proof the association with PSB – not just the BBC – which may not be the sole recipient of PSB funding in future. As the PSB market and the BBC's function within it changes over the next decade, it seems both inevitable and rational that government consider collection of monies to transfer to a household fee, similar to the German model.

The level of the fee should be decided by parliament, with advice from Ofcom, and taking into account evidence from the BBC executive and trust (or whatever governance function may replace it) and the NAO audit. Alternatively, adopting the German model of an independent panel of experts (which periodically examines PSB requirements) and taking its recommendation on appropriate level of funding may be preferable. Survival of the licence fee is not a matter of corporate life or death, as devotees claim, but if we want to change the funding mechanism, the BBC needs to be given a clear flight path to change, with an indicative timescale, coupled with long-term policy commitment to the future size and independence of the BBC.

References

BBC (2014) Written evidence submitted by the BBC [FBB0097] to DCMS select committee inquiry on the future of the BBC. Available online at http://www.parliament.uk/business/committees/committees-a-z/commons-select/culture-media-and-sport-committee/inquiries/parliament-2010/future-of-the-bbc/?type=Written, accessed on 29 June 2015

BBC Trust (2013) *Purpose Remit Survey UK Report: Winter 2012-2013*. Available online at http://downloads.bbc.co.uk/bbctrust/assets/files/pdf/review_report_research/ara201 2_13/prs_reports/uk.pdf, accessed on 29 June 2015

Curran, J. and Seaton, J (1981) *Power without Responsibility: The Press, Broadcasting, and New Media in Britain*. London: Routledge

DCMS (2015) *Select Committee Inquiry on the Future of the BBC*, February. Available online at http://www.parliament.uk/business/committees/committees-a-z/commons-select/culture-media-and-sport-committee/inquiries/parliament-2010/future-of-the-bbc/, accessed on 29 June 2015

Elstein, D. (2014) The licence fee and the question of BBC funding, Mair, J, Tait, R. and Keeble, R. L. (eds) *Is the BBC in Crisis?* Bury St Edmunds: Abramis Publishing pp 274-284

Franklin, B. et al. (ed.) (2005) *Key Concepts in Journalism Studies*, London: Sage Publications

Preston, P. (2014) A licence (fee) to kill? Changing BBC funding needn't be so dramatic, *Guardian* 30 March. Available online at http://www.theguardian.com/media/2014/mar/30/licence-fee-kill-bbc-funding-dramatic-tv, accessed on 29 June 2015

Noonan, C. (2008) *The Production of Religious Broadcasting: The Case of the BBC*. PhD thesis, University of Glasgow, December. Available online at http://theses.gla.ac.uk/614/1/2008noonanphd.pdf, accessed on 29 June 2015

Richards, E. (2014) Oral evidence to culture, media and sport committee: Future of the BBC, HC 315, 2 July Q508

Ross, T. (2013) BBC could lose right to licence fee over 'culture of waste and secrecy', *Telegraph*. 26 October 2013. Available online at http://www.telegraph.co.uk/culture/tvandradio/bbc/10406971/BBC-could-lose-right-to-licence-fee-over-culture-of-waste-and-secrecy-minister-warns.html, accessed on 29 June 2015

Scannell, P. (2002) Public service broadcasting: The history of a concept, Miller, T. (ed.) *Television: Critical Concepts in Media and Cultural Studies*, London: Routledge

Tambini, D. (2014) Funding reform: First agree what the BBC is for, LSE Media Policy Project blog, 27 March. Available online at http://blogs.lse.ac.uk/mediapolicyproject/2014/03/27/funding-reform-first-agree-what-the-bbc-is-for/, accessed on 29 June 2015

Telegraph (2014) Professor Sir Alan Peacock – obituary. 4 August. Available online at http://www.telegraph.co.uk/news/obituaries/11011038/Professor-Sir-Alan-Peacock-obituary.html, accessed on 29 June 2015

Why Abandoning Some or All of the Licence Fee is a No-Brain Solution

Peter Preston, thinking 'outside the box', argues that if an independent corporation is to survive as far as the eye can see into the 21st century, then BBC charges and initiatives offer the best chance of continuing hegemony

Consider what we glibly call 'our' NHS and 'our' BBC. British public life is littered with institutions upholding sacred-cow principles that have a habit of flaking under scrutiny – both before and after elections. One such principle – health treatment free at the point of need – instantly trusses the National Health Service in supposed red lines of compassion. Another, playing tunes of glory along the corridors of Broadcasting House, preserves the licence fee as some kind of national monument. What comes next for BBC financing? Enter a surprise Tory government promising reform and waving a green paper. So it's high time to step back and lump the fee and NHS funding together for a few moments: because honest contextualisation is a sage counsellor in need. Present reality and future reform arrive, as ever, umbilically linked. You have to decide why you are advocating one answer or another, rather than parroting received wisdom. Reality bites.

Health free at the point of need? Unless a rotten tooth is driving you wild. Unless you have to get, and pay for, another prescription fast. Unless the drug you need is too expensive for the Treasury to fund. Unless the GP practice you use is closed on weekends. Unless the A and E you go to instead belongs to a hospital crippled by too many PFI back-payments. Unless mental health provision has run dry. Unless you want to put your car in a hospital park. And, of course, there are many more of these little exceptions. They don't completely destroy the mantra pinned on the wall of NHS HQ: but they do substantially complicate and nuance its delivery, decades-worth of practicalities piled on top of submerged first principles.

So it is too with 'our' broadcasting best. The BBC licence fee began life in 1923 as a 10 shilling impost on radio listening. By 1928, some 2.5 million people were paying it every year. TV and radio licensing came together in 1946. And the rationale, in most people's minds, still seems simple enough. There should be something called public service broadcasting suitably funded, something seemingly balanced and accurate and pure of heart. Its output should not depend on governments signing cheques, on politicians ducking and weaving to get the spin they desire. There's a clear principle here: if you want what the BBC provides, you should pay for it as a user – one definition of a civilised state, one definition of citizenship. A concept called universality.

But now, just as with the NHS, pile practicality and pragmatism on top. The principle did not apply from radio day one in 1923. Fees were collected by the Post Office, and the GPO took a cut. HM Treasury claimed an excise duty slice for over four decades. Today radio, standing alone, is pushed to one side. No television in the house, no need to pay the fee (but a mandatory television licence if you are registered blind comes at half the going rate). A radio in your car? Irrelevant. Over 75? No need to subscribe: the government will do that for you. The World Service used to be paid for by the Foreign Office; now Joe and Jennie Feepayer pick up the tab (and they also, bizarrely, fund the Welsh language programmes on Channel 4). More, plodding down through the devilish details of digital technology, you needed a licence if you recorded directly on your smartphone – but not if you were downloading some later playback service. (Change coming there). What about fees on the Channel Islands and the Isle of Man? More complications; more devilish glitches.

The whole fee business is a morass of confused past and equally confusing present: and it doesn't even keep the corporation clear of commercialism, because around a quarter of the revenue needed to keep the BBC rolling comes from its Worldwide sales arm (with ad breaks et al if your front parlour happens to be overseas).

Enter the age of Whittingdale, raising new fears

All these exceptions, finagles, curlicues, top slicings – ever more confusing, ever more profuse once you begin probing further – make the thought of a simple fee and a simple bargain increasingly ridiculous. Does the licence fee mechanism defend Broadcasting House from government interference? Not at all. The licence fee was frozen in 2010, the bill for the World Service passed intact for licence fee payment after one fraught meeting between Prime Minister Cameron and the then-director general. The once and continuing PM pushed: Mark Thompson swam to the shore. And now, as royal charter renewal begins, George Osborne plays David Cameron and Tony Hall does a Thompson, accepting a £700 million tab for over-75s 'free' licences in a flurry of panicky non-process. John Whittingdale, committee man incarnate, holds sway at the department for culture, media and sport and produces his green prescriptions not just for fees but for whole systems of governance in which secretaries of state appoint new governing figures, new bosses of Ofcom, new alleged guarantors of BBC freedom. BBC independence, secured by charter?

It needs to be said clearly that this is becoming a bad joke. It needs to be registered – nay, absolutely admitted – that this particular licence fee system where politicians hold all the strings, isn't fit for any principled purpose. The fee doesn't guarantee anything much beyond constant stress and occasional humiliation. It is, straightforwardly, a licence to meddle and bully. There must be better answers around.

Cue an uncanny silence. The politicians propose and dispose – pretty forcefully as the relevant select committee chairman becomes a secretary of state. The pundits pontificate. But the BBC itself stands pat. It may, in occasional moments of frankness, admit that the fee regime needs updating ... but not just yet. Even the slightest change – by, for instance, removing the criminal sanctions that can bring viewers to court for recording a show on their smartphones – has long been resisted, lost amid cries of woe. The BBC prefers to set tracker vans patrolling our streets and exacting penalties in a way that some other public sectors (think of the water industry's limitations over turning off taps) can rightly not envisage. The prime cited virtue of the over-75s deal is to guarantee the stability of another charter licence period. Why? Why on earth so much innate conservatism over an approach that Lord Reith himself might find way past its sell-by date?

Yet, in such matters of life and corporate death, the BBC is profoundly conservative. It devoutly believes that the licence fee helps planning and security. It cherishes fee certainty as a foundation of its existence. It wants no change in a world of profound, often frenetic change because change of any sort exposes further areas of vulnerability: to politicians bent on interfering, to rivals bent on undermining, to the pressures of modern digital life where ideas blossom and wilt in an instant. The BBC – even in current straitened circumstances – can hope to bank on £5 billion or so coming through the door every year. Any alternative seems threatening and uncertain. Hang on to nurse...

Print journalists take a look and see their own future online
Yet there is a different reality all around us. It impinges every time a politician on the hustings tries to claim that the NHS can be fully funded without strain (because the basic facts of an ageing populace are clear for all to see). And just the same sort of reality touches every point of the media world today: digital books, digital movies and music streamed into your home, digital news supplementing and then replacing the printed news that used to drop through your letter box. Newspaper journalists, if they lift their eyes from the terminals, are embroiled in the debate already. Can newspapers survive by ads alone? By firm or by porous pay walls? By mixing and matching approaches according to country and audience? By dead forests falling through letter boxes or by smartphone apps? In sum, we are trapped by the immense uncertainty of digital upheaval, looking for a way – any way – to keep the critical mass of news coverage together. And that upheaval, of course, touches every area of the life we know. Can the high street survive in the world of Ocado? Can DVDs survive

in the forests of iTunes and Spotify? Even my local GP's surgery has produced an appointments app that means they can take the phone off the hook. Why is the BBC so hooked on its £145.50 per annum?

Television can't stand still either. Sky is closing in on 20 million TV subscribers across Europe, well over half of them sitting in UK front rooms. Virgin and BT together add millions more. Those subscribers all expect to pay five or six times the licence fee rate over their average viewing year. Subscriptions, in a flurry of offers and packages, are the name of this game. And then, of course, there is Netflix, Amazon Prime and sundry streaming services.

To glimpse the future on that score, perhaps it's best to see America first – and to look at some of the trends afflicting American network TV. Television viewing, on recent counts: some 9 per cent down year on year. Netflix growth: accounting for 43 per cent of that decline. Pay TV: down by 31,000 over a twelve-month period which first saw 241,000 subscribers added. Ad revenue, as committed up front before the season begins and as it unwinds: between 6 per cent and 7 per cent off the 2014 pace. Digital media ad revenue: up 19 per cent on one authoritative estimate and reckoned to finish more or less equal with TV ad revenues at around $67 billion by the end of 2016. 'We're at the tipping point now where the very role of TV in our mix is under consideration,' one marketing chief at Coca-Cola North America declares. Don't think that the marketing kings at Coca-Cola Europe won't be singing the same song before very long.

This is the world British TV will have to live in many years before the next BBC charter expires. This is the world that will destroy any viability for the once and continuing 1923 fee system. This is the new world politicians will need to come to terms with.

The basics of coverage Leveson didn't understand
It won't be easy. When it comes to changing the name of the media game, politicians – and the lawyers who advise them – can seem lamentably off the pace. (Remember Lord Justice Leveson's blank incapacity to grasp that one click of a button brought any viewer in Britain the wealth of Mail Online. Observe the bemused silks who wander outside the law courts of the Strand, wondering how to enforce British privacy law on American web sites). But the first instinct of politicians about to lose their meddling rights is always to press their fingers on to any passing pie. Thus the culture, media and sport select committee's cautious view that the licence fee could be replaced – a dozen or so years' hence – by a riff on the existing German system, which ensures that every German household is charged a set fee for licensing television (whether or not it has one). The political advantages of that are clear enough. It's a more straightforward tax. Politicians will set the rate, patrol the rules, maintain their veiled pressure on BBC windpipes. But treating television in the late 2020s via some kind of blanket levy is offensively non-flexible, especially in an environment of endless

subscription fees summoned at the click of a smartphone. Horse and cart stuff for the space age.

It isn't necessary to invent a precise subscription formula to see that, for the BBC, abandoning some or all of the licence fee is a no-brain solution. Those who want to hang on to nurse are guaranteed worse. Those who shiver at the thought of competition are faint hearts who have little to offer the continuing corporation. If you want an independent BBC to survive as far as the eye can see into the 21st century, then BBC charges and BBC initiatives offer the best chance of continuing BBC hegemony, modestly guaranteed.

For, quite apart from political depredations, look at the programme crunch already afflicting Broadcasting House. The prevailing mantra – Birt updated – still holds that the BBC must offer something that all licence fee payers can enjoy. Universality. But that long ago ceased to be true for sports fans. Live football has more or less vanished (save for cheaper, less prestigious cup matches). Live golf, like live rugby union, only surfaces for a few days a year. Live tennis – Wimbledon apart – is virtually confined to pay channels. Live motor racing is a fading memory. Live cricket has gone for good. BBC sport is an empty shell. £5 billion won't stretch far enough to revive it.

And the same frailty, sure enough, is coming to afflict BBC drama when set against the competition of HBO and other drama subscription channels; BBC comedy as Modern Family and the Comedy Central collection pour in; BBC cooking, knitting, gardening and the rest as discrete channels offer a complete service. Of course, live TV still rules after a fashion. Of course, free to air remains comparatively fine value. But the growth of the multi-channel world gathers strength year by year – and the growth of streaming sucks the life out of that competition too. Look at what will be left standing in 2016, as the last of the royal charters expires, and ask what will be sustainable then. That's the question-and-answer session real defenders of the BBC should be starting now.

Is the BBC a pond of calm in a storm of change?
What price, for instance, a core news service (24, regular bulletins, current affairs, Radios 4 and 5) funded by a ring-fenced government grant set in stone that could be expanded – PBS-style – by viewer and listener participation? Add paid-for Sports, Arts, Drama and Entertainment channels on demand (as technology moves) and you could still offer a bargain that leaves Sky trailing. The BBC has its reputation for programme-making, its heritage in the front window, a legacy built over generations. Why on earth suppose that millions upon millions of viewers wouldn't want to pay, as long as the transition was carefully managed? Why on earth refuse to think out of the box? Why blandly assume that you can use the existing fee to trample on non-subsidised rivals all around as website opportunities take centre stage. Why shrink from using the riches you have to deliver a worldwide streaming service? The music industry has had to change radically. The written press is in the throes of change. Television itself is in flux. Why should the BBC stay a stagnant pond of calm amid so much turbulence?

There are many variations and many possible constructions down this road. All of them, properly honed, allow the BBC to exist at the heart of national life, to be the number one operator for news, investigations – and probably much more. None of them ring the curtain down on 92 years of existence. None of them play into the hands of Rupert Murdoch or other demon kings: to the contrary. But, in their various ways, they do draw a line under Britain's creaking public service model of broadcasting. We have reached a stage – if you listen to politicians from every party – where an indexed £145.50 seems more than enough, too much to increase, a flat tax without friends. We have reached a point, as digital expansion roars away, where we need to define the boundaries of BBC operation, to decide whether broadcasting means ringing the globe by broadband. (Remember that the licence fee is only there because the airwaves are theoretically few and precious and in need of Whitehall supervision; remember that the world wide web is infinite.)

No bit of old logic works any longer. No wall of conservatism rests on firm foundations. No politician on the make and on the spin is in any way incommoded by licence fee defences. There needs to be a settlement, a fresh set of boundaries and understandings that can last for a decade or three whilst technology fizzes on. In that sense, licence funding isn't the central challenge here – any more than privatised slices of NHS provision tackle basic dilemmas. In fact, there's an eerie overlap. Just before John Whittingdale unveiled his paper in the House, Jeremy Hunt from Health was making his own statement – and hinting that we'll soon need to find new ways of funding the NHS. Principle, schminciple! We're just talking straws in the wind of change.

Section 4:
Here is the News

Richard Lance Keeble

The BBC doesn't just produce the news – the corporation's journalism is rarely out of the news. As I write (July 2015), the saga over the disastrous handling of the Jimmy Savile scandal rumbles on with Meirion Jones, former producer at *Newsnight*, claiming that he and other journalists who complained about the way the corporation handled the affair were pressured to leave. Pretty serious allegations, then. The BBC responded quickly: 'Meirion Jones has made his views known before and we have always been clear that nobody was forced out of the BBC for exposing the Savile scandal.'[1]

Everyone from the political extreme right to the extreme left has their distinctive slant on BBC news. The tabloids, for obvious commercial reasons, miss no opportunity to bash the Beeb. Academics plough into the controversies with their often richly researched analyses of output. The Noam Chomskyite/Buddhist inspired website, www.medialens.org, maintains an ongoing, radical critique of its output and urge those dissatisfied to complain (always politely, of course) to the programme makers directly. People even take to the streets to voice their concerns over BBC coverage. For instance, in September 2014, hundreds gathered at BBC Scotland's headquarters in Glasgow to protest over the coverage of the referendum.[2] Protesters also took to the streets in Manchester over the reporting of Israel's assault on Gaza.[3]

The aim of this section of *The BBC Today* is to bring some clear-headed analysis and commentary to the debate, drawing on the wide-ranging insights of academics and journalists (with some a combination of both). Ian Carter, a former senior BBC journalist and currently editorial director of a publisher with interests in media across Kent, argues that a 'seismic shift' in the relationship between local media and the corporation is needed to enable commercial organisations to innovate and invest. This, he believes, will help create a strong media culture in the UK which will be able to compete successfully with social and digital media services abroad. While the BBC and regional news publishers are so often portrayed as mortal enemies, Carter calls for closer co-operation:

> ... there are areas that we can broadly define as public service journalism – coverage of courts and councils, of tribunals and inquiries – where we could provide content to the BBC without damaging our own independence or audience. The BBC, in turn, could provide a new revenue stream for us whilst investing in an area that also clearly meets its public service remit. We are ready to talk if the will is really there.

Next, Andrew Whitehead draws on his experience as a former editor of World Service News to argue that the funding of the World Service through the licence fee strengthens the BBC's hand in negotiations about a new charter. He concludes:

> Over the past few years, the World Service has avoided the prospect of death by a thousand cuts by innovation and new investment as well as a pursuit of greater efficiency. ... That success offers the BBC the opportunity of remaining a vital force in international news at a time of retrenchment. The new form of funding for the World Service carries risks, and it remains possible that a smaller BBC will turn in on itself and focus narrowly on a public service remit in the UK. That is not only unlikely, it would also be unwise.

Jean Seaton, the official historian of the BBC, warns that in the parochial debate about the licence fee and charter renewal, driven by narrow commercial interests, policy makers may well lose sight of the crucial national and international role the BBC plays. She compares the corporation to the British Museum: 'its authority and reach, just like that of the BBC's (and one similarly based on a visionary idea) is perfectly fitted to the modern conditions of the world.' 'The generous and wide vison of the role of these great institutions,' she says, 'was not merely a gift: it was pragmatically, economically, politically in our collective self- interest.' But such an understanding of what matters was completely missing from the July 2015 green paper on the BBC's future, Seaton argues.

Aidan White, for 24 years the general secretary of the International Federation of Journalists and currently director of the Ethical Journalist Network, interviews Michelle Stanistreet, general secretary of the National Union of Journalists. She stresses that the NUJ has been calling for a short, sharp inquiry into the future of local news 'which has been beset by cuts and closures, creating a democratic deficit in local communities that warrants proper scrutiny and thought given to innovative solutions'. But, she says, that debate should not be confused with the BBC and its future. 'There's an argument that runs parallel to this that points to an absolutely vital need for the future of the BBC as a public broadcaster to be protected.'

For David Lloyd, the charter renewal process can hopefully provide an essential super-charging to the BBC's current affairs attitude, commitment and purpose. Lloyd, with an impressive track record as a journalist (former head of news and current affairs at Channel 4, for instance) and academic, suggests that BBC Four is perfect for current affairs. Moreover he suggests linking current affairs across both radio and BBC Four. 'Why not commission and construct *The Report* or *File on Four* across both Radio 4 and BBC Four? That would not only settle the argument about in-house production – surely vital for recruitment and training – but also better serve the dedicated current affairs production companies which have been moving into radio over recent years.'

The final two chapters in this section, by academics Justin Lewis and Ivor Gaber, both examine (though in very different ways) the seemingly never-ending allegations by the tabloids and right that the BBC news is biased against the Tories – being in the hands of liberal lefties. Lewis concludes from detailed quantitative studies of the 2015 general election coverage on television in general (and not just the BBC) by researchers at Loughborough and Cardiff universities that broadcasters – especially in the final week – went with a Conservative rather than a Labour agenda. Gaber cleverly suggests Ofcom and the BBC Trust mount a joint inquiry into the allegations of left-wing bias at the Beeb. Will that help resolve matters? Hardly. Indeed, one is tempted to say that whatever the inquiry decides, this particular debate will run and run…

Notes

[1] http://www.theguardian.com/media/2015/jul/29/bbc-savile-expose-newsnight-meirion-jones, accessed on 30 July 2015

[2] http://www.bbc.co.uk/news/uk-scotland-29196912, accessed on 30 July 2015

[3] http://www.bbc.co.uk/news/uk-england-manchester-28278951, accessed on 30 July 2015

The BBC and the Regional Press: Time for a New Approach

Ian Carter argues that a 'seismic shift' in the relationship between local media and the corporation is needed that enables commercial organisations to innovate and invest – and creates a strong media culture in the UK which would compete successfully with social and digital media services from abroad

Buried deep within the BBC's labyrinth network of websites lie the six founding principles which guide the workings of the world's oldest and largest broadcaster. At their heart is one simple word – trust. Trusted to be impartial, to be honest and to enrich people's lives. Those guiding principles echo closely those of the KM Media Group (of which I am editorial director), which can trace its roots back even further into the past than the birth of British broadcasting.

The wording may have changed over the years, but our ethos has remained the same – we want to entertain, we want to inform and, above all, we want to make Kent a better place for the people who choose to live and work here. Key to that is retaining the trust of our audience to cut through the deafening noise of today's media landscape to report honestly, independently and accurately on what matters to them.

Our two organisations may differ in scale, but our *raison d'être* is so close as to be interchangeable. Is it not ironic, then, that the BBC and regional news publishers are so often portrayed as mortal enemies? And as the world of regional journalism slowly finds its feet again after a decade of almost unimaginable change, is it not time for an equally seismic shift in the relationship between publishers and the corporation?

Traditional boundaries torn down
In the past, the differences between the two were largely confined to the BBC's habit of plundering local newspapers to provide uncredited inspiration for its regional television and radio bulletins. It was a scenario that would irritate our journalists but, ultimately, make little real difference to our business. By the time

the BBC versions of our stories had made it to air, our papers had long been purchased and digested. But the convergence of journalism and increasing platform-neutrality means the traditional boundaries have been torn down.

Whilst our newspapers remain a fundamental part of our business, we now serve our content across IPTV, radio, the web and social media. That is why the suggestion by the BBC Trust in 2013 that the corporation should invest further in its local websites met such fierce opposition from the publishing industry. And it is why we believe it is now so vital that this symbiotic relationship is now forged between us.

Key to that will be finding a scenario that allows the BBC to meet its public service remit without inflicting damage on traditional commercial publishers. As an industry we are probably guilty of creating a perception that we blame the BBC above all others for the challenges we face; we do not. It is not the fault of the BBC that Google, Facebook and Twitter – despite not having offices or staff in Kent – came out of nowhere a decade ago to become swiftly our biggest competitors.

We are now so hooked on the audience the social media behemoths drive to our websites that we hand over our most precious commodity – our content – for free whilst continuing to protest at the BBC drawing inspiration from those self-same stories.

The skewed logic of the situation struck home whilst I was idly looking at the Facebook page of one of the KM's paid-for newspapers, the *Sheerness Times Guardian*, in the early summer of 2015. The *Times Guardian* serves what is classic local publisher territory – a community literally separated from the mainland and where outsiders remain outsiders until they have lived on the island for decades.

It is the kind of community a Silicon Valley software company traditionally could never have penetrated, yet here we are willingly handing it the best of our reporters' stories every day to provide them with just such a foothold. It was one such story involving the latest controversy over the Sheppey Crossing that sparked a fierce debate in the readers' comments. One leapt out at me: 'Isn't it great now that we've got Facebook? Who needs the *Times Guardian* any more to find out what's going on?' There it was in blue and black – a Sheppey resident reading and commenting on a story uncovered, written and posted by a *Times Guardian* journalist whilst completely overlooking the central role that reporter had played in bringing it to their attention.

You can apply the same scenario to the social media network of your choice as people land on our KentOnline website from a tweet or Google link and leave again as soon as they have snacked on their chosen story, without pausing to consider who prepared it for them. And we continue to partake in this unholy marriage in the full knowledge that an unannounced tweak to the Google algorithm here or the introduction of a Facebook Instant Article there has the potential to cause further massive disruption to our business.

When local authorities masquerade as publishers

Just as worrying are those bodies – such as police and public authorities – who are rapidly recruiting journalists from established publishers on salaries the commercial sector simply cannot afford to pay. You will not have to look hard to find your local force or council masquerading as a publisher, pumping out breaking news across social media, the web and in their own publications. Inevitably, you will have to search a lot longer to find anything resembling a probing question or criticism. Compare this to our relationship with the BBC and you soon question whether the corporation should be the main target of our protests or whether we should, in fact, be working together for the greater good.

It is not just our guiding principles that we share with the BBC; we have none of the blurred lines of the social media giants. Our principles, our tax payments and our revenue streams are transparent. But if a symbiotic relationship is ever to become more than a phrase we must first tackle our differences and divisions.

Is the uncredited story poaching – which even now the BBC is loathe to accept takes place – really a sign of deep-rooted antipathy towards local media from within the corporation? Maybe, but in truth it is more likely to be simply a case of journalistic pride. No reporter, whether working for the *News at 10* or a hyperlocal blog, likes to admit they are following up somebody else's story.

Far better for their ego to make passing reference to the story first appearing in an unnamed 'local paper' or to make no reference to the source at all. Illogically, however, the same BBC reporters are only too eager to namecheck Facebook and Twitter when referring to stories that originated on those platforms. How strange it would sound to hear them talking about 'a social media network' when discussing the latest Twitterstorm, yet really what is the difference?

Our protests may seem trivial but we believe they form part of a wider issue. This continued lifting of our content, coupled with the ongoing reluctance to mention even the name of our titles on air, perpetuates the notion that all news is free. Instinctively, we do not believe people automatically make the connection between the BBC's news – certainly online – and the licence fee.

Importance of BBC attributing stories to their source

Attributing stories to their source would, at the least, remind people this content is originating from real journalists in the regions – and if that journalism did not exist there would be little of value left to curate or share. We believe the BBC has a leading role to play in educating people about how vital a thriving, independent press is for democracy, but it will require a huge shift in mindset. Does this will really exist?

A similar suggestion hangs over the second issue we need to overcome before we can hope to move forward. It is the same word we used at the start of this chapter – trust. In the background of every conversation between commercial publishers and the BBC lies an unhelpful but unmistakable air of suspicion.

Suspicion that we are being used as a pawn ahead of charter renewal; suspicion that the warm words will drop away once funding is agreed for a further decade.

This mistrust came to the fore once again in January 2015, months after a working party featuring leading figures from both the BBC and regional press was established to examine ways to strengthen our relationship. The origins of that working party could be traced, in part, to the KM boardroom at the *Medway Messenger* office in Strood in April 2014 where James Harding, the BBC's director of news, met with Geraldine Allinson, chairman of the KM Group.

Harding had arrived in Medway following an invite from the *KM* to look at our multimedia newsroom operation, which has one team generating content for print, digital, radio and TV. But as the conversation developed, his interest was clearly piqued by the suggestion that the BBC could commission some areas of content from regional publishers in the same way it commissions programming from independent production companies.

It was a suggestion that shortly found its way into Harding's introductory speech as he launched a conference ambitiously titled 'The revival of local journalism' at the BBC's northern headquarters in Salford. That same speech announced the formation of the working party to be chaired by David Holdsworth, the BBC's controller of the English regions.

This subsequent gathering of the clans saw slow, tentative progress being made via a series of meetings at the BBC's Mailbox site in Birmingham – progress that was abruptly halted by the February publication of the BBC's *Future of News* report, commissioned by the self-same Harding. The report did not hold back in its criticism of the perceived failings of the regional press. It named names, bemoaning the lack of local press 'news boots' covering a major hospital scandal in Scarborough, and it seemingly set the scene for an appeal for greater investment in BBC regional journalism as part of charter renewal.

How the *Future of News* report opened old wounds

The report was seen a huge slap in the face by all those who had dedicated their time to attempting to forge a new way forward, and placed another huge question mark over how serious the BBC was about working more closely with us. A new relationship requires a new way of thinking, and the *Future of News* report served only to open the old wounds.

With such mixed messages coming from the very top of the organisation, what hope of genuine progress really exists? Yet hope we must if we are to move forward. We can only reiterate that we are not anti-BBC and do not share the ideological objections to its funding that others clearly do.

The BBC was created to provide unique content and, in our view, it should continue to do that in areas where commercial companies cannot make a business case for doing so. However, when it does occupy such a space it should be closely monitored to make sure said space evolves to enable commercial activity to come in behind it, not just sit there in perpetuity without the need to change and adapt.

To illustrate that point, you need look no further than the UK radio industry where the combined BBC output has an audience share of 54 per cent on an annual content cost base of £480 million. That represents a 12 per cent audience lead on commercial radio – but those 340 commercial stations spend only £75 million on their radio content.

With BBC expenditure so far above the commercial market model, this can only be crushing the potential for investment and innovation in the commercial sector. We do not know the figures for the BBC's online publishing, but we suspect it would be fair to assume similar disparity may be found. We fear the BBC appears to be continuing to stake its claims with no regard to the needs and abilities of commercial organisations in this new media landscape; consequently, the BBC and the local media persist in fighting over territory and letting all the 'new era' digital and social media outfits clean up.

KM Group believes a new relationship between local media and the BBC that gives clear space and enables commercial organisations to innovate and invest would create a strong, sustainable media culture in the UK which would not only compete with social and digital media services from abroad but would also help develop more exportable services at a national and international level.

No one-size-fits-all answer
On a practical level, how would this relationship work? First, we have to make it clear that there is no one-size-fits-all answer, even within the publishing industry. Ashley Highfield, chief executive of Johnston Press (JP), has been vocal in his demands for the BBC to share its content across the board. 'Plant your content offerings on our lawns,' he urged. (Or, less prosaically: 'Give us your stories so we can put them on our websites and in our newspapers.') There is no doubting the former BBC executive's logic. The BBC has content; his company has engaged local audiences hungry for it. Spreading this material across JP's portfolio to reach potentially an even bigger audience helps JP fill its products and the BBC to meet its public service remit.

So would that model work for KM Media Group? Probably not. We have continued to invest in the 'news boots' that James Harding highlighted in the *Future of News* report. We cover courts, we cover councils, we cover Kent in a way nobody else does – including the BBC. Being blunt, the BBC has little original content that would necessarily benefit our titles, whatever the platform. Indeed, under the Highfield model, we could see our own content plundered by the BBC who would then share that content with our commercial rivals – a veritable double whammy.

Of far more interest to us is the model Harding seemed to have a genuine interest in – that of being a provider of news to the BBC on a commissioning basis. There are, of course, areas we would not wish to collaborate. Our reporters are passionate, they are competitive and we would never want to dull that edge.

But equally there are areas that we can broadly define as public service journalism – coverage of courts and councils, of tribunals and inquiries – where we could provide content to the BBC without damaging our own independence or audience. The BBC, in turn, could provide a new revenue stream for us whilst investing in an area that also clearly meets its public service remit. We are ready to talk if the will is really there.

We are also interested in how the BBC can help amplify our own content and profile. We have noted with interest the trials in the north of England where BBC websites take a daily feed of stories from regional publishers and publish them on their own digital platforms – but crucially with prominent branding and links back to the source. Again, we will be a willing partner once this rollout makes its way down the country to our corner of the south east.

And, finally, we will continue to urge the BBC to help educate its audience about the value the regional press adds to people's lives and to democracy itself. We are wary of accusations of being thin-skinned by complaining of the BBC putting a negative spin on its output. However, is it really our imagination or are its journalists quick to jump on 'bad news' stories of circulation declines or title closures and far slower to celebrate success?

We believe the BBC should be set the task of working alongside us and help to re-educate people so they understand that news and timely information may be easy to come by at the moment but it isn't free and cannot be free into the future.

Does the World Service Have a Future?

Andrew Whitehead argues that the funding of the World Service through the licence fee strengthens the BBC's hand in negotiations about a new charter

'We all have to decide what we want to do with the World Service, whether it wants a strategy for growth or managed marginalisation' (Harding, 2015). This was James Harding, the director of BBC News, speaking at the launch of his *Future of News* report in January 2015. When editors declare that part of their empire faces a choice between expansion or decay, they are, of course, not advocating the second option. But the stark manner in which the issue was raised – what do we do with the World Service? – chimes with a debate pursued quietly and fitfully within the BBC in recent years. When the corporation faces such acute funding challenges, and is seen as behind the curve in embracing new platforms, what role is there for what is sometimes perceived as a heritage brand remote from its new funder, the licence fee payer?

If the BBC were designing from scratch a range of global services, it would probably not put as much effort and money in a global English language radio service as it would in television and digital offers. And if it broadcast at all in other languages, it may well be in a small number of widely spoken languages where there is both proven demand and a reliable means of delivery. But the BBC is not new in the game. It is in the privileged position of being the best regarded global news broadcaster with a reach and authority built gradually over decades of endeavour. It is currently attracting three-hundred million viewers, listeners and users around the world and has been set – by director general Tony Hall – the task of raising that to half-a-billion by the BBC's centenary in 2022. The World Service – in English and almost thirty other languages – has increased its audience as its budget has fallen; it offers direct benefit to those paying the licence fee; and it provides a considerable reputational advantage to the BBC, at home as well as abroad. Although it is still sometimes regarded in the UK as fusty, its success with audiences is built on vitality, innovation and a level of digital engagement which could usefully be a model for other parts of the BBC.

What is the World Service?

One of the difficulties in discussing the World Service is deciding what it is. The BBC has not always been kind to itself in naming its component parts. The World Service Group, a fairly recent rebranding within BBC News, stretches well beyond what most, within the BBC and beyond, would understand by that name. By the World Service, we mean those international-facing sections of the BBC that were funded principally by a Foreign Office grant-in-aid until April 2014 when they came under the licence fee: the English World Service, a 24-hour radio network which is also increasingly a content provider for digital as well as audio platforms; and the language services, which now have as big a total reach on television and the internet as on radio. That does not stretch, for the purposes of this chapter at least, to encompass other vibrant and successful components of the World Service Group which have a different funding basis or history: BBC World News television which reaches 85 million viewers around the world and the bbc.com website with 32 million reach outside the UK are largely commercially-funded; BBC Media Action, an ambitious global development communications charity, is supported by donors, governmental and otherwise; BBC Monitoring, based at Caversham near Reading, was funded mainly by the Cabinet Office until 2013, and now sits, a touch awkwardly, under the licence fee.

The transfer of funding responsibility from the Foreign Office to the licence fee was preceded by a reduction of about a quarter in the World Service budget. Those cuts entailed the closure of several language services as well as of transmitters and frequencies. The unceremonious dumping of the World Service on the licence fee produced an undertow of resentment elsewhere in the BBC, faced with the prospect of cuts to accommodate services the Foreign Office no longer wished to support. That anxiety was mirrored within the World Service. Veterans of Bush House, habitually anxious that change portends 'the end', feared that period dramas and all sorts of other fluffy populist programming would filch money meant for the less glamorous international networks. That latter concern has not been borne out. The BBC has lived up to its public commitment to inject additional money into the World Service – though that does not mean that global services will, or should, be immune from the need to achieve further savings.

If the Foreign Office was still the funder, the World Service would certainly have faced, and be facing, cuts much deeper than it has so far endured. And simply on the grounds of convincing our audiences and partners of our editorial independence, the rock on which the BBC's worldwide reputation stands, being funded in the same way as much of the rest of BBC News feels a lot more comfortable than receiving a grant direct from government.

All this coincided with the move out of the World Service's Bush House, a building so resolutely unmodern that it really was an example of managed decline. However much the World Service loved Bush House and the cosmopolitan culture it nourished over seventy years, being at a distance from Broadcasting House and Television Centre created formidable barriers to binding with the broader BBC. The move to the lavishly expanded Broadcasting House, where World Service teams are co-located with the rest of BBC News, has proved to be a blessing. Language services, in particular, have been able to shape and inform the wider BBC's coverage of the world much more actively when they attend the same morning editorial meetings and are just a few minutes, not a few miles, away. And co-location has made the necessary search for synergies and savings easier to achieve.

The 'soft power' argument

The funding change has required a recalibration of the case for public money to fund services which are directed largely to audiences outside the UK. The most difficult argument for the World Service is the one James Harding turned to first when launching his *Future of News* report – that it is 'an ambassador of Britain's values and an agent of soft power in the world' (Harding 2015). The roots of the World Service rest with Britain's imperial ambitions. It began as the BBC Empire Service in 1932 – at a time when, in much of that empire, Britain's power was anything but soft. The big expansion in the number of language services came during the Second World War, and many found renewed purpose during the Cold War.

The reinventing of the World Service, from adjunct of British foreign and war policy to an independent, impartial and trusted provider of news, is a story that has not been fully told or appreciated. The argument that respect for and the reach of the BBC World Service brings benefit to Britain is unexceptional and politically valuable – and it is reinforced by concern that China and Russia are now spending far more on their global channels than the BBC (CMSC 2014). If that extends to presenting the primary purpose of the World Service as exercising soft power for Britain, as an informal aspect of British diplomacy, then a line has been crossed. The main purpose of the World Service is to meet a demonstrable need for impartial, authoritative and engaging news of what's happening around the world. If that is diluted, even if simply to help make a case in Westminster and Whitehall, there is a risk of damaging the trust which is the basis of the service's reputation and reach.

It's the audience size, stupid

The more compelling case for the World Service is its continued success in attracting audiences. Across the world, one in every sixteen adults uses the BBC. Two-thirds of that global reach comes from the World Service. It's what makes the BBC a global rather than a parochial broadcaster and gatherer of news and what sustains the BBC as a universal brand.

The English World Service is by far the BBC's biggest radio network. According to the 2015 Global Audience Measure (GAM 2015), more than 50 million listeners tune in to its programmes and news bulletins every week.[1] The BBC has been in dread of a precipitate fall in global radio audiences. It has not happened. Indeed, the latest figures indicate an impressive year-on-year increase in audience of almost a quarter. The gradual fall-off in short-wave listening has been more than matched by increasing audiences to FM relays in major cities and by World Service content being carried on hundreds of partner stations which dip in to BBC output for part of the day. Half the total English audience is in Africa. Half of the rest is in the United States, where public radio pays (not a huge sum, but in total several million dollars a year) for the right to rebroadcast flagship programmes such as *Newshour*.

Although only 4 per cent of the audience for the English World Service is in the UK – split roughly equally between those listening on digital audio and in the night hours on Radio 4 frequencies – that still delivers a reach of more than two-million, which is about the same audience size as Radio 3. It's a powerful reaffirmation of the direct value of the World Service to licence fee payers.

The network has devised new, more engaging and informal, formats for news and current affairs, with programmes such as *World Have Your Say* and *Outside Source*. It produces the BBC's most widely accessed news podcasts (the *Global News* podcast has approaching half-a-million downloads a day) and has developed a Facebook community, notably in South Asia, which at one point was expanding by 1 per cent a day and at the time of writing (July 2015) is over the three-million mark.[2] Programmes such as *Trending* and *Witness* are not simply radio productions, but have developed a profile across platforms as well as on other networks. The 2016 audiences figures will, for the first time, reflect the success of the newly-launched *BBC Minute*, a 'bite-sized conversation of what's happening now around the globe' refreshed every half-hour, which has a tone and news agenda aimed particularly at younger listeners to mixed genre radio stations in Africa; it will add several millions to overall reach.[3] A radio service which is sometimes seen as unchanging has had a greater pace of change than any other of the BBC's national radio networks – accompanied by greater audience growth.

World Service 'in a sweet spot'
The reputation of the World Service, and the generally high standing it enjoys with parliamentarians and opinion formers (including those who do not tune-in all that often), is a valuable asset to an embattled BBC and threatened licence fee. Some years ago, a senior member of the BBC's audiences and marketing team, in presenting a survey of parliamentary and political opinion about the BBC and its constituent parts, commented lyrically that the World Service was 'in a sweet spot' while the broader BBC was simply 'in a spot'. That's still the case. John Whittingdale who, as the new culture secretary is regarded in some quarters as 'the scourge of the BBC', presided over a select committee report (CMSC 2014)

which lauded the World Service as 'a reliable, respected foreign and English language news service' with 'an increasingly important role in what is a global information war'. Far from acquiescing in the downsizing of the World Service, the committee's main concern, echoed in the valedictory report on the World Service of the foreign affairs select committee (FAC 2014), was about whether the World Service was sufficiently represented in the governance of the BBC and what that might portend for its distinctiveness and share of overall BBC resources.

That outlook is reflected in the government's green paper on the BBC published in July 2015, which emphasises the need for continuing change in the World Service – but to ensure its continued vitality rather than to squeeze value out of it:

> There is increased competition from other international providers ... and new research suggests that digital news is dominated by a few successful brands with others struggling to reach a wider audience. We want to look at how this important part of the BBC's service can continue to compete with other international providers and remain relevant in a changing global environment. ... Making sure the World Service continues to have the funding it needs will be vital to allow it to continue to deliver value for the UK (DCMS 2015: 56).

The pressure on the World Service's budgets (the green paper puts these at £254 million in 2014-15) is likely to come from inside the BBC as the baronies compete for increasingly tight resources rather than from external pressure to reduce the scope of global news provision.

The funding of the World Service through the licence fee strengthens the BBC's hand in negotiations about a new charter – in the words of the *Economist*, 'while the World Service remains a national treasure, it is also a valuable ransom' (*Economist* 2014). The BBC's case for charter renewal is likely to argue that only a sufficient overall settlement will allow the World Service to thrive and, in particular, to implement some of the recommendations put forward by Sir Howard Stringer, former president and CEO of Sony and a non-executive member of the BBC's executive board, about how to reach the half-billion audience target (Stringer 2014). These include consideration of a service in Amharic for Ethiopia, Africa's second most populous nation, and a platform to reach the people of North Korea. Ambitions to regionalise the BBC's services in Arabic to develop audiences beyond Egypt, and to serve the Baltic states and other of Russia's immediate neighbours, are also likely to be wrapped up in a pan-BBC proposal for the future.

Language services
The BBC's language services have been through more profound change than perhaps any other part of the corporation. Once almost entirely radio services, these now gain as much of their reach through television, online and social

media. Television services in Arabic and Persian, with audiences of 32 million and 14 million respectively, are now the main BBC platforms into the Middle East. While radio remains the primary means of reaching audiences in sub-Saharan Africa, TV news services in Swahili and building on the *Focus on Africa* brand in Englishare starting to attract millions of viewers.

The case for broadcasting in the most widely spoken languages, and in a small number of lifeline languages (Somali is a good example) where the BBC has high standing and can meet profound need, is fairly clear cut. Not all the current range of services fit in one or other category. Alongside the language networks with huge reach, there are eight with audiences of under a million. This is in part a legacy of rancour between the BBC and the Foreign Office over the implementation of public spending cuts. The Foreign Office insisted on retaining a right of veto over the closure of languages services while divesting itself of funding responsibility. This curious anomaly may well get ironed out in the charter negotiations. But the enduring veto limited the BBC's scope for a thorough remodelling of the range of languages in which it broadcasts – and it may well wish to return to this issue once a new charter is in place. That certainly is the message from Howard Stringer, who recommended prioritising languages and services with the greatest potential for growth and ensuring that digital and 'mobile first' strategies punch through.

There's no such impediment to starting up, or reviving, language services – as long as it is done from within existing resources. The fifth 'languages' floor at Broadcasting House is now home to a 'pop-up' bilingual Facebook service for Thailand introduced in the wake of political instability there. And new platforms have been used to address emergencies, among them WhatsApp in response to the Ebola outbreak in West Africa and Viber after the Nepal earthquake in April 2015.

Commercialising the World Service
When the BBC's World News TV network and the global-facing website have shown the way in attracting commercial income, the World Service also needs to explore opportunities for topping-up budgets. Some of the bigger language websites have piloted taking adverts, and the success of Arabic TV is likely to prompt consideration of its commercial potential. There's not so much prospect of further commercial revenues from the English World Service – unless it, too, pilots taking advertising, which would be politically difficult and, given the absence of an established advertising market in international radio, may not be all that lucrative.

The direct value to licence fee payers of the language services is necessarily limited. A web-based service in Chinese is the only offer targeted at a UK audience and accounts for most of the language service total reach of a third-of-a million UK residents. There may be more to be done to reach out to diaspora audiences in languages such as Somali and Bengali. But the language services provide a direct benefit to licence fee payers in another way. Their journalists allow the BBC to maintain comprehensive global cover at a time when resources are tight and the newsgathering footprint of other major western news networks is shrinking. Correspondents brought in to the BBC to work for language services – among them Shaima'a Khalil, Tomi Oladipo, Anne Soy, Nomsa Maseko and Rupa Jha – are increasingly familiar faces and voices to audiences in the UK. This sharpens the BBC's journalism, freshens the range of on-air talent and is a more efficient use of the licence fee. It is one of those examples of crisis being a catalyst to changes which are altogether beneficial.

'Our biggest job is not to screw it up'

Over the past few years, the World Service has avoided the prospect of death by a thousand cuts by innovation and new investment as well as a pursuit of greater efficiency. If you measure success by size of audience, the standard benchmark for broadcasters, it has worked handsomely. That success offers the BBC the opportunity of remaining a vital force in international news at a time of retrenchment. The new form of funding for the World Service carries risks, and it remains possible that a smaller BBC will turn in on itself and focus narrowly on a public service remit in the UK. That is not only unlikely, it would also be unwise. The harm it would inflict on the BBC's global reputation, and so its ability to provide comprehensive news for domestic as well as international audiences, would be immense. As James Harding put it in reflecting on the enormous global goodwill the BBC enjoys, 'the BBC is unique, the most trusted, responsible and reliable news source in the world, and our biggest job in the next ten years is not to screw it up' (Harding 2015).

Notes

[1] I am grateful to Ben Robins in the BBC audiences team for providing me with additional information about these figures

[2] The Global News podcast is at http://www.bbc.co.uk/podcasts/series/globalnews, accessed on 2 May 2015

[3] BBC Minute can be found at http://www.bbc.co.uk/news/world-31151544, accessed on 2 May 2015

References

Culture, media and sport committee of the House of Commons (CMSC) (2014) *Fourth Report: Future of the BBC*, 10 February 2014. Available online at http://www.publications.parliament.uk/pa/cm201415/cmselect/cmcumeds/315/31502.htm, accessed on 3 May 2015

Department for Culture, Media and Sport (DCMS) (2015) *BBC Charter Review Public Consultation* (aka the green paper). Available online at https://www.gov.uk/government/uploads/system/uploads/attachment_data/file/4457 04/BBC_Charter_Review_Consultation_WEB.pdf, accessed on 20 July 2015

Economist (2014) Foreign losses: Sweeping cuts have not killed the BBC World Service but steady neglect might, 29 March. Available online at http://www.economist.com/news/britain/21599833-sweeping-cuts-have-not-killed-bbc-world-service-steady-neglect-might-foreign-losses, accessed on 26 May 2015

Foreign affairs committee of the House of Commons (FAC) (2014) *Ninth Report: The Future of the BBC World Service*, 31 March. Available online at http://www.publications.parliament.uk/pa/cm201314/cmselect/cmfaff/1045/104502. htm, accessed on 3 May 2015

Global Audiences Measure (GAM) (2015) BBC Global Audiences Measure, May. Available online at http://www.bbc.co.uk/mediacentre/latestnews/2015/combined-global-audience, accessed on 21 May 2015

Harding, James (2014) Speech on the future of the BBC World Service to the Public Radio Programme Directors, in Portland, Oregon, USA, September. Available online at http://www.bbc.co.uk/mediacentre/speeches/2014/james-harding-portland, accessed on 2 May 2015

Harding, James (2015) Speech to launch the *Future of News* report, January 2015 http://www.bbc.co.uk/mediacentre/speeches/2015/james-harding-future-of-news, accessed on 2 May 2015

Stringer, Sir Howard (2014) 2022: Towards 500 million. Available online at http://downloads.bbc.co.uk/mediacentre/howard-stringer-report.pdf, accessed on 2 May 2015

The BBC: A National Asset in a Globalised World

In the ~~parochial~~ limited outlook debate about the licence fee and charter renewal, driven by narrow commercial interests, policy makers may well lose sight of the crucial national and international role the BBC plays, Jean Seaton, the official historian of the corporation, warns

Since 1927, the BBC has had the motto 'nation shall speak peace unto nation'. One of the corporation's 'public purposes', helpfully written into its constitution, is 'to bring the UK to the world and the world to the UK'. This is more apposite than ever before. In a world where international and national boundaries are utterly porous, where threats and opportunities leak from one realm to another, this global role – developed over decades, professionally expert and principled – is urgently relevant. International affairs are increasingly shaped by cross-national communities of interest. Non-state actors – from terrorist groups, multinational corporations, even entertainment 'brands' and personalities – are powerful in new ways. They have all been successful at exploiting this new fluidity. After all, Apple is wealthier than some countries.

The BBC's international presence combined with the its national role, at the heart of the corporation, makes the BBC one of the few institutions we have that is fit for purpose in the evolving, interconnected world. We need to be able to understand what is happening abroad, react to it, understand the domestic consequences and manage those as well. In addition, there are the inter-connected problems where unilateral solutions are inadequate. Climate change, the control of epidemics, migration, cyber-crime, have thrown up international interest groups and sometimes – at least around epidemics – novel and remarkable forms of organisation. But all of them require complex cross-border, cross-lateral thinking and solutions. The BBC almost uniquely is the right shape for this new world. Dedicated to the national interest and public service it has the right values for grappling with the problems.

But the challenge is larger and takes a different form from before: so the BBC also has to grow confidently into the new shape of communications. There are emerging movements – who make skilled use of the tools of communication – but for the first time also make their own communities. The old certainties of almost 80 years of communications research – that the media may promote messages but the social structure in which audiences lived would bend and adapt the impact of such messages – have to be re-thought. Online – whether you are an anorexic, a member of the radical social movement Occupy or a potential jihadi – you are both the receiver and producer of messages and, more significantly, part of that community (Bartlett 2014). Online interaction (although still dependent on images and narratives often taken from the media) now wrap individuals in close communities of support. McLuhan (1994 [1964]) was wrong (about almost everything): it is not that the media are the message but that the media can be the society, the community, the network of apparently intimate social relationships that bind messages into identity. Powerful musical tastes and concern with fashion and 'celebrities' are also increasingly important: indeed, 'the culture tribes' – the demography of taste – may be more significant politically than political parties.

The BBC is already organically fitted to this new world – its institutional shape matches it. The corporation understands how music and political movements are related. It has the capacity to explore how people feel about things. The new structure of international and national life is being shaped by communications, not borders – and the BBC is in the business of communicating.

The shape of the new threats

Modern threats are not simple. They come in unexpected ways and are hard to calibrate. If the Cold War took place in an alarming but bipolar world (although one that hardly felt simple at the time), today world threats are multi-faceted and waged at home as well as abroad. In many ways we have sleep-walked into a more dangerous situation because for thirty years since the end of the Cold War we have reorganised ourselves as if the end of history were settled. History is now back with a vengeance. The new shape of world power and its links with our backyard need to be taken seriously.

On the one hand an over-abundance of communication, messages, information, images, swamps consumers. On the other, this has led to a new world of rigid silos. Online plenty encourages tunnel vision: it narrows encounters. Meeting different points of view is harder, not easier. Prejudices are re-emerging: research, for instance, has shown how online life encourages homophobia (Klan 2011). As Chris Westcott, the recently-retired director of BBC Monitoring, commented:

> Navigating this radically transformed landscape presents the BBC with new challenges. The old broadcast model – 'standing on a hill and shouting loudly' – is no longer sufficient. The 'one to many media' is at best now co-existing with – and in some cases being usurped by – a new 'many to many' model where the dominant mode is conversation, or at least everyone

having the same ability to stand shoulder to shoulder on the hill and shout loudly at each other.[1]

Distilling that cacophony – often ill informed, partisan and trivial – is the new BBC challenge. Appropriating a term used by audio engineers, it's about improving the 'signal to noise ratio'.

The new communications world sets the BBC other conundrums. Traditionally the BBC has been 'jammed, banned and kept out' by nation states which have excluded reporting by refusing visas for its journalists, jamming its radio and television signals and banning local media from rebroadcasting the BBC. The corporation could work its way around almost all of these impediments. These gatekeepers are still busy keeping the BBC out. But it faces a new, more intractable foe: the multinational digital technology companies which control what is allowed on to mobile phone screens, or what we see when we search for something or, increasingly, what a computer running an algorithm decides we should see when we are conversing with our friends online. As our smartphone's apps become our 'window on the world', how does the BBC get on to 'the first screen'? This is, of course, just a splinter of a much larger problem: how do public goods find a place in such a monopolised world? But surely the dangers of the commercial tyranny of screens ought to be an urgent issue. Governments ought to be grappling with those issues on behalf of the BBC and us – citizens – not seeking to 'downsize', 'limit' and 'reduce' the scope of the corporation.

Indeed, the BBC again is ideally fitted to break down such barriers (though it is a formidable task). It does many things that are linked: newsgathering and BBC Monitoring bring the world to the UK, where it is shaped for the national citizen. The World Service takes the UK to the world. It is a sinuous and strong system – based on the BBC's editorial independence and with the resources to deliver at every point in the chain. Yet editorial independence and the BBC's size and value are under more attack than for many years, largely from commercial rivals who have understandably no immediate concern with the national interest, and for whom the separation of commercial and editorial interests has become increasingly muddied.

Understanding the world

Thirty years ago the *Express* and the *Mail* as well as *The Times* and the *Telegraph* ran news bureaus all over the world. Fleet Street was full of people like Freddie Wills, the Russian affairs correspondent for the *Daily Mirror*, who was an accomplished translator of Russian poetry. The Foreign Office possessed long-term research departments which had the accumulated capacity to assess and think about foreign affairs. It had more deeply developed language skills across a wider range of languages. But now these sources have been hollowed out. The BBC, consequently, becomes even more precious by running one of the last important world-sized news operations left standing, with bureaus and deeply embedded reporting from the local of everywhere else. If it is working right (and that is, in part, an issue of how the BBC prioritises and understands its own news operation) then this ought to nuance every story we are told and bear down on news agendas in an intelligent way. We need to be alert to and make sense of the world we live in. This is where the BBC reporter comes in: translating the deep engagement with stories back to home audiences, condensing yet elucidating. He or she is a very powerful bridge between cultures.

If the creative culture within the BBC is right, then these views of the world get metabolised in current affairs, dramas, comedy. None exists in a vacuum but are part of a wide-ranging rumination on our condition. So the BBC is important and unique in the comprehension it can bring to international developments. In a world where reporters (and diplomats) increasingly helicopter in for short periods, the long, deep understanding of the mood and movement in international affairs that the corporation's unique investment in world reporting brings is more valuable than ever. Which, incidentally, is why writing, the arts, visual culture, music matter *more* not less (and the loss of *The Strand* on the World Service that told us about international culture, tragic) — they let us into the way the world is reflecting and feeling.

News and current affairs, in the considered interrogation of events, provide signposts to things the nation should take up and notice. They can stretch the agenda of concern allowing citizens, governments and institutions to pick up information that may have been missed. But at their best they concisely, elegantly and clearly package information in ways that make it easy to assimilate. Such expertise in a world where a scarcity of information has been replaced by a bewildering cacophony of sources is *more*, not less, important: focusing attention on things that matter — reliably sourced and interpreted — is urgent. More information swirling about does make it harder to command attention — it does not make it less important to do so.

Making our place in the world

The BBC is also important because it shapes how we are seen. It makes a place for us in the world. It does this in one simple way — often unacknowledged by much press and government commentary — simply by being admired and envied abroad. While there are reservations, criticisms and hopes expressed about the BBC, it is also worth saying this: when you travel to, say, Burma, Pakistan or Afghanistan — all countries with reservations about us as a nation, though with continuing deep ties with us — admiration for the BBC is all too evident. In these countries, reliable information, journalism that is not bought, the corporation's reporting that gives a voice to the less powerful is understandably admired. Even in the vibrant, loud, competitive market place of Indian journalism, there are concerns over threats to journalistic independence. In China, they just want to learn how the BBC does it and replicate it in their national interest — without quite grasping that journalism, like money, is an expression of political values. But who would have thought that the BBC Persian Service would have been as popular in Iran, for example, as it is? The power of the corporation to represent our values successfully is something that enemies and competitors, whether commercial or political, want to emulate.

But in a more complicated way the BBC places us in the world because it listens and talks to it. In 1946, the broadcasting white paper (the precursor to the royal charter) put the case well when the BBC started to broadcast into Soviet-dominated Eastern Europe: 'Other powers intend to use the broadcasting medium to put their point of view ... we cannot afford to let the British viewpoint go by default.'[2] In cutting our language services to Russia in the late 1990s (originally formed out of careful attention 'to build up a large and friendly audience' rather than propaganda) – we lost the ability to say what we mean to ordinary Russians. They, however, have invested significantly in telling the rest of the world what they think – not least in the television channel, Russia Today.

The BBC lets the world talk to the world

However, the BBC also almost uniquely allows the world to talk to the world. In this guise, the BBC is a ringmaster for multilateral discussions, so that Afghans can hear what people in the Middle East are thinking and Poles what Africans are doing. Through the World Service they talk to each other in a straightforward way. This particular capacity is fragile. Every time you cut a language service you destroy unexpected and important cross-cultural exchanges. Indeed, let it not be forgotten that the diasporas that live here do attend to these services: for example, more than 60 per cent of the weekly users of the BBC Urdu service access from outside the subcontinent.[3] Communication works only as a two-way process – listening to them as well as broadcasting to them. If languages are cut, we lose a capacity to create and understand synergies.

So the whole BBC news operation, from home news and analysis to world news and the World Service, is an important part of our understanding and expression of our place in the world. In the new communicative space that is the net the BBC's capacity (in its important user-generated content systems) to *verify* and use reliable information coming in from the world's mobile phones is also a vital part of bringing comprehensible order to the excesses of modern information. The professional verification processes are at the cutting edge of creating reliable information in a world where much can be faked, where sources and images are unstable, where images are highly political. All are buttressed by the extraordinary capacity of BBC Monitoring, which by watching the world's open-sourced communications over time (not just when there is a crisis) provides intelligent, reflective analysis of what the world is saying and seeing.

Winning the 'battle' in people's minds at home and abroad

It is what is in people's minds that is, in the end, decisive in shaping societies. The BBC has the unique experience in attending to the moods of audiences both at home and abroad: precisely because it has to serve them when they need fun as well as when they are anxious – or just doing nothing. That's what programmes do. Above all, the BBC as a public service institution has a duty to stir curiosity. But this is not some vague and do-goody aspiration. After all, the Cold War was won in people's minds.

Trident, tanks and Star Wars defences mattered; as did washing machines and fridges: the economic success of the West in giving ordinary people comforts and a vision of an easier everyday life had an impact. So did blue jeans and pop music – a rebellious and yet glamorous vision of being young was powerfully seductive. But it was how people saw the world – how they judged it and what they felt about it that was decisive. All of the hardware of success needed the software of ideas. The way ordinary people saw the world and the sentiments they felt shifted and undermined the authoritarian regimes they lived under. Soviet propaganda failed, not just because the regimes tottered nor because governments could not deliver to their peoples what they needed or wanted or aspired to, but because the people behind the Iron Curtain quite simply stopped believing much of what their governments said. The BBC World Service and BBC Monitoring played crucial roles in this triumph. Not as propaganda (although they were also that) but because they put Western values of freedom of thought, fair-minded care for others, truthful and if necessary challenging accounts of events, respect for opinions, wit, and a very intense attentiveness to the views and ways of life of the audiences they broadcast into.

Nevertheless, it did not feel simple nor easy then and above all it was taken with utter seriousness. No one doubted that the stakes were high and at times Armageddon was on the cards. It is the lack of seriousness in current thinking about the BBC and the world that is so perturbing. Yet credibility over the longer term can be created by the provision of truthful news and analysis and creative engagement with audiences.

Perhaps, to cheer ourselves up, it is also worth recalling that the initial government response to the emergence of the Cold War 1946 was slow. The UK and America dismally failed to coordinate any response to the aggressive Soviet propaganda, and the creation of a new Soviet empire (Applebaum 2012). It took time to disaggregate the threats, isolate the differences and explore the real nature of the Soviet rule. But finally, what was then known as the external services (now the World Service) – about to be run down after World War Two – were re-engineered into a vitally important part of international thinking and communication. 'The peacetime establishment of a publicly funded, editorially independent, multilingual global broadcast organisation was a leap of faith in the austere context of post-Cold War Britain,' observes Alban Webb in his important history of the World Service, *London Calling* (2014). Webb's work ought to be being poured over by contemporary policy makers: it tells the story of the construction of a magnificently successful tool for promoting people's understanding.

The Cold War was running 'hot' during the 1970s and 1980s when a 'potentially lethal combination of Reaganite rhetoric and Soviet paranoia' made both America and Russia more unstable (Andrew and Gordievsky 1999). Understanding the motivations and intentions of the 'enemy' became critically important. But everyone understood it was also a conflict conducted within the minds of the population. In 1991, after the Russian coup which finally brought the Cold War to an end, Sir Percy Craddock, the chairman of the joint intelligence committee, ordered champagne for his fellow committee members and toasted the intelligence community: 'We *didn't* have a war. We *did* win' (Craddock 1997).

Comprehensive, clear-eyed understanding was the most important weapon in the prosecution of that war. Peter Hennessy quotes a former senior mandarin observing that the 'key to all of the indicators is to a) notice any change, and b) assess its significance. Any change is bad news' (Hennessy 2002). We need such indicators even more in the perplexing 21st century.

Indeed, we only understand other places and countries if we consistently observe them – even when apparently nothing much is going on. This is true of BBC Monitoring: in a larger way it is true of news more generally. News is the unexpected, but when done well reporting understands the meaning of shifts. While you can parachute journalists into countries during crises it is harder to air-lift deep understanding out of them.

The importance of preserving the national asset

The BBC's international engagements are clearly of immense value to licence fee payers because they directly benefit from the enhanced service they receive from the BBC. In addition, as citizens they benefit from the less direct advantages the BBC's role in the world gives them. Indeed, the BBC World Service and BBC Monitoring are assets to the nation whose previous editorial independence was allied to a separate stream of funding. The worry is that, in the approach to BBC charter renewal, its international activities are undervalued. After all, the governance of the BBC had to be redrafted following the 2010 licence fee settlement because when the trust had been set up to replace the governors the role of an international trustee with responsibility for, and understanding of the BBC's international role, was abolished. How will the new proposals for internal governance reflect proper care for the BBC as both a national and international service? Don't we need a separate and powerful voice to protect this?

The worry is that in the parochial debate about the licence fee and charter renewal, driven by narrow commercial interests, policy makers lose sight of the crucial national and international role the BBC plays – and the enhanced role it could play. On the other hand it might be all too easy to 'ring fence' World Service funding within the BBC[4] in a way that damaged the capacity of the corporation to make its own decisions. The funding both of the World Service and Monitoring needs proper, separate attention. Yet the BBC sits on the fault line of the modern world: where fun, celebrity, power, news, understanding, information and ideas are nationally and internationally the most valuable commodity. It is that which makes it so important in the contemporary re-shaping of the world.

In 1753, the British Museum was founded as the world's first 'universal museum'. It was to be a national institution dedicated to the enlightenment of the public and, as such, was owned by neither monarch nor Church. It was to be open to all free of charge and was dedicated right from the start to British history and culture but above all that of the entire world. The British Museum, like the BBC, had a global reach but was based firmly here. Quite miraculously, it is, in the 21st century, one of the most successful museums in the world: its authority and reach, just like that of the BBC's (and one similarly based on a visionary idea) is perfectly fitted to the modern conditions of the world. The generous and wide vision of the role of these great institutions was not merely a gift: it was pragmatically, economically, politically in our collective self-interest. Such an understanding of what matters is completely missing from the July 2015 green paper on the BBC's future. We may be sleep-walking into losing what we need in a hostile world. These great, successful, British institutions are global leaders. But will we look after them properly?

- This chapter has been informed by the workshops conducted for an AHRC network grant on *The History of BBC Monitoring 1939-1980*, run by a collaboration between the Imperial War Museum, Sussex University, King's College, Reading University, and Westminster University.

Notes
[1] Interview with Chris Westcott, June 2015

[2] Broadcasting Policy, CMND, London HMSO July 1946, para 58

[3] Pakistan Connection Diasporas. Available online at http://www.open.ac.uk/researchprojects/diasporas/files/diasporas/Pakistan-Connection-Audience-Research.pdf, accessed on 30 June 2015

[4] Private interview

References

Andrew, Christopher and Gordievsky, Oleg (1999) *Comrade Kryuchkov's Instructions: Top Secret Files on KGB 1975-1985*, Stanford, Stanford University Press

Applebaum, Anne (2012) *Iron Curtain: The Crushing of Eastern Europe 1944-56*, London: Allen Lane

Bartlett, James (2015) *The Dark Net*, London: Fourth Estate

Craddock, Percy (1997) *In Pursuit of British Interests*, London: Little Brown

Hennessy, Peter (2002) *The Secret State: Whitehall and the Cold War*, London, Penguin

Klan, Edward (2011) Homophobic and sexist yet uncontested: Examining football fan postings on internet message boards, *Journal of Homosexuality*, Vol 58, No. 5 pp 680-699

McLuhan, Marshall (1994 [1964]) *Understanding Media: The Extensions of Man*, Cambridge, Massachusetts: MIT Press

Webb, Alban (2014) *London Calling: Britain, the BBC World Service and the Cold War*, London: Bloomsbury

The Inside Story: Workers in the Crosshairs of the Struggle to Save the BBC

Michelle Stanistreet, general secretary of the National Union of Journalists, tells Aidan White that she is confident the public will back unions campaigning in defence of the corporation

From its earliest days, more than 90 years ago, the BBC has been an organisation in crisis. Every few years, in war and peace, it has been called to account; accused of bias and propaganda in its output or wasteful in its management of public money.

Just Google the words 'BBC' and 'bias' and up pops accusation after accusation of corporation prejudice – against Tories, against Labour, against UKIP, against Palestinians, against Israel, against Scottish independence, against Russia, and, for the discerning football fan, against Rangers. Just about everyone jostling for prominence on the news agenda has a complaint to make.

In times of crisis the BBC has been a unifying, comforting voice but over the years it has also been in the crosshairs of politics and government, not least over its coverage of wars, in the Falklands (in 1982), Iraq (in 1991 and again in 2003) and the long-running conflict in Northern Ireland. But it has enjoyed tremendous public support thanks to its attachment to the ethos of public service, which has always been its greatest strength, and it has survived.

That may be about to change. The election of a new Conservative government in 2015 with its sights firmly set on cutting public spending and the upcoming review and negotiations over its royal charter and the future of its licence fee may signal the biggest threat yet to what Michelle Stanistreet, general secretary of the National Union of Journalists (NUJ), says is a genuine 'national treasure'.

Over the years the BBC has been forced, time and again, to justify its right to exist. It has had to argue and reargue the case for public service values above market principles and most of the time it has done so with widespread public support. But treasure or not, the ground is shifting. In the wake of a 21st century revolution in the way people consume information and a Conservative election victory, its enemies both political and commercial, are full of confidence.

They will have been cheered by reports in May 2015 of haemorrhaging support for the BBC licence fee and a dramatic drop in the number of people willing to pay it. More than 1.6 million households now claim they no longer own a television set, a half a million rise in 15 months and equivalent to around 1,000 homes a day (Allegretti 2015). This points to a historical and seismic change that is overwhelming broadcast media not just in Britain, but across the globe. As David Elstein, chairman of the Broadcasting Policy Group and a former broadcasting executive, points out: 'The BBC dares not prosecute someone for owning a phone, laptop or tablet capable of receiving live pictures – it would create the same public relations disaster as a music company pursuing a teenager for downloading music without paying' (cited in ibid).

This is the sort of news to put a spring in the step of the BBC's political critics. Emboldened by the support of newspapers such as the *Daily Telegraph* and the *Daily Mail* and the visceral hatred of the corporation from Rupert Murdoch and his media empire, including Sky Television, they will press ahead with demands to strip the BBC of its perceived privileges – abolition of the licence fee and privatisation of all but a basic framework of its public information services.

Whether they succeed or not will depend to a large extent on the fate of the 70 policy proposals currently on the table in parliament, drafted by the all-party culture, media and sport committee which in February 2015 published its report, *The Future of the BBC*. They propose to replace the licence fee within the next 15 years by a compulsory levy on all households regardless of what they watch and how they watch. It's a model already adopted in Germany and some other countries.

Not surprisingly, there is growing anxiety among the thousands of people who work for the corporation, not to mention the tens of thousands in related creative industries who benefit from its support. After having to bear the impact of lacerating cuts in recent years, they are in no mood for yet more trimming of the budget, but they are likely to be disappointed.

The corporation's income is falling sharply because of changing consumer habits and may fall further with parliamentary plans to decriminalise non-payment of the licence fee, which the BBC has warned could cost the corporation up to £200 million in lost revenue.

The scale of the cash crisis was revealed in July 2015 when DG Tony Hall announced a new round of jobs cuts after a sudden £150 million fall in licence fee income. He said up to 1,000 jobs would be axed through 'streamlining management structures' and some internal reorganisation. But it was expected to save only up to £50 million, considerably less than the hole that has opened up in the corporation's budget. Hall blamed the shortfall on an unexpected increase in the number of households opting out of paying the licence fee, claiming they no longer watched live television. He said more than one million fewer people had a television set than had been predicted in 2011 when the last round of cuts was imposed.

The response from the unions was surprisingly guarded, perhaps shaped by weary recognition that more cuts are inevitable and that this time around it is high-earning bosses further up the BBC food chain who are in the firing line. Indeed, Gerry Morrisey, general secretary of the broadcast union, BECTU, heaved a sigh of relief: 'We welcome the aims and the commitment to cutting the layers of management,' he said. For the journalists, Stanistreet agreed: 'To date, Delivering Quality First, the cost cutting programme which has reduced the news budget by a quarter, has hit journalist jobs and programming. It's taken this deficit for the BBC to move to tackling the management layers that have made many staff feel like it's one BBC for them, and a very different BBC for those running the corporation.'[1]

But while the NUJ and BECTU will aim to make sure that their members, particularly in over-stretched editorial areas, are not affected by the latest cuts, the unions have noted that the programme of cuts announced by Hall only accounts for around a third of the cost savings needed. More pain is on the way.

Unions to campaign on both political and industrial fronts

The unions say they will face down the threat of urgent and radical change, but to be successful they must mobilise unprecedented levels of support on a number of fronts, both political and industrial, but most importantly they will have to tap into reserves of public support to defend the independence of the BBC.

Michelle Stanistreet says the unions will mount a major campaign to 'ring-fence and protect' the corporation. She is confident the public will join in. 'It's critical that we have an outward-facing campaign to save the BBC that links with the public,' she says. 'People do see the BBC as a national treasure, even if most people don't feel happy about paying the licence fee. If you ask them to list the things they like about the BBC – and you can ask anyone in any demographic group – you'll find they all have their favourites. Anyone will give you a list of what they would miss if it went. The fact is that the BBC has breadth beyond public service news and values that touch on all aspects of cultural experience, whether through drama, entertainment and music. It's all part of its uniqueness.'[2]

The battle has already begun. The unions were plunged into a full-scale confrontation after the licence fee settlement in 2010 which was imposed by the coalition government as part of the public spending review. The settlement saw a freeze on the licence fee – an effective real-terms cut in funding – when the BBC Trust meekly accepted demands that all kinds of government expenditure, such as the BBC World Service, be absorbed by the licence fee. It was a capitulation condemned by the culture committee in parliament which says the BBC Trust arguably acted in breach of its duties by caving in to more than £500 million of government-imposed costs without any public consultation. The result was a dramatic shortfall in funding and the imposition of a programme designed to cut corporation spending by up to £800 million.

The corporation announced plans to cut 2,000 jobs over five years, most of them through voluntary redundancy. However, plans for the compulsory sacking of 110 staff led to strikes in February and March 2013 by members of the two main unions, the NUJ and the broadcasting staff union, BECTU. The unions argued, with some conviction, that it was impossible for corporation to deliver the same levels of output with many fewer staff.

When the unions went on strike in 2013 it wasn't just over the jobs crisis. Also on the agenda was an internal crisis over 'shocking levels' of bullying and harassment, set out in a detailed report presented by the NUJ to an internal BBC inquiry. The NUJ accused the management of using its cuts programme as a means to harass staff – making worse an already entrenched problem of bullying. This issue was finally resolved early in 2015 when the BBC reached a ground-breaking agreement to stamp out the problem.

A further confrontation between the two sides took place in September 2014 when journalists voted to strike over plans for a further 415 job cuts, with almost 87 per cent of its members in favour of industrial action. In the end that strike threat was withdrawn after talks with Tony Hall, director general, reached a deal which included:

- a recruitment freeze in the news departments;

- a moratorium on compulsory redundancies across news departments for six months, and

- a commitment by management to devise a strategy on how work can be done – and standards maintained – in the event of redundancies.

So a ceasefire is in place, but with every chance of a return to hostilities if a further freeze or worse emerges from the coming review.

Uncertainty at BBC adds to pressures on work force

For people working in the BBC the uncertainty adds to pressures that are hardly recognised outside the corporation. Indeed, at a time when jobs in journalism are ever-more precarious, the news of people working at one of the world's most prestigious news organisations walking off the job might come as a surprise, but there's a sweet and sour side to work at the BBC.

For some it's a dream job; for others it's a nightmare. In a telling report published by the *Press Gazette* in 2014, a selection of 130 current and former employees gave conflicting opinions. While there were many who praised the work-life balance offered by working at the corporation others described life at the BBC as a 'nightmare', 'bureaucratic', even 'Orwellian' (Turvill 2014). Most cited the benefits of internal training opportunities, high-class facilities and the reputation of the BBC and some 78 per cent of people recommended it as an employer, but poor pay and a lack of opportunities for progression were among those frequently highlighted as negatives. One anonymous employee, who *had* worked at the BBC for ten years and praised its journalism, described it as 'the worst employer I have ever worked for. ... It relies on its name and former reputation to keep salaries down'.

The other-worldly image of bumbling management given in the BBC's own self-deprecating series *W1A* is recognised by many employees, but there's a hard-edged reality of intolerable working hours, a failure to develop staff potential and an arrogance in the executive ranks that smacks of 'the old school tie' with those from Oxbridge or the well-connected occupying senior roles.

Michelle Stanistreet has no illusions about the continuing employment challenges: she says that the union's objective is not just to improve the quality of work inside the BBC, but to secure its future as a public broadcaster. And she is not convinced this is the moment for a major overhaul of the corporation as demanded by many of its critics; nor is it the moment to tie the fate of the BBC into a wider discussion about the future of journalism.

'It would be seductive to think that the argument about the funding of the BBC is an opportunity to open up a broader conversation about public funding of public interest journalism,' she says.

NUJ 'calling for short, sharp inquiry into the future of local news'
She faces such calls from 'stalwarts in the industry' including people in local newspapers, where savage editorial cutbacks and closures in recent years have had a telling impact on employment of journalists and their working conditions. But that's a crisis that requires a different approach.

> It's high time for a real public debate about the future of the industry and how to ensure that the vital role of public interest journalism is protected and enabled to flourish. The NUJ has been calling for a short, sharp inquiry into the future of local news, which has been beset by cuts and closures, creating a democratic deficit in local communities that warrants proper scrutiny and thought given to innovative solutions.

But that debate should not be confused with the BBC and its future. 'There's an argument that runs parallel to this that points to an absolutely vital need for the future of the BBC as a public broadcaster to be protected.' She cites the BBC's role in journalism and its contribution to the cultural life of the community. 'It's the biggest single driver of creative industry. Many independent production companies and industry players – musicians, actors, performers, composers, directors, and writers – all benefit. This support is sometimes ignored in the discussion about the nature of the licence fee itself.'

Criticism of the BBC is often used to cover up the failures of media, particular newspapers, to develop quality content to rival that of the corporation. 'The reality is that they haven't done that,' she says. 'They've used the opening up of new platforms as a way of cutting costs and doing journalism on the cheap. They've had their opportunities but they haven't used them.' Many newspapers are also reticent to admit that they have long-enjoyed their own range of state subsidies, particularly zero-rating for VAT, but that has not deterred them from presiding over a massive reduction of investment in news coverage in recent years. 'I'm all for carrots to be given in the form of some sort of support to be given to local newspapers or new start-ups or different online ventures. But media should be giving something tangible back in the form of a commitment to public interest journalism.'

Who will pay for watchdog journalism in the digital age?

In his book *Free Ride* (2011), Robert Levine highlighted how information and entertainment distributors such as YouTube and the *Huffington Post* become 'parasites' on the media companies that invest substantially in journalists, musicians and actors. Therefore, it is not surprising that some journalists, editors and publishers have lashed out at internet rulers – Facebook, Google, Apple, and Amazon – which exploit media content while using technology to plunder advertising revenues. For years there has been a largely fruitless search for an elusive 'new market model' that might breathe new life into journalism funded by private enterprise, whether it's in the form of the open journalism or behind paywalls. So, who will pay for public interest journalism in the future?

Already much investigative reporting is being paid for by philanthropists and foundations. The Bill and Melinda Gates Foundation, for example, pours millions into media programmes for reporting on health, poverty and health, in parts of the world where the journalists can no longer afford to set foot. The arguments for new forms of public subsidy, whether raised through general taxation or some specific targeted tax on mobile telephones or computers, are becoming more urgent and pressing as the decline of public interest journalism continues.

Stanistreet says this discussion is important, but if new support is needed it will require new structures to ensure that where public money is used to provide media subsidies, there must be broad-based and measurable ways to ensure the public can see they are getting value for money. Even though this debate is important for thousands of NUJ members beyond the confines of New Broadcasting House, she insists that it should not be confused with the discussion over the future of the BBC.

'There are lots of opportunities for the BBC and other types of local news provision to flourish. This isn't about either one thing or the other,' she says. Of immediate concern is the need to strengthen BBC commitment to its public service role and the NUJ is already alert to the dangers of creeping commercialism. The union sharply criticised the corporation over the introduction of product placement for a year-long trial on BBC World News in April 2015. Despite promises that product placement would not appear on news and current affairs programmes, and would be subject to careful internal controls, the union says the decision makes no sense, particularly at a time when the BBC's enemies are circling, and when the priority must be to focus on a new licence fee settlement that guarantees quality journalism and programming (Plunkett 2015).

Rather than looking for ever-more sophisticated ways to commercialise news the unions want the negotiations on the future funding of the BBC to focus on improving the financial position of the BBC. But the corporation is already well down the commercial track. Among the issues to be discussed in the upcoming review will be the proposal from BBC director general Tony Hall to create a commercial production entity within the BBC for retaining an in-house production arm.

Stanistreet says one line in the upcoming negotiations will be to review the new financial responsibilities imposed by the government on the BBC in 2010, for instance taking on financial responsibility for the World Service, which was previously paid for out from Foreign Office funds. She suggests the World Service might in future be paid for from another government pot – the budget of the department for international development. This may be wishful thinking given the government's cost-cutting agenda; however, she is adamant that any plans to freeze the licence fee or to remove it without a properly thought-through review of policy alternatives will cut no ice with unions. It would be suicidal for the BBC and 'render it incapable for delivering its core commitments'.

Call for shake-up of management and administration

Although the previous licence fee settlement took its toll on working conditions and jobs, she says BBC staff see themselves not just in the business of job-protection. 'We've been pushing for radical reform of the BBC,' she says. That includes a shake-up of the management and administration. This is a message that DG Tony Hall responded to, in part, in July 2015 with his announcement of management job cuts and plans for fresh internal reorganisation.

She condemns the 'craven capitulation' by the BBC during the 2010 licence fee discussions. 'There was absolutely no consultation in the last settlement,' she says. 'It was a shabby, behind closed doors deal, in which the last director general capitulated. The journalists felt absolutely betrayed. That must never happen again.' There has been a commitment from management and Tony Hall to have full transparency in any negotiations. He has said there would be no repeat of the 2010. But the BBC is a big beast with lots of seats of power and Stanistreet says there is a question mark over the commitment of bosses to fight to save the BBC.

The greatest threat is the impact of cuts by stealth which, she fears, would diminish quality and make the corporation less relevant and less popular. Stanistreet believes the failures of management and administration will see the dismantling of the BBC Trust. The NUJ and others have consistently argued for reform. They blame the trust for caving in to government pressure, for not protecting journalism and programming, for not putting a cap on executive pay levels and for wasting money, for instance in the high-profile bungling of a £100 million computer project under previous DG Mark Thompson (Swinford 2013).

In an age of austerity and cuts across the corporation, the payment of excessive salaries by a leading public body has led to union accusations that the trust has been guilty of trying to protect the people at the top while getting rid of jobs lower down in the organisation. The culling of 1,000 jobs among the ranks of BBC managers and bosses may have weakened the argument but the unions still demand that BBC governance must be reshaped with a greater involvement of the workforce at top levels of management. The unions are determined to build a campaign to defend their demands for a well-funded, independent public service broadcaster and a charter renewal settlement in 2016 that results in a strong, independent BBC, and they hope to create a broad base of support – including from Conservative lawmakers. But they don't kid themselves that they are in for an easy ride.

Notes

[1] See https://www.nuj.org.uk/news/nuj-response-to-1000-bbc-job-cuts/, accessed on 4 July 2015

[2] Interview with the author, 28 May 2015

References

Allegretti, Audrey (2015) BBC licence fee under threat as 1,000 homes a day stop paying and politicians call for overhaul, *Huffington Post*, 18 May. Available online at http://www.huffingtonpost.co.uk/2015/05/18/bbc-licence-fee-threat_n_7304606.html, accessed on 4 June 2015

Plunkett, John (2015) Government to introduce product placement on world news channel, 16 April, *Guardian*. Available online at http://www.theguardian.com/media/2015/apr/16/bbc-world-news-product-placement, accessed on 4 June 2015

Swinford, Steven (2013) Mark Thompson 'misled Parliament' over bungled £100m tech project, *Daily Telegraph*, 11 June. Available online at http://www.telegraph.co.uk/culture/tvandradio/bbc/10112173/Mark-Thompson-misled-Parliament-over-bungled-100m-tech-project.html, accessed on 4 June 2015

Turvill, William (2014) A poorly managed Orwellian holiday camp? Employer reviews website provides insight into life at the BBC, *Press Gazette*, 21 May. Available online at http://www.pressgazette.co.uk/content/poorly-managed-orwellian-holiday-camp-anonymous-reviews-provide-insight-working-bbc, accessed on 4 June 2015

A Charter for Current Affairs

Charter renewal can deliver an essential super-charging to the BBC's current affairs attitude, commitment and purpose on screen, argues David Lloyd (assisted by Catherine Chapman)

'The best years for the BBC are yet to come.' Thus spake Tony, Lord Hall, on appointment as the corporation's nineteenth director general in 2013.[1] It was a strange statement, one now sadly tinged with irony, even by the standards of a corporately engineered press release, boldly delivered in what are judged to be the gloaming years of public service broadcasting, rendered almost tenebral by a Conservative government now getting into its full, triumphalist, stride.

The poor old Beeb, obliged to shoulder the burden of free pensioners' licence fees by a Treasury negotiating in the manner of a wild west shoot-out, faced with a green paper sceptical – at best – as to its future (for all that George Osborne may choose to describe it, in his July 2015 budget speech, as 'our respected public broadcaster'), and now in the excruciating process of delivering yet further redundancies from its 18,000 payroll. Can the future *really* be better than the present, or the very distinguished past, let alone rival either?[2]

For some while I assumed that Tony Hall's assertion could only be explained by his having seen a secret replacement strategy for *The Archers* on Radio 4, but after further thought I have a suggestion that could match Hall's boast in the midst of an impending charter renewal. And it has to do with the re-discovery of BBC current affairs television. In many ways current affairs is seen as the definition of public service broadcasting: informative, beyond the news, never likely to deliver consistently large ratings and yet, at the same time, a duty of intelligent television, at the core of upholding public service values. This is where, unfortunately, the BBC has failed.

It is no accident that charter renewal should thrust the commissioning and production of current affairs programming to the foreground of negotiation; it could be argued that this genre of documentary was actually *invented* by the BBC, in the Talks department of the 1950s under the legendary Grace Wyndham

Goldie, with others such as Alasdair Milne and Robin Day in attendance. Nor is it accidental that it should be *the* most appropriate call on public money years later – to sustain it consistently, at adequate levels of funding and at a high level of quality, since in today's marketplace, it struggles more than ever for audience and, in most weeks, delivers reputation rather than ratings to any channel. After all, ITV has greatly enhanced its standing and status by being the only channel to have *added* to its current affairs repertoire, with a new weekly strand *Exposure* – albeit scheduled late at night – in recent years (*vide* its Jimmy Savile scoop). If neither this initiative nor the current stasis at Channel 4 in finding new journalistic formats can shame the BBC into action on this front, we have to look to charter renewal to administer the necessary 'prod' to oblige the corporation to respect its roots.

This is not an argument that you will find in any paragraph of the department for culture, media and sport's (DCMS) green paper, since while charter renewal can be the signal to refresh and re-energise a genre of programming that is traditional to British television, politicians, nonetheless, detest it, believing that they, or some other fellow politician, rarely specified, on some unequally unspecified occasion has been worsted (aka 'done over', 'stitched up', 'taken to the cleaners' etc) by it.

How the BBC uses public money

It is, therefore, worth pointing out at the outset that there are two, quite opposing, angles from which to approach the BBC's use of public money: the first, most recently storming the news headlines and verging on the ideological, driven by the Treasury, a function of financial austerity and making good an inadequate tax take, the latter an answer to viewer need and choice and to supplying a creative marketplace satisfactorily.

These two parallel lines may perhaps meet at infinity, but in my opinion, should only converge there, and there is nothing whatsoever punitive in intent in what follows; rather, when the fog of political war settles, it may be possible – outside the headlines – to decide upon the BBC's funding in a clearer, more coherent and transparent manner, and one that can enrich content for the viewer, in Britain and across the world. In that sense, it might even be that the corporation's best days do, indeed, lie ahead of it, as could – and should – be true for its viewers, and listeners.

Imagine, then, a series of discussions between teams led by Tony Hall and John Whittingdale, where the latter not only demonstrates that he is not at the service of Murdoch or other dark powers, but the talisman has to be the proper and most appropriate use of public money in what is now a mature, multi-channel, internet-challenged, commercial marketplace. I put it like that because in the last ten or twenty years, under different governments and successive director generals, it could be argued that public money was needed, and should be deployed to free the BBC to compete in that burgeoning, dynamic, marketplace on level terms.

But consider the consequences, mostly unintended, of throwing public money to compete with rampant commerce, validated in the two most recent charter renewal negotiations; it is the BBC's commissioning culture that has been most insidiously affected, with upwardly mobile managers and execs looking to mimic the market rather than supplement, broaden and refresh it; for factual programming of any kind the commercial broadcasting 'argot' of 'How will it play at 10pm' reigns supreme at New Broadcasting House, or, alternatively, 'Is that imam sexy enough for 9pm?' rather than 'Does he give us a true insight into Shi'ism?'

Programming unhindered by fear of low audience ratings

Allowable and understandable at Channel 4, perhaps, which has to earn its living from advertising income and audience share, but is it really pardonable on the public purse? God knows how many projects of creative distinction founder on the philistine altar of market mimicry, and reduce the distinctive difference of a publicly funded broadcaster, which can alone attempt and deliver programming unhindered by a fear of low audience ratings.

Disastrously, this attitude of commercial competition would seem now to have visited almost every sector of the BBC labyrinth, with the possible exception – admittedly – of local radio. One of its most pernicious outcomes has attracted the attention of the DCMS green paper, which is to be congratulated on homing in on *The Voice* on BBC One; indeed, it would be justified in delivering a more aggressive judgement upon it.[3] On the surface, it may have delivered an audience and employment for Sir Tom Jones, but behind it lies the deployment of the licence fees of a modest-sized town to purchase the franchise of this format from John de Mol's Talpa Media[4] simply in order to block ITV's Saturday night audience ratings. This just cannot be an appropriate use of public money, but BBC management has now travelled so far in its current direction that it seems to prompt no second thoughts. A similar point could be made about *The Apprentice*, another franchise purchase and, indeed, about its interminable spin-offs (*The Apprentice: You're Fired!* – I wish).

But for the avoidance of doubt, given that it is our enjoyment at stake, and despite the hyperbole of the 'red tops', the same argument does not apply to *Strictly Come Dancing*, which stands as a tribute to the BBC's continuing ability to invent and be creative to contemporary effect – in this case, jumping upon the celebrity bandwagon, without any hint of slavish copy-catting, and which takes its place in the distinguished canon of BBC entertainment. The issue is not that the corporation should forsake that entertainment pedigree, but that it should hold to it only for creative, rather than cynically competitive reasons.

However, the effect of this cultural shift goes beyond individual programmes, of whatever genre, to the character of whole television channels. In terms of factual programmes, and current affairs, in particular, the overall effect can be seen most dramatically at BBC Two, which has been hollowed out intellectually by successive controllers – without, it seems, so much as an internal argument, in the belief that the likes of Professor Brian Cox can provide covering fire for the gadarene rush to lifestyle competition formats, and no genre of programming has suffered so grievously as that of current affairs.

In the last decade, the *Money Programme* has been put to a quiet death – hardly appropriate or justifiable, surely, at a time when the markets and financial services reign supreme, and the hedge funds remain unaccountable and unaccounted for, while structural dysfunction in the form of low productivity and investment persist in the British economy, and sovereign bond yields have dominated European politics.

BBC's international current affairs commitment 'hidden under a bushel'

At the same time, the international current affairs commitment has had its journalistic light hidden under a bushel in the form of the *This World* title, lest any viewer – in search of natural history – might take fright at the prospect of some tough content. When last checked out, the slot had been determinedly 'Simon Reeved'. Nice guy, but current affairs?

Eh? Doesn't this bloke understand the changed role for BBC Two? This isn't the 1980s, you know, and we see he does not mention information feature series such as *Coast*. Okay, okay, he once edited the *Money Programme*, but what does he suggest? Bringing back Valerie Singleton? Besides, Robert Peston's BBC Two series on China did a better job, surely, than any weekly, multiple subject financial series. With these major initiatives and *Dragons' Den* we have finance well-covered and watched.

(In the interest of due impartiality, I needed an attributable statement from the BBC press office, but that egregious institution is by all accounts in defensive and uncooperative mode. However, thankfully their arguments, if complacent, are commonplace and can be authentically reproduced as a running Greek chorus to lift, and fully deliver, the dynamic of this debate, straight from the heart of W1A 1AA...)

Should you put my arguments down to the sentimental gurning of an old traditionalist, I call in aid the following statistics from the BBC Trust's 2014 review of current affairs output on BBC One and Two, which confirms that the two channels' current affairs hours fell from 557 in 2010-2011 to 554 in 2012-2013 and just 539 in 2012-2013.[5] An insidious erosion, by any standards.

Since what feels like time immemorial, the BBC has argued that, to justify its income from the licence fee, it has to be seen to be used and enjoyed by an adequate number of viewers and listeners, perhaps even up to 90 per cent of the population, and behind that argument lies its drive for audience share, even when that share bears no immediate relevance to its income.

Twin controllers of BBC's Two and Four have seemed to regard BBC Four as the 'dumping ground' for the historical and the uncontroversial. As a result, BBC Four remains a current affairs-free zone, yet could badly do with a stronger sense of the contemporary; if *Storyville* can bring the channel distinction, as a refugee from BBC Two, why not a refreshed and remodelled *Money Programme*?

In addition, some developments in technology should have changed the whole character of the BBC's attitude to audience share, most notably their own pioneering of on-demand viewing through the iPlayer. However, instead of this being promoted as an opportunity for intelligent viewing of programmes of lasting quality at the viewer's leisure, the BBC has failed to deploy it to widen its programme ecology, rather than consolidate its overnight audience obsession.

But we're not there yet, and people still expect a well-constructed daily programme schedule to enjoy, so for the time being we will expect commissioners to deliver for viewing as live broadcast, particularly with something as topical as current affairs.

I have focused on BBC Two, when discussion of BBC current affairs normally stops at the fortunes of BBC One's *Panorama*, but in the context of charter renewal it is the *range* on offer that alone justifies the use of public money – an extraordinary privilege of which the BBC all too easily loses sight. Indeed, while the retrenchment that has recently occurred in Channel 4's current affairs output is at least understandable as that channel arm-wrestles for audience share, it simply cannot be credited or indulged at the BBC.

Doesn't this guy understand that current affairs just doesn't get watched? It just doesn't rate. It's all we can do to get half an hour of *Panorama* away every Monday night and our audience share only survives because Channel 4 is doing the same.

Needed: The will to deliver

Yet the corporation has the structures and resources to call on to reverse this retrenchment and it only needs the will to deliver, powered by a change in this same culture. It should, by the way, be noted that none of the suggestions that follow involve any additional money to the BBC but seek to reconfirm its proper use by delivering a more appropriate and consistent range of current affairs journalism.

Of course, at this point in argument, comes inevitably, the tricky and tiresome question of what current affairs actually is. Naturally, it includes panel discussions such as *Question Time*, the lunchtime politics chatter brand on BBC Two, the *Daily Politics*, not forgetting *The Agenda* on ITV, but in peak-time weekly series form, current affairs is essentially defined by documentary narrative.

However, it has not helped the BBC that, since John Birt, there has been something of a schism within the corporation as to the role and style of such programming; during his time in charge he declared it to be analytical in purpose, and even required that it be devoted to policy discussion. But whereas the best current affairs documentary may have analytical *effect*, it is surely to misuse the documentary form to debate policy itself rather than drive to a *point* of policy.

Certainly, Channel 4's *Dispatches* could never have launched itself against *Panorama* to any effect on that basis.

Some years on I would settle for the following definition of high-end, documentary current affairs: that is to break original news stories, use fair and objective evidential method to redefine the public interest on any particular topic, and drive to that point of policy, duly impartially. My case rests. Case closed, even? Thank you, kind reader.

But one can understand if a broadcasting newcomer such as the BBC's director of news, James Harding found the broadcasters' distinction between news and current affairs – so foreign to the newspaper ecology – puzzling and hard to grapple with during his early stages in the post; it may explain the lack of action to date in this area while the news division has been buzzing with change. All of which leads one to hope that charter renewal can, indeed, deliver an essential super-charging to the BBC's current affairs attitude, commitment and purpose on screen.

The first resource at the BBC's command is BBC Four itself which, by a near-perfect irony, would seem to brand itself as intelligent television for the over-forties, irrespective of audience ratings. Why, that's *perfect* for current affairs, so what's stopping them? Even in a period of very limited funding, a re-balancing of budgets between the four television channels could surely supplant the endlessly recycled series on the Incas or the Hittites (yes, really, we've now got the *point*) or *Top of the Pops* repeats with the only origination texted updates on long-forgotten bands, with something a little more energetic.

Then there is bi-media (though here I have to declare a quasi-interest, as I never expected this enforced alloy of very separate resources and production disciplines to work, as it so demonstrably has in BBC News). Now the opportunity exists to extend this success to current affairs, and build a similar synergy between the radio current affairs stable and its television channels; why not commission and construct *The Report* or *File on Four* across both Radio 4 and BBC Four? That would not only settle the argument about in-house production – surely vital for recruitment and training – but also better serve the dedicated current affairs independent production companies which have been moving into radio over recent years. Such a bi-media offer would also enhance the BBC's competitive position against the rival Channel 4 *Dispatches* and acknowledge that, led by the work in BBC Radio, creative storytelling structures have come closer together across both media.

(For 'new listeners' it should be pointed out that *The Report* covers the story of the week at some depth and great fleetness of foot, sometimes with real investigative 'bite'; *File on Four* is the stalwart of the stable, more eclectic and analytical. Any TV channel controller professing themselves dedicated to content should be happy to inherit them, but, surely, they are not the only options, and creative journalistic input, brokered with technological advance, can open up limitless new avenues. It only needs the will and a dedicated signal from Danny Cohen, the director of television, and James Harding.)

Disseminating quality journalism via the World Service

These initiatives surely play well to the BBC's ability to disseminate quality journalism beyond these islands through the World Service and even to play its part in – to coin a David Cameron phrase, of 8 May, following the Tory general election victory – 'making Great Britain greater still'.[6]

Why all this obsession with factual programming? That isn't the only outlet for public service broadcasting. What about *Wolf Hall*? Yes, what about drama? Surely *Wolf Hall* was the public service broadcasting success of the year. Or doesn't he read the reviews?

As I started writing this, I was simply bowled over by a production of *Peter Grimes* on BBC Four, mounted on Aldeburgh Beach.[7] Absolutely superb! It went so, so far beyond the path-finding work of Brian Large and John Culshaw to bring Benjamin Britten's great opera to the screen (yes, I was there-ish, in the Sixties, as a very humble trainee).

This *Grimes* was a fundamental testament to public service broadcasting, supported by public funds, beyond ratings' chasing or competition blocking, not obsessed by audience share or by 'how sexy will Alan Oke be?' I can think of no better lodestar to guide these imminent charter renewal negotiations across the most distinctive public service programme genres. Public service broadcasting, properly resourced from public funds, *works*, and we British must never sell this birthright.

So bring on the Whittingdale and Hall show! This is not the Field of the Cloth of Gold, and the DCMS is not the Pas de Calais, but – despite much of the press, from Murdoch to the *Mail* – there is no good reason to believe that these long-overdue, purposive, discussions, if conducted in good faith, need be catastrophic for the BBC, so much as cathartic.

Viewed from Mars, and with the benefit of no little hindsight, I suspect history will judge every governing political party very poorly for how they have dealt with the BBC over recent decades – a uniquely British force for culture, whatever its prevailing institutional flaws. Under New Labour, with John Birt at the helm, its leaders were prompted to think of themselves as global media players, with rewards and status to match. But the privilege of public funding is now their nemesis, with some members of the cabinet shuddering at the mere mention of the public sector. We must hope that charter renewal will be negotiated rationally rather than punitively, and that Tony Hall will take this opportunity to lead the corporation back to its uniquely public service roots, particularly mindful of his own BBC current affairs training. While he entered the BBC as a news trainee, he spent his formative years in current affairs.

Thus, assisted by contemporary technology and editorial, and the infinite 'can-do' of digital, and an enviable World Service reputation, might the BBC's best days truly lie ahead of it. Indeed, this political/media switchback, set in train by Mrs Thatcher's removal of Alasdair Milne as director general in 1987, could make a fascinating piece of TV current affairs, penetrating the inner sanctum of

Whitehall and laying bare the mysteries of successive governments, with many of the leading players and witnesses contributing; I might even think of pitching it, but will it *rate?*

Notes

[1] BBC News (2013) BBC director general Tony Hall 'confident' about future, 2 April. Available online at http://www.bbc.co.uk/news/entertainment-arts-21997492, accessed on 24 July 2015

2 HM Treasury (2015) Chancellor George Osborne's summer budget speech, 8 July. Available online at www.gov.uk/government/speeches/chancellor-george-osbornes-summer-budget-2015-speech, accessed on 12 July 2015

3 Department for culture, media and sport (2015) *BBC Charter Review Public Consultation*, 16 July-8 October. Available online at https://www.gov.uk/government/uploads/system/uploads/attachment_data/file/445704/BBC_Charter_Review_Consultation_WEB.pdf, accessed on 24 July 2015

4 See http://www.bbc.co.uk/pressoffice/pressreleases/stories/2011/06_june/17/voice.shtml

5 BBC Trust (2014) *BBC Trust Review: BBC Network News and Current Affairs*, April. Available online at http://downloads.bbc.co.uk/bbctrust/assets/files/pdf/our_work/news_current_affairs/news_current_affairs.pdf, accessed on 17 July 2015

6 Prime Minister's Office (2015) Election 2015: Prime Minister's speech, 8 May. Available online at https://www.gov.uk/government/speeches/election-2015-prime-ministers-speech, accessed on 1 July 2015

7 BBC Four (2015) *Peter Grimes* on Aldeburgh beach, 24 May. Available online at http://www.bbc.co.uk/programmes/b05x2wfg, accessed 24 May 2015

BBC Bias Revisited: Do the Partisan Press Push Broadcasters to the Right?

[handwritten: a strong supporter of a party]

Justin Lewis reports on new academic research which suggests that, while all the broadcasters favoured the Conservative agenda, the BBC did so more than most

[handwritten: Traditional attitudes toward change]

Bias, balance and bluster

In the first edition of this book, I reviewed evidence that might shed light on accusations of bias at the BBC (Lewis 2014). The data, I suggested, gave very little credence to claims of a leftist bias at the corporation. Rather, research indicated that in recent years there were signs that the BBC may have shifted its centre of gravity from a broadly impartial position towards the adoption of a discernible rightward tilt.

[handwritten: change; treating equally; perceptible]

When the *Independent* ran a story based on the chapter I received a slew of emails: some were thoughtful and considered, others were dismissive and/or abusive. Those who questioned the evidence I presented (a phrase that does not really do justice to the Basil Fawlty-style spleen exhibited by some respondents) were, in most cases, ideologically motivated. This does not mean their views were not sincerely held, but when it comes to the issue of BBC bias it indicates the presence of two parallel universes.

In one of these worlds the idea that the BBC leans to the left is so obvious that little systematic evidence is needed to support it. When evidence is offered, it is usually anecdotal, but it is reinforced by being widely-shared amongst a range of influential groups – including a number of journalists. The main principle informing an assumption of a leftist bias is a plausible one: namely that the BBC, as a public sector organisation, will lean to the left. What is generally left unspoken is the corollary to this sociological premise: that commercial broadcasters, as part of the business world will, just as the UK press do, lean to the right. This would be equally problematic in a sector bound by the same rules of impartiality.

In this world academic research is generally ignored – consigned to remain in the more obscure spaces of academic books and peer-reviewed journals

182

(although I suspect that this might change in the event of independent academic research which *did* demonstrate a leftist bias at the BBC). When research is conducted it is usually small-scale and by vested interests – such as Norman Tebbit's famously selective analysis of Kate Adie's reporting of the US bombing Libya in 1986 (Higgins and Smith 2011).

A number of the BBC Trust's impartiality reviews have been commissioned in response to these claims. So, for example, the 2012 study commissioned by the trust's (then) Conservative chair, Chris Patten, chose to focus on the three topics most often identified by right-wing critics as areas of concern: immigration, religion and the EU. It is worth noting that neither this, nor any of the other BBC Trust commissioned studies, have corroborated such fears. A series of studies have shown that the BBC is *not* 'pro-Palestinian' (Downey et al 2006), 'anti-business' (BBC Trust 2007), 'pro-EU', 'pro-immigration', 'anti-Christian' or by inference, 'pro-Muslim' (Wahl-Jorgensen et al 2012).

This brings us firmly into the space occupied by the other universe – the generally more polite domain of academic research. Most academics have used two kinds of evidence to explore claims about media bias: an analysis of content (both quantitative and qualitative), and a more structural analysis of the pressures that shape news content (such the ability of powerful institutions to set the political agenda). This world is not without controversy, but the broad range of debate is between those who see the BBC as occupying a kind of establishment middle ground (which, in keeping with the class background of most media professionals, tends to be liberal on social issues and more conservative on economics) and those who see most broadcasters favouring the more powerful voices in society – notably in business and government – which tend to lean more to the right than to the left.

Indeed, for many academics, the idea that the BBC occupies a position hailing somewhere from the middle to the right of the establishment has long since been settled. As a consequence, research into bias (outside the BBC Trust studies) has become less fashionable in recent years. This is, in some ways, as problematic as the assumptions made in the other parallel universe. Amidst a slew of anecdotes and accusations – some from powerful vested interests – we need regular, systematic and independent reviews of political impartiality. These should not focus solely on the BBC, but examine broadcasting as a whole, all of which is supposed to be even-handed and which remains by far the most influential news medium in the UK (Ofcom 2014).

The importance of such research was brought into sharper focus after the 2015 general election. Shortly after polling day, we saw reports that senior figures in the Conservative Party were unhappy with the broadcasters' election coverage (in particular, for their refusal to agree fully to David Cameron's terms for the live television debates). This ire was, somewhat predictably, directed mainly at the BBC, with speculation that the Conservatives would take revenge on the corporation by cutting their funding. This threat was made more palpable by the appointment of John Whittingdale – known for his antipathy towards the

BBC – as the secretary of state for culture, media and sport, and carried through, in part, by the first budget, which required the BBC to fund a political commitment to subsidise the licence fee for the over-75s.

Herein lies the gaping flaw in the apparent independence of the BBC. The corporation's reliance on the government of the day to sanction, tamper with or reduce their funding makes them directly susceptible to political pressure. This is a far more serious and – because of their importance as a news source – more consequential form of political intervention than any of the measures proposed by Lord Justice Leveson for the press. The possibility that the BBC may soften its coverage of the Conservative government in order to appease its more hawkish voices increases the need for careful monitoring of broadcast output in the months and years to come.

Impartiality in the era of multi-party politics

Against this highly charged political backdrop, we have a new body of evidence that offers recent insights into political impartiality. Cardiff and Loughborough universities (with well-established track records for independent news monitoring) both conducted separate studies looking at news coverage of the 2015 UK general election. The Cardiff study focused on television news, while the Loughborough team – who regularly monitor UK election coverage – looked at both press and broadcasting. While there are small variations (resulting from the use of different samples and slightly different coding categories), both studies reported very similar sets of findings.

The most obvious – if somewhat crude – test of political bias is the time allocated to political parties to speak. This traditionally means giving the main two parties equal time, although in this multi-party age, there is no clear or systematic basis for allotment of time to other parties. Table 1 (from the Cardiff study) shows that, broadly speaking, the broadcasters afforded Conservatives and Labour similar levels of coverage. Channel 5 is something of an outlier here, their coverage clearly being weighted in favour of the Conservatives and Liberal Democrats and against Labour. The Loughborough research found an even more dramatic bias on Channel 5, with Labour coming a poor third to the Conservatives and the Liberal Democrats (an issue I shall briefly return to). The Loughborough study also shows the stark contrast between broadcast and newspaper coverage, the press clearly favouring the Conservative Party in both volume and tone (Deacon et al 2015).

Table 1: Volume of Party Coverage during the 2015 Election campaign

	BBC	ITV	Channel 4	Channel 5	Sky News
Con	28.3%	28.3%	26.4%	32.9%	25.6%
Lab	27.5%	24.7%	28.3%	24.2%	24.3%
Lib Dems	14.8%	15.4%	18%	23.2%	14.3%
UKIP	6.4%	10.2%	14.7%	8.8%	10.9%
SNP	15.1%	13.8%	5.3%	7.6%	18.3%
Green	2.4%	4.5%	3.3%	0.9%	3.5%
Plaid	2.5%	2.6%	2.1%	0.9%	3.1%
Other	3.0%	0.5%	1.9%	1.5%	/

The differences between the broadcasters' treatment of the other parties is more varied, especially in the amount of time give to the UK Independence Party (UKIP) and the Scottish National Party (SNP). The BBC and Sky gave significantly more coverage to the SNP than UKIP, while Channel 4 favoured UKIP by nearly three to one. Apart from the SNP, the BBC and Channel 5 tended to give the smaller parties less time than the other broadcasters – so, for example, ITV gave the Green Party nearly twice as much coverage as the BBC.

While this is not a glaring breach of impartiality, it shows the lack of any agreed formula for fair representation in a multi-party age. The BBC and Sky, by paying credence to the likely representation in a first-past-the-post system, appear to have been least responsive to the increasingly fragmented nature of UK politics, while Channel 4's coverage is closer to levels of polling support across the UK. No rules are being broken here because there *are* no rules – an absence that it will be increasingly difficult to justify following an election in which UKIP, the Greens, the SNP and the Welsh nationalists, Plaid Cymru, all increased their share of the vote.

Selection and elections: The role of the press in setting a partisan agenda
The volume of coverage given to parties is, of course, a very blunt measure of political impartiality. It takes little account of the style and flavour of the coverage – time given to a party leader on the defensive, for example, is very different to featuring a party leader on the front foot. The Loughborough research was able to categorise the extent to which the parties received positive or negative coverage in the press, where political bias in this election was fairly blatant.

Overall, they found that the press gave the Conservative Party the most positive coverage by some distance, while being remorselessly negative about Labour (and to a lesser extent, the SNP) – a bias that increased when weighted by circulation (Deacon et al 2015). Indeed, a number of newspapers were not so much reporting the campaign as becoming part of it, the major Conservative titles often following Central Office's lead in unison.

Capturing the political flavour of television news – bound by a commitment to impartiality – is much more difficult. For this reason both studies preferred to explore more verifiable indicators to convey a possible slant in style and tone. The most obvious of these is to look at the time given to non-party sources to see if they favour a particular ideological perspective. Table 2 (from the Cardiff study) shows that the two dominant non-party sources were journalists themselves and business leaders. Apart from being somewhat inward-looking, the prominence of journalists *as sources* raises an important question. Given the emphatically one-sided nature of press coverage suggested by Loughborough study, did the widespread use of journalists as commentators mean that the press's biases push broadcasters to the right?

Table 2: Airtime given to non-party sources (excluding citizens) on TV election news

Journalist/media figure	27%
Business	18.3%
Pollster	12.3%
Academic	12.6%
Think tank	10.3%
Other	19.5%

Although these figures do not give us the answer to that question, they are indicative of what is, for me, the most tangible threat to the broadcasters' impartiality: the extent to which a partisan press shape or influence broadcast news.

We saw indications of this earlier in the campaign. A poll indicating that two thirds of leading economists disagreed with the government's austerity measures was ignored by most newspapers and subsequently disregarded by most broadcasters. By contrast, a letter to the *Telegraph* from 103 business leaders supporting the Conservative's handling of the economy became a headline story on a series of broadcast news bulletins.

It would be hard to argue that the *Telegraph* letter was more newsworthy than the poll of economists – especially since the first was fairly unsurprising while the latter called one of the Conservative's main claims about economic competence into question. The difference was that the press made more of it, and this appears to have shaped the judgement of broadcasters.

The presence of business leaders as the second most quoted group during television's coverage of the election emphasises this point. While business leaders tend to lean to the right (indeed, Labour's inability to line up businesses in their corner became a talking point), trade unionists lean to the left. There is an opportunity here for television news to balance one against the other – and yet trade union voices were conspicuous by their absence on television news.

This raises a more general question about agenda-setting. In broad terms, what was the election on television about? This is a particularly important issue for the two main parties, who want to make sure that during the (roughly equal) time they are allotted they are able to talk about the issues they choose to feature in their campaigns, while avoiding those areas where they poll badly.

The broadcasters should remain impartial during this agenda-setting battle. They need to cover the campaigns while remaining focused on the issues that matter to the electorate. The survey company Ipsos Mori regularly asks people what they feel is the most important issue facing Britain. Responses to this question were fairly stable during 2015: going into the election campaign in April, the NHS was at the top of the list of people's concerns (named by 47 per cent), followed by immigration (40 per cent), the economy (40 per cent), education (22 per cent), unemployment (18 per cent) and housing (15 per cent) (Ipsos Mori 2015a).

For the two main parties, the battleground was fairly clear. Surveys showed that the Conservatives had a clear lead on the economy, while most people trusted Labour on the NHS and, to a lesser extent, housing. Predictably, the Conservatives sought to make the election about the economy, while Labour stressed the NHS. Since the polls showed both issues were top on the list of people's concerns, impartiality required the broadcasters to give roughly equal time to both. Table 3 (from the Cardiff study) suggests that *this did not happen*, the economy receiving four times as much coverage overall as the NHS. This was true of all broadcasters, most dramatically on Channel 5, but with the economy/NHS ratio noticeably higher on the BBC than on ITV or Sky.

Table 3: Election news airtime by topic

	BBC	ITV	Ch.4	Ch.5	Sky
Polls/Horse Race	19.5%	19.7%	17.5%	22.1%	5.9%
Campaigning strategies	11.1%	10.1%	12%	21.4%	19.7%
TV leaders' debates	10.9%	16.5%	4.9%	6.1%	19.3%
Economy	12.1%	7.1%	8.8%	17.7%	8.7%
Coalition deals	8.1%	9.2%	8.5%	10.7%	10.1%
Taxation	11.5%	7.6%	3.7%	4.8%	5.4%
Political tensions/clashes	3.1%	4.8%	5.4%	4.8%	6.6%
Immigration	1.2%	3.5%	9.9%	1.7%	1.8%
Housing	2.3%	4.4%	4.5%	2.1%	5.5%
NHS	3.6%	2.9%	1.1%	2.3%	3.1%
Other	16.6%	14.2%	23.7%	6.3%	13.9%

During the later stages of the campaign the Conservatives also pushed hard on the prospect of a SNP-Labour coalition, with the nationalist party (led by Nicola Sturgeon, dubbed 'the most dangerous woman in Britain' by the Conservative press) pulling the strings. They were bolstered by a poll for the *Sun*, published on 22 April, suggesting that up to 8 per cent of the electorate were sufficiently concerned about such a prospect to consider changing their vote. This hardly amounts to a public outcry, and yet Table 3 shows that the broadcasters gave more time to a discussion of coalition deals – with a possible SNP-Labour deal getting the most attention – than most other issues.

If we compare the three main 'Conservative issues' – the economy, taxation and coalition deals – with the two main 'Labour issues' – the NHS and housing, we also find a significant imbalance. This was, once again, most marked on Channel 5 where the ratio of 'Conservative issues' to 'Labour issues' was more than 7 to 1. Channel 5's record on political impartiality rarely receives attention, but this, combined with the unequal airtime given to the main parties, suggests a pattern of coverage favouring the Conservatives, one that merits further investigation. The other outlier here is the BBC, where the ratio was more than 5 to 1 (the other broadcasters were all between 2.8 to 3.6 to 1). So while all the broadcasters favoured the Conservative agenda, the BBC did so more than most.

Table 4 shows that this trend was exacerbated during the crucial final week of the campaign, when the Conservative Party pushed hard on two issues – the economy and fears of an SNP-Labour deal. The broadcasters clearly followed this agenda, these subjects receiving *thirty times* as much airtime as the NHS – even though the NHS, according to Ipsos Mori (2015b), remains at the top of the electorate's list of concerns.

Table 4: Airtime spent by broadcasters on top ten election topics

	Final week	Across the 5 week campaign
Opinion Polls/ Horse Race	22.7	16.0
Political tensions / clashes	3.8	4.7
Campaign strategies	10.9	10.9
Coalition deals	13.4	9.3
TV leaders' debates	12.9	12.1
NHS	0.7	2.7
Taxation	7.6	7.7
Housing	1.4	4.1
Economy / Business	8.1	10.8
Immigration	6.1	5.3
Other	12.4	16.4

In sum, the evidence suggests that broadcasters – especially in the final week – went with a Conservative rather than a Labour agenda. It is difficult to say whether this was instrumental in pushing undecided voters into the Conservative camp, but given the enduring importance of television news as an information source (Ofcom 2014) it seems unlikely to suggest it would have had *no* impact.

The effect of vociferously pro-Conservative press on the electorate has been much debated – and deserves more serious investigation than the generally ill-informed commentary it has received thus far. What recent research *does* appear to show is that regardless of its effect on its readers, newspaper partisanship directly influenced the broadcast news agenda. The question of whether it was the press 'wot won it', extends to its influence not only on its readers but upon the wider media sphere.

Over the coming months, we are likely to see much debate about the impartiality of the BBC. This should be based on evidence rather than who has the loudest voice. We need more independent research and less speculation. But the question raised by the election campaign is fairly clear: do our partisan press have too much influence on our broadcast news? The answer, at the moment, would appear to be 'yes'.

References

BBC Trust (2007) *Report of the Independent Panel for the BBC Trust on Impartiality of BBC Business Coverage*, London. Available online at http://www.bbc.co.uk/bbctrust/news/press_releases/2007/business_impartiality, accessed on 1 June 2015

Deacon, David, Downey, John, Stanyer, James and Wring, Dominic (2015) *News Media Performance in the 2015 General Election Campaign*. Available online at http://www.electionanalysis.uk/uk-election-analysis-2015/section-1-media-reporting/news-media-performance-in-the-2015-general-election-campaign/, accessed on 8 June 2015

Downey, John, Deacon, David, Golding, Peter, Oldfield, B. and Wring, Dominic (2006) *The BBC's Reporting of the Israeli-Palestinian Conflict*. Available online at https://dspace.lboro.ac.uk/dspace-jspui/handle/2134/3158, accessed on 8 June 2015

Higgins, Michael and Smith, Angela (2011) Not one of us: Kate Adie's report of the 1986 Tripoli bombing and its critical aftermath, *Journalism Studies*, Vol. 12, No. 3 pp 344-358

Ipsos Mori (2015a) *All Change at the Top as Concern about the NHS and the Economy Surges Prior to the Election*, 30 April. Available online at https://www.ipsos-mori.com/researchpublications/researcharchive/3566/EconomistIpsos-MORI-April-2015-Issues-Index.aspx, accessed on 8 June 2015

Ipsos Mori (2015b) *Issues Index*, May. Available online at http://www.slideshare.net/IpsosMORI/ipsos-mori-issues-index-may-2015, accessed on 8 June 2015

Lewis, Justin (2014) How the BBC leans to the right, Mair, John, Tait, Richard and Keeble, Richard Lance (eds) *Is the BBC in Crisis?* Bury St Edmunds: Abramis pp 114-120

Ofcom (2014) *News Consumption in the UK*. Available online at http://stakeholders.ofcom.org.uk/binaries/research/tv-research/news/2014/News_Report_2014.pdf, accessed on 8 June 2015

Wahl-Jorgensen, Karin et al. (2013) *BBC Breadth of Opinion Review: Content Analysis*. Available online at http://downloads.bbc.co.uk/bbctrust/assets/files/pdf/our_work/breadth_opinion/content_analysis.pdf, accessed on 8 June 2015

Beeb-Bashing by the Right:
Is it Justified?

Critics of the BBC argue that the real power lies behind the scene, where the left dominates. Or does it? Ivor Gaber ponders the crucial question – and suggests Ofcom and the BBC Trust mount a joint inquiry into the allegations

My entry for the prize for the most unsurprising allegation of the year was the uncannily similar complaints that emanated from a number of Conservative MPs who claimed that the BBC's reporting of the 2015 general election had been overtly pro-Labour (fat lot of good it did them, one might opine).

In this chapter – which is not about BBC bias as such, but about perceptions of bias – I am focusing on the corporation's political coverage (mainly) on television, the medium that the research indicates is still the most used and most trusted source when it comes to political news.

Let me state at the outset that I believe that political journalists need not, indeed should not, be political eunuchs. If you are interested in politics, and one would have thought that that was a basic requirement of working in the area, one is going to have political views. Hence, the fact that some BBC journalists have, or had, left- or right-wing leanings should not be a cause of surprise, nor of concern. In fact, I would argue that if your own political opinions are 'on the record' then it is that much easier for colleagues and, more importantly, the audience to judge whether you are allowing those opinions to influence your output.

Indeed, I worry about those political journalists I know who proudly state they have no political views. I worry because everyone has political views and, if you are not conscious of your own, then how are you going to take them into account when you are reflecting on the fairness, or otherwise, of your own reporting?

The most shining example of someone who has a 'political past' but has developed into one of the most highly-regarded political journalists of our time is the BBC's (now former) political editor Nick Robinson and now *Today* programme presenter. As is well known (I think), many aeons ago Nick Robinson was chairman of the Young Conservatives, a fact that much exercised Alastair Campbell when he was Labour's director of communications.

But, based on my evaluations of Robinson as a former colleague and now as an academic researcher and a viewer, I would argue that his political analysis and commentary has been, indeed are, generally fair and perceptive. So is Robinson an exception, that is a former (or could be current for all I know) Conservative working for the BBC in a leading political role, but doing a decent job of work; or is he more of a norm than people (and the right-wing press in particular) might think?

Well to begin with there's the BBC political journalist who gets the more political air-time than any other – Andrew Neil: he presents or co-presents five hours of television programmes a week including *This Week*, the *Daily Politics* and *Sunday Politics*. Neil is a penetrating interviewer exposing weaknesses in the arguments advanced by politicians of the left, right and centre. Obviously a man of the left, if one were to believe the BBC's critics, except that Neil is a former Murdoch editor, was a researcher for the Conservative Party and is chairman of the Conservative-supporting *Spectator* magazine and stoutly argued his free market views at the Hayek lecture at the right-wing Institute of Economic Affairs in November 2005.

Tories in top positions at the BBC

But the real power, the critics might argue, is behind the scenes, where the left dominates. Or does it? Nick Robinson's former senior producer was Thea Rogers, who left in 2012 to become special advisor to the chancellor of the exchequer, George Osborne. Then there's Robbie Gibb, the excellent editor of all BBC TV's political programmes; he was a vice-chairman of the extreme right-wing Federation of Conservative Students and went on to become chief of staff to the senior Conservative MP Francis Maude before joining the BBC. And we should not overlook that David Cameron replaced his previous press secretary, Andy Coulson, with the then-editor of BBC News, Craig Oliver, and around the same time London's Tory Mayor, Boris Johnson, recruited BBC political correspondent Guto Harri, to head his media team (and when Harri moved on to the Murdoch Empire he was replaced by Will Walden, a BBC news editor at Westminster).

But in the context of Tory-aligned personnel in influential positions within the BBC, one thinks of the recently retired chair of the BBC Trust Lord Patten, a former Conservative cabinet minister. Hands up those who can remember the last time a former Labour minister chaired the BBC – the correct answer, is never. Patten was, by my reckoning, the tenth BBC chair to sit in either the Commons or Lords on the Tory benches; the equivalent Labour total is two – Phillip Inman – who was chairman of the governors in 1947, for less than a year and he was succeeded by Ernest Simon, 1st Baron Simon of Wythenshawe.

As for the BBC's Labour links – the last chairman with any Labour connections was Gavyn Davies who was, as will be recalled, forced to resign by a Labour government. A former Labour minister, James Purnell is currently working as a senior BBC executive, specifically on charter renewal and presenter Andrew Marr had a well-publicised flirtation with Trotskyist grouplets in his youth. The only other current or recent Labour connections I am aware of are political correspondent, Lance Price, who left the corporation to become Labour's director of communications; Joy Johnson, one of his predecessors at the Labour Party, who had been the BBC's political news editor at Westminster and was told, after she had ceased to work for the party, that she could not expect to return to the BBC (and she didn't) and broadcaster Melvyn Bragg who, when he became a Labour peer, was immediately banned from appearing on any programmes that might have any political content.

So why, despite the demonstrable connections between the BBC and Conservatives and the paucity of connections on the other side, and the plethora of academic research that demonstrates that if there is a bias in the BBC's reporting of politics it is against the left rather than the right, do Conservative newspapers, politicians, and presumably voters, think the opposite?

BBC seen as almost one of the last vestiges of nationalised industries
First, on a very basic level of political instincts, those on the right are not sympathetic to public bodies *per se*. There is an innate belief that in virtually all areas of life the private sector does things better. Hence, the BBC is seen as almost one of the last vestiges of the nationalised industries created by the post-war Labour government, even though the corporation came into being two decades earlier under a Conservative government.

There is another explanation to be found in the DNA of those on the right, and that is that Conservatives tend to believe that the left produces 'propaganda' whilst they deal with the facts. I recall some years back, as a local newspaper reporter, that I was sent to cover allegations from the local Conservative MP that the Labour candidate in his constituency was being allowed into schools to 'spread Labour propaganda'. I phoned the school concerned and was told that slots were given to spokespeople from all three main parties (there were only three in those days) to come into school to talk to pupils during civics lessons. I called back the Conservative MP who confirmed that he did go into the school. 'But then I only talked about the way the country was run in constitutional terms, my Labour opponent goes in to spread propaganda.'

Third, there is the nature of journalism itself. It attracts curious, slightly obstreperous, people who like to ask awkward questions, usually of the establishment. This very activity can be seen as an essentially left-wing activity, and way of thinking but the very same description applies to journalists of the right as well as the left.

The final reason is, in my view, that the right tend to make more noise about these matters. This is because those on the left of the political spectrum feel highly conflicted about the BBC, so their case goes by default. This is partly because they tend to have a broadly positive view of the BBC – they regard the very concept of public service broadcasting as a societal good – and as a result are extremely reluctant to join the right in their campaign of Beeb-bashing.

To what extent does the BBC misrepresent large swathes of our society?

Although there are some on the left who feel less constrained. The sustained and well-argued critique of the BBC's news output that the Glasgow Media Group has been offering over many years starts from the premise that power relations in a capitalist society are innately unbalanced in favour of the economic and political elites and such views tend to be reflected by the BBC because, as they see it, it is very much the creature of these elites. Hence, their criticism of the BBC is based on an ideological perspective that sees the BBC as part of the mainstream media – a media that under- or mis-represents large swathes of our society and narrows political debate to essentially that reflected by the political divisions in parliament. This narrowness of perspective is a criticism that the BBC itself has recognised as an ongoing problem.

All the above suggests that we are dealing with genuinely-held beliefs about media bias, one way or another. However, it would be foolish to ignore the fact that what drives the Conservative-supporting newspapers to attack and seek to undermine the BBC has as much to do with profits as it does with politics. All newspapers see the BBC as a formidable competitor, not just for audiences but for income as well. Conservative-supporting newspapers are outraged by what they see as 'public money' – in fact, income from the licence fee – being used to fund a direct competitor. Indeed, the *BBC News Online* site, according to the most recent research from the Reuters Foundation, dwarfs the sites of the *Mail Online* (and the *Guardian* for that matter) in terms of both readership and trust. An additional motivation for the Murdoch-controlled papers seeking to undermine the BBC is that its BSkyB network competes with the BBC head-for-head, for audiences and hence it would almost be foolish of them not to attack the BBC.

These ongoing political attacks on the BBC as a bastion of left-wing thinking would be an irritation, a severe irritation, at any time. But with a Conservative majority government in office, an upcoming renewal of the BBC's charter and licence fee settlement pending and a secretary of state not seen as one of the BBC's most passionate supporters, these attacks could have very serious consequences, not just for the BBC but for the country as a whole.

Conclusion: The role of the regulators

There is not a great deal the BBC can do about this without sounding self-serving and defensive and nor, in this author's view, would it help if there were 'balancing' attacks from the left accusing the BBC of a right-wing bias. However, there are regulators and maybe they could assist. Both Ofcom and the BBC Trust, whilst subject to criticisms of their own, have not (as yet) been characterised as in the hands of left-wing troublemakers.

Might they ponder mounting a joint investigation into the torrent of allegations about the BBC's supposed left-wing bias? Such an inquiry, if it found such charges to be untrue, would lay the issue to rest, at least until the charter and licence fee settlement had been finalised.

On the other hand, if the inquiry found such charges to be substantiated...

Section 5:
The New BBC, Programme Making and the Creative Industries

John Mair

At the end of the day, the BBC is about, er, broadcasting. What appears on screens and on the radio is how they are judged by the audience. Quality is the ultimate benchmark. How you make that 'content'/'product' (or whatever you label it) and how you find and get it to audiences is the essence of broadcasting.

Until two decades ago, all (or most) television and radio programmes were produced in-house by the corporation. Then, in 1982, along came Channel 4 and the flourishing of the independent production sector. Little Thatcherite acorns spun out of the broadcasters to set up on their own. Soon, the BBC had to face reality and 25 per cent of its television output made, by law, by independents. That figure went up in 2007 with the BBC opening of the WOCC (Window of Creative Competition): 50 per cent guaranteed in-house, 25 per cent to indies and 25 per cent up for grabs between the two. In some genres – drama and comedy for example – the WOCC has led to predominantly indie suppliers.

Some of the acorns started small and became very big through garnering commissions from broadcasting, through mergers or takeovers of other minnows or, latterly, the injection of capital from bigger players in world broadcasting such as Sony. In the very recent past, the conglomerates have taken over and the perfect supply market of the 1990s was soon on the way to oligopsony today. Big has become beautiful again.

Inside, the BBC still continued to train and nurture talent. Many of the great programme makers have a BBC pedigree. Those who stayed enjoyed the security but found they too were ever dependent on the capriciousness of the commissioners, many of whom had previously been their colleagues. For some it proved better to be rich and insecure outside than poor and insecure inside.

How to move forward and level that playing field? Director general Tony Hall announced in 2015 that he wanted to create a BBC Studios – at arm's length from the corporation – which would compete for commissions within the BBC but most importantly outside it too: on ITV, on Channels 4 and Channel 5, Sky wherever. This move has yet to have the sanction of the new charter but Hall has appointed a BBC Studios head, Peter Salmon. The indies, long protected, squealed with horror at this move. How will it all play out? Watch this space.

In 2013, Hall had announced that he wanted to personalise the BBC for each and every audience member: thus was created 'myBBC' with the audience becoming their own curators and schedulers. Lis Howell is a distinguished broadcaster and now a professor at City University London. Her assessment of that initiative is none too positive:

> Broadcasting, particularly news broadcasting, is an open, universal, discursive, communal activity. Despite Lord Hall's rousing language, we cannot let the BBC become all things to all viewers and listeners in a private world where we might only hear one voice.

BBC 'Britain's creative kickstarter'

Alex Connock is a mover and shaker in the independent sector. Formerly co-founder and CEO of Ten Alps, he now heads Shine North, well placed to harvest the fruits of TV and digital growth at Media City Salford. Shine is the Elizabeth Murdoch-originated indie company now merged with Endemol to form one of the largest global production groups. Connock issues a *cri de coeur* for the BBC as 'Britain's creative kickstarter' and shows this well by comparing and contrasting the North West of England with the North East. One has had BBC pump priming, the other not. In one, the creative and digital industries are growing fast, in the other less so. His is a surprising 'hands-off-the-BBC' voice:

> As a nation, we have devoted seven decades of remarkably stable national investment into the BBC. It is repaying us. Not only with a cultural richness that keeps us entertained; not only with an employment cluster in Manchester that is helping to drive a dynamic rebirth of the city's economy as a digital production and tech hub: but also as an entire nation with a production industry that is British and world-class like very few others today'.

Let the children eat ... cartoons. In the flexible definition of public service broadcasting that followed the 1990 Broadcasting Act, commercial ITV broadcasters soon wriggled out of supplying unprofitable genres like properly resourced regional news and original children's programming. Others more surprising, such as Channel 4, followed suit. Even the BBC has gone part of the way along the road and ended up creating two specialised digital channels for the young: CBeebies (for younger) and CBBC (for older) children, both in the digital space used by BBC Three and Four in the evening.

The children's anchor programme *Blue Peter* vanished from its twice weekly slot on BBC One in 2012. The BBC has now become almost the only provider of original children's programmes in the UK. For the rest, the next generation has to rely on US-originated cartoons (and similar) provided cheaply at marginal cost by the big studios. This is not a situation Fiona Chesterton, a former senior executive in the BBC and Channel 4, welcomes. She says:

> We have sleepwalked into a situation where the BBC now has a near-monopoly, or more correctly a 'monopsony' (being a single buyer of goods or services as opposed to a single supplier) in certain genres of children's television

And what of the 'senior service' (as it was known in the BBC), namely radio. It is where the BBC started in 1922 and which it still does superbly nearly a century later. The corporation has segmented that market with some aplomb. There is something for everyone on the five analogue services, five digital and fifty other stations throughout Britain. All niches are covered. Radio 2 is the most popular station in the land, the nations each have at least one station, forty towns and counties have a local station and the chatterati have BBC Radio 4. The *Today* programme sets the agenda for the day. It looks impregnable.

Sadly, it is not. Radio is a classic of market failure. Independent local radio has never properly taken off. Put simply, it does not pay. Small stations have been subsumed under bigger brands whose only 'localness' is in their jingles. Too many are simply jukeboxes with chatter and much of that not live. My local commercial station in Oxford, JackFM, broadcasts live for just three hours out of 24.

Gillian Reynolds is truly the doyenne of writers on radio. She has spent a lifetime listening, making and criticising for the *Daily Telegraph* and the *Guardian*. She remains optimistic, though, about new platforms helping rather than hindering the radio star.

> Radio fits that world perfectly. Its portability is an obvious advantage and, as time has gone by, manufacturers have realised it. Radio is no longer just a box in a room. It can be in your hand, on your phone. It will only stay there, however, if what comes out of it is appealing. The online world is global, the choice of listening it brings is massive.

But she is concerned that the BBC undervalues radio. She writes: 'Both corporate BBC and the media seldom acknowledge BBC Radio's creative and communicative power. Why is radio, in the words of the old music hall song, "always the bridesmaid, never the blushing bride"?'

The BBC's journalistic range does not end there. John Birt, when director general (1992-2000), was very prescient in spotting the upcoming digital revolution. He got the BBC (news and programmes) online as soon as practical.

They are still the gold standard in cyberspace, yet still they face criticism for distorting a market which they created. Living or dying by output – on radio, on television, online – that's the BBC's past and future. It is what they do.

Should the BBC ever be Mine? A Look at the Personalisation Promised by the New DG, Tony Hall

The 'myBBC' development could well give viewers a false sense of objectivity with a personalised news service which is so 'one-to-one' that all sense of context has gone, argues Lis Howell

So what is 'myBBC' and why was it so central to Lord Hall's first major speech as the new director general in October 2013? He talked categorically about named developments such as BBC Store, BBC Playlist, BBC Music, and The Space. But the idea of 'myBBC' permeated the speech. The BBC of the future would

> ... have a two-way, closer, warmer relationship with our audiences. People would think – not 'the BBC', but 'my BBC, our BBC'...

He added that by 2022...

> ... you will also have noticed another trend: towards a much more personal BBC; something different perhaps for every single one of us. Not one to everyone, but one to one. ... If we get all these ideas right, we'll be taking a step into new territory – we will be inviting the audience into the BBC. No longer a paternalist BBC, but a personal one... At the moment we treat audiences like licence fee payers. We should be treating them like owners. That's what I meant when I said that we wouldn't be THE BBC, but My BBC, Our BBC. The public owns us and that is what it needs to feel like...

At the time I referred to it rather tritely as 'more net curtain than Netflix', meaning that a veil had been drawn over what was happening and that it was rather a vague view inside, if you could see inside at all. The 'my' thing sounded like a fashionable marketing ploy. Back in 2012/13 everything was 'my' and it has stuck: 'My Sainsbury's', 'My M&S', the Co-operative Bank has three of them, and Tesco has 'Our Tesco'. There is now 'My Liverpool FC' and 'My List' at the National Gallery (though that is more sedately presented). In 2013, the 'my' word was almost as ubiquitous as the magic word 'community', and often appeared in the same promotional blurbs. But a personalised 'myBBC' seemed close to Lord Hall's heart and an essential part of his strategy. The BBC was to be all things to all people at all levels. It would be...

>...the only public service that pretty much everyone chooses to use each week. We would still be the place everyone goes to for the big events. We would still be the pre-eminent provider of trusted news and information, not just locally, not just nationally but all over the world.

But also ...

>Audiences will be invited to sign in. They'll get personalised recommendations. They'll be able to rate our programmes, to discuss, participate and vote. That will influence what we commission, when we schedule, how we run the BBC. They can become their own schedulers, our next creators, our future innovators.

At the time I found this confusing and still do – to be both personally tailored for individual choice, but also the guardian of the nation's shared heritage. I was intrigued then, and still am, about how this can work. But first, 'myBBC' should be put in the context of the other developments which Lord Hall talked about in 2013. So, where are they now?

Lord Hall's other developments...
Googling reveals that BBC Store launched a closed trial in June 2015 and hoped to be open for business in the autumn of 2015. When you search BBC Store, you first hit the BBC Shop which sells souvenirs at New Broadcasting House, and that's not incongruous. BBC Store is also a shop where you can buy programmes – a sort of Amazon for BBC boxed sets, but digital. It's just what Lord Hall said when reading the label on the tin. It's 'a new commercial online service which will offer people in the UK the chance to buy a whole range of programmes to watch and keep forever'. Lord Hall has a way with emotive language – the 'keep forever' sounds more like a marriage than buying the full run of *Bad Education*, but it's not inaccurate. You can buy shows at BBC Store and keep them – forever. Skystore is not dissimilar and you can keep them forever, too. According to Tim Davie, CEO of BBC Worldwide, as we go to press, BBC Store is doing well and proving popular.

BBC Playlister is described on Wikipedia as 'a personal music platform introduced by the BBC in 2013. It does not carry music itself, but partners with existing online platforms Deezer, YouTube and Spotify to play music from the user's playlist ... curating personalised music playlists based upon listening to radio stations and radio presenters' own choices'. Again, pretty straightforward. The BBC says it is 'fast and free' and there doesn't seem to be anything similar offered by commercial radio groups. BBC Playlister sounds like a winner.

BBC Music is just that – a lush website dedicated to BBC Music. In June 2015, it headlined with the Glastonbury Festival – obviously one of these unique

British events which Lord Hall says the BBC should be covering. Judging by the publicity it seems Glastonbury is up there with the Queen and Westminster Abbey as a national treasure. According to *Radio Times* (which has a unique relationship with the BBC and dedicated five pages to Glastonbury), it is the most successful pop festival in the world and on the social calendar along with Ascot and Henley. But to return to the theme, in terms of what Lord Hall promised in 2013, BBC Music is doing the trick.

The Space is a lot less lavish. Its website is very simple for something promoting the digital arts. It is 'set up by the BBC and Arts Council England. The Space is a commissioner of art that employs technology to push the boundaries of creative expression. We support new talent and great artists from all art forms, creative industries, technical and digital backgrounds, through regular Open Calls, commissions and partnerships'. There is no mention of funding. The Space seems to be a venture which has not had the investment nor interest suggested in the Hall speech. Whether it should, is another issue. But it is there. As promised.

'myBBC': More ethos than technological development

Which brings us at last to 'myBBC'. In fact, Tony Hall never actually referred to it as a new facility. It was just a phrase which recurred throughout his speech. It seemed to be an ethos as much as a technological development – in fact, a BBC spokesman said 'myBBC' was 'much more than a technological development'. Going back to 2011, the new digital strategy for the BBC was formulated based on the 'one-ten-four principle'. This means there is one service, with ten products (news, weather, CBBC, CBeebies, knowledge and learning, homepage, iPlayer, radio, search, sport) available on four screens (mobile, tablet, PC, laptop.). 'myBBC' is part of this.

Phil Fearnley is the director of 'myBBC' and also of Homepage. On the BBC website he is credited with being 'responsible for personalisation projects which help users of bbc.co.uk and other digital services discover the content they're interested in'. His description of 'myBBC' is simple: 'You'll be able to create a BBC experience that you can control [which] recognises you as an individual and brings you the best of our content based on what we know you'll love.' As with all these online clubs, once you subscribe they can 'reach out' to you in return, suggesting things you might like. You can also customise the supply you receive from the ten products.

I tried it with news and it works. I picked the areas I was interested in and I now get alerts every time a woman gets a top job (only joking). You can choose weather for your area, for example, or your local radio station website, and it's all very neat. Another BBC executive told me: 'Anything with "my" in it appeals – it's personal and your choice.' And he suggested that it meant you could 'create your own channel'.

Potential controversies

Which brings us to the first of the four potential controversies I can identify with 'myBBC'. Number one – is it destined to take over from the current channels one day? The BBC officially rejects this idea, but some BBC executives think it may happen. They quote Netflix, for example, which is, in effect, a channel you create yourself. Another phrase used by a BBC manager I spoke to was that this is 'old money turned into new money'. Material which is archived can be re-accessed and placed in your personal favourites. It was suggested that within ten years you could entirely 'make your own channel' with implications for the management structure of the BBC. If BBC production is to become competitive and separately managed, and then channel structure disappears, what is left?

Secondly, this also has implications for funding, as they say in all the best alarmist emails. There is no link between being a subscriber to 'myBBC' and being a licence fee payer. If 'myBBC' achieves the popularity they expect (and there would be no point developing it otherwise – though, by the way, it is impossible to find out how much money is earmarked to develop it), then it means millions of people can access BBC material – maybe all the BBC material they want or need – without paying. The BBC news app had (by July 2015) already been downloaded 25 million times. How many of these people are licence fee payers?

Thirdly – and this is a practical question – how does 'myBBC' work when it comes to the big cultural events which Lord Hall feels we must have because we are British? If we just want our own stuff, how we will know about these big events? I am assured by a BBC spokesman that, as a 'myBBC' user, I will be alerted to the FA Cup Final or the Queen's 90th birthday celebrations, as a matter of course. But who decides what I should be alerted about? Arguably the same is true of traditional broadcasting, but there we currently have a pluralist culture, however weakened, of competition and competitive values between broadcasters, so consumers can be fairly sure of getting more than one provider telling us what is important. Currently there is more than one voice confirming what matters to the nation but if you use 'myBBC' as your sole source of information how can you be sure you really are getting all the nationally important events? The diamond jubilee of *Coronation Street*, for example. That matters more to me than Glastonbury.

There is another issue related to this. We need to ask how instrumental the BBC could be in actually creating a national event. I'm not suggesting for a moment that the modern Glastonbury phenomenon is a creation of the BBC, but surely it is fair to ask whether this is in some way symbiotic. This issue, of course, goes beyond the remit of 'myBBC', but it is worth raising. At what point is it the BBC coverage itself which makes the event matter? We all understand about Wimbledon, Trooping the Colour, and Remembrance Sunday. These events pre-date broadcasting and would probably happen whether they were broadcast or not, by the BBC or any broadcaster. But what about more peripheral happenings? Why does the BBC decide, say, to cover the Hay Literary Festival and not the Cumberland Show? The BBC's ability to create national culture, rather than reflect it, should concern us – unless, of course, you wish to make a fortune by starting the *New Broadcasting House Pop Festival Bake Off* starring Florence Welch, Mary Berry and Nicola Sturgeon.

Fourthly, where does the World Service come into this? You might think this is going really off-piste, but the World Service is already the subject of a quiet but rumbling controversy which must be addressed in the next royal charter. The World Service used to be funded by the Foreign Office and run by the BBC with guaranteed editorial independence. It is now funded by the BBC through the licence fee, and of course it still has guaranteed editorial independence. Or does it? As Lord Birt has pointed out in *Media Guardian*, and at a City University London debate, the Foreign Office still has a say in the shape of the service. It's not entirely clear how this works, but if, for example, the BBC decided that the Lilliput language service should close, could the government insist otherwise if it has an interest in reaching the citizens of Lilliput? Regardless of how costly the Lilliput service is, or what has to go to pay for it?

So what has this to do with 'myBBC'? Two things: first, if 'myBBC' does become the 'build your own channel' of the future, does this apply to overseas users as well, and secondly, if that is the case, where does the famous BBC fairness and balance come in? If I live in Lilliput and I only want to hear about the Lilliput liberation army, can I blank out the news I don't want to hear? And where will the Foreign Office stand on this? It would seem to me that a 'myBBC' for World Service users is not what the Foreign Office wants at all. Of course, the simple answer is to make 'myBBC' available only to UK subscribers. But a BBC spokesman told me: 'We will look to extend "myBBC" to these sites, also.'

Biggest controversy – over fairness and balance

But fairness and balance is, in fact, the biggest controversy of all, for all 'myBBC' users. myNews is great – on the face of it. No more boring football news! But the inevitable result will be that the user does not get an even-handed presentation, and that fairness and objectivity (however chimerical and hard to achieve) go out of the window. It might not matter, on the face of it, if you only want to hear about UKIP. Maybe that wouldn't be a threat to parliamentary democracy. But it is a threat to the BBC's obligation to provide us with balanced information. We are the licence fee payers and because the news is universally provided to all payers, regardless of their views or politics, it cannot be partisan. That's the law. The BBC attempts to be fair and balanced, and relies on composite coverage achieving that balance. Of course, at present viewers and listeners can decide to switch off items which they don't like or agree with, but at least they get those items in the first place. With 'myBBC' it will be far more filtered. It would be possible to not even know that there was a balancing item elsewhere in the schedule or running order.

Of course, we never know about a large amount of news which is dropped. But there is still a big bouquet of different items which are put in order of importance by an editorial team. News by definition is sifted and prioritised by journalists whom we choose to trust when we watch BBC news. We may not always agree with their priorities but we need those benchmarks. If we can over-ride that editorial judgement then we are not getting news – we are getting so many sneezing pandas! It is unfashionable but vital to recognise the importance of editorial judgement in news, and to acknowledge that this is a professional skill which we pay for. In journalism education, one of the hardest things to teach students is how to prioritise both on behalf of others and on behalf of themselves. We crucially rely upon that editorial prioritisation in our news, and we need it in the context of what else is out there. There is a significant danger with 'myBBC' that we miss what matters, in pursuit of what matters to us.

The BBC disagrees, telling me that I will be sent all the breaking news and important stories and that they will be chosen for me by news teams in exactly the same way as they are now. But now, I have to hear all the headlines in order to decide what I want to know. With 'myNews' on 'myBBC' I can by-pass that. In fairness, you still go into 'myNews' through the BBC News homepage. But I tested this with a student, and also with a colleague. The student saw three headlines on the way to 'myNews' – Greece, Heathrow protest, and Wimbledon. She read none of them and in three seconds was into her own selection. The colleague only saw the headline Greece because of the layout on her phone. The prioritised BBC News can be skipped in seconds, and anyway you can only see the top one or two stories. So 'myNews' is not BBC News. On the other hand, if the BBC News homepage dominates, then it is not 'myNews', it is BBC News. It's the dilemma embedded in Lord Hall's speech – the personal versus the public concern. Sometimes, I would contend, it *does* have to be one to everyone, not one to one. That is what news is.

Conclusion: Resolving the potential problems, enshrining plurality of voices

Most of the four potential problems I have raised can be solved by one development – the enshrining of plurality of near-equally resourced and respected voices in our broadcasting environment. I don't mean the BBC in the middle with a lot of little niche news channels or special interest voices clustered around, like small planets around the sun. I mean a choice for viewers between two or three big national players. If other public service, balanced and objective news and events broadcasters are encouraged, perhaps even supported, then the BBC can do all of these things knowing it is in an environment where it is challenged. This would be good for us, good for business and good for the BBC.

Take BBC *News at Ten*. It is watched by about four million people. ITV *News at Ten* only gets about half as many viewers despite being much more than half as good – as the Royal Television Society awards system suggests. But for the last ten years ITV and ITN have seen audiences eroded by three factors –

weaker programmes around ITV News, declining revenues, and the relentless promotion of the BBC, with its guaranteed income and insistence that is the only trusted news provider. But trusting only one source is not healthy for the BBC and it certainly isn't healthy for the viewers. The 'myBBC' development could well add to this danger, giving the viewer a false sense of objectivity with a personalised news service which is so 'one-to-one' that all sense of context has gone.

By 1957, following the launch of independent television two years earlier, the BBC's ratings had slumped to 28 per cent of the audience. Great efforts were made to revive it, and to stop ITV dominating, including putting a £1 surcharge on the combined radio and television licence (which had been introduced in 1946) and so increasing the BBC's income. Now perhaps it should be the other way around and great efforts should be made to protect a rival service. Maybe that means relinquishing some of the features of 'myBBC'. Broadcasting, particularly news broadcasting, is an open, universal, discursive, communal activity. Despite Lord Hall's rousing language, we cannot let the BBC become all things to all viewers and listeners in a private world where we might only hear one voice.

Britain's Creative Kickstarter: The BBC

To see what the creative economy of Britain could be like without the BBC, we have a test case already: the North of England. Compare the North West and North East over the past five years, in the context of the BBC moving substantial assets into one city (Manchester) but not another (Newcastle) and, as Alex Connock argues, we can see a stark result

There is a place a lot like Northern California — where rushing rivers tumble over boulders through rocky outcrops and pine forest. But it's twenty minutes from downtown Stockport. You could spend a sunny day driving about in the Goyt Valley, and confuse the geography with upland California — until you switch on your car radio. At that point, you would fall into a canyon of difference.

In Northern California, 'scan' across the entire FM waveband, and you may never find a station to stop on. It's 24-hour 'adult contemporary' formats, spiced up with religious radio — a small ditch of choice that stretches from Jon Bon Jovi to Kanye, via rehashed Old Testament admonitions.

But in the hills of Northern Britain, your radio choice is epic. Alongside many genres of music, you could hear Melvyn Bragg exploring *Abelard and Heloise*, or the theological differences between Sunni and Shia Islam, or the vacuum of space. You could hear the *Art of Self-Borrowing* as explored through J. S. Bach's *B Minor Mass*. You could listen to an Alan Ayckbourn play or hear Toulouse-Lautrec's *Moulin Rouge* characters brought to life. You could be transported, via broadcasting of unchallenged intellectual richness, to one of the finest libraries in the history of the world. And what makes the difference? The BBC.

For the last 60 years, the BBC has been to radio and television programme-making what Apple is to personal computing today. The world champion. The *sine qua non*. The BBC has quite possibly been the only UK industrial entity that has consistently been in the global premier league in its field for over half a century. Can you name another? British Rail? The Royal Bank of Scotland?

206

Industrially-speaking, the North is also a handy testbed for the wider impact of the BBC on our creative industry, far from where the policies are made in smoke-free rooms – be that Washington or London – and right where the programmes are made and actually enjoyed.

We can see how the BBC impacted on different parts of the North of England when it moved major assets there, and what that might say in microcosm about the corporation's role within the British creative economy as a whole. And since we started with California, we can comparatively think about how the 'cluster' effect of California's long-term embrace of digital creative companies brings extraordinary compound benefits way beyond the value or cost of any given single player.

We can also consider how *unthinkable* it would be to drop that most precious of industrial entities: a truly world class player. Try telling the burghers of San Francisco that Apple isn't worth having any more, and they'll chuck you off a cliff.

The BBC's North experiment

For a simple test of what the creative economy of Britain would be like without the BBC, the North is a case study. We can look at the differing evolutions of the creative economies of the North West and North East over the past five years, in the context of the BBC moving substantial assets into one place (Manchester) but not another (Newcastle). It's not a scientific test (of course) but it does offer a beguiling indication: where BBC North went made a far bigger, wider difference to the creative economy.

Raw metropolitan prejudice, much of which would resonated nicely within the snotty Parisian court *circa* 1750, was directed at the BBC's 2010-2013 implementation of a strategic move of certain departments such as Sport and Children's to Salford (which is in Manchester, unless you are into local council sophistry). A stream of prejudiced negativity, often from nameless BBC staffers, was directed against the very idea of moving programme production out of London to one of the other cities that paid for it.

The general theme was moral outrage: how *dare* they? Max Hastings wrote in the *Daily Mail* (Hastings 2015): 'Like it or not, London is Britain's cultural capital. The attempt to shift one of its greatest institutions to the North makes no more sense than greening Abu Dhabi.'

Clusters

On the Abu Dhabi point, Hastings disregarded that many of the biggest success stories of British broadcasting over the past 60 years had already originated in the North including the world's most successful long-running soap (*Coronation Street*), the two most cerebral long-running formats on British television (*University Challenge* and *Mastermind*), dramas from *Red Dwarf* to *Prime Suspect* and *Colditz* (surely World War Two buff Hastings' ideal show?) plus current affairs from *World in Action* onwards.

Manchester's opponents also arrogantly disregarded the principle that there could be any hypothecated political and democratic logic to locating the production dimension of a publicly-funded entity more fairly across its funding regions. And above all they disregarded the economic desirability of creating a 'northern powerhouse' cluster (to borrow a phrase from George Osborne) of the creative economy in Manchester. The conceit was that creative capital belonged in a single overcrowded political capital – and that conceit was wrong, because the BBC North project has worked.

The BBC with its reported £500 million investment (the exact level depends on whom you ask) kickstarted Media City to the place it is today – a remarkably wide campus of production which encompasses not only major departments but also (often unreported) major teams of BBC digital R&D workers. Media City has concurrently added ITV output spanning drama, entertainment and factual. It has added outposts of large indie groups and distributors (such as the Red Production company, or the one I run, Shine North, part of the global Endemol Shine Group, though I'm writing here as an individual). It now has some 3,000 TV workers. And it has digital and marketing start-ups, a university campus, a brand new college for 14 to 18-year-olds targeting digital employment, and much more.

As Media City came on stream, I sat as chairman of the Royal Television Society North West across a doubling in entries to our annual awards process from 2012-2014 – and by no means just from imported BBC entrants. We viewed entries as a wider production sector bellweather, and we saw cultural engagement rise in doubled attendance at events from quizzes to talks about the how-to of documentary making. In turn, that multiplied beyond, into a wider – if hard to attribute – renaissance in Manchester's creative economy, which saw a jump in the digital sector over exactly the same period. Manchester had 70 per cent growth in new digital companies incorporated between 2010 and 2013, against a nationwide clusters average of 53 per cent, as measured by the Tech Nation report (Morris and Penido 2014).

The report also said there were now 56,145 digital jobs in Greater Manchester, and that 61 per cent to 80 per cent of survey respondents identified access to talent and social networks as the key benefits of being in the region: 'Manchester's long-standing media industry has now gone digital. The average company turnover growth is one of the highest in the UK,' said the report. This was cluster economics at work. 'Some £3.5 billion has been invested to support Manchester's digital and technology infrastructure. For example, Salford's £950 million Media City UK, Europe's first purpose-built business hub for the creative and digital industries.'

What the BBC brought to Manchester was critical mass. It brought strategic scale to a strategic industry. It was a world champion, championing a world class production economy. It worked.

Compare that with the North East

The BBC didn't move any big departments to the Tyne, or digital units. They didn't open any staff canteens or national sports newsrooms or television breakfast shows in Newcastle. Granted, they have made drama and kids productions – estimated at a £6 million annual contribution to the region's economy by Northern Film and Media. Some of them are really good, such as *Wolfblood*. But even the most ardent BBC corporate PR person could not argue the nation's broadcaster invested in Newcastle on the same permanent scale as in Manchester. As a direct result, television output in the region, and the kicker effect that has on the rest of the creative sector, has in relative terms flatlined.

Andy Becket (2014) wrote an article in the *Guardian* titled 'The North East of England: Britain's Detroit?' positing wide decline and an unclear economic *raison d'être*. It was widely derided in the region as untrue and unfair, and certainly in the digital sector there are signs of real progress.

The Tech Nation report identified strength in IT-based software engineering and back-office IT support businesses (not least the FTSE 100-listed Sage and leading games developers including Ubisoft Reflections, Epic Games UK and CCP Games). Some 77 per cent of companies surveyed, in fact, reported belief they were part of a digital cluster. But a critical mass in the creative media industries of television, video content, radio at the same level as was seeded and hot-housed in the North West by the BBC's market intervention was missing. In the Tech Nation's skills mapping, there was no adjacency for North East skills bases with the kind of creative production skills the BBC is bringing to the North West. To Manchester's 70 per cent growth in new digital companies incorporated between 2010 and 2013, the North East had just 23 per cent – which was below the national average. This is not to knock the creativity or entrepreneurialism of the North East: it's to make the obvious point that the lack of an enormous additional BBC spend was a miss for its creative economy.

And why does that matter? Because what happened in the creative elements of the digital content economy in Newcastle – or rather what didn't happen in terms of cluster economics, creative sector jobs growth, 'northern powerhouse' – is a foretaste of what could happen to the British creative sector as a whole without the extraordinary kickstarting effect of the BBC at its heart. And we should watch out for that risk.

The creative industries are worth £76.9 billion per year to the UK economy, according to a department of culture, media and sport report published January 2015. Let's keep it that way. Reform the BBC – sure. But don't deny for a moment the BBC's pivotal role as the UK's region-boosting, world-beating creative kickstarter.

California

In 1913, a young man was sent from New York to Flagstaff, Arizona, to find a location to shoot an 'Indians' movie. Two weeks went by – then a telegram arrived from Flagstaff: 'No good for our purpose. Want authority to rent barn in place called Hollywood.' That was from Cecil B. DeMille, and Sam Goldfish (who later changed his name to Sam Goldwyn) telegraphed back: 'Rent barn but on month to month basis. Don't make any long-term commitment.'[1]

At that point, no feature film had ever been made in Hollywood. These were the first guys in town to do more than a short one-reeler. Their seed investment, and that of others, was one step in the Hollywood cluster being born. And once the cluster was in place, it became unstoppable – an industry worth $679 billion to the US in 2014.[2]

In the 2014 paper, *Why Silicon Valley became Silicon Valley*, Rhett Morris and Mariano Penido concluded that the main reason why it happened was not because it had innate geographic advantages, or a better technological heritage. It was because the entrepreneurs behind key businesses such as Fairchild Semiconductor, who achieved some success in the 1960s and early 1970s, were prepared to pay their success forward by backing others, thereby creating a cluster effect. This did not happen in Dallas where Texas Instruments had better technology (Morris and Pernido 2014). Again – it's clusters of world-beating expertise based on seed investment.

The BBC as core of the UK creative cluster

As a nation, we have devoted seven decades of remarkably stable national investment into the BBC. It is repaying us. Not only with a cultural richness that keeps us entertained; not only with an employment cluster in Manchester that is helping to drive a dynamic rebirth of the city's economy as a digital production and tech hub: but also as an entire nation with a production industry that is British and world-class like very few others today.

If we tinker with the BBC we take a risk of undoing all that and becoming like other countries. Like Belgium or Norway. Perfectly decent countries, with perfectly decent television shows. But without the global impact of a BBC-powered creative economy. Do we remove that creative role from the UK creative equation where someone can take the decision to 'rent a barn' and create a new genre? Do we stifle the pay-it-forward economics of a tech expert who can help another to create the next smash hit tech product? Or do we build on what we already have, without going backwards?

Notes

[1] A barn in a place called Hollywood., by Jesse L. Lasky, *I Blow my Own Horn* (1957) quoted in *Penguin Book of Hollywood*, edited by Christopher Silvester (1998)

[2] See www. statista.com

References

Beckett, Andy (2014) The North-East of England: Britain's Detroit? *Guardian*, 10 May. Available online at http://www.theguardian.com/uk-news/2014/may/10/north-east-avoid-becoming-britains-detroit, accessed on 21 June 2015

Hastings, Max (2015) Decent TV shows? No, the BBC prefers splurging your cash on a bloated army of jobsworths, *Daily Mail*, 16 June 2015. Available online at http://www.dailymail.co.uk/debate/article-3125632/MAX-HASTINGS-Decent-TV-shows-No-BBC-prefers-splurging-cash-bloated-army-jobsworths.html, accessed on 21 June 2015

Morris, Rhett and Penido, Mariano (2014) How did Silicon Valley become Silicon Valley. Available online at http://share.endeavor.org/pdf/HDSVBSV.pdf, accessed on 25 June 2015

Who's Looking After the Children?

Fiona Chesterton makes the case for the BBC to continue to take the lead on children's television, especially on the 'tougher stuff' – helping young people to develop an understanding of the wider world and supporting their learning and skills development

Introduction

The *Teletubbies* are back, updated for children born in the second decade of the new millennium – in a very different world from that which originally transported them to La La Land from BBC Two every morning back in the 1990s. Those toddlers are now graduating from college and joining Generation Rent, while a slightly older generation, nostalgic for the era of Britpop, are comforted that they can introduce their own children to the big bad media world through the safe portal of CBeebies.

So can there be much to worry about the state of British children's television and the BBC's custody of it, if the *Teletubbies* thrive? Superficially no, but as this chapter will argue there are warning signs flashing, and much evidence that British-produced children's programming is at risk. This is not to do with the BBC's own commitment to this section of its audience, which is not questioned, but to do with the wider ecology of the industry, as I will explain. While children's viewing is also becoming increasingly focused around entertainment, I will argue that there needs to be a continuing commitment to the tougher stuff: enabling children to understand their own society and the wider world, supporting their learning and skills development. It's to be hoped that the charter review will focus on such issues, rather more vital as they are than stars' pay. The green paper did not augur well. As Professor Jeanette Steemers has pointed out (Media Policy Project 2015), there are only a few references to children's services, continuing as she puts it 'the long tradition of marginalising children' in the public service broadcasting debate.

Children's television: Sleepwalking to disaster?

There is no doubt that parents, and grandparents for that matter, greatly value a wide range of high-quality and, crucially, UK-made programmes for children. When Ofcom asked people in 2014 to rate what they call public service broadcasting objectives, an overwhelming 85 per cent agreed this was important, second only to the provision of high-quality news (Ofcom 2014). Interestingly, this rating had actually gone *up* considerably from that recorded five years previously, when two thirds had agreed. So, in a landscape of boundless and increasing choice, what does that tells us? Maybe it speaks to the quality kitemark that the BBC and the other PSBs, including Channel 4, provide? Or that people prefer British productions when so much comes with an American accent?

In case you are thinking that this is all outmoded, because all the children you know are watching videos and playing games via their phone or tablet, then the same Ofcom report also firmly states, on the basis of its most recent surveys, that 'TV continues to play an important role in the lives of all children' and that children up to the age of seven spend double the number of hours per week watching television rather than the internet. Of course, no one would deny that trends away from traditional viewing are accelerating rapidly, particularly amongst older children and teenagers, but much of this is about the move towards on-demand and mobile viewing rather than to scheduled channels, and does not necessarily argue for a declining need for high-quality, long-form programmes. So, for example, there were nearly 11 million downloads per week from CBBC on the iPlayer in 2013 (BBC Trust 2013).

Clearly internet platforms such as YouTube and social media have provided new content in a form that is particularly attractive to young people, especially as so much of it is made by their peers – but watch those vloggers become television celebs in time! Surely this will not replace, but will sit alongside the high-budget, high-quality long-form content, the drama, the comedy, entertainment, animation, news and documentary that television can offer.

Yet, the past exciting decade when there has been such technological transformation, putting iPads into the hands of toddlers while television has become a truly global business, has seen a withdrawal and reduction in investment by the traditional UK-based broadcaster/commissioners, such as CITV, saved only by the BBC's continuing commitment. CBBC and CBeebies' budgets have not been immune from efficiency savings and the cuts following the freezing of the licence fee in 2010, but budgets in other children's departments have fallen off a cliff.

We have sleepwalked into a situation where the BBC now has a near-monopoly, or more correctly a 'monopsony' (being a single buyer of goods or services as opposed to a single supplier) in certain genres of children's television. The Ofcom statistics (op cit) are pretty astonishing. These tell us that by 2013 the BBC contributed 97 per cent of all spend on first-run originated content, with the BBC the only commissioner/producers of first-run originated UK drama, news and factual programmes. In the five years from 2008, spend on the commercial PSB channels fell from £13 million to £3 million and some 90 per cent of children's content across these channels were repeats. To be clear, this was not replaced by investment in the UK by the fully-commercial channels such as Disney and Viacom.

Children's television: A way forward

So does this matter, if the BBC continues to provide? There are several reasons why it does. Firstly, of course, the BBC's budgets are virtually certain to be squeezed further given the 2015 licence fee settlement. Secondly, the BBC relies on a creative and sustainable independent production sector specialising in children's content. Thirdly, while the BBC serves some of the children's audience very well, it struggles with older children and teenagers and, indeed, as with adults its tone and content has less appeal the further away from London you go. CBBC reaches less than a third of its target audience (BBC Trust 2013).

The BBC's in-house department supplies probably just over half of its commissioned programmes. As PACT, the trade lobby for the independent production sector together with the Ragdoll Foundation, in a recent submission to Ofcom (Keeny and Suter 2015) and the campaigning group, the Children's Media Foundation (seewww.thechildrensmediafoundation.org) have argued recently, the children's production sector is increasingly unsustainable with its business model described as broken.

While many independents have been increasingly skilled at operating in a global marketplace and can be confident that their ideas are world-beating, it can now take years to get children's productions off the ground, with the BBC providing usually only a minority of the budget and producers having to sell off their secondary rights (which may give them a long-term return) to secure funding from elsewhere.

PACT has made two suggestions for reform – the first, already achieved, persuading the government to extend tax breaks for productions from film and high-end adult drama, to animation, and now to all children's programming. There is not enough evidence yet to know what difference this will make, but in the case of film and drama it seems to have been primarily effective in increasing inward investment and getting more international producers to film in the UK, using British talent and locations. It would be a good outcome if the major global children's players, such as Disney, Viacom and new kids on the block, like Netflix and Amazon, saw opportunities to invest here. It is not sufficient though to fix the bigger issue – particularly if, as some producers fear, the BBC 'prices in' the tax break in setting their budgets.

PACT has also floated a bigger and more radical idea which would see in-house BBC production departments, including children's, spun off in management buy-outs, opening up more of the BBC's commissioning budgets to independents, and leaving the BBC as a publisher/broadcaster like Channel 4

(PACT 2014). Such an idea may be tempting to government keen to hold down the licence fee (although PACT argues for an index-linked one).

Even this idea still does not address the 'monospony' issue. We surely need competition to the BBC from other home-grown broadcasters. Maybe the end of recession will encourage ITV, and Channels 4 and 5 to re-invest in children's content, or more probably some tightening of regulation will be needed. Some now see it as a mistake that children's programmes were put in a lower tier for regulatory obligation after the 2003 Communications Act.

The Children's Media Foundation, amongst others, has also floated the idea of some sort of contestable PSB funding, a separate pot accessible for children's television production. This would fit with other calls for some sort of public broadcasting commission, but surely the risk is that this could be translated into further top-slicing of the licence fee, rather than increasing the total pot.

It's not just about the economic arguments, it's also about diversifying the range and tone of content beyond CBBC. Channel 4's somewhat cooler brand may better appeal to older children. The BBC Trust, in reviewing the children's services in 2013 (BBC Trust 2013), recognised that there were some real limitations to the corporation's engagement with some young audiences, not just older children, but young people outside the South of England, and with ethnic minority audiences.

So, as well as expecting the BBC to continue to invest in children's television, we should expect more from Channel 4, E4 and other public service broadcasters as well. Not just with entertainment and drama, where Channel 4 has recently invested in series such as *Youngers* and *My Mad Fat Diary* but it would be good to see more factual programmes and current affairs for younger viewers as well.

Tough love for children: Factual television

There are a wealth of entertainment options for children now: games, music, YouTube vlogs, as well as TV. Not surprisingly the most popular programmes on CBBC and Disney alike are the entertainment and drama shows. Indeed, CBBC programmes such as *Tracy Beaker*, *The Next Step* and *Horrible Histories* regularly make it into the overall Top 40 iPlayer downloads. It is harder now to get an audience for real world programmes, let alone ones with a more obvious educational intent – and as we have seen only the BBC is committed to that range.

The easy response, of course, is that, given a choice, outside of school, young people will always prefer undemanding entertainment. Partially true, as it is for adults – but there is some evidence that children do value programmes about the world they live in. Let's look at one example – news and current affairs.

Newsround has been going strong for more than 50 years. As I write (in June 2015) one of their specials on *Growing up Black in America* has recently dealt with some tough issues around policing and racism in the troubled inner cities of the United States. Its audience may have decreased from earlier years but who says that this is too challenging stuff for young people? Research undertaken by Cynthia Carter, of Cardiff University's School of Journalism, Media and Cultural Studies, shows the value of learning how to evaluate and understand news from an early age. She did some work initially with a Glasgow school that was studying 9/11 with the aid of the then-Channel 4 children's news programme, *First Edition*. More recently, she did work with older children in conjunction with the BBC, and found that there was a real appetite for having news presented in a style they could relate to (not 'boring' bulletins) and preferably in a supportive learning environment, i.e. school or college (Carter 2014).

Might this be a challenge that new BBC Three service could take up online? Not sixty second headlines, but something with real depth and context alongside their *Free Speech* debates (which I hope will survive the move online).

Education and the BBC: Rising from the ashes

In the first edition of this book, I made the case for reviewing the role of education at the BBC for both children and adults and told the rather sorry story of the demise of the so-called Jam project (Chesterton 2014). Schools television as it used to be delivered, in daytime and overnight on BBC Two (and also on Channel 4) had had its day by the early years of the 21st century.

The BBC set out to reinvent the service for the digital age by committing £100 million of licence fee funds for the development of a comprehensive range of video-rich interactive resources mapped to the national curriculum. It was an ambitious, probably over-ambitious project that won the support of the Blair government but then foundered in the face of opposition from commercial publishers who successfully made the case that it breached EU state aid rules. The government support wavered, and the BBC Trust called a halt to the plan (Michalis 2012).

The effect of this reverse was devastating on BBC Learning, and may have stopped the BBC from becoming a world-class provider of interactive resources for formal learning – a role which others have now occupied. In the last few years, online education has really come into its own. UK plc, given its educational heritage and reputation, may have ceded hegemony as in other fields to the big brains and the big bucks of Silicon Valley.

So services like TedEd, Khan Academy, Discovery, and Education City now provide an astonishing quality and range of services. In their recent report for Ofcom, Enders Analysis identified no fewer than 180 services for education including high-quality mobile apps (Enders Analysis 2014). So the BBC having had its fingers burned, seems to have settled back into a more modest role, emphasising partnerships with its former rivals and with the new innovators: updating its educational online content underneath the Bitesize and iWonder umbrellas.

Bitesize is a strong BBC brand and should be able to combine caretaking the historic content with a regular programme of renewal. I am not so sure about the sustainability of iWonder. Meanwhile the BBC Learning brand seems to have been quietly abandoned: if you Google it now you see this message: 'This page has been archived and is no longer updated.'

There is one area, though, where the BBC seems to have rediscovered its educational ambition and that is in the commitment to campaigns. The director general, Tony Hall, has given his personal support in a speech in the autumn of 2013 not long after he had taken the reins to a big educational initiative a year for the following three years (Hall 2013). The big campaign of 2015 is to encourage digital creativity in children, 'Make it Digital'. This campaign was fired by the report the Royal Society produced in 2012 (Furber 2012) calling for a complete shake-up of what children learned about computing in schools. It condemned IT lessons as boring, and not designed to produce the creative skills that young people and the UK would need to compete globally in the coming decade. The report's author had unique authority to make this warning. Professor Stephen Furber had designed the BBC Micro, which 30 years previously had helped inspire a previous generation of programmers. He urged the BBC to take the lead again.

So 'Make it Digital' (www.bbc.co.uk/makeitdigital) has a fine pedigree – not only the Micro campaign in the 1980s, but also 'Computers Don't Bite' and 'Webwise' in the 1990s. There are some significant differences with this campaign reflecting the changing times and the strengths and weaknesses of where the BBC finds itself now. So the offer this time is to work with industry to offer a million Microbit (*working title*) coding machines to every 11-year-old child in the country. These would be small, low-cost, engaging, programmable and wearable LED boards. The BBC is at pains to say there would only be one million machines made and they would be 'springboards' to more complex machines – betraying a nervousness not to tread on commercial toes (following criticisms of the BBC Micro and Jam). The campaign website stresses the role of its partners – which this time round are not the local library and college of years past, but big companies, including Barclays, Google, Microsoft and smaller social enterprises.

You won't notice much TV programming, although there is much on Radio 4 (to reach parents and opinion formers rather than the children, one suspects) and there is harnessing of what are now called BBC 'brands', such as *Dr Who* (a coding game), *EastEnders* (online) rather than the old-style and now off-the-screen science and computer magazine programmes on BBC One and Two of yore. BBC Two has commissioned a drama about the Grand Theft Auto company, which seems a bit of a stretch from the original idea of encouraging digital creativity, but I am not going to knock it – as in my former role in Learning, I know the tortuous negotiations needed to get a programme idea to support a campaign past the channel controllers. Note to those seeking to reduce the BBC's scope: no one making educational programmes wants them to be boring – and some can actually turn out to be both popular and entertaining.

Let's hope this new campaigning spirit survives the charter review period and that this zeal can crack one final commitment Tony Hall made in his 2013 speech. This was to unlock the whole BBC archive and release its potential as a cultural and educational resource for this generation and generations to come. There have been heroic efforts before but rights issues have foxed them. Please BBC don't put it back in the 'too difficult' box again.

References

BBC Trust (2013) *Review of the BBC's Children's Services*, September. Available online at http://www.bbc.co.uk/bbctrust/our_work/services/television/service_reviews/childre ns_services.html, accessed on 11 June 2015

Carter, Cynthia (2014) *The Point of News: Young People, Critical News Literacy and Citizenship.* Available online at https://www.academia.edu/7658925/The_Point_of_News_Young_people_critical_new s_literacy_and_citizenship_2014_, accessed on 11 June 2015

Chesterton, Fiona (2014) Who cares about BBC education? Mair, John, Tait, Richard and Keeble, Richard (eds) *Is the BBC in Crisis?* Bury St Edmunds: Abramis pp 215-222

Enders Analysis (2014) *How Online Media Services Have Fulfilled the Public Service Objectives.* Report for Ofcom. Available online at http://stakeholders.ofcom.org.uk/consultations/psb-review-3/supporting-documents/enders-report/, accessed on 11 June 2015

Furber, Stephen (2012) *Computing in Schools, Shut Down or Restart?* Report of the Royal Society Advisory Group chair Professor Stephen Furber. Available online at https://royalsociety.org//media/education/computing-in-schools/2012-01-12-summary.pdf, accessed on 11 June 2015

Hall, Tony (2013) Speech given by Lord Hall, BBC director general, 8 October. Available online at www.bbc.co.uk/media centre/speeches/2013/tony-hall-vision.html

Keeny, R. and Suter, T. (2015) *Children's Television: A Crisis of Choice.* A report for PACT and RagdollFoundation. Available online at http://stakeholders.ofcom.org.uk/binaries/consultations/psb-review-3/responses/Pact_Ragdoll.pdf, accessed on 11 June 2015

Media Policy Project (2015) *BBC Charter Green Paper: Where will Children's TV be in 10 years' time?* Available online at http://blogs.lse.ac.uk/mediapolicyproject/2015/07/17/where-will-childrens-tv-be-in-10-years-time-with-this-green-paper/, available online at 23 July 2015

Michalis, Maria (2012) Balancing public and private interests in online media: The case of BBC digital curriculum, *Media, Culture and Society*, Vol. 34, No 8 pp 944-960

Ofcom (2014) *Public Service Broadcasting: Report.* Annexes: Children's PSB Summary. Available online at http://stakeholder.ofcom.org.uk/binaries/broadcast/reviews-investigations/psb-review/psb3/Annex_6.i_PSB_Review_Childrens_summary.pdf, accessed on 11 June 2015

PACT (2014) *A New Age of UK TV Content Creation and a New Role for the BBC*, prepared by Oliver and Ohlbaum Associations Ltd. Available online at http://www.pact.co.uk/support/document-library/documents/bbc-oando-full-report/2014-08-19-final-v20.pdf, accessed on 11 June 2015

Listen: This is the Case for BBC Radio

Why listen to the BBC when you have access to the world's radio and all its podcasts? Because the BBC still offers radio in more varieties, with high standards and star names at a bargain price, argues Gillian Reynolds

Everyone expected the new government in 2015 would try to cut the BBC down to size. No one anticipated DG Tony Hall would agree before the process of charter renewal had even began, to the first big snip. Accepting the cost of free television licences for over-75s will be an effective revenue cut about the size of the whole budget of the BBC domestic radio.

Nowhere in the world are services as various as those of BBC Radio, whether funded by the state, advertising or subscription. We take for granted the day-in, day-out, week-on-week richness of Radios 3 and 4, the creativity and enviable variety of all BBC Radio, its direct contribution to national culture.

New online services (e.g. Apple and Google) now offer streamed music, funded by subscription, advertising and revenue that accrues from possession of subscribers' data. They do not support live and new music to the extent of Radios 1, 2 and 3. American Public Radio enjoys occasional success with the documentary-in-episodes *Serial*, for example. These are rare. Documentaries, features, comedies and drama are the lifeblood of Radio 4.

BBC Radio's slice of the licence fee income is necessarily smaller than that of BBC Television but the effect of year-on-year 'efficiencies' is evident. Repeats abound, programmes vanish. Live editions of Radio 2's *Friday Night Is Music Night* have been halved. Radio 4's investigative *Face the Facts* has disappeared. Those are two examples. There are many more. Yet both corporate BBC and the media seldom acknowledge BBC Radio's creative and communicative power. Why is radio, in the words of the old music hall song, 'always the bridesmaid, never the blushing bride'?

Always the bridesmaid

BBC Radio reaches 34.872 million UK listeners and costs each UK household 8p per day. It is hugely popular at home, widely admired abroad. As a medium, radio slots neatly into online and interactive communications.

Whenever Tony Hall makes a speech about BBC arts or music, news or sport, radio always gets lower billing than television, meriting at best a passing mention. Surely he has noticed that BBC Radio has a far greater direct patronage of music in all genres, more drama and new comedy than BBC Television? That Radio 4's *Today* has more impact than BBC 2's *Newsnight*? BBC Radio still matters to so many millions of people that its part in the charter renewal process should be seriously acknowledged. In May 2015, I asked Tony Hall how valuable BBC Radio was to the BBC's total offer? He replied:

> BBC Radio is a unique and precious part of what we do – not least because our listeners are passionate about it. With so much to choose from, it's a remarkable accolade to BBC Radio that it continues to attract 35 million people in our country every week – and 130 million across the world. It's something only the BBC does in such amazing quality – locally, nationally and internationally. There's nothing else like it in the world, and it's a service our country can be very proud of.

I believe he means it. It would be more convincing if he cited some of the reasons why. Consider, for instance, the six 'public purposes' the current charter sets out for the BBC, set out below. Then consider how well BBC radio fulfils each one. I offer a few reminders. My list is far from complete.

The BBC's public purposes

1. Sustaining citizenship and civil society: by providing accurate news and information services throughout the day across England, Scotland, Northern Ireland and Wales through local and regional radio, plus four FM and one AM national networks. (Radio 1's *Newsbeat* attracts one million 16 to 24-year-old listeners each week.) By direct engagement with the public through such programmes as Radio 1's social action campaigns, Radio 2's daily *Jeremy Vine* show, Radio 4's *Woman's Hour, You & Yours* and all Radio 5 Live's presenter-led programmes.

2. Promoting education and learning: Chris Evans' *500 Words* initiative on Radio 2, a competition for writers aged five to 13, now in its fifth year, attracting more than 120,000 entrants this year. Radio 4's cooperations with the Open University (*Thinking Allowed*), the British Museum (*A History of the World in 100 Objects*) and the Natural History Museum (*Natural Histories*).

3. Stimulating creativity and cultural excellence: some 64 per cent of Radio 1's daytime music is new; Radio 2's support for folk, jazz and specialist music and its comedy competition; Radio 3 and 4's support of writers,

composers and artists. The *Ten Pieces* music education initiative. BBC Radio is by far the predominant purchaser of programmes from independent producers.

4. Representing the UK, its nations, regions and communities: four Scottish radio stations, two in Wales, two in Northern Ireland. And there are 40 BBC local radio stations across England, from Cumbria to the Channel Islands.

5. Bringing the UK to the world and the world to the UK: BBC World Service, (the latest audience research shows it remains the world's favourite; the English language service shows a remarkable 25 per cent leap in listening, reaching an audience of 52 million with the highest growth in Nigeria, USA, Pakistan and Tanzania). Radio 4 Extra re-broadcasts American Public Radio (*Serial* and *This American Life*), Radio 4's Reith and Alistair Cooke Lectures give a platform to the world's leading thinkers (such as Harvard University's Michael Sandel, and Cambridge's Onora O'Neill).

6. Helping to deliver to the public the benefit of emerging communications technologies and services: an area in which BBC radio has excelled, encouraging listeners to all their networks to engage with it online, via text or Twitter. Globally, there are more than 70 million podcasts downloaded per month. In the UK, the total is 35 million. There were 17 million downloads of Radio 4 programmes in February 2015 alone.

My examples are the tip of a huge iceberg. BBC Radio has consistently fulfilled charter obligations while surpassing all industry expectations in remaining so popular for so long. Licence fee funding has ensured its radio services have survived, evolved, developed not just in line with charter commitments but in pace with demographic, societal and technological change. In this, BBC Radio leads the world. A subscription service or 'radio only' licence fee could not achieve this as BBC Radio, being part of a greater whole, benefits from the BBC's corporate funding but offers huge value in return.

The wider context

A common media assumption is that radio is quaint, old fashioned, outdated. In fact, British radio in general and BBC Radio in particular has large and loyal audiences. As a communications medium, radio has kept in swifter step than television with social, technological and aesthetic change. Still, in discussions of 'wither the BBC?' radio gets small, if any, mention. We seem to take for granted that it always will be there.

Perhaps this is because radio has been part of everyday British life for so long. The BBC's founding service in 1922, it became the prime source of public information and entertainment throughout World War Two, survived its partial eclipse by television in the 1950s and remains today a seedbed for talent, a showcase for national achievement. BBC Radio, with its long history, secure funding and range of programming, still sets the pace for the whole radio industry.

BBC Radio has had commercial competition since 1973. What was then called Independent Local Radio had a rocky financial start in a time of political instability and recession. Since then it has grown and consolidated as a business, as an advertising medium and a cherished source of entertainment. Both sectors now co-exist while competing vigorously, in particular for music audiences. All of UK radio has grown, changed, adapted while remaining part of local and national life. Yet UK commercial radio, while competing strongly for the big audiences popular music brings, seldom offers speech radio that goes beyond the phone-in.

In the new, less regulated internet era, radio is expanding in range and reach. The most significant recent development by commercial stations has been into online. Since 2013, when London's local speech service, LBC, went online (and thus became nationally and internationally available) it has heightened its profile and made headlines with phone-in programmes such those hosted by Nick Ferrari and James O'Brien. LBC had its best ever-quarter in the first quarter or 2015, according to RAJAR, (Radio Joint Audience Research) with a share of 1.3 per cent; Radio 4's was 12.8 per cent; Radio 5 Live's 3.7 per cent. Although pirate radio stations still crop up, there is no need for piracy in the online age. Anyone can, and many do set up internet radio stations such as London's Soho Radio requiring no allocation of AM or FM airwaves and, therefore, no Ofcom supervision. The popularity of the service each offers will determine its future but, for the moment, internet stations pay few staff and have yet to make a mark on the wider cultural scene.

What BBC Radios 3, 4 and 5 Live broadcast is beyond the means of commercially funded radio. If it were not, the market would have provided alternatives by now. Most of commercial radio is owned by two internationally owned groups, Global and Bauer. The total revenue of all commercial radio in 2014 was £575.4 million, its best year since the start of the recession in 2008. The RAJAR survey for the first quarter of 2015 reveals that both BBC and commercial radio still have large and devoted audiences. Total hours of listening are over a million, shared 54.4 per cent by the BBC and 42.8 per cent by commercial stations.

Radio in the UK is valued by its listeners and remains a highly valued platform for the widest expression of ideas by politicians and other opinion formers. In contrast, the local commercial television services, launched in direct competition with commercial radio by Jeremy Hunt in 2011 when he was secretary of state for culture, media and sport, and put out to tender by Ofcom in 2013, have so far had no significant success in attracting audiences or advertisers.

This, I suggest, has to do with the nature of radio. It is an intimate medium, one which appears to speak personally to listeners while making us feel part of a special community. It is a traditional medium. Listeners over 30 have grown up within the homes of their parents/guardians and, as adults, have built into their own daily lives, waking up to it, driving with it, turning to it when there is an emergency (bad weather, strikes, disasters) for fast, frequent and trusted information, staying with it for entertainment and company. Change, however, is afoot.

Revolution

Listeners under 50 grew up with UK commercial radio. Listeners under 30 now turn first to websites for music, news, practical information and fun. All radio's loss of listening hours among the 15-35 age group is of concern (a concern shared just as anxiously by television companies). It is significant that the BBC has steadily been moving into the online world for more than two decades. For this the BBC must thank John Birt, As BBC director general, Birt spotted the digital revolution as it began, observed its development, and grasped the communications opportunities it held.

> It offered the prospect of an abundance of channels and thus an end to scarcity; better pictures and sound quality; the facility to order programmes on demand; the opportunity for consumers to interact, participate or track down information of their choosing; the ability to hold one's own massive archive, in the home; and increasing mobility, with access to video and audio on the move (Birt, John, *The Harder Path*, Time Warner Books, 2002).

His strategy to integrate it within the BBC was gradual. His managing director radio Liz Forgan announced the plan for BBC digital-only radio stations in 1993. Birt set up a steering group for digital broadcasting in 1995, launched BBC online in December 1997, called for a rise in the licence fee to fund new digital services in July 1999. In February 2000, the Blair government approved an above-inflation rise in the licence fee over a seven-year term. In December 2002, Jenny Abramsky (having succeeded Forgan as managing director radio) launched the first three digital-only stations, Radio 1Xtra, 6 Music and Radio 7 (later to become Radio 4 Extra, joining two further digital services, the Asian Network and 5 Live Sports Extra).

The massive investment required for such a leap into the future, one that would serve audiences, fulfil charter obligations and maintain the BBC as a world leader in broadcasting, thus came via the licence fee. Persuading the public, the politicians, even his own executive of the necessity of taking such a bold step was not easy but, with the growth of satellite television, it rapidly became clear that Birt's vision of the BBC's public service role in this new media world was wise, well informed, practical and in the national interest.

It also gave the BBC a huge advantage over commercial rivals, in newspapers as well as broadcasting, one growing more apparent every year since. The hostility of the press to the BBC's online news services is unremitting. Every listener and viewer, however, is in the debt of Birt and the digital apostles he fostered throughout the 1990s for securing a major role for public service broadcasting in the new international communications world.

Radio fits that world perfectly. Its portability is an obvious advantage and, as time has gone by, manufacturers have realised it. Radio is no longer just a box in a room. It can be in your hand, on your phone. It will only stay there, however, if what comes out of it is appealing. The online world is global, the choice of listening it brings is massive. Why listen to the BBC when you have access to the world's radio and all its podcasts? Because the BBC still offers radio in more varieties, with high standards and star names at a bargain price.

Show me the money

BBC Radio delivers 43 per cent of (total BBC) consumption for 19 per cent of the licence fee. Of the total BBC licence fee spend, national services get £270 million; digital radio services £27 million; local radio £115 million; nations' radio £69 million. BBC World Service, the cost of which was transferred to the BBC from the Foreign Office in 2015 as part of the last licence fee settlement, receives £245 million.

These figures seem astronomical to commercial rivals. Last year's total annual revenue of UK commercial radio stations was £575.4 million. They are businesses and must make a profit to keep on air. Their formats are simpler, their obligations fewer. It costs listeners nothing to be part of their audience. BBC Radio costs each household 8p per day. That supports five orchestras (£29 million) as well as everything on the national networks, from Radios 1 to 5 Live, digital 1Xtra to the Asian Network, Chris Evans on Radio 2 to the Reith Lectures on Radio 4. Curiously, not everyone who pays the licence fee realises that they get radio for it, too. Perhaps it's not so curious, since it's called the television licence.

Why it matters

Every public discussion about 'the Netflix effect' i.e. the shift to subscription for additional television services, omits to calculate the impact that losing licence fee funding would have on BBC Radio. A frequently made charge against the BBC generally and radio in particular is that it spreads itself too widely, thereby choking commercial competition. Financial columnist Jeremy Warner, commenting in the *Daily Telegraph* (13 May 2015) on the appointment of John Whittingdale as the new secretary of state for culture, media and sport, discussed funding options.

> I doubt the subscription model would work for the BBC. Reform should rather start with a significant cut to the licence fee, the enforced sale or closure of stations already well catered for by the private sector, such as Radios 1 and 5, and some kind of curtailment of the BBC website, which has wrecked the regional press and denied national titles the salvation of meaningful subscription models.

He speaks for many BBC competitors in regard to the website. He seems unaware, however, that any further reduction in licence fee income will directly hit beyond networks, slicing into the Proms, *Today, In Our Time, The Archers*. As to audiences of Radios 1 and 5 being 'already well catered for by the private sector', he is seriously under-informed. Four decades of UK commercial radio have demonstrated that the market cannot provide radio which offers more than recorded music and live conversation. BBC Radios 1 and 5 Live serve different audiences from those addressed by the commercial sector. BBC Radio 1 and its digital sister 1Xtra both offer a wider spectrum of new music and features than any market-led radio station requires for attracting a lucrative audience. Radio 5 Live is fundamentally different in content and style from talkSport and, because of its roots in both BBC News and local radio, can instantly switch when necessary to national coverage of breaking stories. BBC Local Radio still speaks to a huge audience that no commercial operator wants because it's older, quieter, poorer. It is also devoted. Ask any backbench MP.

BBC Radio isn't perfect. What all the research shows, however, is that all radio is alive and developing. In many ways, the licence fee underwrites the future of any radio with social and intellectual purpose, the BBC and independent producers who supply it, the communications business racing to keep up with it, on radio, online, on tablets and iPhones. Prospero's old Shakespearean magic of invisible music and voices in the air shows no sign of fading.

Section 6:
White on White? Diversity
(the Test Card)

John Mair

Britain is now truly a multicultural and multiracial society. As the BBC moves towards its centenary in 2022, it has to try to reflect that.

Some simple facts and figures from the 2011 census. The UK population was 63.2 million – 53 million in England, 5.3 million in Scotland, 3.1 million in Wales and 1.8 million in Northern Ireland. Ethnic diversity is increasing – 86 per cent were white (4.3 per cent less that in 2001 and 8.1 per cent less than in 1991) while 80.5 per cent described themselves as 'white British'. London was the most ethnically diverse area, Wales the least. Integration was on the rise: 12 per cent of households in 2011 had a partner from a different ethnic group. Immigration too: of the 7.5 million born outside the UK in England and Wales, more than half (3.8 million) had arrived in the previous decade.

Christianity was on the wane with four million fewer ticking the Christian box on the census form than ten years previously. The United Kingdom was simply becoming a patchwork in all sorts of ways: nation, race, class, place and country of origin and destination.

Television found it technically easy to move from black and white to colour in the 1960s. It has found it more difficult to recognise colour on- and off-screen in the last three decades. As the then-director general Greg Dyke put it in 2001, the BBC was 'hideously white'. The non-white faces were to be found among the cleaners, in the canteen and engaged in more menial tasks; the white faces were seen on the editorial and executive floors and on screen. Apartheid by job description. Dyke determined to do something about it. Others have before and since. They have sadly failed. The ethnicity balance in the BBC has probably gone backwards.

There was some progress on screen at first. But it seemed to this observer that the doors to the studios opened to a cadre of young Anglo-Asian, usually female, presenters eager to take their place on set. Black faces were not really any more present on screen than they had been before the Dyke revolution. That had been stillborn. Numbers and percentages of BAME (Black and Minority Ethnic) people working in the television industry had gone down rather than up.

It was a guilty and undiscussed secret of the industry. It took one of the best known black faces on British television, Lenny Henry (now Sir Lenny), to point this out at a BAFTA speech in 2014. That lit the blue touch paper of guilt. Only then did the broadcasters, including the BBC, start to take proper notice to set up various positive action programmes in some haste. What effect they will have – only time will tell.

Sir Lenny's distinguished (black) friend, Marcus Ryder, the head of current affairs at BBC Scotland responsible for many of the best investigative programmes of recent years, has contributed on diversity issues for this volume. The Ryder scorecard is not entirely positive:

> It is vital that our dramas and television hold a true reflection of the audience they serve or else they will be failing those very people. However, often the broadcasters' discussion around on-screen diversity lacks a maturity that is essential to make a real difference.

In the previously uncharted waters of British multicultural broadcasting, Farrukh Dhondy is a Sir Walter Raleigh figure. Over fourteen years at Channel 4 he put (and financed) diversity on screen in drama, comedy and current affairs. His footprint will be there for a long time. In his own professional life, Dhondy had written some of the great early multicultural hits such as *Tandoori Nights*.

Back in prehistory (the 1970s), all the broadcasters were reaching out to ethnic niches. New audiences existed from the waves of Commonwealth immigration and their progeny. Britain had changed. The BBC set up a special unit in Birmingham, Channel 4 a multi-cultural commissioning editor. Good programmes like *Black Britain* and *The Bandung File* (1985-1991) came out of those initiatives. Today, BAME programmes on television are noticeable only in their absence. Sir Lenny Henry is right. Dhondy comments:

> Looking back it becomes clear that the impulse to what is now called diversity arose from an attempt at assimilation of the new communities. It was stimulated by the militancy that expressed the socio-political dissatisfactions of these communities. If these communities were to be integrated into Britain's settled population they had to be understood, appreciated and absorbed and television had to play its central part.

Not much action to level the gender playing field

And what of women (in number terms actually a majority, according to the 2011 census)? On screen, their representation has changed to take in tougher, grittier roles as senior policewomen or similar, even women's soccer is getting substantially more coverage. Off screen, there was an awareness but not that much action to level the gender playing field. Grace Wyndham Goldie (1900-1986), a leading BBC producer and executive, may have been a legend but she did not break the BBC glass ceiling forever. Women have been channel controllers, even directors of television but none has made it to the Himalayan peak of the director generalship. Caroline Thomson, the corporation's chief operating officer (2011-2012) got closest, coming second to George Entwistle in the 2012 DG race. She fell at the final hurdle.

Professor Suzanne Franks, in her contribution, worries that a smaller BBC, downsized by default through the poor licence fee settlement in July 2015, may see even fewer opportunities for women in the corridors of power at the corporation:

> There is no question that there have been impressive efforts made to enhance the progress of women in a range of ways within the corporation such as the 'Women in Leadership' group targeting middle managers. Now the concern (based on the experience of other institutions) is that an organisation that downsizes may find such initiatives a 'luxury' and 'dispensable' in such an environment.

So away from the huge financial and political challenges, the BBC faces the great challenge of being all things to all men and women in the United Kingdom. No mean task.

Notes

[1] http://www.ons.gov.uk/ons/rel/census/2011-census/population-and-household-estimates-for-the-united-kingdom/index.html, accessed on 1 August 2015

[2] http://www.theguardian.com/media/2001/jan/07/uknews.theobserver1, accessed on 2 August 2015

[3] www.bafta.org/television/.../lenny-henry-annual-television-lecture-2014, accessed on 1 August 2015

[4] http://www.imdb.com/title/tt0088623/, accessed on 3 August 2015

[5] http://www.imdb.com/title/tt3646052/, accessed on 3 August 2015

Diversity: The Way Ahead

There is little doubt that all the broadcasters want to achieve both a more diverse workforce and on-screen representation: nearly all of them have set a series of actions to try to achieve this. But, according to Marcus Ryder, the fear is whether this can achieved without genuine changes in culture and working practices

As far back as the second century BC there are records of people trying to solve one of the world's great geographical mysteries: what is the source of the Nile? In the nineteenth century the riddle was solved when it became apparent there were actually two answers. The world's longest river has two main branches – the White Nile, which flows 4,230 miles from its remotest central African sources to the Mediterranean, and the Blue Nile, which rises high up on the Ethiopian plateau and flows for 1,450 miles.

For a black man working in British television for more than twenty years, I have been trying to solve a far more mundane mystery: how has diversity in television become such an important issue in the last year? And just as over the source of the Nile there are two answers.

On 14 May 2013, Creative Skillset published its Creative Industry census which finally confirmed what many of us working in television already suspected: that things were bad for ethnic minorities working in the industry and were getting worse. In 2006, BAMEs (Black Asian and Minority Ethnics) made up 7.4 per cent of the total workforce; by 2009 this had dropped to 6.7 per cent and by 2012 the percentage stood at 5.4 per cent. What made the figures even more striking was that between 2009 and 2012 the industry had actually grown by 4,000 people (the equivalent of 2 per cent) at the same time the number of BAMEs working in the industry had fallen by 2,000. This meant that for every BAME person who had left the industry two white people had been employed. This was not an industry in crisis: it was growing healthily. The crisis was over what was happening to ethnic diversity in the industry.

Damning figures fail to penetrate industry

But these damning figures hardly penetrated the industry, let alone the public consciousness. As someone who takes a keen interest in diversity, I saw no increase in the discussion around the issue either in public or behind closed doors. Which takes us to the second source.

Almost a year after the Creative Skillset figures were published Lenny Henry gave a speech at Bafta. Henry had given speeches before about the subject of under-representation of non-white people in the television industry but this one differed in two crucial aspects. The first is that he had empirical evidence from the Creative Skillset census and, second, he was able to point to solutions that had actually worked in increasing diversity. Increasing diversity did not have to be a liberal lost cause on a par with achieving world peace and ending poverty.

In the proceeding ten years, the American Network ABC had increased on-screen ethnic diversity from approximately 3 per cent to more than 25 per cent. ABC achieved this at the same time they appointed a non-white head of casting, Keli Lee, who takes a keen increase in diversity and Shonda Rhimes, a black woman, became one of their most important showrunners. Closer to home in the same ten years before Lenny Henry's speech he was able to point to the increase in regional diversity. In 2003, 3.7 per cent of the core programming budget was being spent in Scotland, despite Scotland having around 9 per cent of the UK population while 91 per cent of BBC produced network programmes were made in and around London. The BBC made a financial commitment to increasing regional diversity and by the time Lenny Henry gave his speech 50 per cent of network spend was outside the M25. Scotland accounted for more than 9 per cent of network programmes and the number of network programmes produced in the English regions had increased by 400 per cent.

So what, since the census and Henry's speech, has been achieved?

Creative Skillset's census and Lenny Henry's speech provided the perfect storm and TV diversity was firmly put on the agenda and continues to be so. The question now is: has anything been achieved since the issue has become so high profile? First of all there has been a raft of initiatives announced and new targets announced by most of the major UK broadcasters – BBC, ITV, Channel 4 and Sky.

The BBC announced a new senior leadership programme in which six people from BAME backgrounds are given a year's experience working at the most senior levels of the BBC. An assistant commissioner development programme was set up giving a further six people training in programme commissioning. These two initiatives were seen as obvious attempts to address the problem of the glass-ceiling faced by so many BAMEs at the BBC whose careers seem to stop at the producer level.

The BBC also set aside £2.1 million of its programme development spend for diversity programmes. The definition of what constitutes a 'diversity programme' has been vague and seems to include criteria ranging from production staff such as writers from a BAME background to on-screen diversity and subject matter. Although it would appear that the primary focus is on-screen diversity, it is doubtful if a production could qualify for any of the £2.1 million in development funds irrespective of how diverse its staff are if the subject matter on screen was not also specifically black or Asian – but this is not yet clear. At entry level, the BBC will take 20 graduate trainees from diverse backgrounds as well as working with grassroots organisations such as the Mama Youth Project and the Stephen Lawrence Trust to widen its pool of apprenticeships.

The ultimate goal for the BBC is to increase BAME on-screen diversity from 10.4 per cent to 15 per cent and behind the camera to achieve 14.2 per cent representation of BAME staff by 2017 and 15 per cent of senior staff by 2020. While the BBC was announcing these initiatives Sky set out a far simpler set of goals although no less ambitious. By the end of 2015, the broadcaster wants 20 per cent of its on-screen talent and writing teams to be BAMEs. Sky estimates it could impact on as many as 100 shows across Sky 1, Sky Atlantic, Sky Living and Sky Arts (although Sky News was noticeably absent in this drive).

Channel 4's approach to increasing diversity
Channel 4 has taken a different approach to increasing diversity. It has not only doubled its spending on diversity to £5 million a year which covers all commitments laid out in its diversity charter and includes an annual £2 million Alpha Fund. It also has its growth fund of £20 million to be invested in independents over three years from January 2014 and has invested in two BAME companies at undisclosed cost. In addition, senior executives will have to hit diversity targets to trigger bonuses and it is aiming for 20 per cent of all staff to be BAMEs by 2020. But its most ambitious proposal has been its new commissioning process. To qualify for money, all new programme commissions must demonstrate diversity in specified criteria both on-screen and behind the camera in a 'two tick' process.

ITV has set a 14 per cent of BAME representation on air – to match Britain's population – by 2016, although it has set no targets for employment or executive roles behind the camera. Most remarkably, ITV is now seen as unambitious by most people in the industry. It is a sign of just how far the diversity debate has moved that a 14 per cent BAME on-screen target is seen as the bare minimum in discussing television diversity. In fact, the culture around diversity has changed so much that even Viacom, owners of Channel 5, who had previously stayed silent on the issue, has rejoined the Creative Diversity Network – the industry body overseeing television diversity – and is currently assessing its performance and monitoring diversity before announcing what it will do.

Talking of the Creative Diversity Network (formerly the Cultural Diversity Network), there has been general agreement that, since its inception more than ten years ago, the organisation has failed to deliver on its objective of increasing diversity in the industry. Over the last year it has undergone a major restructure and set up pan-industry training schemes and is currently rolling out an industry standard of how diversity should be monitored.

Finally the Equality and Human Rights Commission has been given £130,000 by the department of culture, media and sport to give advice on equality issues to the television industry.

The list and range of initiatives to increase diversity has been so extensive in the last year that it even prompted a Royal Television Society debate titled 'Diversity: Job Done?' The answer to that debate question is a resounding 'Not yet'. Indeed, there are still a number of obstacles and possible pitfalls facing all the industry's initiatives. Depending on how the broadcasters tackle these problems will determine if there will be a genuine cultural shift in British television or whether the recent initiatives will just be added to a long list of diversity initiatives which have had no long-term impact. The statistic that most sceptics like to quote is the Freedom of Information request that revealed that over 15 years the BBC rolled out 29 initiatives to increase BME diversity while at the same time diversity actually fell. But it was against this background that most people had given up on ever being able to increase diversity and precisely why the renewed efforts taking place now following the Lenny Henry call to arms are so exciting.

So what are the problems that the latest initiatives face and the industry has to overcome in general? First of all it should be recognised that the situation is getting worse. *Broadcast* magazine recently published the results of a Freedom of Information request that revealed the number of BAME staff leaving the BBC is at a five-year high (incidentally it is only a 'five-year high' since this is as far back as the figures go). In 2009, the number of BAME resignations made up 8.6 per cent of the total – roughly in line with the percentage of BAMEs employed at the BBC. Every year since then, BAME staff have been over-represented in the resignation figures ranging from 14 per cent to 16.1 per cent last year.

The London problem

First of all most people do not believe that the industry has become racist or the culture has become less welcoming to non-white staff. In fact, the BAME diversity figures are far worse than they first appear. The non-white population of the UK is 12.5 per cent. It is bad enough that the Creative Skillset figures point to an industry with just 5.4 per cent BAMEs but the bulk of the industry is based in London which has a BAME population of 40 per cent. When you realise that BAME representation is not just half of what it should be but almost an eighth considering where it is based the uphill struggle can appear daunting.

The London factor also goes some way to explaining why BAME diversity has reached crisis point in the last ten years. The BBC has made tremendous strides in increasing regional diversity in both its output and spend. But this has meant relocating productions to parts of the country with a far lower BAME population. The four main BBC production bases outside of London are Glasgow, Belfast, Cardiff and Greater Manchester. Scotland has a BAME population of 4 per cent, Northern Ireland 1.7 per cent, Wales 4.4 per cent and Manchester 16.2 per cent. All a far cry from London's 40.4 per cent.

Many people have argued that it has been easier for white staff to relocate out of London compared to their non-white colleagues who do not have the same support structures away from the capital. This certainly would explain why there is a higher rate of BAME resignations over the last five years directly mirroring the production move.

In January 2015, when Channel 4's licence was renewed, Ofcom revealed Channel 4's out-of-London commissioning quotas were set to be tripled to £12 million. Regionality is simply a reality in British broadcasting now and the trend looks set to continue. Assuming that increased regionality and decreased BAME diversity are related, then any diversity initiatives need to address the 'London problem'. The workforce in London needs to more accurately reflect the community it comes from. On top of this when relocating staff 'colour-blindness' is not a luxury the industry can afford. Television is a tough enough business at the best of times demanding long hours combined with creative pressures. The only way staff can survive these is through strong support structures. It is naive to think that all the support structures are the same for everybody in different parts of the country.

Critical mass strategy
In increasing regional diversity the BBC has specifically focused on the idea of critical mass. It designated certain nations and regions as being 'centres of excellence' for specific programme genres. For example, Northern Ireland is a centre of excellence for current affairs; Scotland is a centre of excellence for daytime programmes and arts, and it is no coincidence that half the universe's aliens seem to enter earth in *Doctor Who* via Cardiff. This focus on specific genres provides an environment for productions to grow together and concentrate skills and resources. Another crucial component of the BBC's critical mass strategy is that the corporation gave a clear indication as to the level of commitment and commissions it was concentrating in each region and genre for several years into the future. This enables both in-house BBC staff and independent productions to make long-term plans.

But when it comes to BAME staff, one of the most important aspects of the critical mass strategy is that it provides a structure in which they can help one another. This was evident when it came to increasing female participation in the BBC in the late 1980s and early 1990s when many women were in specific departments such as features (which included *That's Life*, *Watchdog* and *Crimewatch*). This concentration created an environment that nurtured talent which then went to flourish throughout the BBC.

However, in any discussion about critical mass there is a fine line between a 'centre of excellence' and a 'ghetto'. Certainly, the most productive critical mass for women has been where they have been working on general journalism – not where they have been working on 'women's issues'. In the same way, it is doubtful that regional diversity would have had the same success if BBC Scotland had focused on haggis and kilts and BBC Wales on sheep and daffodils.

The current BAME diversity plans of all the broadcasters make no mention of critical mass. Instead, the different targets will be dispersed throughout the production output. They are colour-blind policies that might derail genuine ambitions in a culturally specific world.

On-screen diversity by numbers

Everyone acknowledges that on-screen diversity is vital in a modern Britain. To quote Shakespeare's Hamlet, plays hold 'the mirror up to nature'. Here, Hamlet echoes classical authors, who insisted that drama be a form of truth, not mere entertainment. It is vital that our dramas and television hold a true reflection of the audience they serve or else they will be failing those very people. However, often the broadcasters' discussion around on-screen diversity lacks a maturity that is essential to make a real difference. Although more non-white faces on television is an essential first step in achieving Shakespeare's 'mirror' it cannot end there. While there are often strong individual black and Asian characters in television dramas and high profile BAME presenters they are invariably isolated, surrounded by white colleagues or placed in a white community. As Lenny Henry questioned in his Bafta speech: 'Where are Luther's black friends?'. Black and Asian communities are still all too often represented as dysfunctional, populated by forced marriages, gangsters and potential terrorists. And there are rarely BAME presenters who culturally identify themselves as from an ethnic minority the way that Jamie Oliver has a clear cultural background or Graham Norton does.

This is an incredibly tough diversity 'nut' to crack. There is a clear recognition that genuine on-screen representation is dependent on BAME representation behind the camera. Hence both Sky and the BBC have specifically highlighted the importance of BAME script writers in their drama output. The concern, however, is that on-screen targets could be achieved without a cultural shift in people's perceptions about the output.

Defining diversity

How do you define a 'diverse programme'? At one end of the spectrum the BBC currently has no clear definition and so productions are often at a loss as to what would and would not qualify for the £2.1 million development diversity fund. At the other end of the spectrum is Channel 4 with its 'two tick' system. The problem is that the 'two tick' system is so broad covering so many aspects of diversity it is difficult to see how any production could not qualify as a diverse production with a few tweaks and with possibly no noticeable increase in on-screen or behind-the-camera diversity. One would be foolish to underestimate abilities of production staff to get around criteria.

Again, we may want to look at what has been successful in the past. We do not allow broadcasters to define an 'out of London production'. Instead, there is an industry-wide definition as defined by Ofcom, an independent body overseeing the television industry. With this track record it may be advisable for Ofcom to play the same role again and define what is a 'diverse production' though only after public consultation and scrutiny.

Conclusion

There is little doubt that all the broadcasters want to achieve both a more diverse workforce and on-screen representation. Nearly all of them have set a series of actions to try to achieve this. The fear is whether this can achieved without genuine changes in culture and working practice and genuine upheaval. This was the case with increasing regional diversity, while incredibly successful industry insiders still talk about the 'pain' they went through and still experience to achieve the increase in out-of-London productions. Currently, the BAME diversity attempts still amount to reshuffling of existing funds and setting new targets. The real test will come when broadcasters start to face difficulties in pushing through these initiatives.

The Poverties of Diversity

Black and Asian communities have, through the growth of the second and third generation of 'ethnic' or 'diverse' Brits, invaded its meritocracy with a vengeance, argues Farrukh Dhondy. Their talents should carry them through the Kafkaesque labyrinth of the BBC. Yet the hideousness is not in the lack of numbers but in the missing dimension of penetrative perspectives

Introduction: Beyond Greg Dyke's 'hideously white' comment

If you catch the BBC news each evening or watch *Newsnight* on weekdays you may note a strong presence of black and Asian reporters and newsreaders. Most of them project the local news or report on 'ethnic affairs' – which is fair enough. I am sure that Secunder Kermani for *Newsnight* will have easier or a more sympathetic access to the Muslim husbands of women from Bradford who have run away to join the Islamic State, than say a white woman reporter.

That's not to say that Kermani is not deployed on stories that have nothing to do with Muslim culture or background. He is not a token figure. Neither are the newsreaders who present the regional news. They have become institutions in themselves and, at the Asian or black celebrations I have attended, are invited as chief guests and celebrities. Moreover, if one reads down the list of credits at the end of news and particular documentary programmes, the number of Asian names and occasionally the clearly African ones stand out. As far as people of West Indian origin are concerned, a name like Darcus Howe may indicate the individual's 'diversity' but a name like Tamara Howe would not.

When Greg Dyke was appointed director general of the BBC in January 2000, one of his first remarks was that the institution was 'hideously white'. Dyke has a background in race relations and I suppose he instinctively began to count, once he had passed the security guards, receptionists and canteen staff, to assess the numbers of people of colour in the corridors of broadcasting power through which he was being guided. His comment was a volley in the numbers game.

Poles apart

So how did this particular numbers game get started? There are today thousands of European citizens living and even settling in Britain. It's what Nigel Farage and his party, UKIP, are on about. There is as yet, and unlikely in the near future, to be any agitation for the BBC or other broadcasters to recruit Polish or Hungarian newsreaders, reporters, actors, writers or directors. The diktat of 'diversity' does not yet apply to them.

Go a bit further back in the diversification of Britain and note the fact that the Jewish population of the country, long-settled here with a boost in numbers before and during World War Two, fought against anti-Semitism but were never considered, through criteria of 'diversity', as candidates for recruitment to broadcasting outfits or for that matter to parliament. They made their own way into both without what the Americans first called 'positive action' driven by liberal traditions. Disraeli was not made leader of his party because its great and good thought it was about time a Jew was given a shot at being prime minister. I hesitate to name the Jewish individuals who have risen in broadcasting and journalism through their own talent and perseverance, and though there are no statistics and should not be any, the reader is free to count.

Levellers and intruders

The history behind Greg Dyke's exclamation, and behind the expression he used, is that of post-war immigration from Britain's ex-colonies to the sceptred isle. It is no secret that the experience of World War Two was one of levelling in the class set-up of Britain. Those who were sent to lay down their lives for the sake of King and Country, and didn't through luck or strategy make the ultimate sacrifice, counted their entitlements within the body politic. They replaced the icon of victory with the Labour Party and Clement Attlee. Laws were passed to expand universal education and health care for all.

British meritocracy established itself firmly for the first time. The literary movement reflecting the change came to be known as 'kitchen sink'. Novels about the socially mobile 'cad' stealing the colonel's daughters and plays about the sons of miners returning from university and the professions to misunderstandings in the homes to which they were born made up the bulk of this oeuvre. The 'kitchen sink' movement failed, if my reading is adequate, to portray the young men and women who abandoned the textile mills of Yorkshire and Lancashire, or at least refused to work the night shift in these and other dark, satanic enterprises. OK, there was a bit of dark and satanic in driving underground trains for eight or twelve hours a day, but perhaps not in cleaning the streets, manning the buses of the cities as conductors and attending to the nursing and doing the dirty jobs in hospitals. Thousands of citizens of the ex-colonies of India and Pakistan, and of the Caribbean and African colonies agitating for the independence that the subcontinent had gained, were willing to come to Britain and fill the vacancies.

They came as not quite an underclass, but as whole communities who found themselves working at the lowest rungs of employment in the manufacturing and service sectors. The houses they occupied, say, in Dewsbury, Bradford, High Wycombe, Huddersfield or even Brixton and Catford were the cheapest accommodation for rent. It would be inaccurate to call Bradford or Dewsbury a ghetto. It would be more accurate to designate them as 'mill-and-mosque' towns as the Muslim communities, largely of Mirpuri origin from Pakistan, found work and established communities there.

In the middle and late 1960s, the spectres of discontent began to haunt the immigrant communities of 'ethnic' descent. Dissatisfaction with wages, conditions, schooling, housing, treatment at the hands of the police and a general apprehension of racial exclusion and tension gave rise to restlessness and then to agitation. Groups such as the Indian Workers' Association and the British Black Panther Movement carried this restlessness and agitation forward. Enoch Powell's 1968 'Rivers of Blood' speech did not result in any deterioration of race relations or worsening of conditions for what were still seen as immigrant communities. It marked the divide between this 'immigrant' status and the declaration of these communities that 'Come what may, we are here to stay'. There was a general realisation, given official sanction through social initiatives, that Britain was now a 'diverse' population.

At the time of Powell's speech the number of people from the subcontinent, the Caribbean and Africa did not amount to more than 3 or 4 per cent of the population of Britain. The Jewish population of Britain had even fewer numbers, but they had established their permanence and without fuss or fury had more than 50 members of parliament representing different parties.

In the late 1960s and early 1970s there was a lot of rhetoric about 'revolution', not least amongst the groupuscules of the immigrant population and strongly from the far-left parties calling themselves Marxist or Maoist. What became evident, even at the time, that if the revolution was not imminent, the only way out of the restlessness and an answer to perceived discrimination was liberal reform and anti-discrimination laws. Broadcasting had not entered the numbers game yet. What was it doing?

Multicultural TV and the liberal impulse to assist assimilation

Multicultural broadcasting began through the liberal impulse to assist the immigrant population to assimilate. There were programmes on the BBC which instructed subcontinental immigrants in the ways of their new home: how to greet people, what the festivals of Britain mean, how not to bargain at supermarket counters in an attempt to bring the bill down, where to look for assistance of all sorts and other useful tips. There were also programmes about good neighbourliness.

These patronising programmes were accompanied by attempts at providing culture. It began with early Sunday morning programmes featuring classical Indian music and dance, which were to the majority of the immigrant population like playing Wagner at a Justin Bieber gig. There were the noble-minded attempts at providing comedy beginning with a programme featuring a black and a white family called *Love Thy Neighbour*. There was a comedy called *Mind Your Language* about a language school whose humour depended on the mispronunciation of English by immigrants and the howlers and malapropisms in their usage. It was an attempt to portray culture-clash and was a popular programme which was enthusiastically bought by Indian television stations but fell foul of the political considerations of later British critiques.

There was a response to the political protests for equality and the perception of racism which came from London Weekend Television. They recruited or promoted from their ranks people of colour to be producers of a programme called *Skin*. Its very title told you that it was an anti-racist effort but its televisual content soon turned into a mission to complain. *Skin* would pick a theme and demonstrate that blacks and Asians were subject to racist attitudes and racial discrimination in education, in housing, in employment, in treatment by the police, the courts etc. The project was destined to run out of steam or repeat itself. Television presents and debates political and social problems and should not make the mistake of thinking it is able to solve them.

Through the 1980s, the BBC, commendably the drama department at Pebble Mill, ventured into the commissioning of work from black and Asian writers. The drama series *Empire Road*, written by Guyanese writer Michael Abensetts, was an entertaining insight into the life of one of the new communities in the Midlands. There had been attempts at introducing black and Asian characters in series such as *Crossroads*, but the characterisation and plots demonstrated no intimacy with the increasingly enclosed life of these immigrant communities.

Ego trip

David Rose and Peter Ansorge who commissioned *Empire Road* went on to commission me to write *Come To Mecca*, a series of six short plays about young Asians. Five of them were adaptations of short stories from two or three of my collections. The sixth story, *Romance Romance*, written as an original television play, won the Samuel Becket prize for the best single play that year.

The way the stories and the plays came to be written is possibly, in some small way, illustrative of the literary evolution of 'diversity' in Britain. In the 1970s, while I earned my living as a school teacher, I was a member of a black radical group which published a weekly newspaper and distributed it through the few black and Asian shops who consented to stock it and through members of the group selling it outside tube stations and in markets. The newspaper, four to eight pages in tabloid presentation, was strongly influenced by C. L. R. James, the Marxist historian and writer, who exhorted the group and its editors to avoid Marxist rhetoric and write about the experience of life and work of the members. He saw that the members of the group, all black and Asian, were part of a new phase of Britain's history and he urged us to be truthful chroniclers of the detail of it. The injunction was simple. If you are a bus conductor, write about an incident that took place in the garage or on the bus. The more dramatic the better.

I enthusiastically responded to the directive by writing about the incidents of the week in the school where I taught. It was a mixed race South London school and there were plenty of 'stories' that presented themselves: an accusation of theft that turned racial, a fifth-form disco which was invaded by black boys from Brixton seeking revenge in some love triangle, a pupil who threw a bench at an art teacher without being provoked, a strike by the white boys who defied the ban on long hair which was joined by black boys with very short hair. The pieces were short and unsigned. After a few months of such contributions, a young man in a pin-striped three piece suit drove into the school looking for me. He was directed to the staff room. He turned out to be an editor at a publishing house.

We went for a drink to talk about publishing my work over in the pub. I supposed the short pieces were technically the property of the newspaper and were not what I would call proper short stories. The significant thing he said at that first meeting was that a readership existed for stories about the young immigrant experience before the stories existed. He, perhaps prematurely, used the word 'literature'. We struck a deal. I would write him a fresh set of stories and he would draw up a publisher's contract. That first book led to a demand for another and several other publishers asking for a third and then a fourth. Over those three years I decided I could quit teaching and concentrate on trying to earn a living through writing, an ambition I had from my schooldays in India. And now it seemed possible.

These first books of stories attracted the attention of Peter Ansorge, the BBC producer at Pebble Mill, who contracted me to turn them into television plays. At the same time, a young company called the Black Theatre Cooperative, who had had a success with their first play by Trinidadian playwright Mustapha Matura, invited me to adapt one of my stories for the stage. I persuaded them to accept a fresh reggae musical instead. It worked and transferred from their base in a Paddington community centre to the Institute of Contemporary Arts and then to the Arts Theatre in the West End for a short run.

The work of the Black Theatre Cooperative came to the notice of Humphrey Barclay, the supremo of light entertainment at London Weekend Television (LWT), and he proposed that we devise a sit-com through a workshop for which LWT would pay and the product of which LWT would produce. Mustapha and I wrote a series called *No Problem*. It was 1982 and Channel 4 was to begin broadcasting in November. It was given the remit to represent 'minority' interests and that brief was interpreted as making programmes that the BBC and ITV would not make. A situation comedy about five young West Indian siblings, in their late teens and older, fitted the brief and Channel 4 broadcast *No Problem*.

The then commissioning editor for multicultural programming at Channel 4 was Sue Woodford, who had worked as a producer in ITV. After the relative success of *No Problem.* she approached me to write an Asian sit-com and I came up with the idea of *Tandoori Nights*, a rivalry between two Indian restaurants called *The Jewel in the Crown* and *The Far Pavilions*, names ironically stolen from the ground-breaking and vastly popular television series which featured the Raj. The BBC followed my *Come to Mecca* series by commissioning a four-part drama called *King of the Ghetto* which was shown on BBC Two. So no shortage of work. I happened to be in the right place at the right, or ripe, time.

Here to stay

Looking back it becomes clear that the impulse to what is now called diversity arose from an attempt at assimilation of the new communities. It was stimulated by the militancy that expressed the socio-political dissatisfactions of these communities. If these communities were to be integrated into Britain's settled population they had to be understood, appreciated and absorbed – and television had to play its central part.

Channel 4's specific multicultural brief altered the perspective of all British television. To put it in its most general form, the mission to complain was dead and this most social and socialising of all media, the box in the home, had to penetrate the drama, the truth, the tragedy, the comedy and the nuances of existence within the new communities. The sit-coms were not commissioned, written or acted to project a 'positive image' of immigrants, to protest against racism or to provide 'role models'. They were written to entertain audiences, to make them laugh through dramatic conflict. The profundity of the comedy would be its exploration, exposure or exposition of the vanities, the nuances of perception and perspective of characters who were fresh to the screen. The drama had to be a demonstration of the dilemmas of a complex and fast-changing society, warts and all. *Othello* wasn't written to provide role models for bad young blacks or to project a positive image of Moors.

Channel 4 assumed the brief of using commissioners and production teams which had a background in the communities about whom they were making documentaries, drama, situation comedy or any other genre of television. This gave rise to the employment of people of colour on- and off-screen. I had the privilege of being, for fourteen years, Channel 4's second multicultural commissioning editor and was obliged to commission those who could bring intimacy and insight to the schedule. There was no question of counting numbers and calculating percentages of the population.

Greg Dyke's remark was stimulated by a perception that there was a shortage of both on- and off-screen presence in the BBC. This concern translated itself into the numbers game. Strictly speaking, if the black and Asian population of Britain still constitute fewer than 5 per cent of the total, the BBC should be, at least in some departments, sacking some of its ethnic newsreaders, journalists and production staff to adjust to the 'correct' ratio. That would be, absurdly, the conclusion that a number count could lead to.

Though the BBC DG Tony Hall has publicly announced an effort towards greater 'diversity', there really is a diminished need today for a positive discrimination policy in employment. The black and Asian communities have, through the growth of the second and third generation of 'ethnic' or 'diverse' Brits, invaded its meritocracy with a vengeance. The talents of these individuals should and will carry them through the Kafkaesque labyrinth of the BBC. Of course, the numbers game is the easiest one to play and to publicise.

Conclusion: Let's stop counting

The more difficult task is the penetration of the ever-changing culture of the diverse communities. Television, the most potent social force to inform, educate and entertain has, through each of its forms, be it observational, investigative or discursive documentary, drama, comedy or history, failed to penetrate the lives and cultures within these communities. Witness the mass bewilderment of the country and the media when three married sisters take their children and abscond from Bradford to join the 'Islamic State' in Syria, using the ploy of going on pilgrimage to Medina. Who are these women? What do they think they are going to? What are they getting away from? And in Tower Hamlets? In April 2015, a mayor is forced to step down amid allegations of corruption, electoral fraud and religious coercion. The media reported the fall and cursorily traced the rise of Lutfur Rahman, but what in the life of that East London borough bred, spread and condoned that corruption?

In danger of adding to the negativity of these examples, has there been any dramatic or investigative inkling about how and why the grooming of young girls for sex by gangs of men from Rochdale and other towns – exposed in 2012 – was allowed to happen? Is it merely the failure of the police and social services? How is one to get access to these increasingly enclosed cultures in the heart of Britain? Turning to a lighter question, has the rise of the meritocratic Asian and black individuals occasioned the same cultural dislocation and mismatch of generational and class perspective that the 'kitchen-sink' writers from the white working class explored?

Yes, there are stray examples of some depth to investigation into the enclosures of culture on the BBC. There are black and Asian faces in the soap operas and there are ethnic names on the list of credits. The hideousness is not in the lack of numbers but in the missing dimension of penetrative perspectives.

Women Finding their Place at the BBC

There is no question there have been impressive efforts made to enhance the progress of women at the corporation, argues Suzanne Franks. The concern now is that an organisation downsizing may find such initiatives a 'luxury' and 'dispensable'

In its earliest days, the BBC, as an innovatory new service, displayed a comparatively progressive and enlightened attitude towards employing women. Lord Reith saw 'no reason why a woman should not become a station director' even though he added that 'it would be difficult to find one suitable ...' (Franks 2011: 126). The first head of talks, a forerunner of the documentaries department, was a woman – the formidable Hilda Matheson. She also established the BBC's first news service in 1926 during the general strike. And the origins of *The Week in Westminster*, still on air today, was as a programme made by and for women, to enlighten them about politics (ibid: 125).

The first BBC television producer was Mary Adams. In 1932, the marriage bar was imposed, so that in common with many other public institutions, women employed in the BBC were obliged to resign from employment after their wedding. But even then exceptions were permitted so that a number of talented married women could circumvent the bar and continue to work (Murphy 2014). And once the war began all these regulations were overturned and women filled a wide range of posts, both on- and off-air. There was even a day nursery set up in 1943 to help BBC mothers cope with childcare obligations.

The post-war period saw a steady decline in the progress of women within the corporation. Only a small handful rose to senior roles and those few who had on-air or on-screen roles were usually confined to female ghettoes such as women's or children's programming or departments such as personnel. Managing departments, presenting mainstream programmes or roles such as news reading and reporting, were now firmly out of bounds. Even brilliant women like the television current affairs supremo Grace Wyndham Goldie, one of the very few to succeed, may not have fulfilled their potential. Woodrow

Wyatt, reflecting upon Goldie in 1985, considered 'she could have run the BBC far better than any of Reith's successors ... but the prejudice against women was and is nearly insurmountable' (Higgins 2015: 90).

Meanwhile, the day nursery was shut down immediately the war was over and the BBC did not re-open a crèche until 1990 (except for a brief trial in 1974). Women in any kind of senior role became a rare sight until well into the 1980s. A former BBC governor, Thelma Cazalet-Keir, concerned about this imbalance, had written to *The Times* in 1962 asking why only four of the top 150 posts at the BBC were held by women (*The Times*, 21 March 1962). Her comments were ignored and twenty years later that figure had halved to only two, neither of whom were mothers (Murphy 2003).

Equality rules

As the women's movement gained ground in the late 1960s, wider social attitudes towards equality and gender began to shift, culminating in UK legislation on equal pay and sex discrimination. Yet the BBC as an institution was strangely slow to reflect such progress. Behaviour and practice within the corporation was still relatively backward for an organisation that prided itself as speaking for and to the nation. Elspeth Howe, as vice-chair of the new Equal Opportunities Commission in the 1970s, made clear her frustrations with the BBC: 'It had a duty to lead when half its audience were women. ... I really lost my patience' as she observed it was a place 'where able women worked and where they should have been recognised better' (Seaton 2015: 212).

Those women who *were* employed in the corporation may not have always had the most comfortable times. As recent revelations have made clear, the practice of harassment and in some cases outright abuse were not spoken about, but were very much part of the fabric of the BBC workplace (ibid). Of course, other areas of public and, indeed, private life may well have been just as susceptible, but somehow the intensity of programme-making, where creative teams worked closely together, combined with long anti-social hours and frequent travel may have made it more prevalent.

Eventually as a response to the general political and social re-configuring of women's roles in society, the BBC board of management in 1973 commissioned a report enquiring into the progress of women within the corporation. It produced some breathtaking revelations and evidence of staggering prejudice and discrimination. *Limitations to the Recruitment and Advancement of Women in the BBC* collected observations from across the corporation. They included remarks that 'toilet facilities and moral danger' were reasonable justifications to limit women in certain areas of the BBC. Similarly it would 'be wrong to have mixed sex shifts'. According to the editor of *Radio News*: 'Women are simply not able to do hard news stories as they see themselves as experts on women's features.' He had 'never found a woman with the remotest chance of working as a reporter' despite having interviewed many of them. And women in the report were damned either way: although there was agreement it 'would be good to have women as they understand the audience' apparently, 'those who are dedicated are not really women with valuable instincts, but become like men' so there is no point in having them (BBC Board of Management 1973).

Numerous complaints were made that women's voices were unsuitable on air as they 'lacked authority' and 'attracted too much attention', unlike a man's voice 'which is suited to all occasions'. And according to the head of television light entertainment, 'performers find it difficult to deal with female assistant producers on the studio floor' and he further commented that he personally did 'not like to see trousered girls charging about the studio in a sexless way'. Meanwhile, the report noted that, according to the head of sport, there were plenty of female PAs around but 'none of them has ever expressed any desire for advancement' (ibid).

Senior heads shook in disbelief at the report's revelations but not that much changed. A year later another report was commissioned to measure what had improved in the interim. And the embarrassing answer was: nothing much. In 1975, women *were* finally allowed to read the television news, but it was only some years later with the commissioning of the Sims report in 1985 that real institutional shift became apparent. Monica Sims, a retired controller of Radio 4, one of a tiny handful of women who had held such a senior post, was asked to investigate the position of women in BBC management. She produced 19 key recommendations – not all of them were implemented, but enough to make a cultural shift within the organisation (Sims 1985). As Jenny Abramsky, former director of BBC audio and music, commented: 'The impact of Monica's report cannot be underestimated … There were great expectations after publication and inevitably a sense of disappointment, but it was very important in setting a framework for change' (Franks 2011: 138).

In response to these changes, more women took on senior roles, there were more female voices on the airwaves, there was a serious effort made to accommodate mothers with flexible working and job-shares – a nursery opened opposite TV Centre. Women on air were no longer rare and exotic exceptions. An institution which was supposed to reflect the nation began to feel a little closer to including more diverse voices in its output and in its upper management.

Getting on and getting old

In some ways, the past four or five years have seen a similar awakening and awareness of the need for genuine gender representation in an organisation which receives licence fees from the whole population. Criticism from within and also from external lobbying highlighted several areas where women were still facing an unequal position in the BBC, both on- and off-air. A series of targets and initiatives were established to encourage women to progress to senior roles within the BBC. And a number of prominent women – this time including several with children – have, indeed, achieved success at high levels within the BBC. Although as Jana Bennett observed, after she was appointed director of television in January 2002, she could not see why a target of 30 per cent senior female managers was appropriate when the last time she looked, women were 50 per cent of the population. She said it felt sometimes as if the 'glass ceiling' had been replaced by a 'bamboo ceiling' and there was still a way to go beyond the well-meaning intentions (Franks 2013: 37).

One very visible area which began to gain far higher prominence was the issue of older women on screen. The combination of an old, grey haired male presenter, partnered by a much younger woman, had become an established trope. As Caitlin Moran observed watching television in 2011:

> Men visibly age everyday… but women are supposed to stop the decline at 37, 38 and live out the next 30 or 40 years in some magical bubble. So Moira Stewart and Anna Ford got fired when they were 55 whilst 73-year-old Dimbleby slowly turns into an f***ing wizard behind his desk … the BBC makes finding older newsreaders seem like the Holy Grail, but all they have to do is look through the list of people they have sacked (Moran 2012: 291).

In 2011, Miriam O'Reilly, a presenter of *Countryfile*, went to an employment tribunal accusing the corporation of age discrimination. She was largely successful and the BBC DG Mark Thompson said publicly that something would definitely be done to make sure that older women were not pushed out (Revoir 2012). Several other women also revealed to a Lords inquiry (see below) they had been asked to leave for similar reasons – some of them had been obliged to sign confidentiality agreements restricting them from discussing in public the circumstances of their departure. It is clear that age discrimination is a wider issue than just a gender problem but there is certainly a distinct awareness now within the BBC that older women appearing on screen should not be treated differently from men.

It was not only television, but also radio, where gender imbalances were being highlighted. A departing local radio reporter wrote an impassioned blog in 2012 about the paucity of female presenters – observing that there was only one single presenter of a breakfast show (Dixon 2012). Soon after he became DG, Tony Hall made a bold intervention over the small number of female radio presenters. He set a target where half of the local radio breakfast shows should have women in the presenting chair. As part of that initiative, a special BBC Academy programme to train women in radio was set up in venues across the country. There are quibbles about whether the target has been met as very few women are in solo roles, but certainly there has been a big increase in co-presenters.

Expert opinions

Another recent campaign was launched over the issue of gender amongst 'experts' featured on the BBC. There was a general awareness that especially on heavyweight news and current affairs, not only were there fewer female reporters but a huge disparity in those whose views were being sought as experts.

Several surveys (Women in Journalism 2012; Gender Media Monitoring Project 2010) show that women were often in the news as 'victims' or celebrities, but rather fewer featured as authority figures with expertise. This disquiet as far as broadcasting was concerned became a clamour in 2012 when on two successive days the Radio 4 *Today* programme covered breast cancer and teenage pregnancy without including any female interviewees. At one point John Humphrys was reduced to asking a male contributor to 'imagine what it would be like if he had a tumour on his breast'.

City University London had already begun a research project to count and compare the gender of experts used in broadcast news and current affairs. In many programmes such as *Today* the ratio when the surveys began had been as high as 5:1 or 6:1 (Howell 2014). Not surprisingly, the campaign argued that in many areas (and not just, of course, teenage pregnancy or breast cancer) there are plenty of female voices – but the problem is that producers may need to work a little harder to find them and then to encourage them to participate. The *Today* figures fed into the debate and led to the setting up of a successful online 'expert women' website where women who may be suitable contributors could register their details (see http://thewomensroom.org.uk/index.php). Thousands duly did so and this started to filter through to the airwaves, so for example the gender ratio of experts on heavyweight news shows such as *Today* improved to 1:4. Not perfect, but at least some improvement (Howell 2014).

The momentum behind this campaign and the publicity surrounding the other issues of older women or the paucity of radio presenters all combined to persuade the House of Lords communications committee in 2014 to launch an inquiry into women in news and current affairs. I was amongst those invited to give evidence and it was clear from the questioning that their Lordships were taking this issue seriously and determined to urge for change. This was confirmed in the report itself which made a wide range of suggestions to improve the gender balance in news and current affairs broadcasting (House of Lords 2015).

One innovative scheme which was set up just before the House of Lords inquiry was the establishment by the BBC of a series of 'expert women days' which were opportunities for potential contributors to receive training and advice for appearing on air. They were pioneered by the BBC Academy under Anne Morrison. When the first day was advertised 2,000 women applied for 30 places, from engineers to scientists to academics (City University 2014). It was evident that there was certainly no reluctance by women to participate and the scheme was extended to regional training days. Four sessions were held and 164 women were trained, a large proportion of whom subsequently appeared in a range of BBC programmes. This is an interesting example where a public service broadcaster used its position and profile to extend the reach of the institution and thereby enhanced its provision. It is just a pity that this initiative could not be extended further to include more potential female expert contributors.

Unpleasant memories

Tony Hall's arrival as DG in 2013 was a catalyst which prompted a number of these initiatives and changes – a new awareness of who was speaking on air, a wider consciousness of the BBC's need to set an example to the nation in how women were portrayed externally and also involved internally. But in many ways the most profound initiative was one that extended back over several decades. This was prompted by the Jimmy Savile revelations which indirectly led to the rapid exit of George Entwistle as DG in November 2012 and his replacement by Hall. A high profile inquiry was set up under Dame Janet Smith to examine the culture and practices of the BBC which had allowed widespread sexual abuse of children to go allegedly unnoticed and certainly unchecked. Her inquiry, to which I and a number of former producers and other programme makers gave evidence, was also tasked with finding out about the wider culture of sexual mores within the BBC throughout the period of Savile's work there. Although publication has, alas, been significantly delayed – due to legal proceedings – it will undoubtedly throw light upon a workplace environment that, although only a few decades ago, appears almost unrecognisable.

In parallel to the Smith inquiry, another report was commissioned by the BBC management board. The *Respect at Work* review was intended to examine whether, in the light of the revelations about past abuse, the BBC's current policies, culture and practices with respect to confronting sexual harassment and potential workplace bullying were sufficiently robust. It is full of fine words such as 'People expect more from the BBC. Our audiences and licence fee payers expect high standards of creativity, impartiality and distinctiveness. They expect us to behave with the utmost integrity and decency. They expect us to live up to our stated values' (BBC 2014).

An interesting dimension to the review is that it questioned if there were a possible causal link between extra pressures in the workplace (which might lead to bad practices) and a rapidly changing technological environment combined with the impact of continual cutbacks. This raises a broader issue. It will be interesting to observe whether the initiatives to address inequalities, diversity and workplace culture are sufficiently embedded as the BBC goes into what will be a period of further rapid change, in response to charter renewal.

Conclusion

There is no question that there have been impressive efforts made to enhance the progress of women in a range of ways within the corporation such as the 'Women in Leadership' group targeting middle managers. Now the concern (based on the experience of other institutions) is that an organisation that downsizes may find such initiatives a 'luxury' and 'dispensable' in such an environment.

Severe cutbacks may also mean less flexibility in terms of hiring and advancement. Or maybe the efforts to include women have been so widely accepted this time that the progress will remain, despite any surrounding turmoil in the corporation. It will be interesting to find out.

References

BBC Board of Management (1973) *Limitations to the Recruitment and Advancement of Women in the BBC*, BBC Written Archive Centre, Caversham

BBC (1981) *Women in the BBC. Report to the Board of Management*, BBC Written Archive Centre, Caversham

BBC (2014) *Respect at Work*. Available online at http://downloads.bbc.co.uk/aboutthebbc/insidethebbc/howwework/reports/bbcreport_dinahrose_respectatwork.pdf, accessed on 28 July 2015

City University (2014) *Women on Air*. Available online at http://www.city.ac.uk/centre-for-law-justice-and-journalism/projects/women-on-air, accessed on 28 July 2015

Daily Mail (2014) Miriam O'Reilly attacks BBC for giving John Simpson indefinite contract, 17 October. Available online at http://www.dailymail.co.uk/news/article-2797440/ageism-row-presenter-miriam-o-reilly-attacks-bbc-giving-john-simpson-indefinite-contract-s-man.html, accessed on 9 June 2015

Diversity Unit (BBC Written Archive Centre, Caversham) Abbreviated version available online at http://www.bbc.co.uk/historyofthebbc/research/culture/women, accessed on 28 July 2015

Dixon, Ruth (2012) Poetry killed the radio star: Hello, 21 September. Available online at http://ruthedixon.blogspot.co.uk/2012/09/dear-george-i-am-broadcast-journalist.html, accessed on 9 June 2015

Franks, Suzanne (2011) Attitudes to women in the BBC in the 1970s: Not so much a glass ceiling as one of reinforced concrete, *Westminster Papers in Culture and Communication*, Vol. 8, No. 3 pp 123-142

Franks, Suzanne (2013) *Women and Journalism*, London, I. B. Tauris & Co. Ltd in association with the Reuters Institute for the Study of Journalism, University of Oxford

Gender Media Monitoring Project (GMMP 2010) *Who Makes the News?* http://whomakesthenews.org/gmmp

Higgins, Charlotte *(2015) This New Noise: The Extraordinary Birth and Troubled Life of the BBC, London: Faber*

House of Lords select committee on communications (2015) *Women in News and Current Affairs Broadcasting.*

Howell, Lis (2014) Women experts – or the lack of them – on TV and radio news. Blog available online at https://www.nuj.org.uk/news/women-experts--or-the-lack-of-them--on-tv-and-radio-news/, accessed on 28 July 2015

Moran, Caitlin *(2012) How to be a Woman*, London: Ebury Press

Murphy, Kate (2003) *Women in the BBC 1922- 2002*. Unpublished report for BBC
Murphy, Kate (2014) A marriage bar of convenience? The BBC and married women's work 1923-39, *20th Century British History*, Vol. 25, No. 4 pp 533-561

Revoir, Paul (2012) I got it wrong on older women: BBC boss admits there ARE too few on TV, *Daily Mail*, 9 February. Available online at http://www.dailymail.co.uk/news/article-2098498/I-got-wrong-older-women-BBC-boss-admits-ARE-TV.html, accessed on 9 June 2015

Seaton, Jean (2015) *'Pinkoes and Traitors': The BBC and the Nation 1974-87*, London: Profile Books

Sims, Monica (1985) *Women in BBC Management*. Available online at https://www.jiscmail.ac.uk/cgi-bin/webadmin?A2=BBC-HISTORY;34616fb9.0612, accessed on 28 July 2015

Women in Journalism (2012) *Seen But Not Heard: How Women Make Front Page News*. Available online at http://womeninjournalism.co.uk/wp-content/uploads/2012/10/Seen_but_not_heard.pdf, accessed on 28 July 2015

Section 7:
The BRITISH Broadcasting Corporation?

John Mair

The United Kingdom is in a febrile state: Scotland is on the slipway to independence with Wales and Northern Ireland both devolved and wanting more. How does a *British* Broadcasting Corporation serve such disparate audiences?

The May 2015 general election produced a Scottish National Party landslide. Scotland, Wales and Northern Ireland will vote for their devolved parliament/assemblies in 2016. The nationalist tide does not appear to be at an ebb. Plaid Cmyru may well follow the SNP into the political driving seat. Northern Ireland, meanwhile, keeps all the plates in the air with the Democratic Unionist Party and Sinn Fein sharing power by necessity.

In Scotland, the SNP are quite clear. They would like to see a Scottish Broadcasting Corporation super-serving the nation they claim is now under-served by the BBC. During the 2014 referendum campaign, there was a broadcasting first with the BBC's Pacific Quay headquarters in Glasgow targeted by nationalist demonstrators claiming BBC bias, especially from the then-political editor Nick Robinson. That pressure has not abated. Maurice Smith is well placed to test the current temperature north of the border. A former business editor of BBC Scotland, he is clear:

> Despite the rhetoric, there is plenty of evidence that Scots enjoy BBC radio and television services. The sticking points tend to be the quality and scope of its news and current affairs, and the on-screen representation of Scottish life, including sports, arts and culture.

Wales has the BBC, ITV and its own Welsh language channel S4C (Sianel Pedwar Cmyru). It has had that for more than three decades. But S4C is losing audience, being marginalised and under severe budget pressures. Since the 2010 licence fee settlement, S4C is now part of the BBC licence fee 'top slicing'. It played no part in the July 2015 shotgun licence fee marriage between George Osborne and Tony Hall. They will, as a result, suffer even more. BBC Wales has all but abandoned Welsh language programming.

Elis Owen is in the unique position of having been a senior executive in both ITV and BBC Wales. He applies his microscope to the future of broadcasting in the principality and recalls the heady days of the past.

> The early years of S4C through the 1980s to the 1990s were years of 'comparative plenty'. ... That plenty meant that the channel was a catalyst for the growth of broadcasting and other creative industries in Wales. As S4C was a commissioner, not a maker of programmes, the independent production companies flourished in north, west and south Wales. In those days before the competition of the digital world, S4C enjoyed growing viewing figures and had an international reputation with one film, *Hedd Wynn*, being nominated for an Oscar.

BBC 'social cement in society riddled with fissures'

In Northern Ireland, peace holds. Anna Carragher, formerly the controller BBC Northern Ireland (the top job), forensically examines the future need for the BBC as a social cement in a society riddled with fissures. The BBC is seen to be impartial by both communities even after the thirty year 'Troubles'. Without that legitimacy, it is a busted flush. She concludes:

> Nationalism in Northern Ireland is in no small measure a cultural rather than a civic construct and where not only politicians but the general populace are unable to agree on a shared identity, broadcasting is too important and its role too significant to risk its politicisation or the danger of appropriation by any of the communities.

Meanwhile back in England, has the BBC neglected its own backyard? Roger Laughton too has been a senior executive in both the BBC and ITV. He is the 'go to' man when the BBC needs an independent voice. Here, he offers an analysis on their England performance. Shifting the centre of gravity northwards to Salford, in his view, works. Five major departments/strands based there de-metropolitanising the BBC. He thinks they have got it right:

> I doubt if the BBC needs to change course again in England over the next ten years. Media City has the potential to grow further. There is a case for Birmingham to be given a specialism. But, after years of upheaval, it would make more sense to encourage excellence where it emerges and to ensure that the networks of regional and local programming are resourced well enough to meet their objectives.

The BBC and Scotland:
At the Centre of the Storm over
Constitutional Change

There is an opportunity for the BBC to turn the negativity in Scotland of recent years to real advantage, argues Maurice Smith. A commitment to embrace change and take an innovative approach to additional Scottish programming would make that possible

With the BBC pondering its future direction, how does the corporation respond to the novel and tumultuous realities of Scottish politics? As it campaigns for a winning outcome to its royal charter negotiations, there can no greater testing ground for the BBC's aspirations than Scotland.

Certainly, there are all the familiar issues concerning future funding, the competitive environment, audience appreciation indices, and all the familiar buzzwords that make up the decennial lexicon of charter renewal. But Scotland adds several twists. Wittingly or not, the BBC finds itself at the centre of the heightened and long-running storm that is Scotland's constitutional debate. The corporation has straddled the fence uncomfortably during the recent years of SNP government in Edinburgh, particularly during the 2014 independence referendum campaign and the electoral 'tsunami' of the 2015 general election.

The SNP won minority power at Holyrood in 2007, turned that into unprecedented majority government in 2011, pushed the Unionist parties to the brink in 2014, then grabbed 56 of Scotland's 59 Westminster seats less than a year later. This is no flash-in-the-pan flirtation with nationalism; it represents a distinct parting of the ways in British politics, whose conclusion is less predictable than at any time in modern history. At the very least it will end with a constitutional settlement that will disrupt the current BBC model in some way.

These events have, of course, been reported exhaustively by BBC Scotland's news programmes. Each nuance, every breath, each set-piece speech has been fed into the 24-hour news machine, however relevant. For the BBC, the stuff of Scottish politics – much of which concerns whether and to what extent Scots believe their country is different from the rest of the United Kingdom – carries a hefty sting in its tail. The broadcaster has become part of the story. This should be no surprise to the Scottish reader: in the eyes of many, the BBC itself had come to represent the political ruling class in Scotland, whose long-held soft power and parallel sense of entitlement is steadily being swept away by political change.

BBC's referendum coverage: Focus of discontent for independence supporters

The BBC's coverage of the referendum became an unhappy focus of discontent for independence supporters. Large groups held noisy protests outside BBC Scotland HQ in Glasgow, the last of these after a fractious exchange between then-first minister Alex Salmond and the BBC's then-political editor, Nick Robinson. Post-referendum, things were no less heated. Angry talk of mass licence fee non-payment and even a rash attempt at creating an online nightly news 'rival' could be dismissed in some circumstances as the inevitable knee-jerk reactions of a defeated campaign. But we have since witnessed a rare case of the 'losing' party going on to win, and seeming likely to keep winning in Scotland for the foreseeable future.

Scots certainly seem willing to engage in debate about the future structure and direction of Britain's much-vaunted national broadcaster, but perhaps not in the way the corporation might have wished. As if the warning shots of the 2014 referendum were not enough, the Scottish National Party's virtual whitewash of its opponents in 2015 does not bode well for the BBC north of the border.

How will the Scottish revolution be televised?

So how will the Scottish revolution be televised? It is easy to get caught up in the political ping-pong, and much more difficult to separate out the issues and make reasonable headway with them. The BBC's role in covering Scottish politics is at the very heart of fevered constitutional debate where rumour becomes fact and 'fact' is amplified by the modern political discourse of social media.

Amidst angry language about BBC coverage from supporters, the SNP – or rather the Scottish government the party controls – will have unprecedented influence over broadcasting, assuming the royal charter is renewed in 2017. The reason for this lies in the outcome of the referendum itself. The Smith commission, a hastily cobbled together response to the Unionist parties' last-minute appeal to the Scottish electorate a fortnight before the referendum, includes clauses covering broadcasting.

The resulting Scotland Bill, which first came before the Commons in the summer of 2015, gives an indication of the level of influence that the UK government is willing to grant Edinburgh as a result of the Smith commission proposals. These were backed by all four main parties, but remain open to widely differing interpretation to the two groups that matter right now, the Conservatives at Westminster and the SNP at Holyrood.

The UK government stands accused already of seeking to water down the Smith agreement, and naturally the SNP wants the current legislation to go further in many areas. The initial debate has concerned welfare spending and control over taxation. These are the nitty-gritty issues of government. Broadcasting will join them. So what is at stake?

The gap between fee income raised and spend: The key issue in Scotland

The key issue in Scotland is that licence fee receipts north of the border total £320 million, but spend on local content by BBC Scotland is due to decline to £86 million by 2016-2017. This fact alone represents a 'no brainer' for critics. Scottish viewers contribute nearly four times more than is spent on local programming; therefore, there should be more spent in Scotland, they reason.

Even when it is taken into account that Scots television viewers enjoy watching many 'national' UK programmes, the gap still seems inarguable. At the height of the referendum campaign, when the 'Better Together' group seemed to be hinting that an independent Scotland might mean no BBC at all – no more *Strictly*, no more *Doctor Who!* – it emerged that the BBC's commercial arm, BBC Worldwide, had been happily selling those programmes and many more to neighbouring broadcasters in Ireland, the Netherlands and elsewhere, at very affordable rates.

So, reasons the SNP, in an independent Scotland a Scottish Broadcasting Corporation could simply originate its own programming and buy-in BBC services just as other friendly national broadcasters do. That gap between fee income raised and actual spend seems very inviting from the nationalist perspective. With that sort of cash, perhaps an independent Scotland may include the existing BBC channels – pretty much the same as currently broadcast – plus a new English-language Scottish channel, and a beefed-up version of the existing Gaelic channel, BBC ALBA. There may even be enough for a second Radio Scotland service (one music, one speech-based), and so on.

But Scotland is not independent. Only a 'Brexit' in a future European poll is likely to give the SNP the 'material change' that could lead to a second Scottish referendum in the near future. Let us assume, therefore, that Scotland remains part of the UK for the lifetime of the BBC's next royal charter. What then?

The Smith commission's references to broadcasting survived the government's white paper on Scotland, *Scotland in the United Kingdom: An Enduring Settlement*, published in January 2015. The SNP, in acknowledging the constitutional reality, still believes that much can be done to establish increased Scottish content on BBC services in Scotland. Broadly, the Smith-inspired proposals will give the Scottish parliament and government greater access to, and influence over, both the regulator Ofcom and the BBC, but no direct control.

Scottish ministers will have sole power to approve the appointment of a Scottish member to the Ofcom board, as well as overseeing Ofcom appointments to the board of MG ALBA (the BBC's partner in the Gaelic channel, BBC ALBA); and a formal consultative role for both Scottish government and parliament in setting Ofcom's strategic priorities in Scotland.

Ofcom will be required to lay its annual report and accounts before the Scottish parliament and submit reports to its committees.

The Scottish government and parliament will have a formal consultative role in the royal charter review, and the BBC will also be required to lay its annual reports before the parliament, and appear before parliamentary committees, as it does at Westminster. This all sounds like mere process, even if it is welcome. Until now, BBC management could refuse to appear before the Scottish parliament, and those appearances that have occurred have been at times testy affairs. We can assume that the relevant committees in Holyrood will exploit that power to a greater degree in future. Many MSPs have viewed the BBC's attitude towards Holyrood as rather high-handed, to say the least.

BBC having to re-state its *raison d'être*
In that context the Scottish position confronts the BBC with the thought of having to re-state its *raison d'être*: if it wants to keep the licence fee, it must serve its audiences, even if it does not like the implications of spending more north of the border, or having to 'pander' to Scottish interests. Former director general John (now Lord) Birt is said to have warned Tony Blair's Downing Street that devolution could 'lead to the break-up of the BBC', a truly self-important statement that betrays some truth within the context of British public life.

The BBC has always had problems confirming its relevance to all of the UK. Long before devolution, it was criticised for 'super serving' certain groups mainly in the south-east of England. As a mythical licence fee collector travelled north and west from London, he or she would find resistance to payment grow stronger. Only in Northern Ireland – where the BBC's status as the 'British' broadcaster is obviously unpopular in some quarters – have there been traditionally higher avoidance rates. Now, a smaller proportion of Scots – 50 per cent – believes the licence fee offers value for money than any other part of the UK, except Northern Ireland (47 per cent).

There is still majority support for public service broadcasting (PSB) across the UK, according to an Ofcom review covering the period 2008-2013. Viewing figures for the PSBs – BBC, ITV, Channels 4 and 5 – remain high. Some 77 per cent of people in the UK are satisfied with them, up from 69 per cent in 2008. Despite increased multi-channel competition, PSB channels are still watched by the majority. In Scotland, support for PSBs (which include STV in Scotland) remains high, although it has declined. Significantly, 90 per cent of Scots told Ofcom in 2013 that they believed it was important that news programmes were 'trustworthy', but only 70 per cent were satisfied in that respect.

Here we get to the nub of the BBC dilemma in Scotland: the corporation is spending less on 'first run' programmes – down 12 per cent between 2008 and 2013, although some of that cut is the result of efficiency improvements. However, the perception that Scotland does not get its fair share of BBC spending becomes potentially explosive in the context of a critical audience, a significant part of which perceives its news coverage to be unfair.

Significantly, the BBC Annual Report for 2014-15 recorded that only 48 per cent of people in Scotland felt that the BBC 'is good at representing their life' through its news and current affairs coverage, compared to 61 per cent in England and Northern Ireland, and 55 per cent in Wales. The Audience Council Scotland (part of the BBC's consultative apparatus) criticised 'network' coverage of the referendum, commenting in the under-stated manner of such quangos that there had been an 'Anglified perspective' during the independence debate and that it had focused too much on the official campaigns 'at the expense of the wider civic and community engagement'.

The council, which advises the BBC Trust, said BBC Scotland should be given greater authority and resources to commission programmes for Scottish audiences, and that the BBC should review its approach to the coverage of controversial political issues, 'to ensure that perceptions of impartiality remain strong across all audiences'.

BBC Scotland, I would argue, came under severe criticism during the referendum campaign of 2014 partly because of the slavish devotion of its news operation to the political party system, and partly because its editorial guidelines are geared towards delivering conventional election coverage. During an election campaign, the stop-watches come out and the appeals of the party spin-doctors are waylaid by producers who can demonstrate that this party or that received its fair share of coverage. Journalists in Scotland have been long-used to a four-party system (Conservative, Labour, LibDem and SNP), and are perfectly capable of producing conventionally 'fair' election coverage.

The referendum campaign seemed to throw that familiar algorithm into disarray. Where three parties were Unionist and one pro-independence, audiences were frequently witness to programmes where one party representative appeared to be shouted down by three others. Many people's sense of fairness rubbed up against those kind of odds.

How the BBC appeared 'unnecessarily defensive'
Curiously, the BBC made little attempt to explain the difficulties it faced in covering a campaign where Scots were beginning to 'take sides' and passions were rising very quickly. Its reaction to a critical academic report into television news coverage in early 2014 by Professor John Robertson, of the University of West of Scotland, appeared disproportionate, and it remained open to criticism that it only covered that report when it had been criticised for not doing so. In short, however well-intentioned the BBC position, to many outside the organisation it seemed unnecessarily defensive: the drawbridge was pulled up and the blinds closed tight.

Whereas Scottish-based journalists (and audiences) had heard and digested most of the finer points of the debate, the publication by *The Sunday Times* of a YouGov poll claiming a narrow 'Yes' lead just 12 days before before polling day sparked a frenzy of coverage as London journalists (and politicians) scuppered north. Suddenly, the debate about a post-independence currency, or whether there would be border posts at Carlisle, were repeated *ad nauseam*. It was as if London had been unaware of the campaign that had raged for the previous two years.

The Scottish government has been frustrated that BBC Scotland declined to initiate or take part in any scenario planning for independence, or even to discuss whether or not it was undertaking any such exercise. BBC Scotland director Ken MacQuarrie may have become better known as the senior executive drafted in to review *Newsnight*'s calamitous coverage of the Lord McAlpine child abuse 'story' in 2012, and later to investigate Jeremy Clarkson's assault on a producer in March 2015 during an argument about a hot meal. In fact, MacQuarrie is known within the corporation as something of a 'blue sky thinker', and it is hard to believe that certain scenarios embracing constitutional change have not been considered.

What happens next may depend on whether the BBC sees itself as a leader or follower in response to constitutional pressure. Let us assume it adopts the position of follower. The corporation is always happy to lead on professional and technological innovation. For example, Birt's digital strategy matched Rupert Murdoch's BSkyB back in the 1990s, and placed the organisation way ahead of ITV and others in terms of readiness for the impact of the web and digital broadcasting. However, the BBC is much more reticent on the political front. It will prefer to take its lead from government (London, that is, not Edinburgh). If it perceives that the Conservatives view the Smith commission proposals as a means of containing the SNP and preserving the Union, albeit in changed form, the BBC may become a little bolder in presenting a 'solution' for Scotland.

The changed political scene does make life a little different for the BBC as it calculates possible concessions. Immediately before and after devolution, the internal case for a 'Scottish Six' – whereby Scotland would effectively take over responsibility for the television news hour at 6pm – was heavily compromised by strong pressure from Labour. Its leading figures viewed the 'Six' debate as too big a concession to the SNP at a time when Labour had introduced devolution and had every reason to assume that it would retain power at Holyrood *sine die*.

Birt's outright opposition to the 'Six', therefore, had tacit support from Downing Street, and especially the then-chancellor Gordon Brown, who attempted to 'control' Scotland from afar. The Scottish case was dismissed, and a hybrid version of *Newsnight* – whereby Scotland 'opted out' of the news flagship halfway through transmission at 11pm, much to the chagrin of Jeremy Paxman – was agreed instead. Now, with Labour in disarray, the only relevant voice on the future of the BBC is the SNP, a potentially excruciating position for the corporation in London and Scotland.

So let us assume that the main players in the settlement of a BBC charter, the protection of the licence fee and the satisfaction of Scottish concerns include Downing Street, Holyrood, the BBC and Ofcom (which may become the BBC's new regulator). The SNP want more Scottish programming on BBC One and Two, a Scottish TV channel and an enhanced Radio Scotland. It is also being lobbied by independent producers to demand that the BBC sticks to its promises about commissioning network programmes from Scotland. This latter point is worth millions to the industry in Scotland, including in-house producers.

The omens are not great for those who might hope for a new enlightenment. Having signed a memorandum of understanding with the Scottish government about consultation on the future of the BBC in June 2015, the UK government then did the over-75s deal, published its green paper, and appointed an advisory 'reform panel' that included no Scots, without telling Edinburgh. Perhaps to underline the point, culture secretary John Whittingdale reminded an SNP critic that 'BBC' stands for 'British' Broadcasting Corporation.

Conclusions: Need for greater transparency and accountability

The Scottish government spent the summer months of 2015 preparing its case. It wants to achieve real action in terms of firm spending commitments in Scotland, as well as the greater transparency and accountability envisaged by the Smith proposals. In London, the real 'battle' will be over the future structure and direction of the BBC. The corporation remains a big player in the UK broadcasting market, and needs to be kept in check as it attempts to manoeuvre itself into a position that maintains that very power. Scots are not the only ones questioning the BBC's relevance in an age of Netflix, Amazon, and the web. Whittingdale's green paper voices aloud the notion of the BBC becoming more of a publisher-broadcaster than a producer of all things, everywhere.

These factors might encourage BBC Scotland to do some real blue-sky thinking and embrace some of the ambitions of the Scottish government. There is speculation that BBC Scotland executives have modelled a new all-Scottish channel, possibly pulling together local content with network programming. The BBC could also mount its own campaign to convince more Scots that it really does care about their country. Scottish television content on BBC One and BBC Two remains very popular. Despite the rhetoric, there is plenty of evidence that Scots enjoy BBC radio and television services. The sticking points tend to be the quality and scope of its news and current affairs, and the on-screen representation of Scottish life, including sports, arts and culture.

There is an opportunity for the BBC to address these issues, and to turn the negativity of recent years to real advantage in Scotland. A commitment to embrace change, achieve a new and realistic settlement that bridges that licence fee spending gap and perhaps even take an innovative approach to additional Scottish programming, would make that possible.

The question is whether London will allow it.

The Consequences of Language

In Wales, the future of S4C is inextricably tied into the royal charter debate. Here Elis Owen outlines the issues and argues: 'Welsh viewers need strong programmes about Wales in both languages'

It was a rare occurance. A Welsh language television programme praised in the Westminster parliament. On 4 June 2015, when questioned about the future of S4C (the Welsh language channel), culture minister Ed Vaizey praised the 'excellent *Hinterland*' as evidence the channel was going 'from strength to strength'.

The minister had been questioned on whether the future funding of S4C was going to be guaranteed since five years ago the government had decided that most of the channel's funding would come out of the BBC licence fee. S4C says that by 2017 it will have seen a 36 per cent cut in its budget which puts a severe strain on their programme making capability.

Y Gwyll/Hinterland, to give the Celtic *noir* drama series its full title, has been hailed in Wales, the UK and internationally as a genuine hit despite those budget cuts. With its gritty storylines and stunning locations around Aberystwyth in west Wales, the detective drama was a result of a co-production with many partners. S4C was the main co-producer and one of the others was BBC Wales. Significantly, the film was shot in two languages – English and Welsh. It proved that good programmes succeed whatever the language.

Since then S4C has been hit by a series of political decisions. The hastily agreed licence fee deal between the government and the BBC means that the corporation will face more cuts. And there is a prospect of even more cuts as a result of the proposals in the green paper on broadcasting. Culture secretary John Whittingdale said: 'S4C will be expected to find similar savings to those in the BBC.' In Wales, the future of S4C is high profile and is inextricably tied into the charter debate.

It is English, the predominant language in Wales, which is one of the main concerns for BBC Wales. In a speech to mark the 60th anniversary of the BBC in Wales in April 2014, Lord Hall, the director general, said: 'English language television broadcasting for Wales has been declining for over a decade and some aspects of Welsh life like comedy and entertainment and culture are not sufficiently covered by the BBC [in Wales].' This was underlined in July 2015 by the Audience Council for Wales in the BBC annual report which said that English language television broadcasting for Wales was 'close to the cliff edge'. The negotiations over the rest of 2015 and beyond are expected to go a long way towards deciding the future of broadcasting in both languages.

A political beginning
It was a political decision to set up S4C. The channel was born from the campaign to save the Welsh language. In the 1960s and 1970s the future of Welsh was threatened after census figures had shown a decline in the number of Welsh speakers – from 26 per cent of the population in 1961 to 20 per cent ten years later. There were angry protests for bilingual road signs, more government literature to be published in Welsh, the establishment of more Welsh language schools and many other aims. None symbolised the fight more than the campaign for a Welsh language television channel. Activists staged sit-down protests in television studios and climbed television transmitters.

Before S4C, Welsh language television programmes were shown as opt-outs on the main channels – BBC and ITV. This infuriated the Welsh language lobby as they saw a separate channel a way of helping to save the language. It also irritated non Welsh speakers who did not want Welsh language programmes to interfere with their viewing. Thousands of people retuned their aerials to receive the service from England, receiving local news of Bristol in South Wales and Manchester in North Wales.

Margaret Thatcher's Conservative victory in 1979 brought matters to a head. In its manifesto, the Conservatives had promised to create a Welsh language channel but in 1980 the home secretary Willie Whitelaw decided against a Welsh fourth channel when announcing the creation of Channel 4 in the UK. There were immediate protests from all sides of the Welsh language establishment and Gwynfor Evans, the charismatic former leader of Plaid Cymru, (the Welsh nationalist party), threatened to go on hunger strike. Willie Whitelaw relented and Sianel Pedwar Cymru (Channel 4 Wales) went to air on 1 November 1982 with 22 hours a week of Welsh language programming. Channel 4 in England launched the following day. 'This was an important moment for the Welsh language as it was an act of parliament that set up S4C and it is seen as a milestone in the recognition of the language,' said Elan Closs Stephens, a former chair of S4C and now the BBC trustee in Wales.

Initially S4C was responsible to the Home Office and received a grant which was linked to the level of television advertising income in the previous year – in the days before a multi-channel service, advertising grew every year and so did the S4C grant. The channel could also raise their own advertising revenue. It was agreed that BBC Wales would supply 520 hours of programming a year at no charge to S4C. These were mainly news and sport and the popular soap opera *Pobol y Cwm (People of the Valley)*.

In those days of analogue television, the channel was able to access the best of Channel 4's programmes to supplement the Welsh language peak-time service. Huw Jones, the current chair of S4C's authority, said: 'S4C was set up as a unique public service broadcaster to serve the Welsh language in all genres from news and sport to entertainment, the arts and drama. It provides a service on one channel that is spread across many channels in English.' The S4C authority was appointed by the Home Office which was responsible for the governance of S4C.

Growth of an industry

The early years of S4C through the 1980s to the 1990s were years of 'comparative plenty', according to Roger Laughton, then head of Bournemouth Media School who wrote an independent report on S4C in 2004. That plenty meant that the channel was a catalyst for the growth of broadcasting and other creative industries in Wales. As S4C was a commissioner, not a maker of programmes, the independent production companies flourished in north, west and south Wales. In those days before the competition of the digital world, S4C enjoyed growing viewing figures and had an international reputation with one film, *Hedd Wynn*, being nominated for an Oscar.

One of those independent companies, Tinopolis, based in Llanelli, in west Wales, is now one of the largest in the UK, but it has diversified from its Welsh language content. 'It's important that production companies in Wales do not just depend on S4C but try to get as much commissioning as possible from other broadcasters and platforms,' said Ron Jones, the executive chair of the Tinopolis group.

With the growth of Welsh language television there was also a demand for the growth of English language programming about Wales. 'ITV and BBC were each producing over ten hours of programming a week in English for television viewers in Wales and it was not just news and current affairs but drama, entertainment and the arts,' said Rhodri Williams, the director of Ofcom in Wales. Times were so good that in 2001 BBC Wales launched its own digital channel BBC2W when it opted out of the BBC2 network during the evening and provided English language programming about Wales on a range of topics.

Changing fortunes

Today, the broadcasting landscape in Wales is very different from those heady days of 2001. In 1996, the Broadcasting Act linked S4C's grant to the retail price index – the income still went up. By 2004, the channel's income from the department of culture, media and sport (DCMS) was £86 million plus the £20 million or so the BBC contributed with their 520 hours a year of programming. In addition, there was also a few million pounds in advertising revenue.

S4C expanded their services in a growing digital world. As well as S4C analogue, there was S4C digital and S4C2 and they developed their own catch-up service Clic. In 2008, they launched Cyw daytime children's programming and there were ambitious plans for the future including a full HD service in this decade.

But in 2010, the digital switchover was complete and one of the consequences of this was that Channel 4 (English) was now freely available in Wales. This meant that Channel 4 (English) programmes were no longer available to S4C and their output from now on was entirely in Welsh. There were more hours to fill and there was less revenue from advertising, and, as with all terrestrial channels, because of the digital revolution, falling viewing figures. S4C was also troubled by internal wrangling between the authority and the executive over its future direction.

In October 2010, Jeremy Hunt, the coalition's culture secretary, announced the removal of the statutory provision that increased S4C's funding annually in line with inflation. Most of the funds from 2013 onwards would come from the BBC licence fee and an operating agreement was set up with the BBC. Huw Jones, who was appointed chairman of the S4C authority after the infighting, said: 'The effect on our funding has been dramatic. By 2017, we will have seen a 36 per cent cut in our budget compared with what it would have been under the old funding system.'

In this current year (2015), S4C gets around £76 million from the BBC licence fee. The DCMS still directly funds £6.8 million and about £2 million is raised from advertising. A crucial part of the original package remains – BBC Wales still contributes ten hours a week of programming which costs about £20 million. The cuts have hit the channel hard. S4C2 disappeared, the HD service was suspended and programme budgets were cut. 'Original programme budgets fell from £52,700 an hour in 2009 to £31,100 an hour in 2014,' said Ian Jones, S4C's chief executive who was also appointed after the infighting at the channel. S4C's staff were cut from 219 to 129 by 2015. He is proud of the children's service: 'It's one of the most comprehensive services of its kind in the world and an essential part of our programme offering.'

In the year to March 2015, S4C broadcast 1,929 hours of original programmes which does not include the 531 hours the BBC provides. This is a decrease of around 500 hours from the previous year, which means there are more repeats. Huw Jones goes even further in the annual report which came out in July 2015: 'It is a matter of concern that most of the channel's broadcast hours – 57 per cent – are filled by repeats.'

The latest threat of more cuts because of the licence fee deal and the green paper led Huw Jones to say: 'The fact that S4C is funded primarily by the licence fee means that the future of the Welsh language channel must be considered.'

Viewing figures

S4C's viewing figures have come under scrutiny. Some sections of the London broadcasting establishment have resented that a large chunk of the licence fee should go to fund a Welsh language minority channel. In March 2010, the *Daily*

Telegraph headlined: '£100 million taxpayer-funded Welsh TV channel where one in four shows get zero viewers'. Ed Vaizey, the culture minister, told the Welsh select committee in January 2011 that S4C was not making sufficient impact. 'I feel low viewing figures are at the heart of the issue,' he said.

Certainly S4C like all other terrestrial broadcasters faces significant challenges to attract viewers in this multi-platform age. Another challenge facing the broadcaster is that there was a slight fall in the number of Welsh language speakers according to the 2011 census – to 562,000, approximately 19 per cent of the population. The worrying trend for S4C is that it is the Welsh heartlands – west and north Wales – which have seen the biggest decline. Viewing figures are always open to interpretation. If you look at consolidated figures from the Broadcasters' Audience Research Board (BARB) in 2010, the average viewing in peak time for S4C was 28,300. By 2014, this had declined to 19,000. In May 2014, Rhodri Talfan Davies, the director of BBC Wales, said at a BBC Welsh audience council meeting that there had been a fall in viewing figures of 17 per cent for programmes made by the BBC for S4C. The council thought this was a real worry in terms of providing value for money and serving the Welsh language audience.

But S4C believe that relying merely on share gives an incomplete picture. They rely, in particular, on the three-minute reach (which is a person watching a channel for at least three minutes). Ian Jones said there had also been a digital dividend for S4C because the channel was now available on various platforms and devices outside Wales. 'That has contributed greatly to an increase in our overall reach each week,' he said. Another benefit of the S4C agreement with the BBC is that their programmes are now available on iPlayer as well as Clic.

S4C's annual report published in July 2015 declares that audience figures have fallen by 6 per cent from the previous year. The weekly reach was 383,000 in 2013/14 – that has fallen to 360,000 in 2014/15. But the channel points out that across the UK, S4C has seen an increase in its viewing figures from 551,000 in 2013/14 to 605,000 in the last year. Commenting on the shifting viewing patterns, Huw Jones said: 'It appears that we are seeing a situation where people who have moved out of Wales are using technology to keep in touch with Welsh life and language in increasing numbers. At the same time younger viewers are turning away from the television screen towards new media and young Welsh speakers are on average less likely to use the language than older people.'

Ian Jones says that S4C has faced significant challenges including the budget cuts and increasing competition for sports rights. Sport, especially rugby, has been one of the cornerstones of the S4C schedule but as with all terrestrial broadcasters, they face being outbid for top class sport by Sky and BT. He also points out that S4C used to benefit from an increased BARB panel in Wales to gain a more accurate sample of Welsh language viewers. But in recent years that panel has gone. Independent companies such as Tinopolis and TAC, the umbrella organisation for the independent companies in Wales, are also sceptical of the share figures.

Huw Jones, the chair of S4C, says viewing figures are not the only way to measure the channel's success. 'We have eight key indicators which include viewing patterns but also other factors such as economic impact of the channel, audience appreciation and, impact on how the Welsh language is used and learned.'

S4C's position has always been that it is one of the main broadcasters in Wales. It does not compare well with BBC1 which gets 21 per cent of the audience in Wales or ITV1 which gets 14 per cent. S4C gets around 1 per cent of the audience but performs well when compared with BBC Four which only gets 0.7 per cent or Sky Sports 0.7 per cent. Other much admired channels such as Discovery get far less. Ian Jones is dismissive of the niche channel argument though. 'S4C must be seen as a main public service channel as it covers all genres, niche channels only cover specific genres,' he said.

Perhaps S4C should pay heed to the words of Alun Cairns, the Welsh Office minister who has broadcasting as part of his remit. 'I accept that S4C must be measured by other criteria, not just the viewing figures. But ignoring the share figures is not an option. If the number of Welsh speakers watching the channel is falling then you have to question some of the output,' he said.

Broadcasting in English in Wales
Despite apprehension that the operating deal would lead to a BBC takeover of S4C, the channel has retained its editorial independence. Elan Closs Stephens, who is now a member of the S4C authority as well as being the BBC trustee for Wales, and Huw Jones, agree that both sides get on well. Indeed, the future of English language broadcasting for Wales is one of the main issues facing BBC Wales.

The BBC in Wales faces the same pressures as the rest of the corporation in the UK. By 2017, it will have made £10 million savings as a result of the cuts imposed after the 2010 licence fee settlement. Radio Wales, Radio Cymru (the Welsh language radio service), online and the BBC Welsh National orchestra and other departments have all had to make cuts. Before further cuts, the BBC spend on English language programmes in Wales for 2014/15 was £20.2 million. Despite the cutbacks, the programmes are performing well.

Measured on a 15-minute reach (not the three-minute reach measurement used by S4C), 900,000 people a week tuned into BBC's English programmes in Wales. This was a fall of 70,000 on the previous year. Cuts have been made to BBC Wales internal programming staff across the board. It is still uncertain what will happen to the BBC staff in Wales in features, music, documentaries and drama if the BBC studios production project (a plan to commercialise the production division) is applied throughout the BBC. 'The staff in those areas work on local programmes in Wales as well as network programmes. It's uncertain where they will sit if the BBC Studios plan is applied to the nations,' said Rhodri Talfan Davies.

On the face of it, BBC Wales is doing well. *Dr Who, Casualty, Sherlock* and other dramas are made in Wales. *Crimewatch* is made in Cardiff. And the BBC Wales logo sits proudly in the end credits. These programmes are still commissioned by the BBC centrally. How much say does BBC Wales have?

ITV Wales still has a service agreement with Ofcom on what they have to deliver. There is no such agreement for BBC Wales in the provision of English language programmes. Those programmes form part of a licence agreement for BBC One and BBC Two – they are part of the BBC network. A service licence agreement defines what channels have to produce. As there is no such agreement for BBC Wales their hours are not defined – nor protected.

English language television programmes in Wales are broadcast as opt-outs from the regular network schedule on BBC One or BBC Two Wales, so unlike S4C, there is no designated channel for these programmes. The cutback in the number of hours of English language programmes in Wales being broadcast is troubling Ofcom. In their latest review of public service broadcasting, they say: 'It is of concern that the BBC output for Wales in English television programmes has fallen by more than 100 hours since 2008.'

'ITV in Wales cut back to a mainly news and current affairs operation with some additional programming five years ago. That left BBC Wales. The decline in English language programming for Wales there has been drastic,' said Rhodri Williams, Ofcom's director for Wales.

The experiment that was BBC2W has long gone and was not a success with viewers. English language programming at the BBC has fallen from 716 hours a year in 2008 to 592 hours in 2013, according to Ofcom. Rhodri Talfan Davies, director of BBC Wales, sees this the reduction in English language television for Wales as one of his main challenges. 'There has been a decline of 25 per cent in five years. Outside news, current affairs and sport, we only produce one hour a week of other genres,' he said. This has not escaped Lord Hall, director general, who called for more coverage of comedy, entertainment and culture in Wales.

Elan Closs Stephens, a BBC trustee, agrees, but adds: 'There is not enough representation of Wales in drama on the network. The last drama on BBC One network that had Wales as central to the plot was *Gavin and Stacey* and that was five years ago. This should be addressed.' (*Hinterland* is a co-production broadcast on S4C and BBC Four – it is broadcast on BBC One only in Wales.)

Since the 2015 deal on the licence fee and the threat contained in the green paper that there will be more cuts to the BBC, there is now a further worry for English language programmes in Wales. Rhodri Talfan Davies has said it is important that there is a public debate about BBC Wales's programming.

The politics of language
Inevitably it is the support for the Welsh language channel S4C which has got up a head of steam. There is always political noise about any threat to the Welsh language, but there has been little protest about the decline of English language programmes in Wales. S4C wants to protect its funding and editorial

independence. Huw Jones is adamant that they should remain a public service broadcaster for the Welsh language with its own independence.

Most of the public statements made the summer of 2015 about the threatened cuts have been about the future of S4C – with shadow culture secretary Chris Bryant threatening to hold John Whittingdale over a fire if S4C is cut further. Other bodies like TAC, the independent companies' organisation, have called for an increase in funding for the channel the Welsh language. But in Cardiff, the Welsh Assembly recognises there is a threat to broadcasting in both English and Welsh. Three of the parties, Labour, Plaid Cymru and the Liberal Democrats said in a statement on 10 July 2015 that broadcasting in Wales was in serious jeopardy.

The Welsh government has no direct control over broadcasting but it insists it must be consulted in the charter renewal process. Ken Skates, the Welsh minister for culture, said in a speech to the Institute of Welsh Affairs in December 2014: 'There should be a clear commitment to safeguarding and strengthening the core services aimed at Welsh viewers and listeners – in both languages but especially in English.' There is also concern that the panel who will advise John Whittingdale in the charter renewal process does not include any representative of the nations (Wales, Scotland and Northern Ireland) of the UK.

The future

A decision will have to be made on the £6.7 million S4C receives from the DCMS. This government department, like most others, faces cuts of up to 40 per cent as part of George Osborne's spending review. The main decision on funding will be the £76 million that is currently part of the BBC licence fee. The operating agreement with the BBC will end in 2017. In answer to a question from Plaid Cymru during the green paper debate, John Whittingdale said: 'S4C is publicly funded and I do not think it is possible to exempt any publicly funded body from the necessity of seeking greater efficiency savings and making a contribution to the overall objective of mending the economy.'

A lot depends on what happens to the BBC Trust. If it disappears how will S4C fit into a future governance structure in the BBC? Whatever happens the political lobby campaign to protect S4C's funding will continue. Representatives are already having their own meetings with John Whittingdale and the government about the channel's future.

English language programming faces a more difficult lobbying problem and has always had less evident political support. But when asked, Alun Cairns said that there should be more English language programming in Wales and 'funding for Welsh language programming shouldn't be at the expense of English language spend. I would also want to see more Welsh representation on network programmes, particularly drama'.

There is a belief in some quarters that a solution to the English language problem could be in the charter renewal process. A service licence for Wales could be created. It would include aims for all Welsh services such as Radio Wales, Radio Cymru, online and specifically English language television for Wales. Such a licence could also call for more national and regional representation on network programming. Alun Cairns is not so keen on the service licence idea. 'The internal governance of the BBC should be so strong and transparent that it delivers the needs of the nation.'

One thing is certain. By 2018, both BBC Wales and S4C will have changed headquarters. For the last 30 years both empires have been housed a few miles from each other on the outskirts of Cardiff. The BBC plan to move into a new state of the art building in the centre of Cardiff. They are also negotiating with S4C to share transmission departments which will bring the organisations close together. S4C meanwhile has ambitious plans to move 70 miles west to Carmarthen to be near to the Welsh language heartlands and hopefully help the local economy. They will still keep some corporate presence at the new BBC studios.

In the end it's all about providing a service for viewers in Wales. English language programmes about Wales are popular and there have been memorable successes in recent years such as the series *Coalhouse*, Rhod Gilbert's *Work Experience* and, in Wales, *Weatherman Walking* which highlights different walks in Wales. But despite the popularity of programmes like this it will be a far more difficult task to campaign for English language programming for Wales than for S4C. This is because funding for English language programming is tied up with the decision on the whole future funding of the BBC. If the corporation has to cut back more then there could well be more cutbacks in English language programming.

This, according to Welsh newspaper columnist and broadcaster Carolyn Hitt would threaten Wales' national identity. 'How ironic that the more devolved, culturally successful and secure in identity we become, the less able we are to reflect the plurality of the Welsh nation through drama, factual programming, sport and entertainment. We're switching off our own story.'

Welsh viewers need strong programmes about Wales in both languages. Ron Jones, of Tinopolis, said: 'If the English language programmes in Wales are unprotected then you will eventually threaten Welsh language programming. They are interconnected.' The debate will continue with the Welsh select committee in Westminster debating the future of Welsh broadcasting in the autumn of 2015.

The BBC, Northern Ireland and Charter Renewal

When the BBC's founding father, John Reith, gave it the words emblazoned on its coat of arms: 'Nation shall speak peace unto nation' he was, no doubt, considering the further reaches of Empire. Today, argues Anna Carragher, the BBC needs to apply those words to the nations of the United Kingdom in its purpose for the next ten years

Introduction: Post-2015 general election realities

Until 10 pm on Thursday 7 May 2015 those who watch these things with keen interest were uncertain as to the climate in which the BBC charter renewal would be conducted. The exit polls were as sure a guide as the shipping forecast, with promises of gales and stormy weather to come. But as the tide of results poured in confirming those exit polls, and in the following days as the choppy seas of forming a new government settled into calmer waters, some themes emerged clearly.

Despite the lurid headlines, the man charged with overseeing charter renewal, John Whittingdale, believes in public service broadcasting; he is a friend albeit an, on occasions, highly critical one. The licence fee as a basis of BBC funding looks set to stay for some years more – truncated, frozen, with possibly different configuration to take account of household size or income, maybe with the criminal sanctions lifted or modified. The BBC will have to accommodate to this new reality and implement efficiencies, decide what stays and what goes, look at the shape of its management and its production base. The BBC Trust which replaced the old governance system ten years ago is itself widely seen as not fit for purpose and it seems probable that we will see further regulatory and accountability structures.

There is another reality which clearly emerged during that election which the BBC, like other national institutions, has also to respond to with imagination and innovation, the changing shape of the United Kingdom, most starkly exemplified by the results in Scotland but evident to in Wales, Northern Ireland and the regions of England. When the BBC's founding father, John Reith, gave

271

it the words emblazoned on its coat of arms 'nation shall speak peace unto nation' he was, no doubt, considering the further reaches of Empire. Today the BBC needs to apply those words to the nations of the United Kingdom in its purpose for the next ten years of its existence.

The 18 seats of the 'Others'

As the United Kingdom general election results tumbled in through the early hours of 8 May visitors to the BBC website who wished to update themselves on the state of the parties would have found a curious statistic on the 'results' strapline: Con, Lab, LibDem, SNP, UKIP, PC, Grn were all meticulously recorded, from the tall column of Con, through to the one seat each faithfully recorded for UKIP and the Green Party. But there was a final column named 'Others" comprising 18 seats. They were the Northern Ireland seats and while the BBC NI site faithfully recorded eight DUP, four SF, three SDLP, two UU and one IND, it would have been easy to conclude that the BBC did not consider the NI results of sufficient interest to the rest of the UK to fully document them on the election home page. This was even though the DUP gained exactly the same number of seats as the Liberal Democrats and the Ulster Unionist parties were, as was the case in the previous parliament, the fourth largest grouping in the House of Commons. Nor was it sufficient to argue that the omission was justified because they only contested seats in one part of the UK as the SNP and Plaid Cmyru seats were faithfully documented.

It was an appropriate finale to the bitter dispute the NI parties and, in particular, the DUP had had with the BBC over the tortuous negotiations regarding the party leaders' election debates; while it is understandable that the BBC balked at the prospect of including five NI parties on the already overcrowded podium it, nonetheless, appeared, in particular to the DUP, that they were being marginalised and belittled by the national broadcaster and that they, a voice speaking for the union, were excluded while separatist parties from Scotland and Wales were being given a national platform. Nigel Dodds, writing in the *Guardian*, attributed the SNP's success in part to the BBC's decision:

> The decision of the broadcasters, led principally by the BBC, to invent a format for the UK-wide television debates that included the SNP has had entirely predictable results. Last time, a Clegg bubble was created by the TV debates. This time, a Sturgeon surge has been the consequence. The SNP are entitled to fair coverage by the national media: they did not require utterly disproportionate coverage for reasons the BBC still hasn't fully explained (Watt and McDonald 2015).

The outworking of that decision may yet come back to snare the BBC during the debate and negotiations over charter renewal and the licence fee in 2016 and 2017. While the DUP and the Ulster Unionists do not hold the balance of power in parliament as they had hoped they might, should David Cameron's slim majority in any way stumble they will be crucial allies for him and they will take a keen interest in the future of the BBC nationally and particularly locally.

Nationalism in the UK nations is very different – for England, the sense of being the cultural definer of the UK, blessed by history, by its population size compared to the other nations, by its dominance of political and cultural institutions, and among them, up there with the monarchy, the Treasury, the Church of England and the City of London is the BBC. In Scotland, overwhelmingly in 2015, it seems to me its nationalism is civic – we speak in Northern Ireland of the 'nationalist' parties whereas the SNP is the 'national' party, aiming to speak for the Scottish nation in a way in which neither the Unionist parties nor the nationalist parties in NI attempt to.

BBC's complex relationship with its audience in Northern Ireland

But the BBC's position in Northern Ireland and its relationships with its audience is, and always has been, complex and nuanced from the inception of both entities: the British Broadcasting Company was formed in 1922, as was the political entity of Northern Ireland. It is the British Broadcasting Corporation: its very name distances it from those whose instinctive allegiance is not British and makes them distrust its impartiality and its editorial independence. Paradoxically, its name also angers those from a Unionist background when they perceive it as being unpatriotic, airing views which are critical of the United Kingdom and of Britishness itself. But in a further paradox, both Nationalists and Unionists have a strong sense of its intrinsic importance to Northern Ireland. NI audiences value it and recognise what it does; the BBC in Northern Ireland is a force for real cultural good; it nurtures creative talent; it encourages, develops and employs writers. For instance, the young Seamus Heaney supplemented his teacher's salary by writing wonderful scripts for the BBC NI education department; it gave actors such as Sir Kenneth Branagh and James Nesbitt their first major UK television roles; without it musical life in Northern Ireland would infinitely poorer; it is by far and away the largest employer of journalists in Northern Ireland. And the importance of all of this must not be underestimated in a place which is smaller and presents far fewer opportunities than are available in most other large cities in the UK: cutting BBC orchestral provision in London or Glasgow would hurt; in Northern Ireland it would be fatal.

There are three elements of the charter review debate which have particular significance for the BBC in Northern Ireland: news, production and governance.

News

The royal charter granted in October 2006 sets out six public purposes for the BBC, one of which is 'representing the UK, its nations, regions and communities'. The agreement, which fleshes out the charter, briefly adds that in fulfilment of this purpose the BBC shall ensure that it:

a) reflects and strengthens cultural identities through original content at local, regional and national level, on occasion bringing audiences together for shared experiences; and

(b) promotes awareness of different cultures and alternative viewpoints, through content that reflects the lives of different people and different communities within the UK.

It adds that the BBC shall have regard to:

a) the importance of reflecting different religious and other beliefs; and

(b) the importance of appropriate provision in minority languages.

Much of this public purpose is delivered through news output – local news for the audience in Northern Ireland and produced in NI for radio, television and online, and national news, largely produced at the centre of the BBC for UK-wide audiences. This latter category acts as both the window and the mirror through which audiences in NI can come to know the lives of others across the UK while at the same time letting audiences elsewhere see what matters to people in Northern Ireland and letting them understand their social, political and economic ecology. As the BBC approaches the charter renewal for this decade it is, I believe, the latter to which it must pay particular attention. In his book, *The British Constitution*, Professor Anthony King (2007) presciently wrote that:

> … the extent to which Scotland and Wales are developing their own political culture is emphasised by the pattern of communication north of the border … on some mornings, apart from their international coverage the *Today* programme and *Good Morning Scotland* could be reporting from different planets because in a sense they are. … Moreover, the tendency is wholly symmetrical. Just as Scottish reporting is increasingly focused on Scotland and Welsh reporting on Wales so British and UK wide reporting is increasingly focused on England. Without the English realising it [they] are in danger of becoming isolated within their own dominion.

While he was speaking about Wales and Scotland his comments are, if anything, even more true about Northern Ireland which is not part of the body politic in the way in which Wales and, overwhelmingly so in the wake of the 2015 election, Scotland are. Since he wrote this words another factor has skewed the asymmetry of the UK's emotional geography: the growing dominance of London and its separateness from much of the UK. At the most basic level the average income in NI is £21,836 whereas in London it stands at £35,238 (Office for National Statistics, 2014 figures). This creates a gulf of understanding, particularly among the mandarin class of the BBC which, in London, operates in a pool where six figure incomes are not exceptional. And it should be noted that while there is a yawning gulf in housing costs between the two cities other essentials – fuel, heating, food, transport – tend to be more expensive in NI.

So how does the BBC perform in reporting NI to the rest of the UK? It could be argued that for decades the story was covered more fully, that more resources were put into reporting and investigating what are still referred to as the 'Troubles' than in other parts of the UK. But is this still the case? I increasingly sense that the British public feel the 1998 Belfast/Good Friday agreement solved the problem, sorted it all out: yes, there's bound to be some unfinished business but to all intents and purposes it's over and sensible people should just get on with their lives. This is, of course, a view some in Northern Ireland also take but it has not proved to be the case for many. First, there is the legacy of 'the Troubles':   the many hundreds of unsolved murders, the allegations – some of which have been shown to be true – of the involvement of security forces in collusion which resulted in deaths, and there are the thousands of people who bear the scars of physical and mental injury. There is also the fact that those who now hold high public office were implicated in atrocities and their victims have to see them on television and hear them on the radio.

While I would not wish to denigrate or dismiss the many outstanding programmes which the BBC has made on the legacy of 'the Troubles', a remit from which commercial television is largely conspicuous by its absence, it has sometimes proved difficult to engage the wider BBC in taking these issues as seriously as they might in the daily news coverage. For example, when a young woman, Mairia Cahill, came forward on the BBC NI's *Spotlight* programme in October 2014 and told how she had been raped and abused as a child by a senior IRA man and had then been forced to appear before an IRA 'court', local news executives found it almost impossible to interest London even though in Belfast and Dublin the story dominated headlines and shone a powerful light on the behaviour of the Sinn Fein president, Gerry Adams. Equally, the current impasse over implementation of welfare changes has received virtually no network coverage. One of the effects of this is that when a crisis then erupts it takes the rest of the UK by surprise and leaves them baffled.

A second factor is the deep and underlying hostility that in some areas continues to exist between Catholics and Protestants and which can find expression in dreadful violence against individuals – for example, the death in June 2015 after nine years in a vegetative state of a young man, Paul McAuley, who had been viciously attacked in Derry by a group of thugs simply because of his religion; the case was aggravated by a sense that the police investigation had been flawed. If this kind of hate crime had happened in London I have no doubt that it would have received far more coverage and scrutiny.

Then there are the more subtle ways in which coverage can appear to marginalise or dismiss the Northern Irish dimension. For instance, when Margaret Thatcher died on 8 April 2013, I watched the news channels with increasing anger as much airtime was devoted to her role in the Falklands conflict of 1982, the miners' strike of 1984-1985, the reshaping of the economy and Europe but no reference was initially made to the 1980s IRA hunger strikes or the 1985 Anglo-Irish Agreement which laid the foundations for the 1998 Belfast Agreement.

Sport, as any Celtic viewer will attest, is another minefield for the BBC. In February 2015, I listened to a headline which celebrated England coming through the first two weekends of the Six Nations Rugby Championship unbeaten; I waited in vain for it to add that so, too, had Ireland. (Rugby is played on an all-Ireland basis as are virtually all sports with the exception of soccer and the Irish rugby fan base in Northern Ireland is large and loyal.) For the many NI fans this smacked of both arrogance and insensitivity. However, it made it even more pleasing when a few weeks later it was Ireland who lifted the Championship!

So what does the BBC need to do in the next charter period to rectify these shortcomings? I think it needs to recognise that as relationships within and between the four nations which make up the UK shift and develop, the corporation needs to reinvent its current relationship in which, broadly, the centre decides and allow the nations and regions much more power to ensure that the national news properly and truthfully reports on the whole UK.

We may also need to go further and consider whether or not at some point the nations and regions should be free to decide the national news running order locally. Perhaps the time has come to rethink what was known in 1998 as 'the Scottish Six' – the notion of an integrated 6pm-7pm news programme which was edited locally to take account of local news priorities, much as happens with the locally-produced *Good Morning Ulster*. At the time, John Birt was deeply opposed to the proposition; his view, as expressed in his autobiography was that:

> It would have dire consequences for the BBC and unintended consequences for the United Kingdom ... Once the Six was conceded there would be no argument for resisting the takeover of the One and then the Nine. Within a few years there would be no UK-wide news on the BBC (Birt 2002).

He feared a weak, federal BBC or a broken-up and diminished BBC with four separate regional broadcasters. Out of this bitter debate came the still current arrangement to make a more integrated bulletin with a common set, graphics etc and the handover phrase from London of 'Now the news where you are'. This rather clumsy phrase came about because the original suggestion – 'News in your part of the country' – was unacceptable in Scotland which is a country in its own right; that was followed by 'News in your part of the UK' which was vetoed by both the Isle of Man and the Channel Islands on the obvious grounds that they are not part of the UK. The next suggestion – 'Your part of the British Isles' – was rejected by BBC Northern Ireland for equally obvious reasons.

While John Birt's argument had considerable validity in 1998, perhaps it should be revisited in 2016; in 1998, the News channel was still at an embryonic stage whereas now it is fully established and online gives instant access to international, national and local news.

The production base

One of the considerable challenges during the next decade is deciding the shape of the production base; can or should the BBC maintain a production base with all those inherent costs? Would the creation of BBC Studios enhance the quality of content and the choice of commissioners or would a BBC child leaving home jeopardise the future of all other independent production companies? The debate should certainly not overlook the potential implications for the BBC in Northern Ireland where, unlike other parts of the UK, both the purchasers and the supplier bases locally are limited and inherently low cost. UTV's commissions are, in the main, high volume, low-cost-returning series while there is a very low level of commission from other broadcasters on the island – RTE and TG4. What this means is that talent naturally goes where more money and commissions are available which usually means London and increasingly Salford. The risks in this are considerable: the BBC's historic role as trainer would wither; quality of locally produced programming may well suffer and, consequentially, the ability of the BBC to commission programmes for the network from the production base in Northern Ireland. This could, in turn, jeopardise both the BBC's ability to make programmes which represent the culture and experience of those who live in Northern Ireland. Without such a showcase, the licence fee payers in Northern Ireland, many of whom already feel disaffected from the BBC and that the networks fail to reflect their lives and their priorities, may become even more disinclined to support the BBC, especially if the criminal sanction for non-payment is removed in the new charter.

Northern Ireland Screen has certainly had its successes over the last decade in attracting high end, high cost production into NI – most notably the production of *Game of Thrones* but also through series such as *The Fall* and *Line of Duty* and films like *Philomena*. While much of the creative talent is bought in from elsewhere there is no doubt that these productions have built the local production and craft base, provided employment and boosted the tourism sector. While outsourcing the production base may challenge BBC Northern Ireland's current local factual output it could result in building a thriving production sector, supported not only by the broadcasters on the island but by the multinationals such as Sky, Netflix and HBO with a worldwide reach. The challenge then for the BBC nationally may, ironically, be the affordability of locally produced product.

Governance

One of the surer bets on the charter renewal process is that the BBC's governance structure will undergo fundamental change. The compromise negotiated ten years ago which saw the august and long-standing board of governors metamorphose into the BBC Trust while the board of management became a joint board with both executive and non-executive members has proved inherently unstable and, critics say, ineffective. The scars of the Savile crisis, the short tenure of George Entwistle as DG in 2012 for just 54 days, the public and political outrage over the massive payouts to departing executives, the perceived bloated bureaucracy and the high salaries paid to public servants probably make change inevitable. Add to this the recommendations of the 2014 commission on devolution, led by Lord Smith of Kelvin, and the implications for the nations are considerable. This is especially so for the BBC in Northern Ireland since it has little political muscle at Westminster – with the caveat that those ten Unionist MPs may yet exercise significant influence.

Smith recommended a formal consultative role for the Scottish government with accountability to the Scottish parliament for matters which related to Scotland – an interesting point of definition here in relation to network output which refers or does not refer to Scotland, for example, sporting coverage. The government response tempered this somewhat by proposing a memorandum of understanding (MOU) giving the Scottish government and parliament a formal role in both charter review and the ongoing scrutiny of the BBC but maintained the independence of the BBC by keeping its governance away from the statute book.

While there is a temptation to adopt a 'me too' approach to any devolutionary proposals for broadcasting proposals, as many organisations and institutions have cautioned, devolution throughout the UK is, and always has been, asymmetrical, with widely differing patterns in the different nations – Scotland with its distinctive and different education and legal systems, Wales, with its emphasis on linguistic diversity and Northern Ireland with its own parliament for fifty years and now its very particular power-sharing executive.

Conclusion: Caution required over devolution of broadcasting accountability to NI

In the case of Northern Ireland, particular caution should be exercised in the realm of devolution of broadcasting accountability. Nationalism in Northern Ireland is in no small measure a cultural rather than a civic construct and where not only politicians but the general populace are unable to agree on a shared identity, broadcasting is too important and its role too significant to risk its politicisation or the danger of appropriation by any of the communities. Where legitimate journalistic scrutiny can be interpreted as either undermining the forces of law and order or doing the securitat's bidding it is the responsibility of the guardians of broadcasting to preserve its integrity. And this is not theoretical: early in 2015, a minority report from a Stormont committee excoriated the BBC for refusing to appear before it to justify an investigative programme into links between the DUP and commercial companies. And Sinn Fein have ridiculed and condemned programmes which probed its treatment of young people who were sexually abused by members of the IRA as 'just what they might expect from a state broadcaster'. Accountability to the locally devolved parliaments and assemblies may be a fine ambition but may not be the preferred outcome in Northern Ireland.

So what might a new dispensation look like? If regulatory responsibility passes to Ofcom it seems unlikely that there would be protected places for representatives of the nations; equally, is a joint board really going to make space for designated and protected national voices at the top table? Is the Ofcom model of content boards in the nations who meet as a national content board feeding upwards to the main Ofcom board adequate?

I would urge both government and the BBC to reflect long and hard before excluding representation from the nations and especially Northern Ireland from the gubernatorial top table. Northern Ireland is often accused of pleading special case circumstances but in the case of broadcasting it seems to me to have some justification. Northern Ireland trustees and governors played a significant role during both 'the Troubles' and the peace process (which remains unstable) in ensuring that the BBC is respected and trusted by the audience. And broadcasting plays a vital role in creating a shared space for communities to meet and both explore their differences and recognise their commonalities.

References

Birt, John (2002) *John Birt: The Harder Path*, London: Little, Brown

King, Anthony (2007) *The English Constitution*, Oxford: Oxford University Press

Watt, Nicholas and McDonald, Henry (2015) Democratic Unionists: We'd seek a review of BBC in hung parliament talks, *Guardian*, 28 April. Available online at http://www.theguardian.com/politics/2015/apr/28/democratic-unionists-wed-seek-review-of-bbc-in-hung-parliament-talks, accessed on 26 June 2015

How the BBC's strategy for Devolution to the Nations and Regions of the UK has Broadly Been Achieved

More than 50 per cent of BBC employees live and work outside the London conurbation and over half of the overall output is generated in the nations and regions. Not many 10-year plans can point to this level of achievement, according to Roger Laughton

Introduction

Historically, the BBC's instinct has been to cover all the bases. World, the United Kingdom, the nations of the UK, the English regions, the localities – wherever there were licence payers or a public interest, you were likely to find the BBC. That said, whilst the BBC can reach far corners of the digital universe, it has had to accept it cannot be everywhere in the physical world all the time. Getting it right in England is still a work in progress.

The BBC's heart beats most powerfully in London. I should know. But it took me fifteen years to be certain. I started as a trainee in Bush House in 1965, then moved to my first proper job as a production assistant in Bristol in 1967. Two years later I progressed to the role of roving film producer/director for *Nationwide* in the north of England – very conscious and sometimes resentful of the knowledge that final editing decisions about my short films were being made in London. I had chosen to base my family in my home city of Sheffield. It may have been close to striking miners, but it felt a long way from the BBC's weekly news and current affairs meeting and the corridors of Lime Grove.

Three years as deputy editor of *Pebble Mill at One*, based in Birmingham and living in Worcester, followed. Then it was time to complete a full house of English regional experience by moving to Manchester. I edited *Brass Tacks* for three years, a rough-edged topical discussion programme in which most of the voices were northern. But we hit the jackpot, not with current affairs, but with a series of films about *Great Railway Journeys of the World*, produced from the region where railways began.

By 1980, it was time to bow to the inevitable and, much to the relief of my wife and daughter who had experienced enough house moves, to transfer to

London to head a new department called Network Features. Brian Wenham, then controller of BBC Two, believed this could act as an umbrella department for feature programmes from the English regional network production centres. Fat chance. Quite understandably, producers in Birmingham, Bristol and Manchester saw this as their worst nightmare and me as a broadcast quisling. Network Features became yet another London-based features production department. In due course I left the BBC in 1990 to head an ITV franchise bid that saw TVS replaced by Meridian. By then, Network Features, the department, had run its course.

ITV is now almost as London-centric as the BBC was in my day. But, twenty-five years ago, before the companies were able to merge, it retained strong regional identities – notably the Granada stronghold in Manchester, home of *Coronation Street* and *World in Action*. Network production was generated from all the national and regional franchises. Regional news programmes served local audiences.

Meridian's first initiative, on award of its licence, was to create a third news sub-region. TVS had split its large and diversified territory into two – with opt-out news services from Southampton and Maidstone. Meridian added a third news service for viewers in the north of the franchise area, based in Newbury, serving the Thames Valley. There were a few embarrassments at first; viewers in the Isle of Wight whose aerials were aligned to the Hannington transmitter, were understandably irritated by having to watch the headlines from Newbury. But, once teething problems had been resolved, audiences rose and, later, the BBC offered a similar choice of news service. Local news matters to viewers.

ITV's network news provider was then, as it is now, ITN, firmly based in London. The ITV sub-regions remain, broadcasting news and features. But ITV itself is no longer a federation of regional broadcasters in which Granada, based in Manchester, is top dog. For it was Granada which came out on top in the struggle amongst the regional ITV companies for supremacy at the turn of the century. ITV is now a single company, listed on the Stock Exchange with a Head Office in London, not Manchester.

Political and media power in England 'overwhelmingly based in the capital'

The voices for more English media devolution remain, for the most part, muted. Political and media power in England is overwhelmingly based in the capital. The speed of modern communications – physical and digital – has strengthened London's position at the heart of all the national broadcast networks.

That said, the BBC's policy statement of 2004, *Building Public Value*, committed the corporation to ensure more than half its public service staff would be based outside London by the end of the upcoming charter period. This target was reached in 2014, ten years later and earlier than the 2016 deadline which the BBC had set itself.

Scotland, Wales and Northern Ireland have been given a clearer voice and a sharper sense of identity by the BBC as a result of this strategy. However, the same cannot yet be said of the BBC's strategy for network output from the English regions. Put simply, Manchester (or, to be strictly accurate, Salford) has evolved into Media City. Bristol has continued to be home for world-beating natural history programmes. Birmingham has left its leafy headquarters in Edgbaston and not yet rediscovered a solid network production identity. Elsewhere, regional and local news centres are the link between the BBC and audiences outside London.

It is interesting to speculate whether Media City has played a part in triggering the concept of a 'northern powerhouse'. George Osborne, a Londoner, born in Paddington but as political as they come, has argued the case for more devolution of political powers to a northern region – centred in Greater Manchester, not far from his constituency in rural Cheshire. Perhaps administered by a mayor with powers to match those of the mayor of London? As yet the boundaries of such a region are as unclear as the responsibilities that may be devolved.

What is clear, in the broadcast landscape, is that the investment in Media City at Salford Quays ten years ago has been accompanied by swathes of network programme-making being located and editorially controlled in the north. Radio 5 Live, children's programmes, breakfast TV, BBC Sport, religion are all areas where day-to-day editorial decisions are taken in Manchester. Media City appears to be far and away more vibrant, as a programme-making centre, than the Oxford Road BBC of the seventies. No coincidence that Media City is also the base for the director of BBC England.

In contrast, the BBC's commitment to the production of networked programmes from its centre in Birmingham appears to have weakened. Thirty years ago, Pebble Mill provided the network with a daily lunchtime programme, broadcast from the building's lobby, as well as a stream of high quality drama from David Rose's stable. But the Pebble Mill building has been demolished and the move to the Mail Box in the centre of Birmingham has not been accompanied, as yet, by a distinctive brand of network programmes. The controller of English regions is based in Birmingham – but his writ is limited to the twelve news and opt-out regions of the present, not production for the national networks.

Whereas the three English network production centres could once be seen as equal in status, now Manchester is clearly at the centre of the action. Apart from anything else, both Birmingham and Bristol have the disadvantage of being too close to the capital. You can be in Central London within two hours of leaving either city by road or rail. Manchester feels just that bit further away, just that bit more independent.

In sum, the BBC has had to trim its ambitions in recent decades and has chosen to strengthen the three smaller nations of the United Kingdom and to prioritise, in England, one out-of-London production centre for network programmes in the north of England.

Should local BBC radio stations evolve into multi-media broadcasting hubs?

Perhaps the most difficult decisions facing the BBC have not been about the scale and volume of network programme production, but rather about the nature of local and regional programmes. Should local radio stations evolve into local multi-media broadcasting hubs?

The BBC twice experimented with this approach. Between 2001 and 2004, under Greg Dyke, the BBC launched a major initiative, 'Connecting Locally', with the declared aim of making the BBC more relevant to communities in Humberside and Lincolnshire than before. There was a new news region, a broadband trial, two BBC buses and a big screen in the centre of Hull. Calendar, ITV's regional news programme, took the biggest hit. But the fiercest opposition to the experiment came from the local paper, the *Hull Daily Mail*, even though its circulation between 1994 and 2006 declined more slowly than the average decline in circulation across the UK.

Two years later, the BBC decided to try again, mounting a nine-month pilot in the West Midlands, offering six distinct local television services in an area where the BBC already had four existing local radio broadcast areas. If such a model had been adopted nationwide, there may have been 66 local broadcasting stations in the UK – 48 of them in England. Each of the pilot areas was allotted five additional video journalists to provide on-demand and scheduled services to their local areas.

Once again, the BBC faced hostility from other local media and, although there was evidence that public value had been achieved, the BBC's board of governors decided against taking the BBC further into competition with local media interests. Nowadays, the BBC looks to work alongside local media rather than setting itself up as a potential competitor. So the BBC now broadcasts television news programmes in 12 English regions. In addition it has 40 local radio stations as well as a range of websites. Altogether around 7 per cent of the licence fee is spent on providing these services.

The BBC has not achieved all the targets it set itself in *Building Public Value* for broadcasting outside London. Competitors have succeeded in ensuring that the certainty of the licence fee will not be used to create a virtual monopoly in the digital world, which is probably in the public interest. That said, looked at as a whole, the BBC's strategy for devolution to the nations and regions of the UK – developed over the past decade – has broadly been achieved, although the nations and Media City should be adjudged the biggest winners. More than 50 per cent of the BBC's employees live and work outside the London conurbation and over half of the overall output is generated in the nations and regions. Not many 10-year plans can point to this level of achievement.

I doubt if the BBC needs to change course again in England over the next ten years. Media City has the potential to grow further. There is a case for Birmingham to be given a specialism. But, after years of upheaval, it would make more sense to encourage excellence where it emerges and to ensure that the networks of regional and local programming are resourced well enough to meet their objectives.

Conclusion: Why the Media City initiative is a success

I began this survey by recalling my own journey around the English regions. Four house moves in 14 years was quite a burden to impose on a young family. We moved to Kew in 1980 and have remained in Kew ever since. Thanks to the M3, commuting to the Meridian studios in Southampton in the 1990s took just over an hour, a few minutes longer than the time it took to reach the ITV Network Centre in Gray's Inn Road.

A major reason why I consider the Media City initiative to be a success is that it provides BBC staff with an alternative network production career structure to what is offered in London without demanding house moves, and the upheaval associated with them, every time a job change takes place. Tinkering with a strategy that appears to be working will be a temptation for BBC policy wonks that should be resisted. They should concentrate now on the quality of the programmes wherever they are produced.

And maybe the policy wonks should move to Manchester?

Dream on.

Section 8:
The Points of Viewers: The BBC and the Public Interest

Richard Lance Keeble

Journalism, media and communications departments in universities hold uniquely privileged positions. They work closely with their respective industries – for instance, in providing a steady stream of well-educated and highly motivated graduates to take up positions in the media (both mainstream and 'alternative'). But they should never subordinate their activities to the demands of industry. Rather, they should preserve and celebrate their 'autonomy'. This 'distance' from industry is crucial since it means that universities can promote models of 'best practice' and intervene critically in often highly charged (and often highly politicised) public debates with authoritative, well-researched, original commentaries on the media.

This book aims to reflect that creative and dynamic dialogue between industry and academia bringing together leading commentators, public intellectuals and researchers from higher education institutions to debate with broadcasting executives and professionals many of the crucial issues surrounding the BBC today. This section maintains that overall theme – with important and insightful contributions from both industry, public intellectuals and academics focusing on some of the many complex issues surrounding the BBC's highly contested 'public interest' mandate.

Britain is an extremely secretive society and thus it is not surprising that the BBC (as a powerful institution within it) should take so many of its most important decisions in secret. Media and entertainment unions, for instance, were quick to condemn the 'secret stich-up' agreement on the licence fee between the government and the corporation in July 2015.[1] This was just the most recent of a long list of secret dealings between the government of the day and the BBC. Colin Browne was formerly director, corporate affairs at the BBC from 1994 to 2000 and is currently chairman of the Voice of the Listener and Viewer. He is understandably annoyed that the corporation should so often, under pressure from government, marginalise the views of those who pay for it. He argues that the BBC should engage with the public far more deeply and innovatively than ever before. He adds:

> Let me be clear. I am absolutely not talking about some Twitter/phone-in universe, where reflecting the opinions of the audience – or at least that part of the audience which has the time and inclination to have its views broadcast on air – is seen as a sufficient form of engagement. What I am talking about is the recognition that the audience has an important role to play in the debate about the kind of public service broadcaster we want – what do we want it to do more of, or less of, or differently from a purely commercial organisation.

Tom O'Malley, emeritus professor of media at Aberystwyth University, has long been associated with the Campaign for Press and Broadcasting Freedom (CPBF) and its many campaigns to democratise the BBC.[2] Significantly, the CPBF includes amongst its aims:

> To defend the principles of public service broadcasting and to argue for democratically accountable forms of broadcasting regulation which actively promote and encourage high programme standards and genuine cultural diversity. The campaign firmly believes that broadcasting is a public service as fundamental to the wellbeing of our democracy as our education and health systems, and should under no circumstances be treated as merely a producer of commodities. Equally, the campaign holds that broadcast audiences must be treated, first and foremost, as citizens with distinct communicative rights, and not merely as consumers of entertainment products.

Staff working in the industry need a voice, too

Here O'Malley argues that the governance of the BBC – and Ofcom – has to be made more democratic by ensuring that members are drawn from a combination of representatives of licence fee payers, groups in civil society with an interest in broadcasting and staff working in the industry. Britain, he says, needs a communications system which has at its core strong, independent public services accountable to the public, not to commercial lobbyists and politicians steeped in neo-liberal orthodoxy.

Sylvia Harvey, visiting professor in the School of Media and Communication at the University of Leeds, is a long-time distinguished commentator on film history and policy, on the political economy of media and on broadcasting policy and regulation. Focusing on what she describes as a 'yawn-inducing' spectrum policy, she argues that, depending on which industry interests prevail, the users of broadcasting who have enjoyed an unmetered abundance of supply since the 1920s face eviction from a public space into the world of privately managed subscription. In effect, Harvey says, the universal service principle in British broadcasting is now under serious pressure. And she warns:

> Firstly, it has been suggested that BBC programmes should in future be encrypted and provided as subscription services; this would mean new forms of conditional access and the end of universal availability within the United Kingdom. Secondly, the emergence of a new kind of spectrum scarcity – stemming largely from the expansion of new mobile phone and data services – is causing spectrum to be withdrawn from broadcasters and re-allocated to mobile providers. Data and video are now the powerful drivers of mobile traffic.

There has been little public debate about these crucial (though complex) issues. Not surprisingly, Harvey ends by suggesting that, as a minimum, 'the public could be kept better informed about the decisions being taken in their name by ministers, regulators and high level groups as well as by the guardians of mobile telecommunications and public service broadcasting'.

Dan Hind's *The Return of the Public* (Verso) received many rave reviews when it appeared in 2010. According to John Brissendon, it was a 'perfectly-timed and comprehensive challenge to conventional thinking on the role of the media in late capitalist society'.[3] Here Hind draws on the ideas of James S. Fishkin to suggest that a deliberative body or jury considers the nature of the media system as a whole and the BBC's place within it as part of a wide-ranging public debate in the run-up to charter renewal.

Notes

[1] https://writersguild.org.uk/unions-condemn-secret-stitch-up-bbc-deal/, accessed on 2 August 2015

[2] http://www.cpbf.org.uk/?k=aboutus, accessed on 2 August 2015

[3] http://www.newleftproject.org/index.php/site/article_comments/return_of_the_public_a_response, accessed on 2 August 2015

It's Our BBC

Despite the 2015 licence fee deal, there is still much to decide about the future of the BBC, writes Colin Browne, and the views of listeners and viewers, not politicians, should be the ones that count

Historically, the BBC has not always been very good at recognising who its real friends are. Spool back to the mid-1990s when I joined the corporation as director, corporate affairs. There was a real and deeply-rooted arrogance towards the audience shown by many programme makers. They were certainly keen to have critical and peer acclaim for a successful, well-received item of television; but they were much less likely to take on board comments or criticism directly from the audience. There was a sense that the professionals knew best – how dare the audience question their decision-making or the quality of their work.

I remember when I first attended, as a guest, a meeting of the television programme review board – a meeting of some fifty or sixty people who had participated in making and broadcasting that week's programmes. Much time was spent taking praise – and some criticism – from colleagues. Other than the somewhat blunt viewing figures, there was no input on behalf of the people who actually paid for the programmes. The esteem of colleagues seemed to matter much more than the view of licence fee payers.

That approach has changed significantly over the years – but perhaps not enough. Faced with a daunting range of potentially existential challenges over the months ahead, the BBC needs to recognise that its real friends are the people who pay the licence fee and who, by and large, enjoy its services and recognise the value for money they offer; and it needs to engage with these audiences more deeply and innovatively than ever before.

A new role for the audience

Let me be clear. I am absolutely not talking about some Twitter/phone-in universe, where reflecting the opinions of the audience – or at least that part of the audience which has the time and inclination to have its views broadcast on air – is seen as a sufficient form of engagement. What I am talking about is the recognition that the audience has an important role to play in the debate about the kind of public service broadcaster we want – what do we want it to do more of, or less of, or differently from a purely commercial organisation.

For example, in an increasingly global and competitive media marketplace, do we want the UK public service broadcasters – and commissioners – to provide high-quality output that reflects the distinctive interests and culture of UK citizens and exploits to the maximum possible extent the huge wealth of talent that exists in the country – both in creative originality and in technological innovation. There is a real problem in arguing for the *status quo* in this area. Clearly, technology is changing both the customer experience and the competitive landscape, hugely.

These trends are mostly beneficial for audiences, both in principle and in practice. However, as a country we have long enjoyed the benefits of a strong broadcasting sector, thanks in the main to the mixed ecology of strong publicly owned broadcasters, the BBC and Channel 4, and a vibrant commercial sector which has *chosen*, in the case of ITV, to retain its public service commitments and obligations. This mixed ecology has given us some of finest broadcasting in the world. Of course, the Americans may do some things better; the Scandinavians may produce some excellent drama; and by no means everything that we see on our screens would meet most definitions of quality. However, by and large we know that we enjoy a rich and diverse range of programming in all the main genres; and almost certainly uniquely good radio.

The question, therefore, is how to sustain this benign environment in a world where so much is changing, both in the marketplace and in technology; and specifically, at this time, how to ensure that the BBC is able to continue to play a leading role?

As I have written elsewhere, this is too important a decision to be left to the politicians – or, for that matter, to the usual circus of industry insiders. Just as the BBC needed to become better at listening to and understanding the needs of different audiences, so now it is important that the people charged with deciding on its future consult widely on that future before taking those decisions; and that they take those decisions on the basis of what is right for listeners and viewers, and not on the basis of political expediency or prejudice. And I believe it is absolutely in the BBC's interest to engage citizens in this debate.

Two shabby deals: 2010 and 2015

In one important area, however, key decisions have been taken before the public has had a chance to have its say. We at the Voice of the Listener and Viewer (VLV) have been very critical of the shabby deal that underpinned the licence fee negotiations in 2010, which were conducted behind closed doors over a long weekend; a deal that damagingly introduced the principle of top-slicing of the licence fee, arguably more important and damaging to the BBC than the actual level of the settlement. We strongly believe that that agreement was not in the interest of licence fee payers – nor, for that matter, of the BBC itself. So we were all the more disappointed to see history repeat itself in the secret negotiations over the licence fee in July 2015. As recently as the spring 2015 publication of the DCMS select committee report on the BBC, it was stressed that the funding agreements should never again be reached in this way. Unfortunately, no one seems to have told the chancellor, whose raid on the BBC's finances to fund welfare policy was political expedience of the worst kind.

Despite that unfortunate start, which pre-empted an important aspect of the debate, both the DCMS and particularly the BBC Trust are now making the right noises about widespread public consultation and we do, of course, welcome that. However, the timetable is already beginning to look very tight; and it is probably the case that, whatever their good intentions, both the government and the BBC actually feel much more comfortable trying to keep control of the debate. Genuine consultation can be scary; you never quite know what it is going to throw up. Over the years, and perhaps particularly in the Birt era, the BBC had an enviable and justifiable reputation for managing these processes very tightly – not least under the iron grip of Dame Patricia Hodgson, the present chair of Ofcom!

While the BBC has clearly tried to adopt the same approach on this occasion, and with some success, the timing of the general election, and of the culture and media select committee's inquiry and report, have complicated matters – as has the appointment of the chair of the select committee as the new secretary of state. To what extent will John Whittingdale feel obliged to be bound by his committee's report, which was broadly welcomed by the BBC – and, indeed, by the VLV?

In her speech at the 2015 Oxford Media Convention, Rona Fairhead, chair of the BBC Trust, suggested that the level of the BBC's licence fee should be set by an independent panel of the great and good. That is an interesting suggestion, with much to commend it – provided, of course, that the panel consults widely; anything that distances BBC funding from short-term Treasury considerations and that underlines its independence from the politicians is to be welcomed. But can you really see the government and the Treasury giving up the power to determine the BBC's revenues – and thus effectively determine what kind of BBC we will have? I really don't think so.

And that brings me back to the core question of what kind of the BBC we will have. While the issue of governance is important, it is in my view secondary to this fundamental issue of the nature of the BBC. Most systems of governance can be made to work when you have the right people in place and a clear definition of respective roles and responsibilities. Not even the most perfect form of governance will work well with the wrong people. So I share Rona Fairhead's hope that we do not allow discussion on esoteric issues of governance to detract from the main debate on the purposes of the BBC and how – and by how much – it is to be funded. One caveat, however. While it is probably the case that that the trust as we know it will not survive – the trust itself seems to have accepted this – it will be important not to lose the very valuable work the trust has done in consulting widely on BBC services and other issues of interest to licence fee payers. This has represented a step-change on previous practice and has gone a long way towards dispelling the old 'we know best' approach.

The cornerstone of UK broadcasting ecology

However, the focus of the debate needs to be on the big issue of the size, shape and method of funding of the BBC. As I have said, from the VLV's perspective, the BBC represents the cornerstone of the UK's broadcasting ecology – an ecology that has served us so well for so many years. Of course, the changes in technology and the market are having a profound effect; but Ofcom's latest figures show that the change in viewing habits is incremental and, as regards the move from terrestrial to online or mobile viewing, is happening more slowly than many would expect. While forecasts are notoriously difficult in this area, free-to-air terrestrial viewing is likely to remain the main way in which UK citizens receive their television for the foreseeable future and probably for the period of the next BBC charter. Sometimes, the BBC, in its concern to be – and to be seen to be – at the leading edge of the new developments may actually be pushing change in a way that is unhelpful to its own interests. Certainly for the VLV, the principle of public service television – and, of course, radio – universally available and free at the point of reception remains as relevant today as it has ever been.

So let the debate begin – assuming it hasn't already been largely pre-empted by the chancellor of the exchequer; and let the BBC recognise that its most potent weapon in that debate might be the – sometimes critical – support of its listeners and viewers.

The Direction of Travel: The BBC in an Age of Neo-Liberal Communications Policy

Tom O'Malley argues that the governance of the BBC – and Ofcom – has to be made more democratic by ensuring that members are drawn from a combination of representatives of licence fee payers, groups in civil society with an interest in broadcasting and staff working in the industry

This chapter contextualises the current debate about the future of the BBC and public service communications, in order to clarify and urge a reconsideration of the direction of policy. Communications policy is an expression not of some set of abstract economic models which, if applied, will lead to the best outcomes all round. It reflects the moral and social perspectives of policy-makers and those who own and control mass communications. It has a direct bearing on the cultural, political and social environment of the world we live in.

In the last thirty years communications policy has become the preserve of self-referential elites, from very exclusive social backgrounds who have pressed forward a pro-market agenda, which relegates the general cultural welfare of the population to the priorities of profit maximisation (Freedman 2008; Sutton Trust 2006). The BBC is caught up in this process. Unless there is rapid and wholesale change in the nature of policy and the way it is made, we can look forward to a communications environment in which public service values, so vital to the well being of society, are relegated to the margins of the system and patronised largely by those who already have the cultural resources, interests and inclinations to take advantage of them. In the meantime, the overwhelming majority of the population will be left to the ever multiplying and manipulative flow of content designed with profit in mind, not public welfare

Neo-liberalism and broadcasting policy

There is extensive debate about the nature of neo-liberalism and its success in riding out the global financial crisis of 2007-2008, which was a product of neo-liberal policies (Mirowski 2013). As Jack Newsinger has argued:

Neoliberalism is best understood as a project of upward capital redistribution as opposed to a fundamentalist theoretical conviction in the natural ubiquity and efficacy of unfettered markets. Neoliberalism is therefore a political/ideological project in which the state can play a significant role in creating and preserving an institutional framework appropriate to the purpose of capital redistribution (Newsinger 2015: 331).

In the UK, since 1979, all the major political parties have become homes to and promoters of variants of neo-liberalism. This has been characterised by the gradual privatisation of the NHS, the undermining of state education, the curtailing of local democracy by cutting the powers and funding of local authorities, the demonisation of people on welfare, the privatisation of key public utilities, successive assaults on trade unions, increased surveillance by the state of political dissent, the reduction in taxation for the well off and a relaxed approach to the regulation of financial markets. The result has been a redistribution of wealth from the working and middle classes to increasingly wealthy upper-middle and upper classes, a growth in social inequality and the curtailing of post-war advances in social mobility (Mendoza 2015; Leys and Player 2011; Meek 2015). Developments in broadcasting policy since 1986, which frame debates about the future of communications and the BBC, are rooted in this context.

The BBC and communications policy since 1986

The BBC was established in 1922, and received its first royal charter in 1926 (Briggs 1961: 356-358). Between 1926 and 1986 communication policy presupposed that the main purpose of broadcasting was to provide programming that enriched and informed the lives of citizens. This was the idea which underpinned the subsequent BBC charters and the statutes that established ITV (in 1954) and Independent Local Radio (1972).

This was an expression of a political settlement, with its origins in the 1920s and 1930s, that led to a broad level of agreement amongst politicians of all parties around the principles of limited state intervention in industry through public ownership, the creation of a system of welfare to aid the poor, the creation of a non-market based education and health system and the promotion of a more egalitarian, socially humane society than had been the case since the emergence of industrial capitalism in the late eighteenth century (Harrison 2011; Greenleaf 1983).

By the 1970s this settlement was under pressure from economic problems and social and cultural change. The solution to this set of problems which became the political orthodoxy was offered by the pro-market, anti-state wing of Conservatism, centred on think tanks such as the Institute of Economic Affairs. This approach, subsequently characterised as neo-liberalism, emphasised the importance of reducing the size of the state, allowing markets to operate as freely as possible, and rolling back the gains of organised labour, all in the name freedom. It developed a strong base in the media and the Conservative Party during the 1960s and 1970s (Cockett 1995). The Conservative election victory in 1979 began a process of neo-liberal reaction against the post-war settlement, one in which communications policy was caught up.

Neo-liberal ideas in broadcasting policy found their most eloquent and well argued expression in the *Report of the Committee on the Financing of the BBC*, chaired by the economist Alan Peacock, published in 1986 (Home Office 1986). This report set the framework for the development of broadcasting policy in the UK thereafter, leading to an increase in under-regulated commercial competition, the decline of ITV's obligations as a regionally-based public service broadcaster, and the growth of the contracting-out of services in broadcasting, through the support given by successive governments to the independent sector. Peacock saw a future in which the majority of electronic communications would be based on market forces, with public service broadcasting being supplied by a public service broadcasting council, that would fund 'those programmes of merit which would not survive in the market'. Once the technology allowed, the BBC would become a subscription service. The market, or as the report claimed, consumer choice, would replace a system dominated by state intervention and control (O'Malley 1994: 112-114; O'Malley 2001).

A succession of statues enacted this framework – the 1990 and 1996 Broadcasting Acts and the Communications Act 2003. The direction of policy was that set by Peacock, only at a much slower pace than was envisaged in the report. The market-orientated regulator Ofcom allowed ITV to withdraw from many of its public service obligations (O'Malley 2011). Ownership rules were relaxed, independent companies were formed and morphed from lots of small ones into fewer, dominant, large ones, and a mass of under regulated satellite, cable and latterly internet-based communications emerged. One consequence was that spending on new, first run public service content declined in the UK by 17.3 per cent between 2008 and 2013 (Department of culture, media and sport 2015: para 7, note 4).

Like policy towards the NHS, the approach was not a full frontal privatisation (Leys and Player 2011), but the hollowing out of the public service elements of the system. In these years the BBC was forced to engage in constant 'reforms', designed to make it behave more like a commercial enterprise, whilst not competing 'unfairly' with the emerging competition. This involved the introduction of an internal market under director general John Birt (1992-2000) and the steady increase in the amount of outsourcing of programmes to the private sector, under the guise of promoting diversity by commissioning independent producers (Curran and Seaton 2010; O'Malley 1994).

As the years went by the demands for more market based 'reforms' and the curtailing of the BBC's activities continued from groups associated with the Conservative Party (Broadcasting Policy Group 2004) and the media. This was within a context of policy-making in which ministers were in constant touch with those elements in the media whose political support they felt they needed and whose interests were rooted in curtailing the competition posed by the BBC and maximising the opportunities for profit making (Freedman 2008; Leveson 2011; Davies 2015). In 2010, the Conservative and Liberal Democratic government froze the BBC licence fee for six years and forced it to take on the funding of the World Service and S4C, previously funded by the Foreign Office and the department of culture media and sport respectively, thereby forcing the BBC down the road of major cuts (BBC 2010).

The point of all this pressure was not lost on Tony Hall, who had been 'regarded as one of Birt's key lieutenants' (BBC 2015), and who took over as BBC director general in 2013. By 2015, he had decided to take the corporation further down the road suggested by Peacock. He announced that a significant proportion of its production capacity would be transferred to a new unit, BBC Studios which, subject to government agreement and charter change, would be transferred out of the publicly-funded part of the BBC. In addition, the internal rule that ensured 50 per cent of programming be made in-house was to be set aside; potentially turning it into an organisation which no longer produced the majority of its television programming in-house. (Conlan 2015). In addition, the Conservative manifesto at the 2015 general election committed the government to keeping the licence fee frozen until the outcome of the charter review (Conservative Party 2015: 42).

The charter review and beyond

One very strong indicator of the thinking in the media industry and Whitehall, in relation to which charter renewal would take place, was the report on the *Future of the BBC* by the House of Commons culture, media and sport committee (2015). It was chaired by John Whittingdale MP, who after the Conservatives won the general election, was appointed secretary of state at the department of media, culture and sport on 11 May 2015.

Its language was permeated by the economistic terminology common in policy documents since the 1980s. The BBC's income was not a 'licence fee' but a 'public intervention of close to £4 billion'. It repeated the opinion of those in the commercial sector, as if it were a proven fact, when it claimed that '… the BBC is a powerful player and unchecked there is danger that it will, by accident or design, crowd out smaller rivals and inhibit their ability to grow'. It also argued that the BBC should be 'reducing provision in areas that are over-served or where the public service characteristics of its output are marginal, or where others are better placed to deliver excellence and better value for money'. In effect, this means that the scope of public service broadcasting should be defined by the BBC's competitors and narrowed down to providing content which is, ultimately, acceptable to them (House of Commons culture, media and sport committee 2015: 3-5, 44). The idea that public service broadcasting should cover all forms of popular and specialist output, across all platforms, giving everyone access to the widest possible range of cultural goods, subject only to their ability to pay and of the BBC to provide it, is implicitly rejected.

Taking a leaf out of the Peacock report, and echoing the recommendations of the Conservative Party commissioned report of the Broadcasting Policy Group (2004), it concluded that a 'degree of subscription could be a possibility in the future'. Less controversially it suggested that the licence fee be replaced by a German-style broadcasting levy on households. The sting in the tale was that some of that money should be removed from the BBC and diverted to other organisations deemed to be providing public service broadcasting. The BBC was to be placed under even more regulation by the neo-liberal regulator Ofcom, its trust replaced by a commercial-like unitary board, and its strategic plan, level of funding and performance scrutinised by a new body, a public service broadcasting commission a descendent of the Peacock report's public service broadcasting council. The new commission would take on the role of managing a 'fund for certain public service content and genres which was open to competition'. The committee also recommended 'removing in-house production guarantees and opening up the majority of BBC commissioning to competition'. That said, it made the important, and valuable recommendation that the BBC's charter be renewed for two years beyond 2016 to allow for a full review to take place (House of Commons culture, media and sport committee 2015: 3-5).

Alternatives
What has been happening to the BBC and to commercial public service broadcasting since the late 1980s has been happening to other public services, such as local government, the health service and education (Leys and Player 2011; Mendoza 2015). As Colin Leys has argued, once 'Public service television and the National Health Service were both considered important for, if not essential to, democratic citizenship. Under market-driven politics both are being displaced by the profitable production of commodities. Television programming is seen less and less as a contribution to public education and debate and is devoted more and more to entertainment' (Leys 2001: 212). What is happening to communication policy is part of a systematic, if not always smoothly implemented, attempt to re-engineer the state in the interests of those groups with commercial and its accompanying political power, often cloaked in the rhetoric of promoting freedom and choice, whilst, in effect, undermining both.

There are alternatives. In the short term there should be a commission of inquiry running for at least two years to explore the future of public service communications, and which is peopled by a majority representing civil society and not the industry; resources should be made available to organisations in the community to research and provide evidence to the inquiry. The BBC should be established by statute and be free of oversight from Ofcom. It should be allowed to operate freely across all platforms providing services to all members of the community and should not be prevented from delivering the full range of those services by the special pleadings of its commercial rivals.

Commercial providers should be given regulatory incentives to become public service broadcasters, not be allowed to undermine the BBC. The role of Ofcom has to be reviewed; its aims must be to foster public service provision across all commercial platforms by the use of new sources of finance, including levies on recording equipment, pay TV revenues, mobile phone companies, and internet companies such as Google and Microsoft.

The governance of the BBC and Ofcom has to be made more democratic, by ensuring that members are drawn from a combination of representatives of licence fee payers, groups in civil society with an interest in broadcasting and the staff working in the industry. Above all, the underlying principle driving public policy since the 1980s, the principle of a market-orientated system of communications with public service relegated to the margins, needs to be overturned. We need, as organisations such as the Campaign for Press and Broadcasting Freedom have argued for decades, a communications system which has at its core strong, independent public services accountable to the public, not to commercial lobbyists and politicians steeped in neo-liberal orthodoxy (Media Reform Coalition and CPBF 2015). The direction of travel for the BBC and all communications services has to change. Otherwise, as has been the case in, health, local government, public utilities, banking and education, it will be the public and our democracy which will continue to suffer the damaging impact of neoliberalism.

References

BBC (2010) Television licence fee to be frozen for next six years, 20 October. Available online at http://www.bbc.co.uk/news/entertainment-arts-11572171, accessed on 9 June 2015

BBC (2015) Director Generals of the BBC. Available online at http://downloads.bbc.co.uk/historyofthebbc/director-generals.pdf, accessed on 10 June 2015

Briggs, Asa (1961) *The History of Broadcasting in the United Kingdom. Volume 1. The Birth of Broadcasting*, Oxford: Oxford University Press

Broadcasting Policy Group (2004) *Beyond the Charter: The BBC after 2006*, London: Broadcasting Policy Group

Cockett, Richard (1995) *Thinking the Unthinkable: Think-Tanks and the Economic Counter-Revolution, 1931-1983*, London: Fontana

Freedman, Des (2008) *The Politics of Media Policy*, Cambridge: Polity

Conlan, Tara (2015) BBC to hive off production of top shows into studios division, *Guardian*, 2 March. Available online at http://www.theguardian.com/media/2015/mar/02/bbc-production-top-shows-studios-division-doctor-who, accessed on 9 June 2015

Conservative Party (2015) *Strong Leadership, a Clear Economic Plan, A Brighter, More Secure Future*, London: Conservative Party

Curran, James and Seaton, Jean (2010) *Power without Responsibility: Press Broadcasting and the Internet in Britain*, London: Routledge, seventh edition

Davies, Nick, (2015) At this election, British politicians can afford to speak out against Rupert Murdoch, *Guardian*, 6 April. Available online at http://www.theguardian.com/commentisfree/2015/apr/06/election-british-politicians-rupert-murdoch, accessed on 9 June 2015

Department of culture, media and sport (2015) *The Balance of Payments between Television Platforms and Public Service Broadcasters: Options for Deregulation. Consultation Paper*, London: DCMS

Greenleaf, W. H. (1983) *The British Political Tradition. Volume One. The Rise of Collectivism*, London: Routledge

Harrison, Brian (2011) *Seeking a Role. The United Kingdom 1951-1970*, Oxford: Clarendon Press

Home Office (1986) *Report of the Committee on the Financing of the BBC*, London: HMSO, Cmnd 9824

Leys, Colin (2001) *Market Driven Politics. Neoliberal Democracy and the Public Interest*, London: Verso

Leys, Colin and Player, Steward (2011) *The Plot Against the NHS*, London: Merlin

Leveson, Lord Justice (2012) *An Inquiry into the Culture Practices and Ethics of the Press, Volume III*, London: The Stationery Office, HC780-III

Media Reform Coalition and Campaign for Press and Broadcasting Freedom (2015) *A Manifesto for Media Reform*, London: MRF and CPBF. Available online at http://www.cpbf.org.uk/files/media_manifesto_2015.pdf, accessed on 10 June 2015

Meek, James (2015) *Private Island. Why Britain Now Belongs to Someone Else*, London: Verso

Mendoza, Kerry-Anne (2015) *Austerity. The Demolition of the Welfare State and the Rise of the Zombie Economy*, Oxford: New Internationalist Publications

Mirowski, Philip (2013) *Never Let A Serious Crisis Go To Waste. How Neoliberalism Survived the Financial Meltdown*, London: Verso

Newsinger, Jack (2015) A cultural shock doctrine? Austerity, the neoliberal state and the creative industries discourse, *Media, Culture and Society*, Vol. 37, No. 2 pp 302-313

O'Malley, Tom (1994) *Closedown. The BBC and Government Broadcasting Policy, 1979-92*, London: Pluto

O'Malley, Tom (2001) The decline of public service broadcasting, Bromley, Michael (ed.) *No News is Bad News: Radio, Television and the Public*, Harlow: Longman pp 28-45

O'Malley, Tom (2011) Wales, ITV and regulation, *Cyfrwng*, Vol. 8 pp 7-22

Sutton Trust (2006) *The Educational Background of Leading Journalists*, London: Sutton Trust

Digital Dreams and Open Skies: Universal Service and the BBC

Depending on which industry interests prevail, the users of broadcasting who have enjoyed an unmetered abundance of supply since the 1920s face eviction from a public space into the world of privately managed subscription, warns Sylvia Harvey

The prospects for national broadcasting

What does it take to make a national broadcaster? A national service should be freely available in all homes for adults and children without the barriers of encryption or subscription. The United Nations' educational and cultural body, UNESCO, suggested in 2005 that public service broadcasting might have 'an important role to play in providing access and participation in public life'; it would serve 'the interests of people as citizens rather than as consumers'; it would assist in 'strengthening civil society' and it would be 'a unique service providing universal access to information and knowledge' (2005). This chapter argues that the universal service principle in British broadcasting is now under pressure in two ways. Firstly it has been suggested that BBC programmes should in future be encrypted and provided as subscription services; this would mean new forms of conditional access and the end of universal availability within the United Kingdom. Secondly, the emergence of a new kind of spectrum scarcity – stemming largely from the expansion of new mobile phone and data services – is causing spectrum to be withdrawn from broadcasters and re-allocated to mobile providers. Data and video are now the powerful drivers of mobile traffic.

Broadcasters can now manage with less spectrum, partly as a benign consequence of digital switchover – signal compression has made it possible to do more with less. However, the pressures for mobile growth are now suggesting to policy-makers, commercial interests and broadcasters alike that there may come a time when broadcasting will no longer be 'broad' – but banished from the airwaves as the age of plenitude and of 'free-to-air' transmission comes to an end. The users – citizens and consumers – have remained largely unaware of the scale and significance of these possible changes.

Spectrum: The oxygen of broadcasting

The allocation of spectrum is an international as well as a national issue with broad spectrum use priorities being determined by the World Radio Conference (WRC) in consultation with national governments. The WRC is due to meet in November 2015 to take decisions, acting on the authority of the International Telecommunication Union (ITU), an agency of the United Nations. It is expected that this conference will agree the re-allocation of the UHF 700 MHz band from broadcasting to mobile use. The European Union also has an interest in these matters and four of its members, Germany, France, Sweden and Finland, have already committed to the sale of these frequencies to mobile providers (Ofcom 2014a: 10). At present in the United Kingdom this same 700 MHz band is used by the Freeview platform to transmit some 60 free-to-air services, including all the BBC's national television and radio channels. The Freeview platform, along with its sister organisation Freesat, is relied upon by the 47 per cent of British homes that have chosen not to pay for subscription television and that make use of an 'open skies' signal entering the home mainly via a rooftop aerial (Ofcom 2014b: 127; 2014c: 109)[1]. In practice Freeview has a wider take-up than the 47 per cent figure suggests, since many subscription homes have at least one additional television set which makes use of the free services delivered by the rooftop aerial; thus Freeview's reach has been estimated at nearer 75 per cent of British homes (Ofcom 2014d: 4). To deliver television signals into the home this platform relies entirely upon the availability of suitable spectrum.

Freeview provides, in digital form, the old five analogue channels (BBC1, ITV1, Channel 4, BBC Two and Five) along with their families of newer channels – ITV2, BBC Four and many more besides. These services are also referred to as Digital Terrestrial Television (DTT), principally to distinguish them from services relayed by cable, satellite or Internet Protocol (IPTV). The 53 per cent of British homes that have signed up to pay TV receive these services principally via satellite or cable (Sky, UKTV, Virgin). More recently internet delivered services such as BT TV and Netflix have emerged as significant players.

However, internet distribution currently is arguably not able to fulfil a public service remit partly because in the UK there remain some 18 per cent of homes that do not have access to the internet and partly because this mode of delivery – unlike the rooftop aerial – involves additional monthly subscription payments and the possibility, even if this is unlikely, that control over content might be exercised by an internet service provider (Ofcom 2014b: 276). By contrast, broadcasting appears to be a highly efficient and cost effective means of delivering audio-visual content to large numbers of people. Some specialists have noted that broadband capacity is at present unable to cope with very high demand for the simultaneous viewing of especially popular programmes, whether sport or drama. The consultants Aetha comment in a recent report:

Linear television continues to be the most effective means of delivering simultaneous content. It is costly and impractical to expect many viewers to stream a programme simultaneously online, as bandwidth can still be constrained.

The report goes on to note some high profile failures of streaming services: for example, when the ITV Player crashed in response to high demand for live coverage of the World Cup in 2014 and Sky's Now TV crashed on the opening of Season Four of *Game of Thrones* in the same year (Aetha 2014: 20).

Other commentators, including the mobile industry itself, as well as the UN agency the ITU, are advocates of the view that, sooner or later, the fixed and mobile broadband that delivers the internet will be capable of replacing spectrum-reliant broadcasting altogether. In the process, spectators may lose the option of a choice between broadcast (over the airwaves and free-to-view) and broadband delivery. And a monthly broadband subscription may have to rise considerably to cover the costs of the providers in developing much greater capacity. If broadband were able to develop the capacity to deliver the current average daily television diet of just under four hours per person it would, of course, also do much more than that – offering a wide range of additional informational and commercial services, as at present. But one small cost-related point may be worth noting for the future. In 2013, the cost to licence fee payers for the distribution of all BBC services was 6.5 per cent of the licence fee or 80p per month (BBC Trust 2013: 1). This amount may subsequently be seen to compare favourably with an enhanced monthly broadband bill.

Bigger kids on the block: The growth of mobile
The ITU develops the long term case for the broadband delivery of television in its *Trends in Broadcasting* report, while the international trade body for the mobile phone and data sector, GSMA, has argued for mobiles to take over not only the 700 MHz band but also the lower 470-694 MHz band (ITU 2013: 27; GSMA 2015). This lower band appears to constitute the last suitable bloc of spectrum for the free-to-air broadcasters including the BBC (EBU 2015).

One significant way of growing the business of mobile providers is the development of mobile video services – a category that includes broadcasting. Here the take-up, though significant in the richer parts of the world, has not been as rapid or extensive as at first thought. The 2013 ITU report cites an earlier Cisco study forecasting that by 2016 'video will generate over 70 per cent of the mobile data traffic' (ITU 2013: 6). A later report by Cisco corrected this forecast to an estimate that '... nearly three-fourths of the world's mobile data traffic will be video by 2019' (Cisco 2015: 3). Given the generally fast pace of change in the mobile field this is a significant downward adjustment; it also seems likely that users are making greater use of Wi-Fi facilities in order to avoid the otherwise significantly higher mobile data fees associated with video use.

Of course, it would be unwise to underestimate the general pace of change and it is important to note significant variability across countries and age groups.

Thus, for example, France is currently the leader in Europe for the reception of television via the internet with 30 per cent of homes receiving television on their main set via internet protocol (IPTV) (Aetha 2014: 70). In the UK, the BBC's iPlayer (also internet delivered) appears to be growing in popularity although its significance in terms of volume can be over-stated. In 2012, it represented just 2.3 per cent of all BBC viewing. The figure will have risen since then, but it will be important to monitor this use as against live or linear TV watching (BBC Trust 2014: 22). There are other popular technologies in play. With regard to smart phones considered as TV reception devices, 22 per cent of adults in Britain have 'ever watched a TV programme on a mobile' and 13 per cent have done this at least once every three months. The figures for children are difficult to compare; 31 per cent of children aged 5 to 15 own a smartphone. For these children tablets are more popular than the mobile phone for watching television programmes though there also seems to have been a small renaissance in watching programmes on the main TV set in the home. For children, the figures for watching television on a mobile appear to have gone down from 14 per cent to 11 per cent between 2013 and 2014 (Ofcom 2014e: 49; 2014f: 39).

In noting these various related developments, the spectrum story, nevertheless, remains a big one. From the point of view of the BBC and other free-to-air broadcasters, the worry, disruption and cost involved in being required to migrate all services away from the700 MHz band to the lower band is considerable. And, as indicated above, the mobile companies have already indicated that they wish to make use of at least part of the lower 470-694 MHz band. GSMA has cited the possibility of a 'co-existence' within this band that the broadcasters believe is not achievable. Moreover, if the spectrum space on offer is insufficient to innovate and develop new services (Ultra High Definition television is one example) this could have damaging effects on the competitiveness of DTT.

At present a cloud of uncertainty hangs over this lower spectrum band. A recent high level report for the European Commission prepared by Pascal Lamy, former head of the World Trade Organisation, proposed that the use of this lower band by broadcasters be reviewed in 2025 (Lamy 2014). GSMA members would like to see the issue resolved sooner – by 2020. Depending on which industry interests prevail, the users of broadcasting who have enjoyed an unmetered abundance of supply since the 1920s face eviction from a public space into the world of privately managed subscription.

In part this process of transition is occurring in most countries as governments understand that the 'free' spectrum space allocated to broadcasting has become economically valuable. In the UK, in 2000, spectrum sales for the development of the 3G mobile phones brought in £22.5 billion for the national Treasury, followed by £2.3 billion for the auction of the 800MHz spectrum for 4G in 2013 (Radio Communications Agency 2000; Ofcom 2013). It is easy to see why some governments might prefer to see the airwaves as generators of public cash not public communication.

Digital TV = Pay TV?

The tension between public and private ownership of communication systems has been with us for a long time. In Britain, there has been some sympathy for public service broadcasting since the creation of the BBC in 1922 and, much later, a special clause in the European Treaty permitted public methods of funding (Goldberg et al. 1998). The current debate and conflict over spectrum allocation is not the first time that universally available public broadcasting, free at the point of use, has faced something of an existential crisis. The early days of transition to digital in the UK were full of uncertainty and conflict. 1998 saw both the satellite broadcaster, BSkyB and its commercial rival ITV launch digital subscription services. BSkyB did well, attracting some 5 million customers by the end of 2000. ITV fared badly and was forced to close in 2002. As one contemporary observer noted: 'Pay TV had in effect colonised the digital TV market' (Starks 2007: 49).

However, in the wake of the ITV closure a surprising new alliance combining the BBC with ITV, Channel 4, Arqiva and BSkyB took over the licences and launched the Freeview digital service in late 2002. It was perhaps in the interests of BSkyB that this new initiative should not emerge as a subscriber competitor and Freeview remained, resolutely, a free-to-air service: 'This was TV through the normal rooftop aerial for people who did not want pay TV' (ibid: 83).

In the following decade many commentators believed the process of digital transition would deliver a predominantly pay TV system. To begin with this seemed to be happening. In 2002, when some 39 per cent of British homes had adopted digital television (mainly through BSkyB) the percentage of digital homes paying for television stood at 87 per cent. Five years later, in 2007, when the proportion of digital homes had grown to 86 per cent the corresponding figure for pay television had fallen to 55 per cent. Five years after that, in the final switchover year of 2012, the figure of 96 per cent of homes adopting digital compares with 51 per cent of homes adopting pay TV (Ofcom 2007: 101; 2010: 97; 2014b: 127). There appeared to be life in the free-to-view model after all.

In 2014, the Lamy report acknowledged DTT as the 'backbone' of European provision, citing the fulfilment of such policy objectives as 'cultural diversity and media pluralism' and 'ensuring universal and free-to-air access for citizens'; but he also noted that the market share of DTT varied considerably between countries with Belgium at 4 per cent and Italy at nearly 80 per cent (2014: 3 and 5).

A national service, free at the point of use

While the BBC appears resolute in supporting the principle of universal access and 'something for everyone', it also seems internally conflicted on the topic of internet delivery with one recent report asserting that:

> By 2025, most people in the UK are likely get their television programmes over the internet. By 2030, possibly everyone will. The TV aerial will have gone the way of the typewriter (BBC 2015: 2).

At the same time senior executives lobbying in Europe and preparing for the possible consequences of the forthcoming World Radio Conference were arguing that spectrum should be retained for broadcasters and that free-to-air reception, via the old aerial, was one of the necessary features of public service.

In 1924, John Reith, first director general of the BBC, spoke of bringing 'the best of everything into the greatest number of homes' and marvelled at the new technology of broadcasting. He considered it to be:

> ...a reversal of the natural law, that the more one takes, the less there is left for others... Most of the good things of this world are badly distributed and most people have to go without them. Wireless is a good thing, but it may be shared by all alike, for the same outlay and to the same extent (Reith 1924: 147 and 217).

Wireless or broadcast delivery is still 'a good thing' and cost effective for users. Living wage or 'minimum income standard' calculations developed in the UK include the cost of owning a Freeview television along with an annual television licence fee to cover content costs (Rowntree 2014: 20). But there are also many homes managing on less than a living wage and some of these may be struggling to pay the licence fee. Government figures indicate that around 17 per cent of UK households are on a 'low income' – defined as less than 60 per cent of median income (Department of Work and Pensions 2014: 4). This 17 per cent figure could be seen to correspond roughly to the already mentioned 18 per cent of homes that Ofcom records as being without internet access.

Low income households with children may be as dependent on Cbeebies and CBBC as high income ones might be addicted to the *Today* programme or *Top Gear*. But little or no research seems to be available on the likely costs of fixed or mobile broadband delivery of programmes – in an age when the option of broadcast delivery might no longer be available. This seems an odd omission.

Democratic governments and institutions have a responsibility to weigh carefully the impact of policy-driven change on all of a nation's homes including the impact of otherwise yawn-inducing spectrum policies. Perhaps, as a minimum, the public could be kept better informed about the decisions being taken in their name by ministers, regulators and high level groups as well as by the guardians of mobile telecommunications and public service broadcasting.

Notes
[1] Except where otherwise noted the figures given in Ofcom's 2014 *Communications Market Report* are for the full year 2013

References
Aetha (2014) *Future Use of the 470-694 MHz Band. Report for Albertis, Arqiva, BBC, BNE, EBU and TDF.* Available online at https://tech.ebu.ch/docs/news/2014_11/Aetha%20Future%20use%20of%20the%204 70-694MHz%20band%20in%20the%20EU%2031%20Oct%202014.pdf, accessed on 14 June 2015

BBC Trust (2014) *The BBC's Distribution Arrangements for its UK Public Services*. Available online at http://downloads.bbc.co.uk/bbctrust/assets/files/pdf/review_report_research/vfm/distribution.pdf,accessed on 31 May 2015

BBC (2015) *Future of News*. Available online at http://newsimg.bbc.co.uk/1/shared/bsp/hi/pdfs/29_01_15future_of_news.pdf, accessed on 31 May 2015

Cisco (2015) *White Paper. Cisco Visual Networking Index: Global Mobile Data Traffic Forecast Update, 2014-2019*. Available online at http://www.cisco.com/c/en/us/solutions/collateral/service-provider/visual-networking-index-vni/white_paper_c11-520862.pdf, accessed on 15 June 2015

Department for Work and Pensions (2013) *Households below Average Income (HBAI) Absolute Low Income*. Available online at https://www.gov.uk/government/uploads/system/uploads/attachment_data/file/207120/absolute_low_income_using_cpi.pdf, accessed on 18 June 2015

EBU (2015a) *Spectrum: What is at Stake?* Available online at http://www3.ebu.ch/member-support/advocacy-policy-development/spectrum, accessed on 12 June 2015

Goldberg, David, Prosser, Tony and Verhulst, Stefan (1998) *EC Media Law and Policy*, London: Longman

GSMA (2015) *Mobile Spectrum Requirements and Target Bands for WRC-15*. Available at http://www.gsma.com/spectrum/wp-content/uploads/2014/05/WRC-15-Public-Policy-Position-Paper-June-2015.pdf, accessed on 13 June 2015

ITU (2013) *Trends in Broadcasting: An overview of developments*. Available online at http://www.itu.int/en/ITU-D/Technology/Documents/Broadcasting/TrendsinBroadcasting.pdf, accessed on 14 June 2015

Lamy, Pascal (2014) *Report to the European Commission: Results of the Work of the High Level Group on the Future Use of the UHF Band (470-790 MHz)*. Available online at http://ec.europa.eu/newsroom/dae/document.cfm?doc_id=8423, accessed on 31 May 2015

Ofcom (2007) *Communications Market Report*. Available online at http://stakeholders.ofcom.org.uk/binaries/research/cmr/cm07_1.pdf, accessed on 15 June 2015

Ofcom (2010) *Communications Market Report*. Available online at http://stakeholders.ofcom.org.uk/binaries/research/cmr/753567/CMR_2010_FINAL.pdf, accessed on 15 June 2015

Ofcom (2013) Ofcom announces winners of the 4G mobile auction. Available online at http://media.ofcom.org.uk/news/2013/winners-of-the-4g-mobile-auction/, accessed on 31 May 2015

Ofcom (2014a) *Consultation on future use of the 700 MHz band. Cost-benefit analysis of changing its use to mobile services*. Available online at http://stakeholders.ofcom.org.uk/binaries/consultations/700MHz/discussion/ftv.pdf, accessed on 31 May 2015

Ofcom (2014b) *The Communications Market Report*. Available online at http://stakeholders.ofcom.org.uk/binaries/research/cmr/cmr14/2014_UK_CMR.pdf, accessed on 15 March 2015

Ofcom (2014c) *Public Service Content in a Connected Society. Ofcom's Third Review of Public Service Broadcasting*. Available online at http://stakeholders.ofcom.org.uk/binaries/consultations/psb-review-3/summary/PSBR-3.pdf, accessed on 12 June 2015

Ofcom (2014d) *The Future of Free to View TV: A Discussion Document*. Available online at http://stakeholders.ofcom.org.uk/binaries/consultations/700MHz/discussion/ftv.pdf, accessed on 31 May 2015

Ofcom (2014e) *Adults' Media Use and Attitudes Report 2014*. Available online at http://stakeholders.ofcom.org.uk/binaries/research/media-literacy/adults-2014/2014_Adults_report.pdf, accessed on 16 June 2015

Ofcom (2014f) *Children and Parents: Media Use and Attitudes Report 2014*. Available online at http://stakeholders.ofcom.org.uk/binaries/research/media-literacy/media-use-attitudes-14/Childrens_2014_Report.pdf, accessed on 16 June 2015

Radio Communications Agency (2000) *Final Auction Results*. Available online at http://www.ofcom.org.uk/static/archive/spectrumauctions/auction/auction_index.htm, accessed on 7 June 2015

Reith, John (1924) *Broadcast over Britain*, London: Hodder and Stoughton

Rowntree (Joseph Rowntree Foundation) (2014) *A Minimum Income Standard for the UK in 2014*. Available online at http://www.jrf.org.uk/sites/files/jrf/MIS-2014-Final.pdf, accessed on 15 June 2015

Starks, Michael (2007) *Switching to Digital Television. UK Public Policy and the Market*, Bristol: Intellect

UNESCO (2005) *Public Service Broadcasting: A Best Practice Sourcebook*. Available online at http://unesdoc.unesco.org/images/0014/001415/141584e.pdf, accessed on 14 June 2015

From Walk-On Part to Featured Player: The Deliberating Public and the BBC

Dan Hind draws on the ideas of James S. Fishkin to suggest that a deliberative body or jury considers the nature of the media system as a whole and the BBC's place within it as part of a wide-ranging public debate in the run-up to charter renewal

'If there is hope,' wrote Winston, 'it lies in the proles.'
George Orwell, *Nineteen Eighty-Four* (1949)

The trouble with the media

Taken as a whole there is something wrong with the British media system. Mainstream media operations were unable or unwilling to resist the Anglo-American propaganda campaign for the invasion of Iraq in 2003. They did not describe what was happening to the global economy in general and to the credit markets in particular in the years before 2007. Since the financial crisis they have consistently failed to explain what happened and why.

The problem is perhaps most acute when it comes to coverage of the media's own operations. Most newspapers and all broadcasters were extremely slow to report on what the Information Commission in May 2006 called 'a widespread and organised undercover market in confidential private information' (Information Commissioner's Office 2006). This illegal trade only became common knowledge in July 2011, a full two years after the *Guardian* began to report on the evidence of criminality accumulating in the civil courts (Davies 2009).

Much like the commercial media, the BBC is unable or unwilling to challenge the elite consensus on matters of great importance to the majority of its viewers and listeners. It is inept and misleading when it attempts to describe the country's political economy and must take a considerable share of responsibility for the fantastical nature of much of our public debate.

The BBC's treatment of the media is every bit as timid as its treatment of other powerful groups. Although it was not involved in the illegal acquisition of data, it never took the lead in exposing what was an open secret in much of Fleet Street. Indeed, it continued to use newspapers that were engaged in questionable practices as proxies for public opinion in its deliberations about the daily news agenda (Lewis 2015). This incuriosity and complacency about criminal behaviour in the media took a particularly sinister turn when an ITV documentary in October 2012 revealed that a famous BBC 'personality', Jimmy Savile, was also a prolific abuser of children. In the months that followed it emerged that the BBC had dropped its own investigation into Savile in late 2011.

To summarise, media institutions in Britain – including the BBC – are significantly constrained by their partial subordination to the interests of political and economic elites. Furthermore, they cannot adequately acknowledge this subordination or their interests as significant power centres in their own right. They are subject to the same mystification that obscures other forms of power.

The usual model of liberal reform, in which a consensus for change is developed in 'civil society' and then publicised in the media before it eventually becomes part of a governing party's programme, is of limited use when we consider the media themselves. The people who own and run the media are not disinterested and cannot be expected to give anything like impartial coverage to proposals that might significantly curtail their powers or reduce their income.

Meanwhile media reform has far-reaching political implications that are constitutional in nature in the sense that they bear on how the game is played, rather than on the outcome of any particular point. To take an obvious example, a media system able to investigate and publicise elite wrongdoing in the 1980s would have led to significant changes in the top ranks of the political class. Whether or not our current politicians are outright villains they are clearly beneficiaries of the communications regime. Inadequate coverage of the financial sector has gone hand in hand with extravagant enrichment for the bankers' many friends in parliament.

The context: Charter renewal

It is against this background of pervasive media failure that the government is making plans for the BBC's new charter and agreement, which will come into effect in early 2017. In the past there has been little public discussion of the charter renewal process. Politicians and special interests preferred to keep things to themselves. This time, though, there are signs that there will be somewhat more *glasnost*. The current DG Tony Hall said in a recent interview that there needed to be an open discussion of how funding levels related to the levels of service we could expect from the BBC:

> This is where the debate has to be out in public, which is: what is the scale of services you want from the BBC? If you want to take out £200m because of decriminalisation, that £200m less for content. That's a whole load of radio services, or a chunk of the drama budget (Kanter 2015).

This is in line with his desire for 'a debate that fair-minded, proper and about the things that really matter to people, which in my humble opinion are the content and the services' (ibid).

Many of us would welcome a fair-minded debate. But a narrow focus on 'content and services' at the expense of the structures that generate them would mean treating citizens as consumers, an ironic stance for an institution whose first 'public purpose' in the last royal charter and agreement was 'sustaining citizenship and civil society' (BBC nd).

Whether we know it or not, what matters to us is the structure of the BBC: how it is funded and how it is governed. This structure determines how it relates to other interests, and hence what kinds of content and services it eventually produces. Those who suffer from the current distribution of power and knowledge urgently need a public debate to address the matters of funding and of governance in the country's most important media operation. But this debate must be substantially free from control by established interests, it must be authoritative, and it must reach large numbers of people.

The method: Deliberative polling[1]

One approach that satisfies these requirements is what James S. Fishkin calls 'deliberative polling' (Fishkin 1997). A representative sample of the relevant population is chosen at random and polled on a matter of public concern. A sub-set of this group – usually more than 150 – then convenes at a single venue. Normally participants receive a modest payment and have their expenses covered. If the proceedings are to be publicised in some way this acts as another incentive. The planners take steps to ensure that those who attend the polling event are also representative of the general population (ibid: 162-168).

Participants are given briefing materials and engage in moderated face-to-face discussions in small groups. They then have an opportunity to question experts and interested parties in plenary sessions. They are polled again at the end of their deliberations. In this way we are able to see a snapshot of raw public opinion and then we see what effects – if any – sustained deliberation has on the participants' general understanding and attitudes. The idea, in Fishkin's words, is 'to model what the public would think, had it a better opportunity to consider the questions at issue' (ibid: 162).

Such deliberative bodies have been used with considerable success in matters of deep controversy and considerable complexity. They have made recommendations on infrastructure priorities at the city level in China and in North America they have helped inform decisions about how utilities companies direct investments (Fishkin 2009: 106-158). This approach has even been tried in the United Kingdom. Channel 4 televised a deliberative poll on crime in May 1994 (Weale 2002: 45).

There is always a danger that established interests will use the process to lend a democratic façade to decisions they have already made by suppressing certain options or manipulating the participants in some other way. This is by no means inevitable, however. In the case of the BBC there are well established, if currently little known, proposals for structural reform that provide a range of options on both funding and governance. So long as each of these proposals are given rough equality of opportunity to make their case to the participants, and those participants are able to shape their deliberations through active interrogation of experts and established interests, elite capture of the process can be prevented.

Indeed, there is some evidence that the process of deliberative polling can change the minds of elite individuals who are involved in the process as witnesses. Fishkin describes how, at the end of a series of eight deliberative polls, the chair of Texas's public utility commission, Pat Wood, revised his position on renewable energy:

Before the deliberative polls he had viewed it as a 'boutique industry' that used 'public money for pet projects'. By the end, reflecting on what he had heard from the public about its priorities after deliberation, he viewed it as an infant industry that had to be nurtured (Fishkin 2009: 153)[2]

A mirror that doesn't reflect itself

In order to answer the two questions that relate to the nature of the BBC after 2016 – how is it funded and how is it structured? – a deliberative body or jury will have to take evidence on the nature of the media system as a whole and the BBC's place within it. This is by no means a simple matter and business will not be concluded quickly. But a series of hearings with time for reflection and debate by members the jury could be conducted over a month or so. This would be adequate to give a group of, say, 151 citizens the time and information needed to express an informed opinion on structural matters of funding and governance.

Audiences outside the process would be able to access raw footage and edited summaries of particular aspects of the discussion. These summaries could be shaped in part by the participants. Testimony and exchanges that struck those present as particularly interesting or relevant could be voted into the final cut of various video outputs.

The general public would have a chance to see 'ordinary people', that is, people who are no more or less implicated in the closed networks of power and privilege than the rest of us, interrogating experts and vested interests and coming to independent conclusions. We would watch people like us exercising responsible authority of a kind that is normally denied us – concerning matters that are normally kept under the tight control of elite interests.

In a Fishkin-type deliberative poll, the participants are not asked to reach a consensus position, a verdict. The process, in his words, 'offers the representative and informed views of the public, sincerely expressed'. As such it is likely to differ in important respects from elite discourse, in both style and content. But there might be grounds for going further and inviting participants to make a more formal report, which would set out the recommendations of at least a plurality of those who have been invited to offer their opinions.[3]

Anthony Barnett, the founder of openDemocracy, who has studied jury forms with respect to the UK's House of Lords (Barnett and Carty 2008), argues that deliberative bodies need to have the power and responsibility for an unambiguous outcome to be effective:

> A jury in a court of law is not a consultative process. Its members are motivated to listen and decide because they know they must reach a verdict. Similarly, with a jury-style process in a governing role. Citizens can be trusted with the wisdom of decision making if they are charged with the final word in principle. Experts and elites say you can't trust people with power in case they take the wrong decision. In fact, they can be trusted to take decisions that are at least as wise as the elites', but only if they have power. Their wisdom follows from their responsibility. Of course, for a citizens' jury to reach a verdict there needs to be due process of evidence, a guiding framework, and a way of setting out alternatives. This might simply be permitting a jury to say it is not satisfied with a proposal achieving the stated outcome that is desired and a rethink is necessary. Just as a judge not a jury decides the sentence after a verdict so how a citizen jury's judgement is implemented need not be up to it. But there has to be a power of basic decision making and then it will work (Barnett 2015).

Once integrated into the governance structure of an institution a deliberative poll becomes an Athenian-style jury – a body chosen by lot that gives form and substance to the self-governing *demos*.

If a political party were to help sponsor a deliberative process, it could undertake to debate this verdict at its next conference. The wider public would be in a position to judge the merits of that response and make their dispositions accordingly. A willingness to engage with, and learn from, public opinion might be a source of advantage in electoral competition. In all likelihood neither the government nor the BBC will agree to be bound by the outcome of a deliberative poll. But publicity itself is a kind of power. People will take the process seriously if they know that their contributions will be shared with a large audience.

Whatever the details of execution, a deliberative process is a promising broadcast format. After all, a reality show in which ordinarily distracted and self-absorbed individuals transform into a public-spirited and engaged body politic seems at least as emotionally engaging as the personal journeys described in any number of televised talent shows.

Motives and agency

Given that the media institutions will not take the initiative in making their own operations accessible and legible to a wider public, we must look elsewhere for support. Plenty of organisations suffer in the current political economy of communications. Trade unions, environmental NGOs and the smaller political parties are all hampered by the extent to which their concerns are excluded from the mainstream debate. If they use some of the money they normally spend in a largely vain attempt to influence mainstream coverage to inform the public about the current structure of the media and the possibilities for reform they may see much better returns on their investment.

The process of public deliberation becomes an opportunity for far broader enlightenment. Those who argue that the BBC is biased in various ways and those who believe that the television licence should be replaced by some other funding mechanism would have a chance to make their case. Those who want to replace the current governance structure with elected officers, or want the public to secure some sort of purchase on the investigative agenda, would have a chance to engage in a debate where the merits of their arguments would not be trumped by the demands of elite self-interest. Similarly, those who want to restore the legitimacy of the BBC funded by a universal charge by establishing it as a provider of a commonwealth of knowledge through universal broadband provision would be able to make their case (Ageh 2015). At present the focus on 'content and services' will exclude all these legitimate concerns and potentially helpful ways forward.

The process of jury-led deliberation lends drama to the process of enlightenment. Assumptions that normally go unchallenged – unnoticed even – in the circuits of elite communication become vulnerable to the tests of evidence and reason. Democracy, in the sense of civic equality, finds expression in a way that can be grasped and appreciated by those – the great majority – who stand to benefit from it.

While the media pose particular and pressing questions there are other subjects that would benefit from being made objects of public deliberation. It is time for banking to be subjected to steady and uninhibited scrutiny by people who are not beholden to it. The social and economic implications of climate change and environmental degradation are also currently little considered by much of the public, for entirely rational reasons. In both instances, as in the case of the media, the views expressed in opinion polls are not likely to be the outcome of sustained and careful deliberation.

A jury – or series of juries – convened to consider the future of the BBC would provide a useful prototype for a larger and more extensive constitutional convention. The BBC is, after all, an institution of overwhelming constitutional significance, even if it is rarely described as such. Its operations have a wide-ranging impact on the way that the state functions. Even if a Conservative government ignores a citizens' jury convened to consider the future of the BBC, its findings will find their way on to the agenda of a constitutional convention worthy of the name.

Dan Hind

Conclusions

Deliberative forms, if convened around a clearly defined agenda and possessed of adequate time and resources, can address matters of deep public interest in ways that an elite-controlled and elite-directed process cannot. Citizens drawn from the general population in society characterised by steep inequalities of power will, by necessity, not be the people who normally control debate. They will be free to consider the public interest without regard to the need to preserve and increase elite power.

In my view, the BBC's record on investigating scandals in the media, the economy and politics is simply not robust enough - and improving the BBC's journalism in these key areas should be at the heart of any public debate about the corporation's future. So too should its persistent failure to offer a factual challenge to the fantasies that currently pass as the conventional wisdom. Whether a representative group of citizens will agree, once they have motive, means and opportunity to assess the evidence, is something that can only be discovered empirically.

What is already clear is that journalists who want to discover and publicise flaws in the current ruling order and its attendant body of shared understandings and assumptions struggle to make a living, let alone find large audiences. Meanwhile, those who tailor their curiosity to the needs of the powerful prosper. It is a situation that should shame us, and that we should move swiftly to remedy. We can only hope to succeed with the help of an informed and representative public.

Notes

[1] The author would like to thank Anthony Barnett for his advice and guidance in the preparation of this chapter.

[2] Deliberative polling does not seem to unduly favour privileged groups. Meanwhile the outcomes of deliberative polls often surprise the organisers, which isn't what we would expect if the mechanism were reliably vulnerable to elite manipulation

[3] If the composition of this plurality proved significantly different from the profile of the group as a whole – if it was older or whiter, for example – this would have to be noted, of course

References

Ageh, Tony (2015) The BBC, the licence fee and the digital public space, openDemocracy, 3 March. Available online at https://www.opendemocracy.net/ourbeeb/tony-ageh/bbc-licence-fee-and-digital-public-space, accessed on 29 June 2015

Barnett, Anthony and Carty, Peter (2008) *The Athenian Option: Radical Reform for the House of Lords*, Exeter: Imprint Academic

Barnett, Anthony (2015) Interview with the author, 15 July

BBC (nd) The BBC's six public purposes. Available online at http://www.bbc.co.uk/corporate2/insidethebbc/whoweare/publicpurposes, accessed on 29 June 2015

Davies, Nick (2009) Murdoch papers paid £1m to gag phone-hacking victims, *Guardian*, 8 July. Available online at http://www.theguardian.com/media/2009/jul/08/murdoch-papers-phone-hacking, accessed on 29 June 2015

Fishkin, James S. (1997) *The Voice of the People: Public Opinion and Democracy*, New Haven: Yale University Press

Fishkin, James S. (2009) *When the People Speak*, Oxford: Oxford University Press

Information Commissioner's Office (2006) *What Price Privacy? The Unlawful Trade in Confidential Private Information*. Available online at http://webarchive.nationalarchives.gov.uk/20140122145147/http:/www.levesoninquiry.org.uk/wp-content/uploads/2012/01/Exhibit-SA-X351.pdf, accessed on 29 June 2015

Kanter, Jake (2015) The *Broadcast* interview: Tony Hall, *Broadcast*, 18 June 18. Available online at http://www.broadcastnow.co.uk/features/the-broadcast-interview-tony-hall/5089486.article?blocktitle=Most-popular&contentID=-1, accessed on 29 June 2015

Lewis, Justin (2015) Newspapers, not the BBC, led the way in biased election coverage, *openDemocracy*, 15 May. Available online at https://www.opendemocracy.net/ourbeeb/justin-lewis/newspapers-not-bbc-led-way-in-biased-election-coverage, accessed on 29 June 2015

Weale, Albert (2002) Public consultation and public policy on risk, Weale, Albert (ed.) *Risk, Democratic Citizenship and Public Policy*, Oxford: Oxford University Press pp 39-48

Lightning Source UK Ltd.
Milton Keynes UK
UKOW01f0216230915

259120UK00001B/38/P